# LEARNING LATIN

# LEARNING LATIN

AN INTRODUCTORY COURSE FOR ADULTS

by John G. Randall

in collaboration with J.C.B. Foster and D.F. Kennedy

 FRANCIS CAIRNS

Published by Francis Cairns (Publications) Ltd

c/o The University, P.O. Box 147, Liverpool L69 3BX
Great Britain

First published 1986

*British Library Cataloguing in Publication Data*

Randall, John G.
  Learning Latin : an introductory course for adults
  1. Latin language—Problems, exercises, etc.
  I. Title    II. Foster, J.C.B.    III. Kennedy, D.F.
  478      PA2087

  ISBN 0-905205-33-2

Printed in Great Britain by
Redwood Burn Ltd, Trowbridge, Wiltshire

# CONTENTS

# MINERVAE
# MERCURIOQUE

# PREFACE

*Learning Latin* began life as an introductory Latin course taught by John G. Randall in Lancaster University from 1969 on. In 1975 a new version of this course was created with the help of Liverpool University's Max Wheeler and Francis Cairns for use on both campuses. In the succeeding years W. Barr (Liverpool), J.L. Creed (Lancaster) and O.A.W. Dilke (Leeds) contributed detailed and valuable advice. *Learning Latin*, a thorough revision made in 1985/86, introduced as collaborators J.C.B. Foster and D.F. Kennedy (Liverpool) and is thus the fruit of a further ten years' teaching experience in both Universities. It has benefited much from the reactions of its students throughout the intervening period.

*Learning Latin* has already attracted UGC/Computer Board funding for its adaptation to microcomputer use: the project team — F. Cairns and M. Haywood (Liverpool) — plans to have available by mid-1987 an interactive IBM-compatible system which will markedly enhance the flexibility and usage of the course (e.g. in remedial teaching) and which will enable students to reinforce their learning at their own pace and in accordance with their individual needs.

We gratefully acknowledge the help of all those named and of many other well-wishers who have encouraged and assisted us towards the publication of *Learning Latin*.

John G. Randall
D.F. Kennedy, J.C.B. Foster
15th February 1986

# INTRODUCTION

This introductory section summarises concepts and terminology which will be essential throughout the course; teachers should ensure that students are familiar with them before turning to chapter 1.

## I THE AIM AND METHODS OF THE COURSE

The aim of *Learning Latin* is to give students a working knowledge of the essentials of the Latin language, that is, of the "morphology" and "syntax" (see (a) and (b) below) which constitute Latin grammar, and of the most common Latin vocabulary. With this knowledge, and with the help of a Latin Dictionary, students will, by the end of the course, be able to read competently and confidently straightforward Latin prose and verse of all periods. The Latin used in the course is drawn largely from major classical writers of the later republic and early empire (approximately 200 BC–AD 150). Since this kind of Latin became the accepted norm for subsequent writers, students will also be able, with very little adjustment, to read most medieval and renaissance Latin.

The course uses traditional grammatical terminology throughout, with only two additional terms, "kernels" and "metaphrasing" (see (b), (c) and (d) below). Thus students will acquire the ability to consult standard reference works such as Latin dictionaries, grammars and commentaries.

The course is clearly structured and requires systematic application on the part of the student. Stress is laid throughout on understanding the structure of Latin sentences rather than on rote memorisation, although naturally an element of memorisation is essential. Each chapter introduces fresh morphology for recognition; this will be assisted by consultation of the Tables at pages 348-363. Students should become familiar with these as they go along; gradual learning of them will prove advantageous. Similarly, each chapter introduces fresh syntax, which needs to be understood and remembered. At the end of each chapter there is a small vocabulary to be learned; other vocabulary will be picked up by use.

The grammatical terminology and concepts essential to the course are dealt with below under four headings: morphology, syntax and the kernels, metaphrasing and the kernels, and "incomplete" kernels. Finally, some suggestions will be made about how the course may be taught; and the principles on which the Latin passages in it were selected will be explained.

## a) Morphology

Latin is an inflected language; the relationships between words are shown by their "endings" rather than by the order in which they appear.

There are nine different types of word (or "parts of speech"), which have different functions in the sentence. They are:

NOUNS: a noun is used to name things both animate (e.g. *arbor* "a tree", *vir* "a man") and inanimate (e.g. *vīnum* "wine", *virtūs* "virtue").

Nouns fall into five "declensions" (or groupings of noun forms); each declension has five main "cases" (or forms indicating different functions in the sentence); and each case has a characteristic "ending" to identify it. Nouns also fall into three "genders"; the gender of nouns referring to people and animals is usually the same as their sex, but inanimate nouns may be of any gender. Nouns are either singular or plural.

In the vocabularies nouns are listed in the nominative singular, followed by the genitive singular ending (a procedure which identifies the declension), followed by the gender and meaning, e.g. homō –inis (m) = a human being, man.

ADJECTIVES: an adjective is used to describe a noun (e.g. *arbor* **fēlix** "a **fruitful** tree", *vīnum* **ācre** "a **sharp** wine"). Adjectives agree in gender, number and case with the noun they describe. They are sometimes used by themselves in place of a noun, when their gender suggests an appropriate noun (e.g. *bonus* "a good **man**", *bona* "a good **woman**", *bonum* "**something** good, a blessing").

Adjectives follow a similar pattern to nouns: some belong to the 1st and 2nd declensions, others to the 3rd declension. In the vocabularies adjectives are listed in the nominative singular masculine, followed by the nominative singular feminine and neuter endings, followed by the meaning, e.g. vērus -a -um = real, true. But 3rd declension adjectives with the same nominative ending for all three genders are listed in the nominative singular, followed by the genitive singular ending and the meaning, e.g. sapiens -ntis = wise. Most 3rd declension adjectives use the same ending for both masculine and feminine in all cases, and the same ending for all genders in the genitive, dative and ablative.

PRONOUNS: a pronoun is used in place of a noun, to indicate things without naming them (e.g. *illud* "that", *tū* "you").

Pronouns follow a similar pattern to 1st and 2nd declension adjectives. In the vocabularies pronouns are listed in the nominative singular masculine, followed by the nominative singular feminine and neuter endings and the meaning, e.g. ille -a -ud = that.

VERBS: a verb is used to refer to an action or state (e.g. *ille saltat* "he dances", *ille insānit* "he is mad").

Verbs fall into four "conjugations" (or groupings of verb forms); each conjugation has an imperfect stem, a perfect active stem, a perfect passive stem; from these stems all parts of the verb are formed.

Verbs are either intransitive (i.e. those which take no direct object) or transitive (i.e. those which take a direct object in the accusative) or "transitive" (i.e. those which take a "direct object" in a case other than the accusative). Verbs may also appear in an "active" form, expressing what the subject of the verb is or does (e.g. *cōgitō, ergō sum* "I think, therefore I am") or in a passive form, expressing what is done to the subject of the verb (e.g. *amātor exclūsus est* "the lover is shut out"); but see also Chh. 5 and 12.

In the vocabularies verbs are listed by their principal parts, the present indicative 1st singular active, present infinitive active (which serves to identify the conjugation), perfect indicative 1st singular active, and supine accusative singular; they are normally assumed to be transitive unless otherwise indicated; their meaning is conventionally given by an infinitive in English, e.g. crescō -ere crēvī crētum (intr) = to grow.

ADVERBS: an adverb is used to qualify a verb, an adjective or another adverb (e.g. *is bene vīvit* "he lives well", *vīnum minus ācre* "a wine less sharp").

PREPOSITIONS: a preposition governs a noun or pronoun and is used to show the relationship between it and the sentence as a whole. Different prepositions govern nouns or pronouns in different cases (e.g. *in vīnō vēritās* "truth **in** wine").

CONJUNCTIONS: a conjunction is used to connect sentences or clauses or words within the same clause (e.g. *dum bibimus, hilarī et laetī sumus* "**while** we drink, we are cheerful **and** happy").

INTERJECTIONS: an interjection is used as an exclamation (e.g. *heu!* "alas!").

INTERROGATIVE PARTICLES: an interrogative particle is used to signal a question (e.g. *an hoc vērum est?* "**can it really be that** this is true?").

## b) Syntax and the Kernels

The formal rules of Latin syntax are set out in Chapters 1-25; they determine the clause and sentence structure of Latin and make possible the accurate analysis of the meaning of an infinite number of individual Latin clauses and sentences.

In spite of their apparent diversity, all Latin clauses fall into one of three basic patterns, *depending on the meaning of the verb*. These patterns are called "*kernels*"; they underlie the structure of the Latin language and are basic to this course. The three kernels are:

**K1**: consisting of

a subject in the nominative

**plus either** the verb *esse* "to be" used in its existential sense:

nox erat.
it was night.

urbs antīqua fuit.
there was an ancient city.

**or** an intransitive verb:

tempus fugit.
time flies.

vēritās numquam perit.
truth never dies.

**K2**: consisting of

> a subject in the nominative

> **plus either** a copulative verb such as *esse* "to be" **and** another nominative or a prepositional phrase:

>> terra ipsa dea est.
>> the earth itself is a goddess.

>> iam ferme in exitū annus erat.
>> now the year was almost at an end.

> **or** a transitive verb **and** a direct object in the accusative:

>> fortēs Fortūna iuvat.
>> Fortune favours the brave.

> **or** a "transitive" verb **and** a "direct object" in a case other than the accusative:

>> nec facta impia caelicolīs placent.
>> and unholy deeds do not please the gods.

**K3**: consisting of

> a subject in the nominative

> **plus either** a transitive verb **and** a direct object in the accusative

> **or** a "transitive" verb **and** a "direct object" in a case other than than the accusative

> **plus** (in either instance) one more element required to complete the sense of the verb:

>> nonnullī erum meum rusticitātis arguunt.
>> some people accuse my master of lack of sophistication.

>> ēbrietās sollicitīs animīs onus eximit.
>> drunkenness removes the burden from anxious minds.

## c) Metaphrasing and the Kernels

The three types of kernel described above condition our expectations about the structure and meaning of Latin clauses and sentences.

The recognition of the different kernels and of the information which they give us about the structure of the Latin clause and sentence is elicited through a technique called "metaphrasing". In general terms this is a method of translating the Latin into English by analysing each word as it comes, rendering it as far as possible at the time, and working by progressive elimination towards the recognition of the particular kernel present. Once recognised, the kernel allows us to predict the pattern of the rest of the clause or sentence.

Thus, through metaphrasing, the reader makes positive identification of the morphology and syntax and becomes constantly more aware of the direction which the sentence is taking. The overall sense of the sentence may however take some time to reveal itself, so that the reader also learns to suspend judgement and to accept an initial period of uncertainty. By the end of the metaphrasing process, the reader has responded to the sentence as a Roman would have done and has produced an acceptable, if not always elegant, translation: understanding the Latin must always be the first step towards a good translation.

Metaphrasing aims then at translating a clause or sentence through recognition of which of the three kernels it contains. The detailed rules for metaphrasing are set out in Chapters 1-25. The symbol "—" (which may be vocalised for convenience as "blank") is used to represent a noun or noun phrase and "★" (which may be vocalised as "star") is used to represent a verb or verb phrase until the "blanks" and "stars" can be filled in with the actual meanings of the words. In this set of terms the kernels can be represented schematically as follows:

**K1:**  | — | ★s
--- | --- | ---
 | blank | stars
e.g. | time | flies

**K2:** | — | ★s | —
--- | --- | --- | ---
 | blank | stars | blank
e.g. | Fortune | favours | the bold

**K3:** | — | ★s | — | —
--- | --- | --- | --- | ---
 | blank | stars | blank | blank
e.g. | drunkenness | removes | the burden | from anxious minds

In metaphrasing a sentence, three questions must be asked about each inflected word:

(a) what is the ending?

(b) what grammatical information does the ending convey?

(c) what kernel does this information suggest and where does the word fit into it?

As the sentence unfolds, each new word which is metaphrased will advance the translation; and the progressive revelation of structure and meaning will enable ambiguities and uncertainties to be resolved. An elementary example of this process can be given here:

## omnia vincit amor. (Verg. *Ecl.* 10.69)

omnis –is –e = every, all

| | | |
|---|---|---|
| omnia | (a) | –ia |
| | (b) | nom/acc pl neut (for the moment it is uncertain which case this is, and so which type of kernel it suggests, whether K1, K2 or K3) |
| | (c) | all — ★ / — ★s all — |

vincō –ere vīcī victum = to conquer, defeat

| | | |
|---|---|---|
| vincit | (a) | –t |
| | (b) | pres indic, 3rd sing act (a singular verb requires a singular subject; *omnia*, being plural, is most probably part of the direct object;this suggests that the sentence is a K2 or K3 kernel) |
| | (c) | — conquers all — |

amor –ōris (m) = love

| | | |
|---|---|---|
| amor. | (a) | –r |
| | (b) | nom sing (the singular subject, anticipated above, now appears; the full stop, by ending the sentence, excludes the possibility of its being a K3 kernel) |
| | (c) | love conquers all —. |

| | |
|---|---|
| Translation | Love conquers all things. |

N.B. *omnia* has no noun to agree with; the neuter gender suggests that "things" should be supplied.

## d) "Incomplete" Kernels

Sometimes a clause or sentence in which a particular kernel is present turns out to lack part of that kernel. The reader, however, is supposed to supply the missing part from the surrounding context. The typical situation in which this happens is where parallel clauses stand side by side, but where elements common to two or more of these clauses are expressed only once. The reader notices that a word or phrase is missing from one or more clauses and supplies it from the parallel clause or clauses in which it does appear. Some examples are:

> ēnumerat mīles vulnera, pastor ovēs.
> a soldier counts his wounds, a shepherd (counts) his sheep.

Here an incomplete clause follows a complete clause.

> nāvita dē ventīs, dē taurīs narrat arātor.
> a sailor (tells stories) about winds, a ploughman tells stories about bulls.

Here an incomplete clause precedes a complete clause.

> neque calce lupus quemquam, neque dente petit bōs.
> no wolf (attacks) anyone with its hoof, no ox attacks (anyone) with its teeth.

Here two incomplete clauses complement one another in different ways.

> pōma, crūda sī sunt, vix ēvelluntur, sī mātūra, dēcidunt.
> fruits, if (they) are unripe, are picked with difficulty, if (they) (are) ripe, (they) fall.

Here several incomplete clauses complement each other.

# II SUGGESTIONS ABOUT TEACHING THE COURSE

At the beginning of the course the teacher should take the students through the introduction, in particular making clear the difference between an inflected language like Latin and a non-inflected language like English, emphasising the importance of "endings" in the one and of word order in the other, and stressing the need to recognise sentence patterns in Latin as an aid to understanding.

At the start of each chapter the teacher should go through the Morphology, Syntax and Metaphrasing sections with the students. The Morphology sections should be used as a guide to the Tables at pp.348-363.

Once the students have understood the opening sections of each chapter they can then metaphrase the Examples in their own time. This must be done conscientiously and systematically. The method is as follows: a card is used to cover up the right hand side of the page, leaving exposed only the items of vocabulary and the series of letters (a) (b) (c) printed down the centre of the page; these letters act as a prompt, to which the students respond. The students, as they respond, move their card down one line at a time so as to check the correctness of their response. After metaphrasing the Examples in this way, the students then prepare the Exercises and the Reading for the next class in their own time.

In the initial part of the next class the teacher then works through this material with the students, giving a running commentary, providing background information, underlining the new points of grammar in each chapter, and solving problems of translation by metaphrasing and kernelling. It may occasionally be necessary for the teacher to help bridge the gap between the sort of English which metaphrasing produces and the more elegant English which is desirable in a translation.

A full vocabulary is provided with each Latin passage in the course. It gives the basic meaning of every word, followed where necessary by a second (or third) meaning more appropriate to the immediate context. The most common words encountered in each chapter are listed at the end of that chapter as vocabulary to learn. They must be learned, since they will not appear again in the vocabularies of subsequent chapters. A complete list of the words to be learned can be found in Appendix C.

As the course goes on and students become more adept, they may well wish to skip the metaphrasing process and move to translation without the intermediate stage. This is perfectly legitimate provided that fluent and accurate translation continues to be the result. But if students begin to guess wildly or to experience difficulties, firm recourse should again be made to metaphrasing.

A determined group of students can average 2 class hours per chapter, which should be reinforced by at least the same amount of private study; but great flexibility is possible and teachers should not be concerned if more leisurely progress sees the course completed in 75-100 class hours.

## III THE LATIN IN THE COURSE

In this course real Latin is used throughout and references are given to the sources from which it is drawn; a checklist of authors and works can be found in Appendix A. In the nature of things, however, it has not always been possible to use the Latin in its full and unaltered form. Any adaptations of any kind in the Latin are indicated by a small asterisk beside the Latin when it first appears. Such adaptations usually involve either omitting words so as not to introduce un-heralded complexities or supplying nouns so as to eliminate obscurities or changing tenses or moods for the same reasons. Passages so altered are assembled in their original form in Appendix B.

The Latin passages used have been chosen as much for their moral, social and political content as for their linguistic value. Although divorced from their original context, they should not be regarded as disconnected pieces of Latin existing in a vacuum. The passages in each chapter have been arranged to form an implicit narrative, dramatic or conceptual sequence, in which one passage can be seen to reinforce, comment upon or contradict another.

Students who work through this course will have read a great deal of real Latin written by the greatest writers of Rome. They will have come into contact with the philosophy, the poetry, the morality and the daily life of the Romans, not in any simplified or mediated form but in the idiom and accent of ancient Rome. If such students go on to read entire works in Latin, they will find themselves, both linguistically and culturally, already at home.

# 1
# NOMINATIVES

## Morphology

The commonest ending for the nominative singular is –*s* or –*x* (which represents the sound of –*cs* or –*gs*). Exceptions are:

> nouns and adjectives which have lost this ending altogether, e.g. 1st declension nouns, which end in –*a*, 2nd declension nouns which end in –*r*, and a variety of 3rd declension nouns;

> nouns and adjectives which use another ending instead, e.g. 2nd declension neuters, which end in –*um*;

> pronouns, which have several unusual forms including the unique neuter ending –*d*.

The commonest ending for adverbs of the 1st and 2nd declension is –*ē*, for adverbs of the 3rd declension –*iter*, –*ter* or –*er*. Exceptions are:

> some 1st and 2nd declension adjectives and some 3rd declension adjectives in the accusative singular neuter used adverbially (see chapter 2 syntax §5);

> some 1st and 2nd declension adjectives in the ablative singular used adverbially (see chapter 3 syntax §9).

Verbs will at first appear only in the present tense. Their use will be restricted to the 3rd singular active and passive, which end in –*t* and –*tur*, and to the present infinitive active and passive, which end in –*re* and –*(r)ī*.

# Syntax

**1.** A nominative singular introduces a singular verb and vice versa:

> **erus** meus bene **vīvit**; **ornātur cēna** sumptuōsa.
> my **master lives** well; a lavish **dinner-party is being prepared.**

**2.** Nominatives are used for:

**(a)** the subject of the verb whether active or passive:

> sī **quis** nimium bibit, **is** rīdētur
> if **anyone** drinks too much, **he** is laughed at.

**(b)** the complement of copulative verbs such as *esse* "to be" and *vidērī* "to seem":

> est enim **rīdiculus** homō male sōbrius.
> for a man barely sober is **laughable.**

The nominative is still used when the copulative verb is in the infinitive:

> is **vīnōsus** esse dīcitur
> he is said to be **addicted to wine.**

But when two nouns are joined in this way, it is not clear from the Latin word order which is the subject and which the complement:

> sed **vīta vīnum** est.
> but **life** is **wine** / **wine** is **life.**

Usually the context resolves the problem unless the speaker is being deliberately ambiguous.

**3.** The infinitive is a verbal noun. As a verb it presents the bare action of the verb stem, e.g. *bibere* "to drink"; as a noun it is neuter, and is used only in the nominative and accusative singular (see chapter 2 syntax §§1 and 2).

**4.** Infinitives are used in the nominative:

**(a)** as the subject of the main verb:

> illud est dulce, **esse** et **bibere.**
> this is sweet, to **eat** and **drink.**

(b) as the complement of copulative verbs such as *esse* "to be" and *vidērī* "to seem":

> hoc est bene **vīvere**.
> this is **to live** well.

# Metaphrasing

**1.** A noun or pronoun in the nominative is metaphrased: — ★s

> homō                   the man ★s

A second noun or pronoun in the nominative suggests a K2 kernel; it is metaphrased predicatively (i.e. after the verb):

> homō erus            the man ★s master

It soon becomes clear how they are related:

> homō erus meus est     the man is my master

**2.** An adjective in the nominative is metaphrased in a similar way:

> rīdiculus             a ridiculous — ★s

But the appearance of a copulative verb later in the sentence or the "feel" of the sentence as it unfolds may suggest that the adjective should also be metaphrased predicatively (i.e. after the verb):

> rīdiculus homō est      a ridiculous man is —
>                         *or* the man is ridiculous

**3.** A relative pronoun in the nominative is metaphrased in a similar way, in brackets, at the beginning of its clause:

> homō quī            the man (who ★s) ★s

But when there is no such antecedent (i.e. no previous noun or pronoun for it to refer to), the relative pronoun is indefinite in meaning:

> quī                 (whoever ★s)

The relative clause is left thus suspended until it becomes clear how it fits into the whole sentence:

| | |
|---|---|
| quī nimium bibit rīdētur | (whoever drinks too much) is laughed at |

**4.** An intransitive verb active suggests a K1 kernel; it is metaphrased: — ★s

| | |
|---|---|
| vīvit | — lives |

A passive verb is metaphrased: — is ★ed

| | |
|---|---|
| rīdētur | — is laughed at |

**5.** An active infinitive is metaphrased: to ★, in brackets:

| | |
|---|---|
| vīvere | (to live) |

A passive infinitive is metaphrased: to be ★ed, in brackets:

| | |
|---|---|
| rīdērī | (to be laughed at) |

The infinitive phrase is left thus suspended until it becomes clear how it fits into the whole sentence:

| | |
|---|---|
| vīvere dulce est | (to live) is sweet / it is sweet (to live) |

**6.** *Est* may need metaphrasing in more than one way since it can suggest a K1 or K2 kernel:

| | |
|---|---|
| est | there / it is — |
| | *or* — is — |

**7.** These basic patterns can then be adjusted when necessary as follows:

**(a)** an abstract noun or neuter adjective in the nominative may need an alternative metaphrase if it can introduce an infinitive or subordinate clause as part of a K2 kernel:

| | |
|---|---|
| dulce | a sweet — ★s |
| | *or* it is sweet |

**(b)** two nominative nouns forming a K2 kernel may need an alternative metaphrase unless the context makes clear which is the real subject:

vīta vīnum est          life is wine / wine is life

**(c)** *est* may be omitted from a K2 kernel in Latin since the structure can suggest the missing word; "is" must be supplied in English at the end of the metaphrasing process and the translation adjusted:

haec rēs rīdicula          this ridiculous matter ★s
                         this matter is ridiculous

# Examples

**1. homō hic ēbrius est.** (Pl. *Am.* 574)

homō -inis (m) = a human being,
    man

|  | homō | (a) | –ō |
|--|------|-----|----|
|  |      | (b) | nom sing |
|  |      | (c) | the man ★s |

hic haec hoc = this

|  | hic | (a) | –ic |
|--|-----|-----|-----|
|  |     | (b) | nom sing masc |
|  |     | (c) | this man ★s |

ēbrius -a -um = drunk, drunken

|  | ēbrius | (a) | –us |
|--|--------|-----|-----|
|  |        | (b) | nom sing masc |
|  |        | (c) | this drunken man ★s |

sum esse fuī = to be

|  | est. | (a) | –t |
|--|------|-----|----|
|  |      | (b) | 3rd sing act |
|  |      | (c) | this man is drunk. |

## 2.   nēmō enim ferē saltat sōbrius, nisi forte insānit. (Cic. *Mur.* 13)

nēmō –inis (m) = no-one
enim = for

|  | nēmō enim | (a) | –ō |
|---|---|---|---|
|  |  | (b) | nom sing |
|  |  | (c) | for no-one ★s |

ferē (adverb modifying words of quantity) = almost, virtually

|  | ferē | (a) | –ē |
|---|---|---|---|
|  |  | (b) | adv |
|  |  | (c) | for virtually no-one ★s |

saltō –āre –āvī –ātum (intr) = to dance

|  | saltat | (a) | –t |
|---|---|---|---|
|  |  | (b) | 3rd sing act |
|  |  | (c) | for virtually no-one dances |

sōbrius –a –um = sober

|  | sōbrius, | (a) | –us |
|---|---|---|---|
|  |  | (b) | nom sing masc |
|  |  | (c) | for virtually no-one dances sober, |

nisi (conj) = if not, unless
forte (adv) = by chance, perhaps

|  | nisi forte | (a) | –e |
|---|---|---|---|
|  |  | (b) | adv |
|  |  | (c) | unless perhaps — ★s |

insāniō –īre –īvī –ītum (intr) = to be mad

|  | insānit. | (a) | –t |
|---|---|---|---|
|  |  | (b) | 3rd sing act |
|  |  | (c) | unless perhaps — is mad. |

|  | Translation | For virtually no-one dances sober, unless perhaps he is mad. |
|---|---|---|

## 3. vērum gaudium rēs sevēra est. (Sen. *Ep.* 23.4)

vērus -a -um = real, true

|  | vērum | (a) | -um |
|---|---|---|---|
|  |  | (b) | nom sing neut |
|  |  | (c) | a true — ★s / it is true |

gaudium -[i]ī (n) = joy

|  | gaudium | (a) | -um |
|---|---|---|---|
|  |  | (b) | nom sing |
|  |  | (c) | true joy ★s / it is true joy |

rēs reī (f) = a thing, matter

|  | rēs | (a) | -s |
|---|---|---|---|
|  |  | (b) | nom sing |
|  |  | (c) | true joy ★s a matter / a matter ★s true joy |

sevērus -a -um = stern, serious

|  | sevēra | (a) | -a |
|---|---|---|---|
|  |  | (b) | nom sing fem |
|  |  | (c) | true joy ★s a serious matter / a serious matter ★s true joy |

sum esse fuī = to be

|  | est | (a) | -t |
|---|---|---|---|
|  |  | (b) | 3rd sing act |
|  |  | (c) | true joy is a serious matter / a serious matter is a true joy |

| | Translation | True joy is a serious matter. |
|---|---|---|

N.B. In the original context the first alternative is the correct one.

## 4. **nihil est bonum nisi quod honestum est.** (Sen. *Ep*. 120.3)

nihil (n.indecl) = nothing

|        | nihil | (a) | –l |
|--------|-------|-----|----|
|        |       | (b) | nom sing |
|        |       | (c) | nothing ★s / it is nothing |

sum esse fuī = to be

|        | est | (a) | –t |
|--------|-----|-----|----|
|        |     | (b) | 3rd sing act |
|        |     | (c) | nothing is — / there/it is nothing |

bonus –a –um = good

|        | bonum | (a) | –um |
|--------|-------|-----|-----|
|        |       | (b) | nom sing neut |
|        |       | (c) | nothing is good / there is nothing good |

nisi (conj) = if not, except
quī quae quod = who(ever),
  which, what

|        | nisi quod | (a) | –d |
|--------|-----------|-----|----|
|        |           | (b) | nom sing neut |
|        |           | (c) | except (what ★s) |

honestus –a –um = honourable

|        | honestum | (a) | –um |
|--------|----------|-----|-----|
|        |          | (b) | nom sing neut |
|        |          | (c) | except (what ★s honourable) |

sum esse fuī = to be

|        | est. | (a) | –t |
|--------|------|-----|----|
|        |      | (b) | 3rd sing act |
|        |      | (c) | except (what is honourable). |

|        | Translation | There is nothing good except what is honourable. |
|--------|-------------|---------------------------------------------------|

## 5. nōn enim vīvere bonum est, sed bene vīvere. (Sen. *Ep.* 70.4)

nōn = not
enim = for
vīvō –vere –xī –ctum (intr) = to
   live

           nōn enim vīvere   (a)  –re
                                  (b)  pres infin act
                                  (c)  for not (to live)

bonus –a –um = good

                        bonum   (a)  –um
                                  (b)  nom sing neut
                                  (c)  for not (to live) ★s good / for it is good not (to live)

sum esse fuī = to be

                          est,   (a)  –t
                                  (b)  3rd sing act
                                  (c)  for not (to live) is good, / for it is good not (to live),

sed (conj) = but
bonus –a –um = good (adv: bene)

                    sed bene   (a)  –e
                                  (b)  adv
                                  (c)  but — ★s well

vīvō –vere –xī –ctum (intr) = to
   live

                     vīvere.   (a)  –re
                                  (b)  pres infin act
                                  (c)  but (to live well).

              Translation     For it is good not to live, but to live well.

# Summary of Examples

1. homō hic ēbrius est.
2. nēmō enim ferē saltat sōbrius, nisi forte insānit.
3. vērum gaudium rēs sevēra est.
4. nihil est bonum nisi quod honestum est.
5. nōn enim vīvere bonum est, sed bene vīvere.

# Exercises

Complete the following sentences on the analogy of the first:

quī sōbrius est sōbrie saltat.
quī sevērus est ..........
quī honestus est .........
quī fortis est ............
quī sapiens est ..........
quī bonus est ...........

# Reading

1. nēmō malus fēlix. (Juv. 4.8)

   fēlix –īcis = fruitful, fortunate, happy
   malus –a –um = bad, wicked
   nēmō –inis (m) = no-one

2. vir bonus est quis? (Hor. *Ep.* 1.16.40)

   bonus –a –um = good
   quis? quid? = who? what?
   sum esse fuī = to be
   vir virī (m) = a man

3. Atticus eximiē sī cēnat, lautus habētur. (Juv.11.1)

   Atticus –ī (m) = Atticus (a man well known for his wealth)
   cēnō –āre –āvī –ātum (intr) = to dine
   eximius –a –um = outstanding, exceptionally good
   habeō –ēre –uī –itum = to have, hold, consider (to be)
   lautus –a –um = well-washed, luxurious, "posh"
   sī (conj) = if

4. num parva causa aut prāva ratiō est? (Ter. *Eu.* 575)

aut (conj) = or
causa -ae (f) = a cause, reason
num? (interrogative particle) = surely ... not?
parvus -a -um = small, negligible
prāvus -a -um = crooked, perverse, faulty
ratiō -ōnis (f) = a reckoning, reason
sum esse fuī = to be

5. sī bene quī cēnat bene vīvit, lūcet, eāmus quō dūcit gula. (Hor. *Ep.* 1.6.56)

bonus -a -um = good (adv: bene)
cēnō -āre -āvī -ātum (intr) = to dine
dūcō -cere -xī -ctum = to lead
eāmus = let us go
gula -ae (f) = the throat, appetite
lūcet = (now that) it is daylight
quī quae quod = who(ever), which, what
quō = whither, to the place to which
sī (conj) = if
vīvō -vere -xī -ctum (intr) = to live

6. sed fugit intereā, fugit irreparābile tempus. (Verg. *Georg.* 3.284)

fugiō -ere fūgī (intr) = to run away, fly
intereā (adv) = meanwhile
irreparābilis -is -e = irretrievable
sed (conj) = but
tempus -oris (n) = time

7. et nunc omnis ager, nunc omnis parturit arbōs. (Verg. *Ecl.* 3.56)

ager agrī (m) = land, a field
arbōs -oris (f) = a tree
et (conj) = and
nunc (adv) = now
omnis -is -e = every
parturiō -īre -īvī (intr) = to be in labour, be giving birth

8. idem est ergō beātē vīvere et secundum nātūram. (Sen. *Dial.* 7.8.2)

beātus -a -um = happy
ergō = therefore, then
et (conj) = and
īdem eadem idem = the same
secundum nātūram = following, in accordance with nature
sum esse fuī = to be
vīvō -vere -xī -ctum (intr) = to live

11

9. omnis opīniō ratiō est, et quidem bona ratiō sī vēra, mala autem
   sī falsa est opīniō. (Cic. *N.D.* 3.71)

   autem = however, but
   bonus -a -um = good
   et (conj) = and
   falsus -a -um = false, mistaken
   malus -a -um = bad
   omnis -is -e = every
   opīniō -ōnis (f) = an opinion, belief
   quidem = indeed
   ratiō -ōnis (f) = reason, an act of reasoning
   sī (conj) = if
   sum esse fuī = to be
   vērus -a -um = real, true

10. cum ratiōne animus movētur placidē atque constanter, tum illud
    gaudium dīcitur; cum autem ināniter et effūsē animus exsultat,
    tum illa laetitia gestiens vel nimia dīcī potest. (Cic. *Tusc.* 4.13)

    animus -ī (m) = the mind, spirit
    atque (conj) = and
    autem = however, but
    constans -ntis = steady
    cum (conj) = when
    dīcō -cere -xī -ctum = to say, call
    effūsus -a -um = impetuous, immoderate
    et (conj) = and
    exsultō -āre -āvī (intr) = to leap up, exult
    gaudium -[i]ī (n) = joy
    gestiens -ntis = elated, unrestrained
    ille -a -ud = this, that
    inānis -is -e = empty, meaningless
    laetitia -ae (f) = gladness, pleasure
    moveō -ēre mōvī mōtum = move, excite
    nimius -a -um = excessive, extravagant
    placidus -a -um = quiet, calm
    possum posse potuī = to be able (to)
    ratiōne = with good reason
    tum (adv) = then
    vel (conj) = or

# Vocabulary to Learn

bonus -a -um = good (adv: bene)
et (conj) = and
sī (conj) = if
sum esse fuī = to be
vir virī (m) = a man

# 2
# ACCUSATIVES

## Morphology

The commonest ending for the accusative singular is a short vowel plus *-m* (which most often appears as *-am*, *-em* or *-um*, and only rarely as *-im* or *-om*). Exceptions are:

> nouns and adjectives which have lost this ending altogether, e.g. a variety of 3rd declension neuter nouns;
>
> pronouns which have the unique neuter ending *-d*.

All neuter forms have the same ending for the nominative and accusative. This can lead to uncertainty about the true subject or object, unless an unambiguous case or the context resolves the problem.

## Syntax

Accusatives limit or define the action of the verb. They are used:

**1.** as the direct object of transitive verbs forming a K2 kernel:

> erus meus **magnam cēnam** dat.
> my master is giving **a big dinner**.

When sentences of this type are turned into the passive, the direct object becomes the new subject:

> **magna cēna** (ab erō meō) datur.
> **a big dinner** is being given (by my master).

Infinitives being verbal nouns (see chapter 1 syntax §3) are used in the accusative in a similar way:

> ille bene ac beātē **vīvere** vult.
> he wants **to live** well and happily.

They can also have a direct object of their own:

> ille **bonam** atque **magnam cēnam** praebēre potest.
> he can provide **a good, big dinner**.

**2.** as the second direct object of certain transitive verbs such as *cēlāre* "to conceal", *docēre* "to teach" and *rogāre* "to ask", which take two accusatives, one of the person and one of the thing, forming a K3 kernel:

> **quid aliud** pauper deum rogat?
> **what else** does a poor man ask god for?

When sentences of this type are turned into the passive, the accusative of the thing remains unchanged:

> **quid aliud** (ā paupere) deus rogātur?
> **what else** is god asked for (by a poor man)?

Infinitives being verbal nouns (see chapter 1 syntax §3) are used in the accusative in a similar way:

> bene **vīvere** is deum rogat.
> he asks god **to live** well.

They can also have their own direct object in addition to that of the main verb:

> **rem** facere is deum rogat.
> he asks god to make **money**.

**3.** as the second, predicative accusative with factitive verbs such as *dīcere* "to call", *facere* "to make" and *reddere* "to make", forming a K3 kernel:

> rēs hominem **beātum** reddit.
> wealth makes a man **happy**.

When sentences of this type are turned into the passive, the second, predicative accusative becomes the complement:

> homō **beātus** (rē) redditur.
> a man is made **happy** (by wealth).

When two nouns are joined in this way, it is not clear from the Latin word order which is the direct object accusative and which the predicative accusative:

> dīves **erum meum hērēdem** facit.
> a rich man makes **my master his heir** (a rich man makes **his heir my master**).

Usually the context resolves the problem unless the speaker is being deliberately ambiguous.

**4.** in various prepositional phrases:

> mortuus est ille: rēs **ad hērēdem** venit.
> he is dead: the estate comes **to his heir**.

But there is no preposition with certain examples of:

**(a)** the accusative of extent in space or time;

**(b)** the accusative of the goal of motion, especially with names of towns, small islands, *domus* "home" and *rūs* "country".

**5.** in certain adverbial expressions which use the accusative singular neuter in place of an adverb. Most frequent are:

**(a)** comparative adverbs (see chapter 4);

**(b)** expressions of quantity such as *multum* "much", *nihil* "not at all", *nimium* "too much" and *tantum* "so much":

> sīc fortūnātus meus erus **multum**que beātus.
> thus my master is lucky and **very** happy.

# Metaphrasing

**1.** A noun or pronoun in the accusative is metaphrased: — ⋆s —

erum — ⋆s the master

A second noun or pronoun in the accusative is metaphrased with the first:

erum nihil — ⋆s the master nothing

It soon becomes clear how they are related:

erum nihil rogat — asks the master for nothing

**2.** An adjective in the accusative is metaphrased in a similar way:

beātum — ⋆s the happy —

**3.** A relative pronoun in the accusative is metaphrased in a similar way, in brackets, at the beginning of its clause:

erus quem the master (whom — ⋆s) ⋆s

But when there is no such antecedent (i.e. no previous noun or pronoun for it to refer to), the relative pronoun is indefinite in meaning:

quem (whomever — ⋆s)

The relative clause is left thus suspended until it becomes clear how it fits into the whole sentence:

quem vult rogat — asks (whomever — wants)

**4.** A prepositional phrase is metaphrased according to the sense of the preposition and its position in the Latin sentence; it is often best placed after the verb in English:

ad hērēdem — ⋆s to the heir

**5.** A transitive verb taking a direct object in the accusative suggests a K2 kernel; it is metaphrased: — ⋆s —

rogat — asks —

Such a verb in the passive is metaphrased: — is ★ed

rogātur                                    — is asked

**6.** These basic patterns can then be adapted when necessary as follows:

(**a**) two accusatives with a factitive verb may need an alternative metaphrase unless the context makes clear which is the direct object accusative and which the predicative accusative:

erum hērēdem facit          — makes the master the heir
                             *or* — makes the heir the master

(**b**) an accusative and an infinitive may need metaphrasing both as a unit and as two separate elements:

erum rogāre          (to ask the master)
                     *or* (to ask —) ★s the master
                     *or* — ★s the master (to ask —)

(**c**) a neuter form may need an alternative metaphrase since it has the same ending for both nominative and accusative:

dulce          a sweet — ★s / it is sweet
               *or* — ★s a sweet —

(**d**) an accusative that can be used adverbially without a preposition may need an alternative metaphrase:

Rōmam          — ★s Rome / — ★s to Rome

If it is a neuter form, it may need more than one alternative:

nihil          nothing ★s
               *or* — ★s nothing / not at all

# Examples

## 1. *ille homō tuam hērēditātem inhiat quasi ēsuriens lupus. (Pl. *St.* 605)

ille -a -ud = that, this

| | | |
|---|---|---|
| ille | (a) | -e |
| | (b) | nom sing masc |
| | (c) | that — ★s |

homō -inis (m) = a human being, man

| | | |
|---|---|---|
| homō | (a) | -ō |
| | (b) | nom sing |
| | (c) | that man ★s |

tuus -a -um = your (own)

| | | |
|---|---|---|
| tuam | (a) | -am |
| | (b) | acc sing fem |
| | (c) | that man ★s your — |

hērēditās -ātis (f) = an inheritance

| | | |
|---|---|---|
| hērēditātem | (a) | -em |
| | (b) | acc sing |
| | (c) | that man ★s your inheritance |

inhiō -āre -āvī -ātum = to be open-mouthed, avid for

| | | |
|---|---|---|
| inhiat | (a) | -t |
| | (b) | 3rd sing act |
| | (c) | that man is avid for your inheritance |

quasi (conj) = as if, like
ēsuriens -ntis = hungry

| | | |
|---|---|---|
| quasi ēsuriens | (a) | -ns |
| | (b) | nom sing masc/fem |
| | (c) | like a hungry — ★s |

lupus -ī (m) = a wolf

| | | |
|---|---|---|
| lupus. | (a) | -us |
| | (b) | nom sing |
| | (c) | like a hungry wolf ★s. |

| | |
|---|---|
| Translation | That man is avid for your inheritance like a hungry wolf. |

## 2.  et genus et formam rēgīna Pecūnia dōnat.
(Hor. *Ep*. 1.6.37)

et (conj) = and
genus −eris (n) = breeding, high
    birth

|  |  |  |
|---|---|---|
| et genus | (a) | −s |
|  | (b) | nom/acc sing |
|  | (c) | and high birth ★s / — ★s high birth |

et (conj) = and
forma −ae (f) = form, shape,
    beauty

|  |  |  |
|---|---|---|
| et formam | (a) | −am |
|  | (b) | acc sing |
|  | (c) | and — ★s high birth and beauty |

rēgīna −ae (f) = a queen

|  |  |  |
|---|---|---|
| rēgīna | (a) | −a |
|  | (b) | nom sing |
|  | (c) | and a queen ★s high birth and beauty |

pecūnia −ae (f) = wealth, money

|  |  |  |
|---|---|---|
| Pecūnia | (a) | −a |
|  | (b) | nom sing |
|  | (c) | and Queen Money ★s high birth and beauty |

dōnō −āre −āvī −ātum = to grant,
    confer

|  |  |  |
|---|---|---|
| dōnat. | (a) | −t |
|  | (b) | 3rd sing act |
|  | (c) | and Queen Money confers high birth and beauty. |

## 3. *pauper locuplētem optāre podagram nec dubitat. (Juv. 13.96)

pauper -eris = poor

| | | |
|---|---|---|
| pauper | (a) | -r |
| | (b) | nom sing masc/fem |
| | (c) | the poor — ★s |

locuplēs -ētis = rich

| | | |
|---|---|---|
| locuplētem | (a) | -em |
| | (b) | acc sing masc/fem |
| | (c) | the poor — ★s the rich — |

optō -āre -āvī -ātum = to wish, pray for

| | | |
|---|---|---|
| optāre | (a) | -re |
| | (b) | pres infin act |
| | (c) | the poor — ★s (to pray for the rich —) / the poor — ★s the rich — (to pray for —) |

podagra -ae (f) = gout

| | | |
|---|---|---|
| podagram | (a) | -am |
| | (b) | acc sing |
| | (c) | the poor — ★s (to pray for the rich gout) |

nec = not even
dubitō -āre -āvī -ātum = to be in doubt, hesitate (to)

| | | |
|---|---|---|
| nec dubitat. | (a) | -t |
| | (b) | 3rd sing act |
| | (c) | the poor — does not even hesitate (to pray for the rich gout). |

| | |
|---|---|
| Translation | The poor man does not even hesitate to pray for the rich man's gout. |

N.B. "Rich" agrees grammatically with "gout" but logically describes the type of man to have the disease.

# 4.  *domum suam istum nōn ferē quisquam vocat.
## (Cic. *S.Rosc.* 52)

domus -ūs (f) = a house, home

                domum    (a)   -um
                                 (b)   acc sing
                                 (c)   — *s a house / to a house

suus -a -um = his, her, its (own),
    etc.

                suam    (a)   -am
                                 (b)   acc sing fem
                                 (c)   — *s his/her house / — *s to
                                           his/her house

iste -a -ud = that, this

                istum    (a)   -um
                                 (b)   acc sing masc
                                 (c)   — *s that — his/her house / — *s
                                           that — to his/her house

nōn = not

ferē (adverb modifying words of
    quantity) = almost, virtually

quisquam quicquam = anyone,
    anything

        nōn ferē quisquam    (a)   -s
                                 (b)   nom sing masc
                                 (c)   virtually no-one *s that — his house /
                                           virtually no-one *s that — to his
                                           house

vocō -āre -āvī -ātum = to call,
    invite

                vocat.    (a)   -t
                                 (b)   3rd sing act
                                 (c)   virtually no-one invites that — to his
                                           house.

            Translation       Virtually no-one invites that man to
                                       his house.

## 5. *sapiens nihil deum rogat nisi quod rogāre potest palam. (Sen. *Ep.* 10.5)

sapiens –ntis = wise

| | | |
|---|---|---|
| sapiens | (a) | –ns |
| | (b) | nom sing masc/fem |
| | (c) | a wise — ★s |

nihil (n.indecl) = nothing

| | | |
|---|---|---|
| nihil | (a) | –l |
| | (b) | nom/acc sing |
| | (c) | a wise — ★s nothing / not at all |

deus deī (m) = a god

| | | |
|---|---|---|
| deum | (a) | –um |
| | (b) | acc sing |
| | (c) | a wise — ★s god nothing / not at all |

rogō –āre –āvī –ātum = to ask (for)

| | | |
|---|---|---|
| rogat | (a) | –t |
| | (b) | 3rd sing act |
| | (c) | a wise — asks god for nothing |

nisi (conj) = if not, except
quī quae quod = who(ever), which, what

| | | |
|---|---|---|
| nisi quod | (a) | –d |
| | (b) | nom/acc sing neut |
| | (c) | except (what ★s / what — ★s) |

rogō –āre –āvī –ātum = to ask (for)

| | | |
|---|---|---|
| rogāre | (a) | –re |
| | (b) | pres infin act |
| | (c) | except (what — ★s to ask for) |

possum posse potuī = to be able (to)
palam (adv) = openly

| | | |
|---|---|---|
| potest palam. | (a) | –t |
| | (b) | 3rd sing act |
| | (c) | except (what — is able to ask for openly). |

| | |
|---|---|
| Translation | A wise man asks god for nothing except what he can ask for openly. |

# Summary of Examples

1. ille homō tuam hērēditātem inhiat quasi ēsuriens lupus.

2. et genus et formam rēgīna Pecūnia dōnat.

3. pauper locuplētem optāre podagram nec dubitat.

4. domum suam istum nōn ferē quisquam vocat.

5. sapiens nihil deum rogat nisi quod rogāre potest palam.

# Exercises

Complete the following sentences on the analogy of the first:

quī sapiens est sapientem ad cēnam vocat.
quī ēsuriens est  . . . . . . . . . . . . . . . . . . . . . .
quī beātus est . . . . . . . . . . . . . . . . . . . . . . .
quī magnus est . . . . . . . . . . . . . . . . . . . . . .
quī locuplēs est  . . . . . . . . . . . . . . . . . . . . . .
quī pauper est  . . . . . . . . . . . . . . . . . . . . . .

# Reading

1.  ★virtūs sōla, sī adest, vītam efficit beātam. (Cic. *Fin.* 5.78)
adsum −esse −fuī (intr) = to be present
beātus −a −um = happy
efficiō −icere −ēcī −ectum = to make
sōlus −a −um = alone
virtūs −ūtis (f) = virtue
vīta −ae (f) = life

LEARNING LATIN

2. *paupertātem nēmō gravem sentit nisi quī putat. (Sen. *Dial.* 12.12.1)

gravis –is –e = heavy, oppressive
nēmō –inis (m) = no-one
nisi (conj) = if not, except
paupertās –ātis (f) = poverty
putō –āre –āvī –ātum = to think, regard (as)
quī quae quod = who(ever), which, what
sentiō –tīre –sī –sum = to feel, perceive (as)

3. *animus dīves, nōn arca appellārī solet. (Cic. *Parad.* 44)

animus –ī (m) = the mind, spirit
appellō –āre –āvī –ātum = to address, call
arca –ae (f) = a coffer, money-chest
dīves –itis = rich
nōn = not
soleō –ēre –itus = to be accustomed (to)

4.      perpetuus nullī datur ūsus, et hērēs
hērēdem alterius velut unda supervenit undam.
(Hor. *Ep.* 2.2.175)

alterius = of another man
dō dare dedī datum = to give, grant
hērēs –ēdis (m) = an heir
nullī = to no-one
perpetuus –a –um = continuous, lasting
superveniō –enīre –ēnī –entum = to come on top of, overtake
unda –ae (f) = a wave (of the sea)
ūsus –ūs (m) = use, enjoyment (of wealth, property)
velut (adv) = just as

5. ita miser quidem esse, quī virtūtem habet, nōn potest. (Sen. *Ep.* 92.14)

habeō –ēre –uī –itum = to have, possess
ita (adv) = so, consequently
miser –era –erum = pitiable, wretched, unhappy
nōn = not
possum posse potuī = to be able (to)
quī quae quod = who(ever), which, what
quidem = certainly, indeed
sum esse fuī = to be
virtūs –ūtis (f) = virtue

24

6. ⋆beāta est ergō vīta conveniens ad nātūram suam, quae nōn aliter contingere potest quam sī prīmum sāna mens est, deinde fortis ac vehemens. (Sen. *Dial.* 7.3.3)

ac (conj) = and
ad (prep w.acc) = to
aliter … quam = in another way … than
beātus -a -um = happy
contingō -ingere -igī -actum (intr) = to come about, happen
conveniens -ntis = appropriate (to)
deinde = from there or then, then
ergō = therefore
fortis -is -e = strong, courageous
mens -tis (f) = the mind
nātūra -ae (f) = nature
nōn = not
possum posse potuī = to be able (to)
prīmum (adv) = first
quī quae quod = who(ever), which, what
sānus -a -um = healthy, sane
suus -a -um = his, her, its, one's (own), etc.
vīta -ae (f) = life
vehemens -ntis = vigorous, forceful

7. potest aliter quoque dēfīnīrī bonum nostrum.'(Sen. *Dial.* 7.4.1)

aliter (adv) = in another way
bonum -ī (n) = something good, a blessing
dēfīniō -īre -īvī -ītum = to delimit, define
noster -tra -trum = our (own)
possum posse potuī = to be able (to)
quoque (adv) = as well, also

8. rēs sōla potest facere et servāre beātum. (Hor. *Ep.* 1.6.47)

beātus -a -um = happy
faciō -ere fēcī factum = to make
possum posse potuī = to be able (to)
rēs reī (f) = property, wealth
servō -āre -āvī -ātum = to watch over, keep
sōlus -a -um = alone

9. nam dīves quī fierī vult, et cito vult fierī. (Juv. 14.176)

cito (adv) = quickly, soon
dīves -itis = rich, wealthy
et = in addition, also
fīō fierī (intr) = to become, be made
nam = for
quī quae quod = who(ever), which, what
volō velle voluī = to want, wish (to)

10. * quid prohibet nōs beātam vītam dīcere līberum animum et ērectum et interritum ac stabilem, extrā metum, extrā cupiditātem positum? (Sen. *Dial.* 7.4.3)

ac (conj) = and
animus -ī (m) = the mind, spirit
beātus -a -um = happy
cupiditās -ātis (f) = desire, greed
dīcō -cere -xī -ctum = to say, call
ērectus -a -um = upright
extrā (prep w.acc) = beyond (the reach of)
interritus -a -um = not terrified, fearless
līber -era -erum = free, independent
metus -ūs (m) = fear
nōs (acc) = us
positus -a -um = placed, set
prohibeō -ēre -uī -itum = to keep off, forbid (to)
quis? quid? = who? what?
stabilis -is -e = standing firm, steady
vīta -ae (f) = life

# Vocabulary to Learn

beātus -a -um = happy
nōn = not
possum posse potuī = to be able (to)
quī quae quod = who(ever), which, what
vīta -ae (f) = life

# 3
# ABLATIVES

## Morphology

The commonest ending for the ablative singular is *a long vowel* (which may be $-\bar{a}$, $-\bar{e}$, $-\bar{\imath}$, $-\bar{o}$ or $-\bar{u}$). Exceptions are most 3rd declension nouns and some 3rd declension adjectives including comparatives (see chapter 4), which have a short $-e$.

## Syntax

The ablative case has a special meaning of its own ("from"), but it has also taken over the meaning of three other cases, i.e. the instrumental ("by"), the sociative ("with") and the locative ("at, in, on"). This gives it four basic meanings:

**1.** the "ablative of separation" refers to the point of departure. It is often signalled by $\bar{a}$ or *ab* "from, away from", *dē* "from, down from", $\bar{e}$ or *ex* "from, out of":

> haud procul **ē conspectū** urbs Rōma est.
> not far **out of sight** is the city of Rome.

It is also used with animate nouns (and personifications) for the agent of passive verbs, from whom the action is regarded as originating. This use is always signalled by $\bar{a}$ or *ab* "by":

> hic diēs festus **ā tōtō populō** agitur.
> today's festival is celebrated **by the whole people**.

**2.** the "ablative of the instrument" refers to the thing by means of which something is done. It is not accompanied by a preposition:

> villa nostra abundat **porcō haedō agnō gallīnā.**
> our villa abounds **in pig, kid, lamb and chicken.**

It is also used for expressions of price:

> erus meus hostiam **magnō** vendere potest.
> my master can sell a sacrificial victim **at a high price.**

**3.** the "ablative of accompaniment" refers to the person or thing associated with the action. It is often signalled by *cum* "with, together with":

> praetor urbānus **cum magnō comitātū** descendit in forum.
> the city praetor comes down into the forum **with a large retinue.**

**4.** the "ablative of time or place" refers to the time when or the place where something is done. It is often signalled by *in* "in, on":

> **hōc diē** praetor immolat pūblicē iuvencam.
> **on this day** the praetor sacrifices a heifer on behalf of the state.

> posteā **in fānō** iuvenca tōta cōnsūmitur.
> afterwards the whole heifer is consumed **in the sanctuary.**

These basic meanings can be seen in the different ways in which ablatives are used:

**5.** as the "direct object" of certain "transitive" verbs which take an ablative (rather than an accusative), forming a K2 kernel:

> quī colit Herculem edācem nōn **cibō** caret.
> whoever worships the gluttonous Hercules does not lack **food.**

**6.** as the indirect or more remote object of certain transitive verbs such as *abstinēre* "to restrain from", *dōnāre* "to present with" and *prīvāre* "to deprive of", forming a K3 kernel:

> quī colit Herculem vīnōsum nōn abstinet sē **cantū.**
> whoever worships the drunkard Hercules does not restrain himself **from singing.**

7. with certain adjectives that take an ablative such as *dignus* "worthy (of)" and *līber* "free (from)":

>dignum **laude** virum Mūsa vetat morī.
>the Muse forbids a man worthy **of praise** to die.

8. in various prepositional phrases:

>dulce est dēsipere **in locō**.
>it is sweet to play the fool **on the right occasion**.

But there is no preposition with certain examples of:

(a) the ablative of time;

(b) the ablative of place and the ablative of separation, especially with names of towns, small islands, *domus* "home" and *rūs* "country".

9. in certain adverbial expressions which use the ablative singular of 1st and 2nd declension adjectives in place of an adverb such as *cito* "quickly", *rectā* "directly" and *sērō* "at a late hour":

>erus **sērō** domum revenit titubantī pede.
>the master comes back home **late** with stumbling step.

# Metaphrasing

1. A noun or pronoun in the ablative is metaphrased: — ★s by/with/from —, as appropriate:

>populō               — ★s by/with/from the people

2. An adjective in the ablative is metaphrased in a similar way:

>tōtō                 — ★s by/with/from the whole —

3. A relative pronoun in the ablative is metaphrased in a similar way, in brackets, at the beginning of its clause:

>hostia quā           a victim (by/with/from which — ★s) ★s

29

But when there is no such antecedent (i.e. no previous noun or pronoun for it to refer to), the relative pronoun is indefinite in meaning:

quā                              (by/with/from whatever — ★s)

The relative clause is left thus suspended until it becomes clear how it fits into the whole sentence:

quā hostiā potest immolat     — sacrifices (with whatever victim — is able)

**4.** A prepositional phrase is metaphrased according to the sense of the preposition and its position in the Latin sentence; it is often best placed after the verb in English:

in fānō                         — ★s in the sanctuary

**5.** A "transitive" verb taking a "direct object" in the ablative suggests a K2 kernel; it is metaphrased: — ★s —

caret                           — lacks —

**6.** These basic patterns can then be adapted when necessary as follows:

**(a)** an ablative of time or place is also metaphrased: at/in/on —, as appropriate:

diē                             — ★s by/with/from/on the day

**(b)** a verb taking a "direct object" in the ablative may make prepositions used earlier redundant:

cibō                            — ★s by/with/from food
cibō caret                      — lacks food

**(c)** a verb of buying, selling or valuing may make prepositions used earlier inappropriate:

magnō                           — ★s by/with/from a great —
magnō vendit                    — sells — at a great price

**(d)** an adjective taking an ablative normally follows the noun in English which the adjective modifies:

dignus laude vir                a man worthy of praise ★s

(e) an adjective in the ablative that can be used adverbially without a preposition may need an alternative metaphrase:

cito                 — ★s by/with/from a swift —

*or* — ★s swiftly

# Examples

## 1.    vetus āra multō fūmat odōre. (Hor. *Carm* .3.18.7)

vetus –eris = old

| | | | |
|---|---|---|---|
| | vetus | (a) | –s |
| | | (b) | nom sing masc/fem/neut *or* acc sing neut |
| | | (c) | the old — ★s / — ★s the old — |

āra –ae (f) = an altar

| | | | |
|---|---|---|---|
| | āra | (a) | –a |
| | | (b) | nom sing |
| | | (c) | the old altar ★s |

multus –a –um = much

| | | | |
|---|---|---|---|
| | multō | (a) | –ō |
| | | (b) | abl sing masc/neut |
| | | (c) | the old altar ★s by/with/from much — |

fūmō –āre –āvī (intr) = to smoke

| | | | |
|---|---|---|---|
| | fūmat | (a) | –t |
| | | (b) | 3rd sing act |
| | | (c) | the old altar smokes with much — |

odor –ōris (m) = a smell, incense

| | | | |
|---|---|---|---|
| | odōre. | (a) | –e |
| | | (b) | abl sing |
| | | (c) | the old altar smokes with much incense. |

## 2. nōn festā lūce madēre est rubor. (Tib. 2.1.29)

nōn = not

festus -a -um = festive, appropriate to a feast or festival

nōn festā     (a)  -ā
                 (b)  abl sing fem
                 (c)  — does not ★ by/with/from a
                       festive —

lux lūcis (f) = light, daylight,
a day

lūce     (a)  -e
                 (b)  abl sing
                 (c)  — does not ★ by/with/from/on a
                       feast day

madeō -ēre (intr) = to be wet,
be drunk

madēre     (a)  -re
                 (b)  pres infin act
                 (c)  (to be drunk) does not ★ / — does
                       not ★ (to be drunk) on a feast day

sum esse fuī = to be

est     (a)  -t
                 (b)  3rd sing act
                 (c)  (to be drunk) is not — / it is not —
                       (to be drunk) on a feast day

rubor -ōris (m) = redness, cause
for shame or embarrassment

rubor.     (a)  -r
                 (b)  nom sing
                 (c)  it is not cause for shame (to be
                       drunk) on a feast day.

Translation     It is not cause for shame to be drunk
                       on a feast day.

## 3. quodcumque invectīcium gaudium est fundāmentō caret. (Sen. *Ep.* 23.5)

quīcumque quaecumque quod
    cumque = whoever,
    whatever

            quodcumque   (a)   -d
                         (b)   nom/acc sing neut
                         (c)   (whatever ★s / whatever — ★s)

invectīcius -a -um = imported

             invectīcium   (a)   -um
                         (b)   nom/acc sing neut
                         (c)   (whatever imported — ★s / whatever
                               ★s imported -)

gaudium -[i]ī (n) = joy

               gaudium   (a)   -um
                         (b)   nom/acc sing
                         (c)   (whatever imported joy ★s /
                               whatever ★s imported joy)

sum esse fuī = to be

                    est   (a)   -t
                         (b)   3rd sing act
                         (c)   (whatever is imported joy)

fundāmentum -ī (n) = a foun
    dation

              fundāmentō   (a)   -ō
                         (b)   abl sing
                         (c)   (whatever is imported joy) ★s by/
                             with/from a foundation

careō -ēre -uī -itum (w.abl) = to
    be without, lack

                 caret.   (a)   -t
                         (b)   3rd sing act
                         (c)   (whatever is imported joy) lacks
                             foundation.

             Translation   Whatever is imported joy lacks
                               foundation.

## 4. *beātus esse sine virtūte nēmō potest. (Cic. *N.D.* 1.48)

beātus -a -um = happy

|  | beātus | (a) | -us |
|---|---|---|---|
|  |  | (b) | nom sing masc |
|  |  | (c) | a happy — ★s |

sum esse fuī = to be

|  | esse | (a) | esse |
|---|---|---|---|
|  |  | (b) | pres infin act |
|  |  | (c) | (to be happy) |

sine (prep w.abl) = without
virtūs -ūtis (f) = virtue

|  | sine virtūte | (a) | -e |
|---|---|---|---|
|  |  | (b) | abl sing |
|  |  | (c) | (to be happy without virtue) |

nēmō -inis (m) = no-one

|  | nēmō | (a) | -ō |
|---|---|---|---|
|  |  | (b) | nom sing |
|  |  | (c) | no-one ★s (to be happy without virtue) |

possum posse potuī = to be able (to)

|  | potest. | (a) | -t |
|---|---|---|---|
|  |  | (b) | 3rd sing act |
|  |  | (c) | no-one is able (to be happy without virtue). |

Translation    No-one can be happy without virtue.

## 5.   magnō ubīque pretiō virtūs aestimātur. (Val. Max. 5.4.1)

magnus -a -um = great

| | | | |
|---|---|---|---|
| | magnō | (a) | -ō |
| | | (b) | abl sing masc/neut |
| | | (c) | — ★s by/with/from a great — |

ubīque (adv) = anywhere, everywhere

pretium -(i)ī (n) = a price

| | | | |
|---|---|---|---|
| | ubīque pretiō | (a) | -ō |
| | | (b) | abl sing |
| | | (c) | — ★s everywhere at a great price |

virtūs -ūtis (f) = virtue

| | | | |
|---|---|---|---|
| | virtūs | (a) | -s |
| | | (b) | nom sing |
| | | (c) | virtue ★s everywhere at a great price |

aestimō -āre -āvī -ātum = to estimate, value (at)

| | | | |
|---|---|---|---|
| | aestimātur. | (a) | -tur |
| | | (b) | 3rd sing pass |
| | | (c) | virtue is valued everywhere at a great price. |

# Summary of Examples

1. vetus āra multō fūmat odōre.

2. nōn festā lūce madēre est rubor.

3. quodcumque invectīcium gaudium est fundāmentō caret.

4. beātus esse sine virtūte nēmō potest.

5. magnō ubīque pretiō virtūs aestimātur.

# Exercises

Complete the following sentences on the analogy of the first:

quī ēbrius est diem festum agit cum ēbriō comitātū.
quī beātus est ...............................
quī sōbrius est ...............................
quī fortis est ...............................
quī sapiens est ...............................
quī pauper est ...............................

# Reading

1. \* lūce sacrā requiescit humus, requiescit arātor. (Tib. 2.1.5)

    arātor –ōris (m) = a ploughman, farmer of arable land
    humus –ī (f) = ground, soil
    lux lūcis (f) = light, daylight, a day
    requiescō –escere –ēvī –ētum (intr) = to rest
    sacer –cra –crum = holy, sacred

2. libet iacēre modo sub antīquā īlice,
        modo in tenācī grāmine.                    (Hor. *Epod.* 2.23)

    antīquus –a –um = ancient, aged
    grāmen –inis (n) = grass
    iaceō –ēre –uī –itum (intr) = to lie
    īlex –icis (f) = a holm-oak
    in (prep w.acc/abl) = into / in, on
    libet = it is pleasing
    modo ... modo (advs) = now ...now
    sub (prep w.acc/abl) = under, beneath
    tenax –ācis = holding fast, clinging

3. parvō famēs constat, magnō fastīdium. (Sen. *Ep.* 17.4)

    constō –āre –itī (intr) = to stand together, cost
    famēs –is (f) = hunger, appetite
    fastīdium –(i)ī (n) = lack of appetite, fastidiousness
    magnus –a –um = great
    parvus –a –um = small, little

4. parva seges satis est, satis est requiescere lectō. (Tib. 1.1.43)

    lectus –ī (m) = a bed, couch
    parvus –a –um = small
    requiescō –escere –ēvī –ētum (intr) = to rest
    satis (n.indecl) = sufficient, enough
    seges –etis (f) = a field or crop of standing corn

5. sed genus ignāvum, quod lectō gaudet et umbrā. (Juv. 7.105)

gaudeō -dēre gavīsus (intr) = to rejoice, be pleased
genus -eris (n) = a breed or kind (of human beings)
ignāvus -a -um = lazy
lectus -ī (m) = a bed, couch
quī quae quod = who(ever), which, what
sed (conj) = but
umbra -ae (f) = shadow, shade


6. * velut haec meretrix meum erum miserum suā blanditiā infert in pauperiem. (Pl. *Truc.* 572)

blanditia -ae (f) = blandishment, charm
erus -ī (m) = a master
hic haec hoc = this
in (prep w.acc/abl) = into / in, on
inferō -rre intulī illātum = to carry or bring into, reduce to
meretrix -īcis (f) = a courtesan
meus -a -um = my (own)
miser -era -erum = pitiable, wretched, unhappy
pauperiēs -ēī (f) = poverty
suus -a -um = his, her, its (own), etc.
velut (adv) = as for example


7. difficile est longum subitō dēpōnere amōrem. (Catul. 76.13)

amor -ōris (m) = love, a love affair
dēpōnō -ōnere -osuī -ositum = to put or lay down, abandon
difficilis -is -e = difficult
longus -a -um = long, prolonged
subitus -a -um = sudden


8. * infēlix quīdam nōn sine voluptāte, immō ob ipsam voluptātem est, quā virtūs saepe caret, numquam indiget. (Sen. *Dial.* 7.7.2)

careō -ēre -uī -itum (w.abl) = to be without, lack
immō = rather
indigeō -ēre -uī (w.abl) = to need, feel the need of
infēlix -īcis = unhappy, unfortunate
ipse -a -um = himself, herself, itself, etc
numquam (adv) = never
ob (prep w.acc) = because of
quīdam quaedam quiddam = a certain person or thing
saepe (adv) = often
sine (prep w.abl) = without
virtūs -ūtis (f) = virtue
voluptās -ātis (f) = pleasure

9. sīc rōbustus animus et excelsus omnī est līber cūrā et angōre. (Cic. *Fin.* 1.49)

angor –ōris (m) = anguish, anxiety
animus –ī (m) = the mind, spirit
cūra –ae (f) = worry, care
excelsus –a –um = lofty, noble
līber –era –erum = free (from)
omnis –is –e = every
rōbustus –a –um = robust, strong
sīc (adv) = thus

10. iam Fidēs et Pax et Honōs Pudorque
priscus et neglecta redīre Virtūs
audet, appāretque beāta plēnō
    Cōpia cornū.            (Hor. *Saec.* 57)

appāreō –ēre –uī –itum (intr) = to be seen, appear
audeō –dēre –sus = to have the courage, dare (to)
beātus –a –um = happy, blessed
cōpia –ae (f) = an abundance, plenty
cornū –ūs (n) = a horn
fidēs –ēī (f) = trust, good faith
honōs –ōris (m) = honour
iam (adv) = now
neglectus –a –um = neglected
pax pācis (f) = peace
plēnus –a –um = full
priscus –a –um = belonging to a former time, old-fashioned
pudor –ōris (m) = a sense of shame, decency
–que (conj) = and
redeō –īre –iī –itum (intr) = to come back, return
virtūs –ūtis (f) = virtue

# Vocabulary to Learn

erus –ī (m) = a master
hic haec hoc = this
in (prep w.acc/abl) = into / in, on
sed (conj) = but
virtūs –ūtis (f) = virtue

# 4
# COMPARATIVES

## Morphology

The commonest ending for comparative adjectives is *–ior* or *–iōr–* followed by 3rd declension case endings. Exceptions are:

nominative and accusative singular neuters, which end in *–ius*;

adjectives ending in *-eus*, *-ius* and *-uus*, which use *magis* "more", e.g. *dubius* "doubtful" but *magis dubius* "more doubtful";

a small group of irregulars.

The ending for comparative adverbs is *–ius*, which is the accusative singular neuter of the comparative adjective used adverbially (see chapter 2 syntax §5).

## Syntax

**1.** Comparatives are used for comparing one thing with another:

hic homō **locuplētior** est
this man is **richer / rather rich / too rich**.

**2.** Adding the standard of comparison makes this more precise. *Quam* "than" is most often used, so that the two things compared are in the same case:

> hic homō locuplētior est **quam erus meus**
> this man is richer **than my master**.

When the two things being compared are in the nominative or accusative, an ablative (of comparison) is sometimes used instead of the more frequent *quam* construction:

> hic homō **erō meō** locuplētior est
> this man is richer **than my master**.

**3.** A further refinement is to add another ablative (of measure of difference) to show by how much the one thing differs from the other:

> hic homō **multō** locuplētior est quam erus meus
> this man is **much** richer than my master.

Two such ablatives enable a pair of comparative clauses to be related to each other:

> **quō** / **quantō** locuplētior hic homō, **eō** / **tantō** beātior est
> **the** richer this man is, **the** happier he is.

# Metaphrasing

**1.** A comparative is metaphrased: more — / —er (or: rather — / too —, according to the context) in the position its case requires:

> locuplētior                   a richer — ★s

**2.** A comparative ending in *-ius* may need four alternatives, since it could be nominative or accusative singular neuter of the adjective, or the accusative singular neuter used adverbially:

> vīlius                   a cheaper — ★s / it is cheaper / — ★s a cheaper — / more cheaply

**3.** *Quam* is metaphrased in the usual way unless the presence of a comparative signals the need for the alternative metaphrase: than —:

locuplētior est quam          — is richer than —

**4.** An ablative is metaphrased in the usual way unless the presence of a comparative signals the need for an alternative metaphrase:

multō locuplētior est       — is richer by/with/than much —

It soon becomes clear whether *multō* is ablative of the instrument ("richer by means of much —"), ablative of comparison ("richer than much —") or ablative of measure of difference ("much richer").

**5.** *Quō* ... *eō* and *quantō* ... *tantō* when followed by comparatives are metaphrased: the (more) ... the (more). Each phrase whatever its case is placed at the start of its clause in English and the metaphrase adjusted accordingly:

quō locuplētior          the richer — ★s
quō locuplētiōrem       the richer — — ★s
quō locuplētiōre        the richer — — ★s by/with/from

If however the Latin word order is inverted (*eō* ... *quō*, or *tantō* ... *quantō*), the metaphrase is: that much (more) ... the (more).

# Examples

## 1.   quī multum habet plūs cupit. (Sen. *Ep.* 119.6)

quī quae quod = who(ever),
    which, what

| | | |
|---|---|---|
| quī | (a) | –ī |
| | (b) | nom sing masc |
| | (c) | (whoever ★s) |

multus –a –um = much

| | | |
|---|---|---|
| multum | (a) | –um |
| | (b) | acc sing masc/neut |
| | (c) | (whoever ★s much —) |

habeō –ēre –uī –itum = to have,
    possess

| | | |
|---|---|---|
| habet | (a) | –t |
| | (b) | 3rd sing act |
| | (c) | (whoever possesses much -) |

plūs –ris (n) = a greater amount,
    more

| | | |
|---|---|---|
| plūs | (a) | –s |
| | (b) | nom/acc sing |
| | (c) | (whoever possesses much —) ★s more / more ★s (whoever possesses much —) |

cupiō –ere –īvī –ītum = to desire,
    want

| | | |
|---|---|---|
| cupit. | (a) | –t |
| | (b) | 3rd sing act |
| | (c) | (whoever possesses much —) wants more. |

| | |
|---|---|
| Translation | Whoever possesses much, wants more. |

## 2. māiōre tormentō pecūnia possidētur quam quaeritur. (Sen. *Ep.* 115.16)

māior –ior –ius = greater

| | | |
|---|---|---|
| māiōre | (a) | –iōre |
| | (b) | compar, abl sing masc/fem/neut |
| | (c) | — *s by/with/from greater — |

tormentum –ī (n) = torture, torment, agony

| | | |
|---|---|---|
| tormentō | (a) | –ō |
| | (b) | abl sing |
| | (c) | — *s by/with/from greater agony |

pecūnia –ae (f) = wealth, money

| | | |
|---|---|---|
| pecūnia | (a) | –a |
| | (b) | nom sing |
| | (c) | money *s by/with/from greater agony |

possideō –idēre –ēdī –essum = to have, hold (in one's possession)

| | | |
|---|---|---|
| possidētur | (a) | –tur |
| | (b) | 3rd sing pass |
| | (c) | money is held with greater agony |

quam = than
quaerō –rere –sīvī –sītum = to look for, acquire

| | | |
|---|---|---|
| quam quaeritur. | (a) | –tur |
| | (b) | 3rd sing pass |
| | (c) | than — is acquired. |

| | |
|---|---|
| Translation | Money is held with greater agony than it is acquired. |

## 3.  et genus et virtūs nisi cum rē vīlior algā est. (Hor. *Serm.* 2.5.8)

et (conj) = and
genus –eris (n) = breeding, high
    birth

|  |  |  |
|---|---|---|
| et genus | (a) | –s |
|  | (b) | nom/acc sing |
|  | (c) | and high birth ★s / — ★s high birth |

et ... et (conjs) = both ... and
virtūs –ūtis (f) = virtue

|  |  |  |
|---|---|---|
| et virtūs | (a) | –s |
|  | (b) | nom sing |
|  | (c) | both high birth and virtue ★s |

nisi (conj) = if not, unless
cum (prep w.abl) = with,
    accompanied by
rēs reī (f) = property, wealth

|  |  |  |
|---|---|---|
| nisi cum rē | (a) | –ē |
|  | (b) | abl sing |
|  | (c) | both high birth and virtue ★s unless accompanied by wealth |

vīlis –is –e = cheap, worthless

|  |  |  |
|---|---|---|
| vīlior | (a) | –ior |
|  | (b) | compar, nom sing fem |
|  | (c) | both high birth and virtue ★s more worthless unless accompanied by wealth |

alga –ae (f) = seaweed

|  |  |  |
|---|---|---|
| algā | (a) | –ā |
|  | (b) | abl sing |
|  | (c) | both high birth and virtue ★s more worthless than seaweed unless accompanied by wealth |

sum esse fuī = to be

|  |  |  |
|---|---|---|
| est. | (a) | –t |
|  | (b) | 3rd sing act |
|  | (c) | both high birth and virtue is more worthless than seaweed unless accompanied by wealth. |

|  |  |
|---|---|
| Translation | Both high birth and virtue are more worthless than seaweed unless accompanied by wealth. |

N.B. *est* is singular because Latin can present a group of subjects as individual items with a singular verb.

# 4.   heu, quantō melior sors tua sorte meā est! (Ov. *Tr.* 5.4.4)

heu = alas
quantus –a –um! = how great! how much!

| | | |
|---|---|---|
| heu, quantō | (a) | –ō |
| | (b) | abl sing masc/neut |
| | (c) | alas, — ★s by/with/from how much —! |

melior –ior –ius = better

| | | |
|---|---|---|
| melior | (a) | –ior |
| | (b) | compar, nom sing masc/fem |
| | (c) | alas, how much better — ★s! |

sors –rtis (f) = a lot, situation

| | | |
|---|---|---|
| sors | (a) | –s |
| | (b) | nom sing |
| | (c) | alas, how much better the situation ★s! |

tuus –a –um = your (own)

| | | |
|---|---|---|
| tua | (a) | –a |
| | (b) | nom sing fem |
| | (c) | alas, how much better your situation ★s! |

sors –rtis (f) = a lot, situation

| | | |
|---|---|---|
| sorte | (a) | –e |
| | (b) | abl sing |
| | (c) | alas, how much better your situation ★s than the situation! |

meus –a –um = my (own)

| | | |
|---|---|---|
| meā | (a) | –ā |
| | (b) | abl sing fem |
| | (c) | alas, how much better your situation ★s than my own situation! |

sum esse fuī = to be

| | | |
|---|---|---|
| est! | (a) | –t |
| | (b) | 3rd sing act |
| | (c) | alas, how much better your situation is than my own situation! |

## 5. dūrum: sed levius fit patientiā quidquid corrigere est nefās. (Hor. *Carm.* 1.24.19)

dūrus -a -um = hard, hard to bear

| | | |
|---|---|---|
| dūrum: | (a) | -um |
| | (c) | nom sing neut |
| | (c) | it is hard to bear: |

sed (conj) = but
levis -is -e = light, bearable

| | | |
|---|---|---|
| sed levius | (a) | -ius |
| | (b) | compar, nom/acc sing neut |
| | (c) | but a more bearable — ★s / it is more bearable / — ★s a more bearable — / more bearably |

fīō fierī (intr) = to become or be made

| | | |
|---|---|---|
| fit | (a) | -t |
| | (b) | 3rd sing act |
| | (c) | but — becomes more bearable |

patientia -ae (f) = endurance

| | | |
|---|---|---|
| patientiā | (a) | -ā |
| | (b) | abl sing |
| | (c) | but — becomes more bearable with endurance |

quisquis quidquid = whoever, whatever

| | | |
|---|---|---|
| quidquid | (a) | -d |
| | (b) | nom/acc sing neut |
| | (c) | (whatever ★s / whatever — ★s) |

corrigō -igere -exī -ectum = to straighten out, put right

| | | |
|---|---|---|
| corrigere | (a) | -re |
| | (b) | pres infin act |
| | (c) | (whatever ★s / whatever — ★s to put right) |

sum esse fuī = to be

| | | |
|---|---|---|
| est | (a) | -t |
| | (b) | 3rd sing act |
| | (c) | (whatever it is — to put right) |

nefās (n.indecl) = a sacrilege

| | | |
|---|---|---|
| nefās. | (a) | -s |
| | (b) | nom sing |
| | (c) | (whatever it is a sacrilege to put right). |

| | |
|---|---|
| Translation | It is hard to bear: but whatever it is a sacrilege to put right becomes more bearable with endurance. |

# Summary of Examples

1. quī multum habet plūs cupit.

2. māiōre tormentō pecūnia possidētur quam quaeritur.

3. et genus et virtūs nisi cum rē vīlior algā est.

4. heu, quantō melior sors tua sorte meā est!

5. dūrum: sed levius fit patientiā
quidquid corrigere est nefās.

# Exercises

Complete the following sentences on the analogy of the first:

quī locuplēs est locuplētior vult fierī.
quī sapiens est .............................................
quī fortis est .............................................
quī beātus est .............................................
quī bonus est .............................................
quī magnus est .............................................

# Reading

1. quis mē ūnō vīvit fēlīcior? (Catul. 107.7)

   fēlix -īcis = fruitful, fortunate, happy
   mē (abl) = me
   quis? quid? = who? what?
   ūnus -a -um = one, alone
   vīvo -vere -xī -ctum (intr) = to live

2. nōn quī parum habet, sed quī plūs cupit, pauper est. (Sen. *Ep.* 2.6)

   cupiō -ere -īvī -ītum = to desire, want
   habeō -ēre -uī -itum = to have, possess
   parum (n.indecl) = an insufficient amount, too little
   pauper -eris = poor
   plūs -ris (n) = a greater amount, more

3. multōque grātius venit, quod facilī quam quod plēnā manū datur. (Sen. *Ben.* 1.7.2)

dō dare dedī datum = to give
facilis –is –e = easy, ready
grātus –a –um = appreciative or appreciated, welcome
manus –ūs (f) = the hand
multus –a –um = much
plēnus –a –um = full (of money or gifts)
quam = than
–que (conj) = and
veniō venīre vēnī ventum (intr) = to come

4. quid lībertāte pretiōsius? (Plin. *Ep.* 8.24.7)

lībertās –ātis (f) = freedom
pretiōsus –a –um = costly, precious
quis? quid? = who? what?

5. nulla servitūs turpior est quam voluntāria. (Sen. *Ep.* 47.17)

nullus –a –um = not any, no
quam = than
servitūs –ūtis (f) = slavery, enslavement
turpis –is –e = ugly, disgusting, shameful
voluntārius –a –um = voluntarily undertaken, undergone

6. omne animī vitium tantō conspectius in sē
crīmen habet, quantō māior quī peccat habētur. (Juv. 8.140)

animī = of the mind, character
conspectus –a –um = visible, conspicuous
crīmen –inis (n) = an accusation, ground for reproach
habeō –ēre –uī –itum = to have, hold, consider (to be)
in sē = in itself
māior –ior –ius = greater
omnis –is –e = every
peccō –āre –āvī –ātum (intr) = to make a mistake, do wrong
tantō ... quantō = that much (more) ... the (more)
vitium –(i)ī (n) = a fault, vice

7. *tuā amīcitiā apud meum animum nihil cārius est. (Sall. *Jug.* 110.3)

amīcitia –ae (f) = friendship
animus –ī (m) = the mind
apud (prep w.acc) = at, to
cārus –a –um = costly, dear
meus –a –um = my (own)
nihil (n.indecl) = nothing
tuus –a –um = your (own)

8. ＊paucīs cārior fidēs quam pecūnia est. (Sall. *Jug.* 16.4)

    cārus -a -um = costly, dear
    fidēs -ēī (f) = trust, loyalty
    paucīs = to few men
    pecūnia -ae (f) = wealth, money
    quam = than

9. ＊nihil est virtūte formōsius, nihil pulchrius, nihil amābilius. (Cic. *Fam.* 9.14.4)

    amābilis -is -e = lovable
    formōsus -a -um = shapely, beautiful
    nihil (n.indecl) = nothing
    pulcher -chra -chrum = beautiful, handsome

10. ad summam sapiens ūnō minor est Iove, dīves,
    līber, honōrātus, pulcher, rex dēnique rēgum;
    praecipuē sānus, nisi cum pītuīta molesta est.
    (Hor. *Ep.* 1.1.106)

    ad summam = to sum up, in short
    cum (conj) = when
    dēnique (adv) = finally
    dīves -itis = rich, wealthy
    honōrātus -a -um = honoured, respected
    Iuppiter Iovis (m) = Jupiter (the supreme being)
    līber -era -erum = free
    minor -or -us = smaller, lesser
    molestus -a -um = troublesome
    nisi (conj) = if not, except
    pītuīta -ae (f) = mucus, catarrh
    praecipuus -a -um = special, above all
    pulcher -chra -chrum = beautiful, handsome
    -que (conj) = and
    rēgum = of kings
    rex rēgis (m) = a king
    sānus -a -um = healthy, sane
    sapiens -ntis = wise
    ūnus -a -um = one, alone

# Vocabulary to Learn

animus –ī (m) = the mind, spirit
homō –inis (m) = a human being, man
nihil / nīl (n.indecl) = nothing
quam (with comparatives) = than
–que (conj) = and

# 5
# PLURALS
# AND DEPONENT VERBS

## Morphology

The commonest ending for both the nominative and accusative plural is *a long vowel plus –s*. This appears in the nominative plural as *–ēs* or *–ūs*, and in the accusative plural as *–ās*, *–ēs* (less frequently *–īs*), *–ōs* or *–ūs*. Exceptions are:

> 1st and 2nd declension forms, which end in *–ae* or *–ī* in the nominative plural;

> most neuter forms, which end in *–a* or *–ia* in both nominative and accusative.

This identity of nominative and accusative plural endings can lead to uncertainty about the true subject or object unless an unambiguous case or the context resolves the problem.

The ending for all ablative plurals is *–īs* or *a vowel plus –bus* (which most often appears as *–ibus* and much less frequently as *–ābus*, *–ēbus*, *–ōbus* or *–ūbus*.

Two new verb endings will now appear, the 3rd plural active and passive of the present tense, which end in *–nt* and *–ntur*.

Deponent verbs are verbs which are passive in form but active in meaning. They will at first appear only in the present tense like other verbs; their use will be restricted to the 3rd singular and plural passive, which end in *–tur* and *–ntur*, and to the present infinitive passive, which ends in *–(r)ī*.

# Syntax

**1.** A nominative plural introduces a plural verb and vice versa:

> tot **cūrae** meum erum dīversae **trahunt**.
> so many **worries pull** my master in different directions.

Two or more nouns in the nominative singular also introduce a plural verb and vice versa:

> **cupiditās** et **libīdō** et **ignāvia** semper eum **excruciant**.
> **greed** and **desire** and **idleness** constantly **torture** him.

The members of such a group however may be presented individually with a singular verb (as in chapter 4 example 3); and when there are both plural and singular nouns in the group, the verb may simply agree with the nearest, singular subject:

> nihil librī, nihil litterae, nihil **doctrīna prōdest**.
> neither books nor letters nor **learning is any help** at all.

**2.** The change from singular to plural does not affect the way in which the different cases are used:

> concupiscunt **hominēs** aliquid semper.
> **men** always long for something.

> et revocat **cupidās** ālea saepe **manūs**.
> and gambling often calls back **greedy hands**.

> plōrātur **lacrimīs** āmissa pecūnia **vērīs**.
> lost money is lamented **with real tears**.

Certain forms however such as the infinitive (see chapter 1 syntax §3) are only found in the singular, and certain case uses such as the adverbial use of the accusative (see chapter 2 syntax §5) and ablative (see chapter 3 syntax §9) are only found in the singular.

**3.** Deponent verbs are passive in form but active in meaning. They can take a direct object in the appropriate case like other verbs:

> et crescentem **sequitur** cūra pecūniam.
> and worry **accompanies** growing wealth.

# Metaphrasing

**1.** Plurals are metaphrased like the equivalent singular form:

cūrae                              worries ★

**2.** Ambiguous forms may need an alternative metaphrase, especially those having the same ending for the nominative and accusative plural:

hominēs                           men ★ / — ★s men

**3.** Deponent verbs are metaphrased like the equivalent active form:

sequitur                          — follows —

# Examples

## 1. rēs hūmānae fragilēs cadūcaeque sunt. (Cic. *Amic*. 102)

rēs reī (f) = a thing, affair

|  |  |  |
|---|---|---|
| rēs | (a) | –s *or* –ēs |
|  | (b) | nom sing *or* nom/acc pl |
|  | (c) | an affair ★s |
|  |  | *or* affairs ★ / — ★s affairs |

hūmānus –a –um = human

|  |  |  |
|---|---|---|
| hūmānae | (a) | –ae |
|  | (b) | nom pl fem |
|  | (c) | human affairs ★ |

fragilis –is –e = fragile, uncertain

|  |  |  |
|---|---|---|
| fragilēs | (a) | –ēs |
|  | (b) | nom pl *or* acc pl masc/fem |
|  | (c) | human affairs ★ uncertain |
|  |  | *or* human affairs ★ uncertain — |

cadūcus –a –um = liable to fall, impermanent
–que (conj) = and

|  |  |  |
|---|---|---|
| cadūcaeque | (a) | –ae |
|  | (b) | nom pl fem |
|  | (c) | human affairs ★ uncertain and impermanent |

sum esse fuī = to be

|  |  |  |
|---|---|---|
| sunt. | (a) | –nt |
|  | (b) | 3rd pl act |
|  | (c) | human affairs are uncertain and impermanent. |

## 2.  \*hominēs caecōs reddit cupiditās et avāritia et audācia. (Cic. *S.Rosc.* 101)

homō –inis (m) = a human being,
     man

|  | hominēs | (a) | –ēs |
|--|--|--|--|
|  |  | (b) | nom/acc pl |
|  |  | (c) | men ★ / — ★s men |

caecus -a –um = blind

|  | caecōs | (a) | –ōs |
|--|--|--|--|
|  |  | (b) | acc pl masc |
|  |  | (c) | men ★ blind — / — ★s blind men |

reddō –ere –idī –itum = to give
     back, make

|  | reddit | (a) | –t |
|--|--|--|--|
|  |  | (b) | 3rd sing act |
|  |  | (c) | — makes men blind |

cupiditās –ātis (f) = desire, greed

|  | cupiditās | (a) | –s |
|--|--|--|--|
|  |  | (b) | nom sing |
|  |  | (c) | greed makes men blind |

et (conj) = and
avāritia –ae (f) = avarice

|  | et avāritia | (a) | –a |
|--|--|--|--|
|  |  | (b) | nom sing |
|  |  | (c) | and avarice ★s |

et (conj) = and
audācia –ae (f) = daring,
     recklessness

|  | et audācia. | (a) | –a |
|--|--|--|--|
|  |  | (b) | nom sing |
|  |  | (c) | and recklessness ★s. |

|  |  |
|--|--|
| Translation | Greed and avarice and recklessness make men blind. |

## 3. *vitia eō magis latent, quō māiōra sunt. (Sen. *Ep.* 53.5)

vitium –[i]ī (n) = a fault, vice

| | | |
|---|---|---|
| vitia | (a) | –a |
| | (b) | nom/acc pl |
| | (c) | vices ★ / — ★s vices |

eō ... quō = that much (more) ... the (more)

magis (compar.adv) = to a greater extent, more

| | | |
|---|---|---|
| eō magis | (a) | –is |
| | (b) | compar, adv |
| | (c) | vices ★ / — ★s vices that much more |

lateō –ēre –uī (intr) = to lie hidden, escape notice

| | | |
|---|---|---|
| latent, | (a) | –nt |
| | (b) | 3rd pl act |
| | (c) | vices escape notice that much more. |

eō ... quō = that much (more) ... the (more)

māior –ior –ius = greater

| | | |
|---|---|---|
| quō māiōra | (a) | –iōra |
| | (b) | compar, nom/acc pl neut |
| | (c) | the greater — ★ / the greater — — ★s |

sum esse fuī = to be

| | | |
|---|---|---|
| sunt. | (a) | –nt |
| | (b) | 3rd pl act |
| | (c) | the greater — are. |

| | |
|---|---|
| Translation | Vices escape notice that much more, the greater they are. |

## 4. multī fāmam, conscientiam paucī verentur. (Plin. *Ep*. 3.20.9)

multus -a -um = much, many

|          |     |               |
| multī    | (a) | -ī            |
|          | (b) | nom pl masc   |
|          | (c) | many — ★      |

fāma -ae (f) = talk, public opinion

| fāmam, | (a) | -am                          |
|        | (b) | acc sing                     |
|        | (c) | many — ★ public opinion,     |

conscientia -ae (f) = knowledge (of oneself), conscience

| conscientiam | (a) | -am              |
|              | (b) | acc sing         |
|              | (c) | — ★s conscience  |

paucī -ae -a = few

| paucī | (a) | -ī               |
|       | (b) | nom pl masc      |
|       | (c) | few — ★ conscience |

vereor -ērī -itus = to respect, fear

| verentur. | (a) | -ntur                 |
|           | (b) | 3rd pl pass           |
|           | (c) | few — fear conscience. |

Translation — Many fear public opinion, few fear their conscience.

57

## 5.  *luxuria immensās opēs avārīs manibus rapit. (Sen. *Oct.* 434)

luxuria –ae (f) = luxury,
    extravagance

                  luxuria   (a)  –a
                                (b)  nom sing
                                (c)  extravagance ★s / it is extravagance

immensus –a –um = im
    measurable, immense

                immensās  (a)  –ās
                                (b)  acc pl fem
                                (c)  extravagance ★s immense —

opēs opum (f.pl) = resources,
    riches

                    opēs  (a)  –ēs
                                (b)  acc pl
                                (c)  extravagance ★s immense riches

avārus –a –um = greedy (for
    money or gain)

                  avārīs  (a)  –īs
                                (b)  abl pl masc/fem/neut
                                (c)  extravagance ★s immense riches by/
                                        with/from greedy —

manus –ūs (f) = the hand

                  manibus  (a)  –ibus
                                (b)  abl pl
                                (c)  extravagance ★s immense riches by/
                                        with/from greedy hands

rapiō –ere –uī –tum = to seize,
    carry off

                  rapit.  (a)  –t
                                (b)  3rd sing act
                                (c)  Extravagance carries off immense
                                      riches with greedy hands.

# Summary of Examples

1. rēs hūmānae fragilēs cadūcaeque sunt.

2. hominēs caecōs reddit cupiditās et avāritia et audācia.

3. vitia eō magis latent, quō māiōra sunt.

4. multī fāmam, conscientiam paucī verentur.

5. luxuria immensās opēs avārīs manibus rapit.

# Exercises

Complete the following sentences on the analogy of the first:

quī honestus est, multī honestī eum sequuntur.
quī caecus est . . . . . . . . . . . . . . . . . . . . . . . . . . . . .
quī fortis est . . . . . . . . . . . . . . . . . . . . . . . . . . . . .
quī dīves est . . . . . . . . . . . . . . . . . . . . . . . . . . . . .
quī sapiens est . . . . . . . . . . . . . . . . . . . . . . . . . . . .

quī caecus est hominēs caecōs reddit.
quī cupidus est . . . . . . . . . . . . . . . . .
quī avārus est . . . . . . . . . . . . . . . . . . .
quī fortis est . . . . . . . . . . . . . . . . . . .
quī locuplēs est . . . . . . . . . . . . . . . . .

quī avārus est cum avārīs vīvit.
quī beātus est . . . . . . . . . . . . . . .
quī līber est . . . . . . . . . . . . . . .
quī pauper est . . . . . . . . . . . . . .
quī dīves est . . . . . . . . . . . . . . .

# Reading

1. fertilior seges est aliēnīs semper in agrīs
vīcīnumque pecus grandius ūber habet.     (Ov. *Ars*. 1.349)

ager agrī (m) = land, a field
aliēnus –a –um = belonging to others, not one's own
fertilis –is –e = fertile, abundant
grandis –is –e = large, big
habeō –ēre –uī –itum = to have, possess
pecus –oris (n) = livestock
seges –etis (f) = a field or crop of standing corn
semper (adv) = always
ūber –ris (n) = a breast, udder, fruitfulness
vīcīnus –a –um = neighbouring, belonging to a neighbour

2. turbant, miscent mōrēs malī: rapax, avārus, invidus
sacrum profānum, pūblicum prīvātum habent, hiulca gens.
(Pl. *Trin*. 285)

avārus –a –um = greedy (for money or gain)
gens –tis (f) = a breed, race
habeō –ēre –uī –itum = to have, hold, consider (to be)
hiulcus –a –um = open-mouthed, insatiable
invidus –a –um = malevolent, envious
malus –a –um = bad, wicked
misceō –ēre –uī mixtum = to mix (up), throw into confusion
mōs mōris (m) = an established practice; (pl) habits, morals
prīvātum –ī (n) = private property
profānus –a –um = profane, secular
pūblicum –ī (n) = public property
rapax –ācis = inordinately greedy, rapacious
sacer –cra –crum = holy, sacred
turbō –āre –āvī –ātum = to stir up, disrupt

3. *quamquam sacrilegium, furtum, adulterium inter bona ha-
bentur. quam multī furtō nōn ērubescunt, quam multī adulteriō
glōriantur! nam sacrilegia minūta pūniuntur, magna in triumphīs
feruntur. (Sen. *Ep*. 87.23)

adulterium –[i]ī (n) = adultery
bonum –ī (n) = something good, a good deed
ērubescō –escere –uī (intr) = to blush, feel ashamed
ferō –rre tulī latum = to carry, bear
furtum –ī (n) = stealing, theft
glōrior –ārī –ātus (intr) = to pride oneself, boast
habeō –ēre –uī –itum = to have, hold, consider (to be)
inter (prep w.acc) = among
magnus –a –um = great
minūtus –a –um = small, petty

multus −a −um = much, many
nam = for
pūniō −īre −īvī −ītum = to punish
quam! = to what an extent! how much! how!
quamquam = although, yet
sacrilegium −[i]ī (n) = theft of sacred property, sacrilege
triumphus −ī (m) = a triumphal procession, triumph

4.  omnibus in terrīs, quae sunt a Gādibus usque
    Aurōram et Gangēn, paucī dīnoscere possunt
    vēra bona atque illīs multum dīversa.          (Juv. 10.1)

ā (prep w.abl) = from
atque (conj) = and
aurōra −ae (f) = the dawn, the East
bonum −ī (n) = something good, a blessing
dīnosco −ere = to know apart, distinguish
dīversus −a −um = turned in different directions, different (from)
Gādēs −ium (f.pl) = Cadiz
Gangēs −is (m) = the river Ganges (acc. Gangen)
ille −a −ud = that, this
in (prep w.acc/abl) = into / in, on
multum (adv) = much, very
omnis −is −e = every, all
paucī −ae −a = few
terra −ae (f) = the earth, a land
usque (adv) = all the way (from, to)
vērus −a −um = real, true

5.  * hoc ēvenit in hīs morbīs quibus afficiuntur animī: quō quis
    pēius sē habet, minus sentit. quārē vitia sua nēmō confitētur?
    (Sen. *Ep.* 53.7)

afficiō −icere −ēcī −ectum = affect
animus −ī (m) = the mind, character
confiteor −fitērī −fessus = to admit
ēveniō −enīre −ēnī −entum (intr) = to happen
habeō −ēre −uī −itum = to have, be (in such and such a way)
minus (compar.adv) = to a smaller extent, less
morbus −ī (m) = a disease, failing
nēmō −inis (m) = no-one
pēius (compar.adv) = worse
quārē? = for what reason? why?
quis qua quid = anyone, anything
quō ... (eō) = the (more) ... the (more)
sē (acc) = himself
sentiō −tīre −sī −sum = to feel, recognise
suus −a −um = his, her, its (own), etc.
vitium −[i]ī (n) = a vice, fault

61

6. quōmodo autem revocārī ad salūtem possunt quōs nēmō retinet, populus impellit? (Sen. *Ep.* 41.8)

ad (prep w.acc) = to
autem = however, but
impellō –ellere –ulī –ulsum = to hit against, push forward
nēmō –inis (m) = no-one
populus –ī (m) = people, the general public
quōmodo? = in what way? how?
retineō –ēre –uī retentum = to hold back, restrain
revocō –āre –āvī –ātum = to call back, recall
salūs –ūtis (f) = safety, health

7. nōn enim gāzae neque consulāris
   summovet lictor miserōs tumultūs
   mentis et cūrās laqueāta circum
          tecta volantīs.       (Hor. *Carm.* 2.16.9)

(N.B. cūrās ... volantīs = cūrās quae ... volant)

circum (prep w.acc) = round
consulāris –is –e = of or proper to a consul
cūra –ae (f) = worry, care
enim = for
gāza –ae (f) = treasure
laqueātus –a –um = panelled
lictor –ōris (m) = a lictor (a magistrate's attendant)
mentis = of the mind
miser –era –erum = pitiable, wretched, unhappy
neque (conj) = and ... not, nor
summoveō –ovēre –ōvī –ōtum = to move, clear out of the way
tectum –ī (n) = a roof, ceiling
tumultus –ūs (m) = an uproar, disturbance
volō –āre –āvī –ātum (intr) = to fly

8. quidquid vult habēre nēmō potest, illud potest, nōlle quod nōn habet, rēbus oblātīs hilaris ūtī. (Sen. *Ep.* 123.3)

habeō –ēre –uī –itum = to have, possess
hilaris –is –e = cheerful
ille –a –ud = that, this
nēmō –inis (m) = no-one
nōlō –lle –luī = to be unwilling, not to want (to)
oblātus –a –um = put in one's path, freely given
quisquis quidquid = whoever, whatever
rēs reī (f) = a thing
ūtor –ī ūsus (w.abl) = to use, make use of
volō velle voluī = to want, wish (to)

9. ＊nam sī ratiō et prūdentia cūrās, nōn locus aufert, caelum nōn animum mūtant, quī trans mare currunt. (Hor. *Ep.* 1.11.25)

animus -ī (m) = the mind, frame of mind
auferō -rre abstulī ablātum = to carry away, take away
caelum -ī (n) = the sky, a region
cūra -ae (f) = worry, care
currō -rere cucurrī -sum (intr) = to run, rush, speed
locus -ī (m) = a place
mare -is (n) = the sea
mūtō -āre -āvī -ātum = to exchange, change
nam = for
prūdentia -ae (f) = practical understanding, intelligence
ratiō -ōnis (f) = reason, the exercise of reason
trans (prep w.acc) = across, over

10. scandit aerātās vitiōsa nāvīs
Cūra nec turmās equitum relinquit,
ōcior cervīs et agente nimbōs
ōcior Eurō                    (Hor. *Carm.* 2.16.21)

(N.B. agente nimbōs ... Eurō = Eurō quī nimbōs agit)

aerātus -a -um = fitted with bronze or brass
agō agere ēgī actum = to drive, bring
cervus -ī (m) = a stag, deer
cūra -ae (f) = worry, care
equitum = of horsemen, of knights
Eurus -ī (m) = the East wind
nāvis -is (f) = a ship
nec (conj) = and ... not, nor
nimbus -ī (m) = a rain-cloud
ōcior -ior -ius = swifter
relinquō -inquere -īquī -ictum = to leave, desert
scandō -ere = to climb up, climb aboard
turma -ae (f) = a squadron, troop (of cavalry)
vitiōsus -a -um = faulty, tarnished

# Vocabulary to Learn

ad (prep w.acc) = to
ille –a –ud = that, this
multus –a –um = much, many
omnis –is –e = every, all
vitium –[i]ī = a fault, vice

# 6
# DATIVES

## Morphology

The commonest ending for the dative singular is $-\bar{\imath}$. Exceptions are:

1st and 2nd declension nouns and adjectives, which end in $-ae$ and $-\bar{o}$;

4th declension neuter nouns, which end in $-\bar{u}$.

The ending for all dative plurals is $-\bar{\imath}s$ or *a vowel plus* $-bus$ (which most often appears as $-ibus$ and much less frequently as $-\bar{a}bus$, $-\bar{e}bus$, $-\bar{o}bus$ or $-\bar{u}bus$). Thus the ending for some dative singulars is the same as for the ablative singular, and the ending for all dative plurals is the same as for the ablative plural. This can lead to uncertainty unless an unambiguous case or the context resolves the problem.

## Syntax

The dative case has two basic meanings. Firstly it refers to the person or thing "to" whom or which something is done. It is used in this sense for:

**1.** the "direct object" of certain "transitive" verbs which take a dative (rather than an accusative), forming a K2 kernel:

> erus meus nīl **linguae** moderārī potest.
> my master cannot restrain his **tongue** at all.

**2.** the indirect or more remote object of certain transitive verbs, forming a K3 kernel, such as:

**(a)** verbs of giving, saying and showing:

aliī aut **Sōlī** aut **Lūnae** miseriās narrant suās.
others tell their sorrows either **to the Sun** or **to the Moon**.

**(b)** compound verbs where the prepositional element defines the sense of the dative:

amīca **illī** molestiam affert (i.e. ad-fert).
his mistress is causing (i.e. bringing to) **him** trouble.

The dative also refers to the person (or more rarely to the thing) "for" whose benefit (or the reverse) something is done. It is used in this sense:

**3.** for the person with reference to whom or for whose advantage (or disadvantage) something is done:

ūna sat est **cuivīs** fēmina multa mala.
one woman is quite enough misfortunes **for any man**.

**4.** with *esse* "to be" to show possession:

eī nōmen Erōtium est.
**her** name is (**for her** there is the name) Erotium / **she** has the name Erotium.

**5.** with certain adjectives that take a dative:

utque **virō** furtīva Venus, sīc grāta **puellae**.
and as stolen love is pleasing **to the man**, so it is pleasing **to the girl**.

**6.** with certain inanimate nouns to refer to the purpose or result of the action:

virtūs sōla neque datur **dōnō** neque accipitur.
virtue alone is neither given nor received **as a gift**.

A dative of this type is often accompanied by a dative of advantage (see §3 above):

virtūs sōla **nēminī** datur dōnō.
virtue alone is given **to no-one** as a gift.

**7.** with passive forms to refer to the agent of the action in preference to an ablative of the agent (see chapter 3 syntax §1). This occurs most often with gerundives (see chapter 7) and past participles (see chapter 18).

# Metaphrasing

**1.** A noun or pronoun in the dative is metaphrased: — ⋆s to/for —, as appropriate:

> hominī — ⋆s to/for a man

**2.** An adjective in the dative is metaphrased in a similar way:

> dīvitī — ⋆s to/for a rich —

**3.** A relative pronoun in the dative is metaphrased in a similar way, in brackets, at the beginning of its clause:

> homō cui a man (to/for whom — ⋆s) ⋆s

But when there is no such antecedent (i.e. no previous noun or pronoun for it to refer to), the relative pronoun is indefinite in meaning:

> cui (to/for whomever/what-ever — ⋆s)

The relative clause is left thus suspended until it becomes clear how it fits into the whole sentence:

> cui grātum est narrat — tells — (to whomever it is pleasing)

**4.** A "transitive" verb taking a "direct object" in the dative suggests a K2 kernel: it is metaphrased: — ⋆s —

> moderātur — restrains —

**5.** These basic patterns can then be adapted when necessary as follows:

**(a)** an ambiguous form having the same ending for the dative and some other case may need an alternative metaphrase:

erō        — ★s to/for/by/with/from
the master

**(b)** a verb taking a "direct object" in the dative may make prepositions used earlier redundant or inappropriate. The prepositional element of compound verbs will often suggest a better translation:

erō affert        — brings — upon the master

**(c)** a dative of possession requires the English sentence to be rephrased:

erō amīca est        there is a mistress for the
master
*or* the master's mistress is —
*or* the master has a mistress

**(d)** an adjective taking a dative normally follows the noun in English which the adjective modifies:

erō grāta puella        a girl pleasing to the master ★s

**(e)** a dative of purpose or result may need a different preposition or none at all according to its sense:

dōnō dat        — gives — for/as a gift

# Examples

## 1. nēmō līber est quī corporī servit. (Sen. *Ep.* 92.33)

nēmō –inis (m) = no-one

|        |     |                |
|--------|-----|----------------|
| nēmō   | (a) | –ō             |
|        | (b) | nom sing       |
|        | (c) | no-one ★s      |

līber –era –erum = free

|        |     |                   |
|--------|-----|-------------------|
| līber  | (a) | –r                |
|        | (b) | nom sing masc     |
|        | (c) | no-one free ★s    |

sum esse fuī = to be

|     |     |                 |
|-----|-----|-----------------|
| est | (a) | –t              |
|     | (b) | 3rd sing act    |
|     | (c) | no-one is free  |

quī quae quod = who(ever), which, what

|     |     |                |
|-----|-----|----------------|
| quī | (a) | –ī             |
|     | (b) | nom sing masc  |
|     | (c) | (who ★s)       |

corpus –oris (n) = the body

|         |     |                              |
|---------|-----|------------------------------|
| corporī | (a) | –ī                           |
|         | (b) | dat sing                     |
|         | (c) | (who ★s to/for the body)     |

serviō –īre –īvī –ītum (w.dat)= to serve, be a slave (to)

|         |     |                                  |
|---------|-----|----------------------------------|
| servit. | (a) | –t                               |
|         | (b) | 3rd sing act                     |
|         | (c) | (who is a slave to the body).    |

|             |                                              |
|-------------|----------------------------------------------|
| Translation | No-one is free who is a slave to his body.   |

## 2.   nec placidam membrīs dat cūra quiētem. (Verg. *Aen.* 4.5)

nec (conj) = and ... not
placidus –a –um = kindly,
    peaceful

|  |  |  |
|---|---|---|
| nec placidam | (a) | –am |
|  | (b) | acc sing fem |
|  | (c) | and — not ★s peaceful — |

membrum –ī (n) = a limb

|  |  |  |
|---|---|---|
| membrīs | (a) | –īs |
|  | (b) | dat/abl pl |
|  | (c) | and — not ★s peaceful — to/for/ by/with/from the limbs |

dō dare dedī datum = to give,
    grant

|  |  |  |
|---|---|---|
| dat | (a) | –t |
|  | (b) | 3rd sing act |
|  | (c) | and — does not grant peaceful — to the limbs |

cūra –ae (f) = worry, care

|  |  |  |
|---|---|---|
| cūra | (a) | –a |
|  | (b) | nom sing |
|  | (c) | and care does not grant peaceful — to the limbs |

quiēs –ētis (f) = sleep

|  |  |  |
|---|---|---|
| quiētem. | (a) | –em |
|  | (b) | acc sing |
|  | (c) | and care does not grant peaceful sleep to the limbs. |

## 3. *aliquī nullī reī nisi vīnō ac libīdinī vacant.
(Sen. *Dial.* 10.7.1)

aliquis –qua –quid = someone,
    something
                aliquī   (a)   –ī
                        (b)   nom pl masc
                        (c)   some people ★

nullus –a –um = not any, no
                 nullī   (a)   –ī
                        (b)   dat sing masc/fem/neut
                        (c)   some people ★ to/for no —

rēs reī (f) = a thing, matter
                   reī   (a)   –ī
                        (b)   dat sing
                        (c)   some people ★ to/for nothing

nisi (conj) = if not, except
vīnum –ī (n) = wine, drinking (of
    wine)
              nisi vīnō   (a)   –ō
                        (b)   dat sing
                        (c)   some people ★ to/for nothing except drinking

ac (conj) = and
libīdō –inis (f) = desire, wanton-
    ness.
             ac libīdinī   (a)   –ī
                        (b)   dat sing
                        (c)   some people ★ to/for nothing except drinking and wantonness

vacō –āre –āvī –ātum (intr) = to
    be empty, have time (for)
              vacant.   (a)   –nt
                        (b)   3rd pl act
                        (c)   some people have time for nothing except drinking and wantonness.

71

## 4. *artibus honestīs nullus in urbe locus.
(Juv. 3.21)

ars –tis (f) = an art, craft, skill

artibus   (a)  –ibus
            (c)  dat/abl pl
            (c)  — ★s to/for/by/with/from skills

honestus –a –um = honourable

honestīs   (a)  –īs
            (b)  dat/abl pl masc/fem/neut
            (c)  — ★s to/for/by/with/from
                 honourable skills

nullus –a –um = not any, no

nullus   (a)  –us
            (b)  nom sing masc
            (c)  no — ★s to/for/by/with/from
                 honourable skills

in (prep w.acc/abl) = into / in,
   on
urbs –bis (f) = a city, the city (of
   Rome)

in urbe   (a)  –e
            (b)  abl sing
            (c)  no — ★s to/for/by/with/from
                 honourable skills in the city

locus –ī (m) = a place

locus.   (a)  –us
            (b)  nom sing
            (c)  no place ★s for honourable skills in
                 the city.

Translation   There is no place for honourable
                 skills in the city.

# 5.   et quisquam pia tūra focīs impōnere cūrat? (Ov. *Am.* 3.3.33)

et (conj) = and
quisquam quicquam = anyone,
    anything

<table>
<tr><td>et quisquam</td><td>(a)</td><td>−s</td></tr>
<tr><td></td><td>(b)</td><td>nom sing</td></tr>
<tr><td></td><td>(c)</td><td>and does anyone ★?</td></tr>
</table>

pius −a −um = faithful to moral
    obligations, reverent

<table>
<tr><td>pia</td><td>(a)</td><td>−a</td></tr>
<tr><td></td><td>(b)</td><td>acc pl neut</td></tr>
<tr><td></td><td>(c)</td><td>and does anyone ★ reverent —?</td></tr>
</table>

tūs tūris (n) = frankincense, a
    grain of frankincense

<table>
<tr><td>tūra</td><td>(a)</td><td>−a</td></tr>
<tr><td></td><td>(b)</td><td>acc pl</td></tr>
<tr><td></td><td>(c)</td><td>and does anyone ★ reverent grains of frankincense?</td></tr>
</table>

focus −ī (m) = a hearth, altar

<table>
<tr><td>focīs</td><td>(a)</td><td>−īs</td></tr>
<tr><td></td><td>(b)</td><td>dat/abl pl</td></tr>
<tr><td></td><td>(c)</td><td>and does anyone ★ reverent grains of frankincense to/for/by/with/from the altars?</td></tr>
</table>

impōnō −ōnere −osuī −ositum = to
    place, put on

<table>
<tr><td>impōnere</td><td>(a)</td><td>−re</td></tr>
<tr><td></td><td>(b)</td><td>pres infin act</td></tr>
<tr><td></td><td>(c)</td><td>and does anyone ★ (to put reverent grains of frankincense on the altars)?</td></tr>
</table>

cūrō −āre −āvī −ātum = to care,
    bother (to)

<table>
<tr><td>cūrat?</td><td>(a)</td><td>−t</td></tr>
<tr><td></td><td>(b)</td><td>3rd sing act</td></tr>
<tr><td></td><td>(c)</td><td>and does anyone bother (to put reverent grains of frankincense on the altars)?</td></tr>
</table>

# Summary of Examples

1. nēmō līber est quī corporī servit.

2. nec placidam membrīs dat cūra quiētem.

3. aliquī nullī reī nisi vīnō ac libīdinī vacant.

4. artibus honestīs nullus in urbe locus.

5. et quisquam pia tūra focīs impōnere cūrat?

# Exercises

Complete the following sentences on the analogy of the first:

quī honestus est honestō grātus est.
quī beātus est ..................
quī līber est ..................
quī fortis est ..................
quī sapiens est ..................

quī honestus est honestīs grātus est.
quī beātus est ..................
quī līber est ..................
quī fortis est ..................
quī sapiens est ..................

# Reading

1. *an ille līber cui mulier imperat? (Cic. *Parad.* 36)

   an? (interrogative particle) = can it really be that ...?
   imperō –āre –āvī –ātum (w.dat) = to order, command
   līber –era –erum = free
   mulier –eris (f) = a woman

2. sīc vīsum Venerī, cui placet imparīs
   formās atque animōs sub iuga aēnea
        saevō mittere cum iocō.     (Hor. *Carm.* 1.33.10)

   aēneus –a –um = made of bronze, hard as bronze
   atque (conj) = and
   cum (prep w.abl) = with
   forma –ae (f) = form, shape
   impār –ris = unequal, ill-matched
   iocus –ī (m) = a joke, fun
   iugum –ī (n) = a yoke (of slavery, of love)
   mittō –ere mīsī missum = to let go, send
   placet (w.dat) = it is pleasing (to)
   saevus –a –um = savage, cruel
   sīc (adv) = thus
   sub (prep w.acc/abl) = under, beneath
   Venus –eris (f) = Venus (goddess of love)
   vīsum (est) = it has seemed good (to)

3. *is videt igne micantīs sīderibus similīs oculōs. (Ov. *Met.* 1.498)

   (N.B. igne micantīs ... oculōs = oculōs quī igne micant)
   ignis –is (m) = fire
   is ea id = this, that: he, she, it
   micō –āre –uī (intr) = flicker, flash
   oculus –ī (m) = the eye
   sīdus –eris (n) = a star
   similis –is –e (w.dat) = similar (to), like
   video vidēre vīdī vīsum = to see

4. tunc gravis illa virō, tunc orbā tigride pēior. (Juv. 6.270)

   gravis –is –e = heavy, fierce
   orbus –a –um = bereaved
   pēior –ior –ius = more harmful, worse
   tigris –idis (f) = a tiger
   tunc (adv) = then
   vir virī (m) = a man, husband, lover

5. * "sed nātūrāle est" inquis "dēsīderiō torquērī, nātūrāle est opīnionibus hominum tangī et adversīs contristārī". nullum est vitium sine patrōciniō; nullī nōn initium verēcundum est et exōrābile, sed ab hōc lātius funditur. (Sen. *Ep.* 116.2)

ab (prep w.abl) = from
adversus −a −um = turned towards or against, unfavourable
contristō −āre −āvī −ātum = to sadden, depress
dēsīderium −[i]ī (n) = desire
exōrābilis −is −e = able to be placated or won over
fundō −ere fūdī fūsum = to pour out, diffuse
hominum = of men
initium −[i]ī (n) = a beginning, starting point
inquis = you say
lātus −a −um = broad, wide
nātūrālis −is −e = natural
nullus −a −um = not any, no
opīniō −ōnis (f) = an opinion
patrōcinium −[i]ī (n) = patronage, excuse
sine (prep w.abl) = without
tangō −ere tetigī tactum = to touch, affect
torqueō −quēre −sī −tum = to twist, torture
verēcundus −a −um = restrained by moral scruples, modest

6. formam optat modicō puerīs, māiōre puellīs
murmure, cum Veneris fānum videt, anxia māter.
(Juv. 10.289)

anxius −a −um = anxious, worried
cum (conj) = when
fānum −ī (n) = a shrine, temple
forma −ae (f) = form, shape, beauty
māior −ior −ius = greater
māter −tris (f) = a mother
modicus −a −um = moderate
murmur −uris (n) = a murmur, whisper
optō −āre −āvī −ātum = to wish, pray for
puella −ae (f) = a girl, daughter
puer −ī (m) = a boy, son
Veneris (f) = of Venus (goddess of love)
videō vidēre vīdī vīsum = to see

7. * nūmina sunt precibus nōn inimīca meīs. (Ov. *Pont.* 2.8.38)

inimīcus −a −um = unfriendly, hostile
meus −a −um = my (own)
nūmen −inis (n) = a divine power, god
prex −ecis (f) = a prayer

8.  \* cui aliquid accēdere potest, id imperfectum est; cui aliquid abscēdere potest, id imperpetuum est: cui perpetua futūra laetitia est, is suō gaudet. omnia autem quibus vulgus inhiat ultrō citrōque fluunt: nihil dat fortūna mancipiō. (Sen. *Ep.* 72.7)

abscēdō –dere –ssī –ssum (intr) = to go from, be taken away
accēdō –dere –ssī –ssum (intr) = to go to, be added to
aliquis –qua –quid = someone, something
autem = however, but
dō dare dedī datum = to give, grant
fluō –ere –xī –xum (intr) = to flow
fortūna –ae (f) = fortune
futūrus –a –um = going to be
gaudeō –dēre gāvīsus (intr) = to rejoice, be pleased
imperfectus –a –um = not complete, imperfect
imperpetuus –a –um = not perpetual, transitory
inhiō –āre –āvī –ātum = to be open-mouthed, avid for
is ea id = this, that: he, she, it
laetitia –ae (f) = gladness, pleasure
mancipium –[i]ī (n) = taking hold of something, possession
perpetuus –a –um = continuous, lasting
suum –ī (n) = something belonging to himself, herself, itself, etc
ultrō citrōque (advs) = to and fro, backwards and forwards
vulgus –ī (n) = the common people, general public

9.  \* nōn īrascitur sapiens peccantibus. quārē? quia condiciōnem hūmānae vītae perspectam habet; nēmō autem nātūrae sānus īrascitur. (Sen. *Dial.* 4.10.6)

autem = however
condiciō –ōnis (f) = a contract, condition
habeō –ēre –uī –itum = to have
hūmānae vītae = of human life
īrascor –ī īrātus (w.dat) = to be angry (with)
nātūra –ae (f) = nature
nēmō –inis (m) = no-one
peccans –ntis (m) = one who makes a mistake, a wrong-doer
perspectus –a –um = fully observed
quārē? = for what reason? why?
quia (conj) = because
sānus –a –um = healthy, sane
sapiens –ntis = wise

10.  \* sed multī mortālēs, dēditī ventrī atque somnō, indoctī incultī-
que vītam sīcutī peregrīnantēs transigunt: quibus profectō
contrā nātūram corpus voluptātī, anima onerī est. (Sall. *Cat.* 2.8)

anima -ae (f) = the breath, soul
atque (conj) = and
contrā (prep w.acc) = opposite, contrary to
corpus -oris (n) = the body
dēditus -a -um (w.dat) = devoted, given over (to)
incultus -a -um = uncultivated, unrefined
indoctus -a -um = unlearned, uninformed
mortālis -is (m) = a human being
nātūra -ae (f) = nature
onus -eris (n) = a burden, nuisance
peregrīnans -ntis (m) = a traveller, foreigner
profectō (adv) = undoubtedly, assuredly
sīcutī (conj) = in the same way as
somnus -ī (m) = sleep
transigō -igere -ēgī -actum = to drive through, pass
venter -tris (m) = the belly
voluptās -ātis (f) = pleasure

# Vocabulary to Learn

atque / ac (conj) = and
is ea id = this, that
neque / nec (conj) = and ... not, nor
nullus -a -um = not any, no
sapiens -ntis = wise

# 7
# GERUNDS AND GERUNDIVES

## Morphology

The ending for both gerunds and gerundives is *-nd-*. Gerunds then add case endings (singular only) of 2nd declension neuter nouns; gerundives add case endings of 1st and 2nd declension adjectives.

## Syntax

**1.** The gerund is a verbal noun. As a verb it is active in meaning (deponents included) and can take a direct object in the appropriate case; as a noun it is always singular and never appears in the nominative nor in the accusative unless introduced by a preposition, the infinitive being used instead (see chapters 1 and 2):

> fundum bene **colendō** fructuōsum facit erus meus.
> my master makes the farm profitable **by cultivating** it well.

**2.** The gerundive is a verbal adjective. As a verb it is passive in meaning (deponents included); as an adjective it agrees in gender, number and case with the noun it modifies. It is used predicatively in two ways, the second of which may be regarded as a weakened version of the first:

**(a)** in the nominative, normally with *esse* "to be", to present an action as something that is going to be or should be done:

> vīneae mātūrē **putandae** sunt.
> vines are **to be pruned** early.

With this "gerundive of obligation" a dative of the agent (see chapter 6 syntax §7) is normally used in preference to an ablative of the agent:

> vīnitōrī sunt vīneae putandae.
> the vines are to be pruned **by the vineyard worker**.

**(b)** in cases other than the nominative to present an action as something that is being or is going to be done:

> fundō bene **colendō** dīves fit erus meus.
> my master becomes rich by the farm **being cultivated** well.

The gerundive construction of §2(b) is often used in preference to the gerund construction of §1; its reference to future action however lacks the sense of obligation conveyed by the gerundive construction of §2(a).

# Metaphrasing

**1.** A gerund is metaphrased: ★ing (or if the verb is not intransitive: ★ing —), in brackets, in the position its case requires:

> ad crescendum          — ★s at (growing)

**2.** A gerundive in the nominative is metaphrased: to be ★ed, after the verb:

> putandī          — ★ to be pruned

**3.** A gerundive in cases other than the nominative is metaphrased: being ★ed, in brackets, after the noun it modifies; an active version however will often make a better translation:

> dē putandā          — ★s about — (being pruned) /
>                        — ★s about (pruning —)

**4.** These basic patterns can then be adapted when necessary as follows:

**(a)** an ambiguous form having the same ending for the gerund and the gerundive may need an alternative metaphrase:

| | |
|---|---|
| in putandō | — ⋆s in (pruning —)<br>*or* — ⋆s in — (being pruned) |

**(b)** a dative is metaphrased in the usual way unless the presence of a gerundive signals the need for the alternative metaphrase: by —

| | |
|---|---|
| vīnitōrī putandī | — ⋆ to be pruned by the vine-yard worker |

# Examples

## 1. ⋆mons pecorī bonus alendō est. (Liv. 29.31.9)

mons montis (m) = a mountain,
   hill

| | | |
|---|---|---|
| mons | (a) | –s |
| | (b) | nom sing |
| | (c) | a hill ⋆s |

pecus –oris (n) = livestock

| | | |
|---|---|---|
| pecorī | (a) | –ī |
| | (b) | dat sing |
| | (c) | a hill ⋆s to/for livestock |

bonus –a –um = good

| | | |
|---|---|---|
| bonus | (a) | –us |
| | (b) | nom sing masc |
| | (c) | a hill good for livestock ⋆s |

alō –ere –uī –tum = to nurture,
   feed

| | | |
|---|---|---|
| alendō | (a) | –ndō |
| | (b) | gndv, dat sing neut |
| | (c) | a hill good for livestock (being fed) ⋆s |

sum esse fuī = to be

| | | |
|---|---|---|
| est. | (a) | –t |
| | (b) | 3rd sing act |
| | (c) | a hill is good for livestock (being fed). |

| | |
|---|---|
| Translation | A hill is good for feeding livestock. |

81

## 2.  aliō locō virgulta serenda. (Var. *R.R.* 1.23.5)

alius –a –ud = different, other

aliō   (a)  –ō
  (b)  abl sing masc/neut
  (c)  — ★s by/with/from another —

locus –ī (m) = a place

locō   (a)  –ō
  (b)  abl sing
  (c)  — ★s from/in another place

virgulta –ōrum (n.pl) = brush-wood, thickets

virgulta   (a)  –a
  (b)  nom/acc pl
  (c)  thickets ★ / — ★s thickets from/in another place

serō –ere sēvī satum = to sow, plant

serenda.   (a)  –nda
  (b)  gndv, nom pl neut
  (c)  thickets ★ to be planted in another place.

Translation    Thickets are to be planted in another place.

## 3. vītis propter fēmineam mollitiam ad crescendum prōna. (Var. *R.R.* 1.41.4)

vītis –is (f) = a vine

|             |     |                                        |
|-------------|-----|----------------------------------------|
| vītis       | (a) | –s                                     |
|             | (b) | nom sing                               |
|             | (c) | the vine ★s                            |

propter (prep w.acc) = because of
fēmineus –a –um = feminine

|                  |     |                                              |
|------------------|-----|----------------------------------------------|
| propter fēmineam | (a) | –am                                          |
|                  | (b) | acc sing fem                                 |
|                  | (c) | the vine ★s because of feminine —            |

mollitia –ae (f) = softness,
    suppleness

|            |     |                                          |
|------------|-----|------------------------------------------|
| mollitiam  | (a) | –am                                      |
|            | (b) | acc sing                                 |
|            | (c) | the vine ★s because of feminine suppleness |

ad (prep w.acc) = to, at
crescō –ere crēvī crētum (intr) =
    to grow

|               |     |                                                              |
|---------------|-----|--------------------------------------------------------------|
| ad crescendum | (a) | –ndum                                                        |
|               | (b) | gnd, acc sing                                                |
|               | (c) | the vine ★s because of feminine suppleness at (growing)      |

prōnus –a –um = leaning
    forward, inclined (to),
    quick (at)

|         |     |                                                                                      |
|---------|-----|--------------------------------------------------------------------------------------|
| prōna.  | (a) | –a                                                                                   |
|         | (b) | nom sing fem                                                                         |
|         | (c) | the vine ★s quick at (growing) because of feminine suppleness.                        |

|             |                                                                              |
|-------------|------------------------------------------------------------------------------|
| Translation | The vine is quick at growing because of its feminine suppleness.              |

## 4. oleam legendam hōc modō locāre oportet.
(Cato *Agr.* 144.1)

olea −ae (f) = an olive

oleam   (a)  −am
        (b)  acc sing
        (c)  — ★s the olive

legō −ere lēgī lectum = to gather, pick

legendam  (a)  −ndam
          (b)  gndv, acc sing fem
          (c)  — ★s the olive (being picked)

hic haec hoc = this

hōc   (a)  −ōc
      (b)  abl sing masc/neut
      (c)  — ★s the olive (being picked) by/ with/from this —

modus −ī (m) = a manner, way

modō  (a)  −ō
      (b)  abl sing
      (c)  — ★s the olive (being picked) in this way

locō −āre −āvī −ātum = to place, contract out for

locāre  (a)  −re
        (b)  pres infin act
        (c)  (to contract out in this way for the olive being picked)

oportet −ēre −uit = it is right (to)

oportet.  (a)  −t
          (b)  3rd sing act
          (c)  it is right (to contract out in this way for the olive being picked).

Translation   It is right to contract out in this way for picking the olive.

## 5. nec domō dominus, sed dominō domus honestanda est. (Cic. *Off.* 1.139)

nec (conj) = and ... not
domus -ī (f) = a house, home

| | | |
|---|---|---|
| nec domō | (a) | -ō |
| | (b) | dat/abl sing |
| | (c) | and — does not ★ to/for/by/with/ from a house |

dominus -ī (m) = the master of a
    household

| | | |
|---|---|---|
| dominus, | (a) | -us |
| | (b) | nom sing |
| | (c) | and the master does not ★ to/for/ by/with/from a house, |

sed (conj) = but
dominus -ī (m) = the master of a
    household

| | | |
|---|---|---|
| sed dominō | (a) | -ō |
| | (b) | dat/abl sing |
| | (c) | but — ★s to/for/by/with/from the master |

domus -ī (f) = a house, home

| | | |
|---|---|---|
| domus | (a) | -us |
| | (b) | nom sing |
| | (c) | but the house ★s to/for/by/with/ from the master |

honestō -āre -āvī -ātum = to
    honour, dignify

| | | |
|---|---|---|
| honestanda | (a) | -nda |
| | (b) | gndv, nom sing fem |
| | (c) | but the house ★s to be dignified by the master |

sum esse fuī = to be

| | | |
|---|---|---|
| est. | (a) | -t |
| | (b) | 3rd sing act |
| | (c) | but the house is to be dignified by the master. |

| | |
|---|---|
| Translation | and the master is not to be dignified by his house, but the house by its master. |

# Summary of Examples

1. mons pecorī bonus alendō est.

2. aliō locō virgulta serenda.

3. vītis propter fēmineam mollitiam ad crescendum prōna.

4. oleam legendam hōc modō locāre oportet.

5. nec domō dominus, sed dominō domus honestanda est.

# Exercises

Complete the following sentences on the analogy of the first:

quī fundum colit dīves fit bene colendō.
quī pecus alit dīves fit . . . . . . . . . . . . . .
quī vītem putat dīves fit . . . . . . . . . . . . .
quī oleam legit dīves fit . . . . . . . . . . . . . .
quī domum honestat dīves fit . . . . . . . . .

quī fundum colere potest, hic fundus eī colendus est.
quī pecus alere potest, hoc pecus . . . . . . . . . . . . . . . .
quī vītem putāre potest, haec vītis . . . . . . . . . . . . . . .
quī oleam legere potest, haec olea . . . . . . . . . . . . . . . .
quī domum honestāre potest, haec domus . . . . . . . . .

# Reading

1. ⋆consulēs trēs virōs colōniae dēdūcendae agrōque dīvidendō creant. (Liv. 8.16.14)

   ager agrī (m) = land
   colōnia −ae (f) = a colony
   consul −lis (m) = a consul (the highest magistrate)
   creō −āre −āvī −ātum = to create, appoint
   dēdūcō −cere −xī −ctum = to lead out, establish
   dīvidō −idere −īsī −īsum = to divide (up), share out
   trēs trēs tria = three

2. quaeritur argentum puerīsque beāta creandīs
   uxor et incultae pācantur vōmere silvae.    (Hor. *Ep*. 1.2.44)

argentum –ī (n) = silver, money
creō –āre –āvī –ātum = to create, bear
incultus –a –um = uncultivated
pācō –āre –āvī –ātum = to pacify, bring under control
puer –ī (m) = a boy, son
quaerō –rere –sīvī –sītum = to look for, acquire
silva –ae (f) = a wood, an area of scrubland
uxor –ōris (f) = a wife
vōmer –eris (m) = a ploughshare

3. * quid satis est ad omnīs miseriās lēniendās? (Sen. *Dial*. 12.5.2)

lēniō –īre –īvī –ītum = to alleviate, mitigate
miseria –ae (f) = a pitiful condition, sorrow
quis? quid? = who? what?
satis (n.indecl) = sufficient, enough

4. * at in voluptāte spernendā et repudiandā virtūs vel maximē
   cernitur. (Cic. *Leg*. 1.52)

at (conj) = but
cernō –ere crēvī crētum = to distinguish, discern, see
repudiō –āre –āvī –ātum = to reject, refuse
spernō –ere sprēvī sprētum = to reject, spurn
vel maximē (adv) = most of all, especially
voluptās –ātis (f) = pleasure

5. quid ergō? virtūs ad beātē vīvendum sufficit? (Sen. *Dial*. 7.16.3)

ergō = therefore, then
quis? quid? = who? what?
sufficiō –icere –ēcī –ectum = to be sufficient, enough (for)
vīvō –vere –xī –ctum (intr) = to live

6. salsa autem tellūs et quae perhibētur amāra:
   frūgibus infēlix ea nec mansuescit arandō.
   (Verg. *Georg*. 2.238)

amārus –a –um = bitter, acidic
arō –āre –āvī –ātum = to plough
autem = however, but
frux –ūgis (f) = a fruit, crop
infēlix –īcis = unfruitful, unfortunate
mansuescō –escere –ēvī –ētum (intr) = to become tame
perhibeō –ēre –uī –itum = to present (as), call
salsus –a –um = salted, salty
tellūs –ūris (f) = the earth, ground

7. neglectīs ūrenda filix innascitur agrīs. (Hor. *Serm.* 1.3.37)

ager agrī (m) = land, a field
filix –icis (f) = fern, bracken
innascor –ascī –ātus (intr) = to be born, spring up (in, on)
neglectus –a –um = neglected, uncultivated
ūrō –ere ussī ustum = to destroy by fire, burn

8. texendae saepēs etiam et pecus omne tenendum. (Verg. *Georg.* 2.371)

etiam = also, even, in addition
pecus –oris (n) = livestock
saepēs –is (f) = a hedge, fence
teneō –ēre –uī –tum = to hold (back), restrain
texō –ere –uī –tum = to weave, form by intertwining

9. est etiam ille labor cūrandīs vītibus alter,
cui numquam exhaustī satis est: namque omne quotannīs
terque quaterque solum scindendum, glaebaque versīs
aeternum frangenda bidentibus, omne levandum
fronde nemus. redit agricolīs labor actus in orbem.
(Verg. *Georg.* 2.397)

actus in orbem = driven or moving in a circle
aeternum (adv) = eternally, unendingly
agricola –ae (m) = a farmer
alter –era –erum = another, a second
bidens –ntis (m) = a two-pronged hoe
cūrō –āre –āvī –ātum = to care for, look after
etiam = also, even, in addition
exhaustī satis = enough exhaustion or effort
frangō –ngere frēgī –ctum = to break (up)
frons –ndis (f) = foliage
glaeba –ae (f) = a lump of earth, clod
labor –ōris (m) = labour, work
levō –āre –āvī –ātum (w.abl) = to lift up, rid (of)
namque (conj) = for, because
nemus –oris (n) = a wood, group of planted trees
numquam (adv) = never
quotannīs (adv) = every year, annually
redeō –īre –iī –itum (intr) = to come back, come round again
scindō –ere scicidī scissum = to cleave apart, split open
solum –ī (n) = the earth, soil
terque quaterque (advs) = three or four times
versus –a –um = backwards turned
vītis –is (f) = a vine

10.  * quid ais? tot praedia, tam pulchra, tam fructuōsa Sex. Roscius filiō suō supplicī grātiā colenda ac tuenda trādit? (Cic. *S.Rosc.* 43)

ais = you say
colō –ere –uī cultum = to cultivate, look after
filius –[i]ī (m) = a son
fructuōsus –a –um = fruitful, profitable
praedium –[i]ī (n) = an estate
pulcher –chra –chrum = beautiful, fine
quis? quid? = who? what?
Sex. Roscius –[i]ī (m) = Sextus Roscius (a member of a
    distinguished family)
suus –a –um = his, her, its (own), etc.
supplicī grātiā = as a punishment
tam (adv) = to such a degree, so
tot ≠ so many
trādō –ere –idī –itum = to hand over, entrust (to)
tueor –ērī tuitus = to watch over, maintain

# Vocabulary to Learn

ager agrī (m) = land, a field
autem = however, but
dīves –itis = rich, wealthy
(in)fēlix –īcis = (un)fruitful, (un)fortunate, (un)happy
quis? quid? = who? what?

# 8
# GENITIVES

## Morphology

The commonest endings for the genitive singular are $-\bar{\imath}$ and $-is$. Exceptions are:

1st declension nouns and adjectives, which end in $-ae$;

4th declension nouns, which end in $-\bar{u}s$;

pronouns which have the unique ending $-ius$.

In each declension however the genitive singular ending can lead to uncertainty unless an unambiguous case or the context resolves the problem:

$-ae$ could also be dat sing or nom pl

$-\bar{\imath}$ could also be nom pl

$-is$ could also be nom sing (for certain forms)

$-\bar{u}s$ could also be nom or acc pl

$-\bar{\imath}$ could also be dat sing

The ending for all genitive plurals is $-(i)um$ or *a long vowel plus* $-rum$ (which appears as $-\bar{a}rum$, $-\bar{e}rum$ or $-\bar{o}rum$).

# Syntax

The genitive case has one basic meaning ("of"), although in practice it is not limited to the idea of "belonging"; it can express any relation suggested by the context. Its chief function is to complete the meaning of another noun on which it depends (referred to below as the "key noun"), but it is also used with certain adjectives and verbs.

Genitives are used:

**1.** to refer to the possessor of the key noun:

> ingenium est **omnium hominum** prōclīve ad libīdinem.
> the nature **of all men** is inclined to wantonness.

A genitive of this type is often used predicatively with *esse* "to be" to refer to someone as possessing a particular characteristic:

> libīdō magis est **adulescentium** quam **senum.**
> wantonness is more **typical of** (is more **of**) **young men** than **of old men**.

It is also used with infinitives in this way:

> sed **cūiusvīs hominis** est errāre.
> but it is **typical of any man** (it is **of any man**) to err.

**2.** to refer to the subject or object of a verb corresponding to the key noun:

> erus meus dēperit amōre **puellae.**
> my master is dying of love **for a girl**.

A genitive of this type is ambiguous: *puellae* could be a "subjective" genitive corresponding to the nominative *puella* in *puella erum meum amat* "the girl loves my master"; or it could be an "objective" genitive corresponding to the accusative *puellam* in *erus meus puellam amat* "my master loves the girl". Only the context can resolve the ambiguity.

**3.** to refer to the whole of which the key noun is a part:

> nēmō **mortālium** omnibus hōrīs sapit.
> no **mortal** (no-one **of mortals**) is wise at all times.

A genitive of this type is also used with pronouns and neuter adjectives of the 1st and 2nd declension:

quid **novī** est sī fīlius lābitur?
what is **new** (what is there **of something new**) if a son falls into error?

**4.** to define or describe the key noun:

quid sonat haec vox **amōris**?
what does this word **love** (this word **of love**) mean?

nē puer quidem **sēdecim annōrum** hoc nescit.
not even a boy **of sixteen years** is ignorant of this.

**5.** with certain adjectives that take a genitive:

rēs est **sollicitī** plēna **timōris** amor.
love is a thing full **of anxious fear**.

**6.** as the "direct object" of certain "transitive" verbs which take a genitive (rather than an accusative), forming a K2 kernel, such as verbs denoting emotion; of remembering and forgetting; of being empty and full:

illa puella nīl **erī meī** miserētur.
that girl does not pity **my master** at all.

**7.** as the indirect or more remote object of certain transitive verbs, forming a K3 kernel, such as verbs of reminding; of valuing, buying and selling; of accusing, condemning and acquitting:

illa erum meum **rusticitātis** arguit.
she accuses my master **of lack of sophistication**.

**8.** to refer to "place at which", instead of the more common ablative of place (see chapter 3 syntax §4), with certain nouns of the 1st and 2nd declension such as *domī* "at home", *mīlitiae* "on campaign", place names of the 1st and 2nd declension singular, and *rūrī* "in the country" (apparently a 2nd declension ending on a 3rd declension noun):

est enim **Rōmae** dīves amātor puellae.
for the girl has a rich lover **at Rome**.

# Metaphrasing

**1.** A noun or pronoun in the genitive is metaphrased: of —

    hominum                      of men

It is left thus suspended until the appearance of the word on which it depends:

    hominum nēmō            no-one of men ★s

**2.** An adjective in the genitive is metaphrased in a similar way:

    sapientis                   of a wise —

**3.** A relative pronoun in the genitive is metaphrased in a similar way, in brackets, at the beginning of its clause:

    homō cūius            a man (of whom — ★s ) ★s

But when there is no such antecedent (i.e. no previous noun or pronoun for it to refer to), the relative pronoun is indefinite in meaning:

    cūius                    (of whomever/whatever — ★s)

The relative clause is left thus suspended until it becomes clear how it fits into the whole sentence:

    cūius ingenium sīc prōclīve   he (whoever's nature is thus
    est is                       inclined) ★s

**4.** A "transitive" verb taking a "direct object" in the genitive suggests a K2 kernel; it is metaphrased: — ★s —

    miserētur                 — pities —

**5.** These basic patterns can then be adapted when necessary as follows:

    **(a)** an ambiguous form having the same ending for the genitive and some other case may need an alternative metaphrase:

    erī meī                   my masters ★
                                *or* of my master

**(b)** a verb taking a "direct object" in the genitive may make the preposition "of" used earlier redundant:

erī meī miserētur                      — pities my master

**(c)** *est* when linked to a genitive may need the alternative metaphrase: it is typical of —. The phrase may then introduce an infinitive or subordinate clause as part of a K2 kernel:

hominum est                      — is of men
                                 *or* it is typical of men

**(d)** an adjective taking a genitive normally follows the noun in English which the adjective modifies:

rēs plēna timōris           a thing full of fear ★s

**(e)** sometimes the preposition "of" may need to be replaced by another, more suitable to the context, or omitted altogether:

amor puellae                love for a girl ★s
vox amōris                  the word love ★s

# Examples

## 1. *censōrēs ad mōrēs hominum regendōs animum advertunt. (Liv. 24.18.2)

censor –ōris (m) = a censor

| | | |
|---|---|---|
| censōrēs | (a) | –ēs |
| | (b) | nom/acc pl |
| | (c) | the censors ★ / — ★s the censors |

ad (prep w.acc) = to
mōs mōris (m) = an established practice; (pl) habits, morals

| | | |
|---|---|---|
| ad mōrēs | (a) | –ēs |
| | (b) | acc pl |
| | (c) | the censors ★ / — ★s the censors to morals |

homō –inis (m) = a human being, man

| | | |
|---|---|---|
| hominum | (a) | –um |
| | (b) | gen pl |
| | (c) | the censors ★ / — ★s the censors to men's morals |

regō –gere –xī –ctum = to make straight, correct

| | | |
|---|---|---|
| regendōs | (a) | –ndōs |
| | (b) | gndv, acc pl masc |
| | (c) | the censors ★ / — ★s the censors to men's morals (being corrected) |

animus –ī (m) = the mind

| | | |
|---|---|---|
| animum | (a) | –um |
| | (b) | acc sing |
| | (c) | the censors ★ the mind to men's morals (being corrected) |

advertō –tere –tī –sum = to turn to

| | | |
|---|---|---|
| advertunt. | (a) | –nt |
| | (b) | 3rd pl act |
| | (c) | the censors turn their mind to men's morals (being corrected) |

| | |
|---|---|
| Translation | The censors turn their mind to correcting men's morals. |

## 2. errat, quī fīnem vēsānī quaerit amōris.
(Prop. 2.15.29)

errō –āre –āvī –ātum (intr) = to
    wander, make a mistake

|  | | |
|---|---|---|
| errat, | (a) | –t |
| | (b) | 3rd sing act |
| | (c) | — makes a mistake |

quī quae quod = who(ever),
    which, what

|  | | |
|---|---|---|
| quī | (a) | –ī |
| | (b) | nom sing masc |
| | (c) | (whoever ★s) |

fīnis –is (m) = a boundary, end

|  | | |
|---|---|---|
| fīnem | (a) | –em |
| | (b) | acc sing |
| | (c) | (whoever ★s the end) |

vēsānus –a –um = frenzied,
    passionate

|  | | |
|---|---|---|
| vēsānī | (a) | –ī |
| | (b) | gen sing masc/neut |
| | (c) | (whoever ★s the end of a passionate —) |

quaerō –rere –sīvī –sītum = to
    look for

|  | | |
|---|---|---|
| quaerit | (a) | –t |
| | (b) | 3rd sing act |
| | (c) | (whoever looks for the end of a passionate —) |

amor –ōris (m) = love, a love
    affair

|  | | |
|---|---|---|
| amōris. | (a) | –is |
| | (b) | gen sing |
| | (c) | (whoever looks for the end of a passionate love affair). |

| Translation | Whoever looks for the end of a passionate love affair makes a mistake. |
|---|---|

97

## 3. *magis illa iuvant quae plūris emuntur. (Juv. 11.16)

magis (compar.adv) = to a greater
    extent, more
ille –a –ud = that, this

| | | |
|---|---|---|
| magis illa | (a) | –a |
| | (b) | nom sing fem *or* nom/acc pl neut |
| | (c) | that — *s more |
| | | *or* those — * / — *s those — more |

iuvō –āre iūvī iūtum = to help,
    delight

| | | |
|---|---|---|
| iuvant | (a) | –nt |
| | (b) | 3rd pl act |
| | (c) | those — delight — more |

quī quae quod = who(ever),
    which, what

| | | |
|---|---|---|
| quae | (a) | –ae |
| | (b) | nom/acc pl neut |
| | (c) | (which * / which — *s) |

plūs –ris (n) = a greater amount,
    more

| | | |
|---|---|---|
| plūris | (a) | –is |
| | (b) | gen sing |
| | (c) | (which * / which — *s of a greater amount) |

emō emere ēmī emptum = to buy

| | | |
|---|---|---|
| emuntur. | (a) | –ntur |
| | (b) | 3rd pl pass |
| | (c) | (which are bought at a greater amount). |

| | |
|---|---|
| Translation | Those things delight more which are bought at a greater amount. |

## 4.  *quis vult in omnium rērum abundantiā vīvere? (Cic. *Amic.* 52)

quis? quid? = who? what?

|  | quis | (a) | –s |
|---|---|---|---|
|  |  | (b) | nom sing |
|  |  | (c) | who *s? |

volō velle voluī = to want, wish (to)

|  | vult | (a) | –t |
|---|---|---|---|
|  |  | (b) | 3rd sing act |
|  |  | (c) | who wants —? |

in (prep w.acc/abl) = into / in, on

omnis –is –e = every, all

|  | in omnium | (a) | –ium |
|---|---|---|---|
|  |  | (b) | gen pl masc/fem/neut |
|  |  | (c) | who wants — into/in/on — of all —? |

rēs reī (f) = a thing

|  | rērum | (a) | –ērum |
|---|---|---|---|
|  |  | (b) | gen pl |
|  |  | (c) | who wants — into/in/on — of all things? |

abundantia –ae (f) = an overflow, abundance

|  | abundantiā | (a) | –ā |
|---|---|---|---|
|  |  | (b) | abl sing |
|  |  | (c) | who wants — in an abundance of all things? |

vīvō –vere –xī –ctum (intr) = to live

|  | vīvere? | (a) | –re |
|---|---|---|---|
|  |  | (b) | pres infin act |
|  |  | (c) | who wants (to live in an abundance of all things)? |

|  | Translation | Who wants to live in an abundance of all things? |
|---|---|---|

## 5. *est proprium stultitiae aliōrum vitia cernere, oblīviscī suōrum. (Cic. *Tusc.* 3.73)

sum esse fuī = to be

|   |   |   |
|---|---|---|
| est | (a) | –t |
|  | (b) | 3rd sing act |
|  | (c) | there / it is —  |
|  |  | *or* — is — |

proprius –a –um (w.gen) = characteristic, typical (of)

|   |   |   |
|---|---|---|
| proprium | (a) | –um |
|  | (b) | nom sing neut |
|  | (c) | it is typical / — is typical |

stultitia –ae (f) = stupidity

|   |   |   |
|---|---|---|
| stultitiae | (a) | –ae |
|  | (b) | gen sing |
|  | (c) | it is typical of stupidity |

alius –a –ud = different, other

|   |   |   |
|---|---|---|
| aliōrum | (a) | –ōrum |
|  | (b) | gen pl masc/neut |
|  | (c) | it is typical of the stupidity of other — |

vitium –[i]ī (n) = a fault, vice

|   |   |   |
|---|---|---|
| vitia | (a) | –a |
|  | (b) | acc pl |
|  | (c) | it is typical of stupidity (★ faults of other —) |

cernō –ere crēvī crētum = to
distinguish, discern, see

|   |   |   |
|---|---|---|
| cernere, | (a) | –re |
|  | (b) | pres infin act |
|  | (c) | it is typical of stupidity (to see the faults of other —), |

oblīviscor –viscī –tus (w.gen) = to
forget (about)

|   |   |   |
|---|---|---|
| oblīviscī | (a) | –ī |
|  | (b) | pres infin pass |
|  | (c) | (to forget about —) |

suus –a –um = his, her, its, one's
(own), etc.

|   |   |   |
|---|---|---|
| suōrum. | (a) | –ōrum |
|  | (b) | gen pl neut |
|  | (c) | (to forget about one's own —). |

| Translation | It is typical of stupidity to see the faults of others and forget about one's own. |
|---|---|

# Summary of Examples

1. censōrēs ad mōrēs hominum regendōs animum advertunt.

2. errat, quī fīnem vēsānī quaerit amōris.

3. magis illa iuvant quae plūris emuntur.

4. quis vult in omnium rērum abundantiā vīvere?

5. est proprium stultitiae aliōrum vitia cernere, oblīviscī suōrum.

# Exercises

Complete the following sentences on the analogy of the first:

quī dīves est ad dīvitis libīdinem prōclīvis est.
quī amātor est . . . . . . . . . . . . . . . . . . . . . . . . .
quī agricola est . . . . . . . . . . . . . . . . . . . . . . . .
quī fīlius est . . . . . . . . . . . . . . . . . . . . . . . . .
quī sapiens est . . . . . . . . . . . . . . . . . . . . . . . .

quī dīves est ad dīvitum libīdinem prōclīvis est.
quī amātor est . . . . . . . . . . . . . . . . . . . . . . . . . .
quī agricola est . . . . . . . . . . . . . . . . . . . . . . . . .
quī fīlius est . . . . . . . . . . . . . . . . . . . . . . . . . .
quī sapiens est . . . . . . . . . . . . . . . . . . . . . . . . .

# Reading

1.  ∗sī istī callidī rērum aestimātōrēs prāta et āreās quāsdam magnō aestimant, quantī est aestimanda virtūs? (Cic. *Parad.* 51)

    aestimātor –ōris (m) = a valuer
    aestimō –āre –āvī –ātum = to value
    ārea –ae (f) = a space clear of buildings, open space
    callidus –a –um (w.gen) = experienced, practised (in)
    iste –a –ud = that (of yours)
    magnus –a –um = great
    prātum –ī (n) = meadowland
    quantus –a –um? = how great?
    quīdam quaedam quoddam = a certain
    rēs reī (f) = property; (pl) goods, possessions

2. * nam amātor meretrīcis mōrēs sibi emit aurō et purpurā.
   pulchra mulier nūda erit quam purpurāta pulchrior:
   poste nēquīquam exornāta est bene, sī mōrāta est male.
   pulchrum ornātum turpēs mōrēs pēius caenō collinunt.
   (Pl. *Mos.* 286)

amator –ōris (m) = a lover
aurum –ī (n) = gold
caenum –ī (n) = mud, filth, ordure
collinō –inere –ēvī –itum = to soil, defile
emō emere ēmī emptum = to buy, procure
erit = will be
exornātus –a –um = adorned, dressed up
malus –a –um = bad
meretrix –īcis (f) = a courtesan
mōrātus –a –um = endowed with certain habits or morals
mōs –ris (m) = an established practice; (pl) morals, compliance
mulier –eris (f) = a woman
nam = for
nēquīquam (adv) = to no purpose, in vain
nūdus –a –um = naked
ornātus –ūs (m) = clothing, adornment
pēius (compar.adv) = worse
poste (adv) = subsequently, afterwards
pulcher –chra –chrum = beautiful
purpura –ae (f) = a purple dye, purple-dyed cloth
purpurātus –a –um = dressed in purple
sibi = for himself
turpis –is –e = ugly, disgusting, shameful

3. * at vērō in M. Caeliō nulla luxuriēs reperītur, nullī sumptūs,
   nullum aes aliēnum, nulla convīviōrum ac lustrōrum libīdō.
   (Cic. *Cael.* 44)

aes aeris (n) = bronze, money
aliēnus –a –um = not one's own, borrowed from someone else
at (conj) = but
convīvium –[i]ī (n) = a dinner-party, banquet
libīdō –inis (f) = desire
lustrum –ī (n) = a muddy place, den of vice
luxuriēs –ēī (f) = luxury, extravagance
M. Caelius –[i]ī (m) = Marcus Caelius (involved in a notorious
    scandal)
reperiō –īre repperī –tum = to discover, find
sumptus –ūs (m) = spending, lavish expenditure
vērō (adv) = in truth, in fact

4. nam dīvitiārum et formae glōria fluxa atque fragilis est, virtūs clāra aeternaque habētur. (Sall. *Cat.* 1.4)

aeternus -a -um = eternal, everlasting
clārus -a -um = clear (to see), bright
dīvitiae -ārum (f.pl) = riches, wealth
fluxus -a -um = flowing, impermanent
forma -ae (f) = form, shape, beauty
fragilis -is -e = fragile, uncertain
glōria -ae (f) = glory
habeō -ēre -uī -itum = to have, hold, consider (to be)
nam = for

5. *vērum sī quis etiam meretrīciīs amōribus interdīcit iuventūtī, est ille quidem valdē sevērus; abhorret nōn modo ab huius saeculī licentiā vērum etiam ā māiōrum consuētūdine atque concessīs. (Cic. *Cael.* 48)

ā / ab (prep w.abl) = from
abhorreō -ēre -uī (intr) = to recoil (from), be at odds (with)
amor -ōris (m) = love, a love affair
concessus -a -um = permitted, allowable
consuētūdō -inis (f) = custom, practice
etiam = also, even
interdīcō -cere -xī -ctum (w.dat and abl) = to debar (from)
iuventūs -ūtis (f) = the youth, young men
licentia -ae (f) = freedom, permissiveness
māior -ior -ius = greater, older; (m.pl) ancestors
meretrīcius -a -um = of or with courtesans
nōn modo ... vērum etiam = not only ... but also
quidem = indeed
quis qua quid = anyone, anything
saeculum -ī (n) = a particular generation or age
sevērus -a -um = stern, strict
valdē (adv) = vigorously, extremely
vērum (conj) = but

6. tardī ingenī est rīvulōs consectārī, fontīs rērum nōn vidēre. (Cic. *de Orat.* 2.117)

consector -ārī -ātus = to go after, make for
fons -ntis (m) = a spring, source
ingenium -[i]ī (n) = the (inborn) character, intellect
rēs reī (f) = a thing, matter
rīvulus -ī (m) = a rivulet
tardus -a -um = slow, slow-witted
videō vidēre vīdī vīsum = to see

7. \*ūnum exemplum luxuriae aut avāritiae multum malī facit: convictor dēlicātus paulātim ēnervat et mollit, vīcīnus dīves cupiditātem irrītat, malignus comes quamvīs candidō et simplicī rūbīginem suam affricat. (Sen. *Ep.* 7.7)

affricō –āre –uī –itum = to rub (against), rub off (on to)
aut (conj) = or
avāritia –ae (f) = avarice, greed
candidus –a –um = bright, white, innocent
comes –itis (m) = a companion
convictor –ōris (m) = a table companion, bosom friend
cupiditās –ātis (f) = desire, greed
dēlicātus –a –um = addicted to pleasure, effeminate
ēnervō –āre –āvī –ātum = to cut the sinews of, weaken
exemplum –ī (n) = an example
faciō –ere fēcī factum = to make, do
irritō –āre –āvī –ātum = to provoke, stimulate
luxuria –ae (f) = luxury, extravagance
malignus –a –um = mean, spiteful
malus –a –um = bad, harmful
molliō –īre –īvī –ītum = to make soft or effeminate
paulātim (adv) = little by little, gradually
quamvīs = as ... as you like, no matter how
rūbīgo –inis (f) = a red deposit, rust, blight
simplex –icis = pure and simple, straightforward
suus –a –um = his, her, its (own), etc.
ūnus –a –um = one, a single
vīcīnus –ī (m) = a neighbour

8. parvula – nam exemplō est – magnī formīca labōris ōre trahit quodcumque potest atque addit acervō quem struit haud ignāra ac nōn incauta futūrī. (Hor. *Serm.* 1.1.33)

acervus –ī (m) = a heap, pile
addō –ere –idī –itum = to add (to)
exemplum –ī (n) = an example
formīca –ae (f) = an ant
futūrus –a –um = going to be
haud = not
ignārus –a –um (w.gen) = ignorant (of)
incautus –a –um (w.gen) = unwary (of)
labor –ōris (m) = labour, work
magnus –a –um = great
nam = for
ōs –ōris (n) = the mouth
parvulus –a –um = small, tiny
quīcumque quaecumque quodcumque = whoever, whatever
struō –ere –xī –ctum = to construct, build
trahō –here –xī –ctum = to drag, haul

9. at nunc dīvitibus cēnandī nulla voluptās;
nīl rhombus, nīl damma sapit, pūtēre videntur
unguenta atque rosae, lātōs nisi sustinet orbēs
grande ebur et magnō sublīmis pardus hiātū.   (Juv. 11.120)

at (conj) = but
cēnō -āre -āvī -ātum (intr) = to dine
damma -ae (f) = deer, venison
ebur -oris (n) = ivory, an ivory column
grandis -is -e = large, big
hiātus -ūs (m) = an opening (of the mouth)
lātus -a -um = broad, wide
magnus -a -um = great
nīl (n.indecl) = nothing
nisi (conj) = if not, unless
nunc (adv) = now, nowadays
orbis -is (m) = a circular object, round table top
pardus -ī (m) = a leopard or panther
pūteō -ēre -uī (intr) = to have a bad smell, stink
rhombus -ī (m) = a turbot
rosa -ae (f) = a rose
sapiō -ere -īvī (intr) = to have a taste
sublīmis -is -e = raised up high, rampant
sustineō -ēre -uī = to hold up, support
unguentum -ī (n) = a scent, perfume
videor vidērī vīsus (intr) = to appear, seem (to)
voluptās -ātis (f) = pleasure

10. *quantō rērum minus, tantō minus cupiditātis erat: nūper dīvitiae avāritiam et abundantēs voluptātēs dēsīderium per luxum atque libīdinem pereundī perdendīque omnia invehunt. (Liv. *pr.* 12)

abundans -ntis = overflowing, abundant
avāritia -ae (f) = avarice, greed
cupiditās -ātis (f) = desire, greed
dēsīderium -[i]ī (n) = desire (for)
dīvitiae -ārum (f.pl) = riches, wealth
erat = there was
invehō -ere -xī -ctum = to bring in, import
libīdō -inis (f) = desire, sexual indulgence
luxus -ūs (m) = luxury, extravagance
minus -ōris (n) = a smaller amount, less
nūper (adv) = lately, recently
per (prep w.acc) = through, by means of
perdō -ere -idī -itum = to ruin, destroy
pereō -īre -iī -itum (intr) = to vanish, perish, die
quantō ... tantō = the (more) ... the (more)
rēs reī (f) = property; (pl) goods, possession
voluptās -ātis (f) = pleasure

# Vocabulary to Learn

ā / ab (prep w.abl) = from, by
amor –ōris (m) = love
at (conj) = but
nēmō –inis (m) = no-one
pulcher –chra –chrum = beautiful

# 9
# SUPERLATIVES

## Morphology

The commonest ending for superlative adjectives is *–issim–* followed by 1st and 2nd declension case endings, and for superlative adverbs *–issim–* followed by the 1st and 2nd declension adverb ending *–ē*. Exceptions are:

those which end in *–errim–* or *–illim–*;

adjectives ending in *–eus*, *–ius* and *–uus*, which use *maximē* "most", e.g. *dubius* "doubtful" but *maximē dubius* "most doubtful";

a small group of irregulars.

## Syntax

**1.** Superlatives are used to express some quality to a very high degree:

vīta haec rustica **honestissima** ab omnibus habētur.
this country life is considered **very / most honourable** by all.

**2.** The same superlative forms are also used for comparing one thing with a group of things:

vīta haec rustica **honestissima** quibusdam vidētur.
this country life seems **the most honourable** to certain people.

The difference may be emphasised by *vel* "quite, altogether" or *quam* "the most ... possible":

> erō quidem meō vīta haec rustica **quam honestissima** vidētur.
> to my master in fact this country life seems **the most honourable possible**.

**3.** Adding the standard of comparison makes this more precise; a partitive genitive (see chapter 8 syntax §3) or a prepositional phrase may be used:

> vīta haec rustica **omnium rērum / ex omnibus rēbus** honestissima eī vidētur.
> this country life seems to him the most honourable **of all things / out of all things**.

With both expressions *rēs* "a thing" is understood as the noun with which *honestissima* agrees.

**4.** A further refinement is to show by how much the one thing differs from the rest; only *multō* "by much" and *longē* "by far" are commonly used:

> haec vīta rustica omnium rērum **multō** honestissima iūre habētur.
> this country life is rightly considered **much** the most honourable of all things.

# Metaphrasing

**1.** A superlative is metaphrased: very — / most — (or: the most — / the —est, according to the context) in the position its case requires:

    honestissimam            — ⋆s the most honourable —

**2.** *Quam* is metaphrased in the usual way unless the presence of a superlative signals the need for the alternative metaphrase: the most — possible:

    quam honestissimam       — ⋆s the most honourable — possible

**3.** *Multō* is metaphrased in the usual way:

    multō honestissimam       — ⋆s the most honourable — by/with/from much —

It soon becomes clear whether *multō* is ablative of the instrument ("most honourable by means of much —") or ablative of measure of difference ("much the most honourable").

# Examples

### 1. fundit humō facilem victum iustissima tellūs.
(Verg. *Georg.* 2.460)

fundō –ere fūdī fūsum = to pour
  out

| | | |
|---|---|---|
| fundit | (a) | –t |
| | (b) | 3rd sing act |
| | (c) | — pours out — |

humus –ī (f) = the earth, soil

| | | |
|---|---|---|
| humō | (a) | –ō |
| | (b) | dat/abl sing |
| | (c) | — pours out — to/for/by/with/ from the soil |

facilis –is –e = easy, easily
  obtained, readily available

| | | |
|---|---|---|
| facilem | (a) | –em |
| | (b) | acc sing masc/fem |
| | (c) | — pours out readily available — to/ for/by/with/from the soil |

victus –ūs (m) = food

| | | |
|---|---|---|
| victum | (a) | –um |
| | (b) | acc sing |
| | (c) | — pours out readily available food to/for/by/with/from the soil |

iustus –a –um = fair, just

| | | |
|---|---|---|
| iustissima | (a) | –issima |
| | (b) | superl, nom sing fem |
| | (c) | the most just — pours out readily available food to/for/by/with/from the soil |

tellūs –ūris (f) = the earth

| | | |
|---|---|---|
| tellūs. | (a) | –s |
| | (b) | nom sing |
| | (c) | the most just earth pours out readily available food from the soil. |

## 2. pascuntur armenta commodissimē in nemoribus. (Var. *R.R.* 2.5.11)

pascō –cere pāvī –tum = to feed,
    pasture

|  |  |  |
|---|---|---|
| pascuntur | (a) | –ntur |
|  | (b) | 3rd pl pass |
|  | (c) | — are pastured |

armentum –ī (n) = a herd; (pl)
    cattle or horses (for
    ploughing)

|  |  |  |
|---|---|---|
| armenta | (a) | –a |
|  | (b) | nom pl |
|  | (c) | cattle are pastured |

commodus –a –um = suitable,
    convenient

|  |  |  |
|---|---|---|
| commodissimē | (a) | –issimē |
|  | (b) | superl adv |
|  | (c) | cattle are pastured most conveniently |

in (prep w.acc/abl) = into / in, on
nemus –oris (n) = a wood (with
    pasturage)

|  |  |  |
|---|---|---|
| in nemoribus. | (a) | –ibus |
|  | (b) | abl pl |
|  | (c) | cattle are pastured most conveniently in the woods. |

## 3. *cāseus lacte fierī dēbet sincērō et quam recentissimō. (Col. 7.8.1)

cāseus -ī (m) = cheese

| | | |
|---|---|---|
| cāseus | (a) | –us |
| | (b) | nom sing |
| | (c) | cheese ★s |

lac lactis (n) = milk

| | | |
|---|---|---|
| lacte | (a) | –e |
| | (b) | abl sing |
| | (c) | cheese ★s by/with/from milk |

fīō fierī (intr) = to become or be
    made

| | | |
|---|---|---|
| fierī | (a) | –rī |
| | (b) | pres infin pass |
| | (c) | cheese ★s (to be made from milk) |

dēbeō –ēre –uī –itum = to be
    obliged (to), should

| | | |
|---|---|---|
| dēbet | (a) | –t |
| | (b) | 3rd sing act |
| | (c) | cheese should (be made from milk) |

sincērus –a –um = unspoiled,
    pure

| | | |
|---|---|---|
| sincērō | (a) | –ō |
| | (b) | abl sing neut |
| | (c) | cheese should (be made from pure milk) |

et (conj) = and
quam (w.superl) = the most ...
    possible
recens –ntis = recent, fresh

| | | |
|---|---|---|
| et quam recentissimō. | (a) | –issimō |
| | (b) | superl, abl sing neut |
| | (c) | cheese should (be made from pure milk and the freshest possible). |

| | |
|---|---|
| Translation | Cheese should be made from milk which is pure and the freshest possible. |

## 4. *vīnum post solstitium acētum ācerrimum et pulcherrimum fit. (Cato *Agr.* 104.2)

vīnum -ī (n) = wine

| | | |
|---|---|---|
| vīnum | (a) | -um |
| | (b) | nom/acc sing |
| | (c) | wine ⋆s / — ⋆s wine |

post (prep w.acc) = after
solstitium -[i]ī (n) = the (winter or summer) solstice

| | | |
|---|---|---|
| post solstitium | (a) | -um |
| | (b) | acc sing |
| | (c) | wine ⋆s / — ⋆s wine after the solstice |

acētum -ī (n) = sour wine, vinegar

| | | |
|---|---|---|
| acētum | (a) | -um |
| | (b) | nom/acc sing |
| | (c) | wine ⋆s vinegar after the solstice |

ācer ācris ācre = sharp

| | | |
|---|---|---|
| ācerrimum | (a) | -errimum |
| | (b) | superl, nom/acc sing neut |
| | (c) | wine ⋆s very sharp vinegar after the solstice |

et (conj) = and
pulcher -chra -chrum = beautiful, fine

| | | |
|---|---|---|
| et pulcherrimum | (a) | -errimum |
| | (b) | superl, nom/acc sing neut |
| | (c) | wine ⋆s very sharp and very fine vinegar after the solstice |

fīō fierī (intr) = to become or be made

| | | |
|---|---|---|
| fit. | (a) | -t |
| | (b) | 3rd sing act |
| | (c) | wine becomes very sharp and very fine vinegar after the solstice. |

## 5.  *tantās opēs optima mātrum terra creat. (Ov. *Met.* 15.91)

tantus –a –um = so great, such
   great

|  | | |
|---|---|---|
| tantās | (a) | –ās |
| | (b) | acc pl fem |
| | (c) | — ★s such great — |

opēs opum (f.pl) = resources,
   riches

|  | | |
|---|---|---|
| opēs | (a) | –ēs |
| | (b) | acc pl |
| | (c) | — ★s such great riches |

optimus –a –um = best

|  | | |
|---|---|---|
| optima | (a) | –a |
| | (b) | superl, nom sing fem *or* nom pl neut |
| | (c) | the best — ★s *or* ★ such great riches |

māter –tris (f) = a mother

|  | | |
|---|---|---|
| mātrum | (a) | –um |
| | (b) | gen pl |
| | (c) | the best of mothers ★s such great riches |

terra –ae (f) = the earth

|  | | |
|---|---|---|
| terra | (a) | –a |
| | (b) | nom sing |
| | (c) | earth the best of mothers ★s such great riches |

creō –āre –āvī –ātum = to create,
   produce, bear

|  | | |
|---|---|---|
| creat. | (a) | –t |
| | (b) | 3rd sing act |
| | (c) | Earth the best of mothers bears such great riches. |

# Summary of Examples

1. fundit humō facilem victum iustissima tellūs.

2. pascuntur armenta commodissimē in nemoribus.

3. cāseus lacte fierī dēbet sincērō et quam recentissimō.

4. vīnum post solstitium acētum ācerrimum et pulcherrimum fit.

5. tantās opēs optima mātrum terra creat.

# Exercises

Complete the following sentences on the analogy of the first:

quī honestus est omnium honestissimus vult fierī.
quī iustus est ...............................
quī pulcher est ...........................
quī magnus est ...........................
quī fēlix est ..............................
quī locuplēs est ..........................

# Reading

1.  \*māiōrēs nostrī virum bonum cum laudant, ita laudant, bonum agricolam bonumque colōnum. amplissimē laudārī existimātur quī ita laudātur. (Cato *Agr.* 1.2)

    agricola –ae (m) = a farmer
    amplus –a –um = ample in size, generous, magnificent
    colōnus –ī (m) = a cultivator, husbandman
    cum (conj) = when
    existimō –āre –āvī –ātum = to value, consider (to be)
    ita (adv) = so, in this way
    laudō –āre –āvī –ātum = to praise
    māior –ior –ius = greater, older; (m.pl) ancestors
    noster –tra –trum = our (own)

2.  \*nec vērō mihi difficile est quamvīs multōs nōminātim prōferre vel tribūlīs vel vīcīnōs meōs quī suōs līberōs, quōs plūrimī faciunt, agricolās assiduōs esse cupiunt. (Cic. *S.Rosc.* 47)

    agricola –ae (m) = a farmer
    assiduus –a –um = settled on the land, busy
    cupiō –ere –īvī –ītum = to desire, want
    difficilis –is –e = difficult
    faciō –ere fēcī factum (w.gen) = to make, value (at)
    līberī –ōrum (m.pl) = children
    meus –a –um = my (own)
    mihi = for me
    nōminātim (adv) = by name
    plūrimus –a –um = very many, very much; (gen.sing.neut) at a very
        great amount
    prōferō –ferre –tulī –lātum = to bring forward, produce
    quamvīs = as ... as you like, no matter how
    suus –a –um = his, her, its (own), etc.
    tribūlis –is (m) = a fellow tribesman
    vel ... vel (conjs) = either ... or
    vērō (adv) = in truth, in fact
    vīcīnus –ī (m) = a neighbour

3. at ex agricolīs et virī fortissimī et mīlitēs strēnuissimī gignuntur, maximēque pius quaestus stabilissimusque consequitur minimēque invidiōsus. (Cato *Agr.* 1.4)

agricola -ae (m) = a farmer
consequor -quī -cūtus = to follow (as a consequence)
et ... et (conjs) = both ... and
ex (prep w.abl) = from, out of
fortis -is -e = strong, courageous
gignō -ere genuī genitum = to create, bear
invidiōsus -a -um = odious, invidious
maximus -a -um = greatest; (adv) most
mīles -itis (m) = a soldier
minimus -a -um = smallest
pius -a -um = faithful to moral obligations, upright
quaestus -ūs (m) = the acquisition of wealth, income
stabilis -is -e = standing firm, steady
strēnuus -a -um = active, energetic

4. trīticī genera complūra cognōvimus, vērum ex eīs maximē serendum est quod rōbus dīcitur. (Col.2.6.1)

cognōvimus = we know
complūrēs -ēs -a = several, many
dīcō -cere -xī -ctum = to say, call
ex (prep w.abl) = from, out of
genus -eris (n) = a breed or variety
maximus -a -um = greatest; (adv) most
rōbus = a kind of wheat, "red"
serō -ere sēvī satum = to plant, sow
trīticum -ī (n) = wheat
vērum (conj) = but

5. et nunc omnis ager, nunc omnis parturit arbōs, nunc frondent silvae, nunc formōsissimus annus. (Verg. *Ecl.* 3.56)

annus -ī (m) = a year
arbōs -oris (f) = a tree
formōsus -a -um = shapely, beautiful
frondeō -ēre (intr) = to be in leaf
nunc (adv) = now
parturiō -īre -īvī (intr) = to be in labour, be giving birth
silva -ae (f) = a wood

6. nusquam nec opera sine ēmolumentō nec ēmolumentum fermē sine impensā operā est. labor voluptāsque, dissimillima nātūrā, societāte quādam inter sē nātūrālī sunt iuncta. (Liv. 5.4.4)

dissimilis -is -e = unlike, different
ēmolumentum -ī (n) = a reward, benefit

fermē (adv) = virtually, hardly ever
impensus -a -um = devoted, painstaking
inter sē = between each other
iunctus -a -um = connected
labor -ōris (m) = labour, work
nātūra -ae (f) = nature, character
nātūrālis -is -e = natural
nec ... nec (conjs) = neither ... nor
nusquam (adv) = nowhere
opera -ae (f) = work, effort
quīdam quaedam quoddam = a certain
sine (prep w.abl) = without
societās -ātis (f) = partnership, affinity
voluptās -ātis (f) = pleasure

7.  at, puto, fructus adest, iustissima causa labōrum,
    et sata cum multō faenore reddit ager.   (Ov. *Pont.* 1.5.25)

adsum -esse -fuī (intr) = to be present, have arrived
causa -ae (f) = a cause, reason
cum (prep w.abl) = with
faenus -oris (n) = interest (on capital), gain, profit
fructus -ūs (m) = the enjoyment (of something), fruit, crop
iustus -a -um = fair, just
labor -ōris (m) = labour, toil
puto = I think
reddō -ere -idī -itum = to give back, repay
sata -ōrum (n.pl) = things sown

8.  *an aliquis mortālium quam Gȳgēs fēlīcior? Apollō Pȳthius
    Aglaum Psophidium eī praefert. is erat Arcadum pauperrimus
    sed parvulī rūris fructibus contentus. (Val. Max. 7.1.2)

Aglaus Psophidius -ī -[i]ī (m) = Aglaus Psophidius (a poor Greek
    peasant)
aliquis -qua -quid = someone, something
an? (interrogative particle) = can it really be that ...?
Apollō -inis (m) = Apollo (god of prophecy)
Arcades -um (m.pl) = the inhabitants of Arcadia
contentus -a -um = content, satisfied (with)
erat = was
fructus -ūs (m) = the enjoyment (of something), fruit, crop
Gȳgēs -is (m) = Gyges (king of Lydia fabled for his wealth)
mortālis -is -e = mortal
parvulus -a -um = small, tiny
pauper -eris = poor
praeferō -ferre -tulī -lātum (w.dat) = to prefer (to)
Pȳthius -a -um = Pythian (cult title of Apollo at Delphi)
rūs rūris (n) = the country, a country estate

117

9. *nunc contrā hominēs villam urbānam quam maximam ac polītissimam habēre nītuntur. (Var. *R.R.* 1.13.7)

contrā (adv) = opposite, on the other hand
habeō –ēre –uī –itum = to have, possess
maximus –a –um = greatest, largest
nītor –tī –xus = to lean (upon), strive (to)
nunc (adv) = now, nowadays
polītus –a –um = refined, elegant
quam (w.superl) = the most ... possible
villa urbāna –ae –ae (f) = the dwelling on a country estate

10. * avāritia latentium indāgātrix lucrōrum, manifestae praedae avidissima vorāgō, neque habendī fructū fēlix et cupiditāte quaerendī miserrima. (Val. Max. 9.4.intr)

avāritia –ae (f) = avarice, greed
avidus –a –um = greedy, insatiable
cupiditās –ātis (f) = desire, greed
fructus –ūs (m) = the enjoyment (of something)
habeō –ēre –uī –itum = to have, possess
indāgātrix –īcis (f) = a tracker, searcher
latens –ntis = hidden, concealed
lucrum –ī (n) = material gain, profit
manifestus –a –um = obvious
miser –era –erum = pitiable, wretched, unhappy
neque ... et (conjs) = neither ... and
praeda –ae (f) = plunder
quaerō –rere –sīvī –situm = to look for, acquire (wealth)
vorāgō –inis (f) = a chasm, devourer

# Vocabulary to Learn

cum (prep w.abl) = with, together with
ē / ex (prep w. abl) = from, out of
fortis –is –e = strong, courageous
labor –ōris (m) = labour, toil
miser –era –erum = pitiable, wretched, unhappy

# 10
# PRONOUNS

## Morphology

Pronouns have a pattern of case endings similar to those of the 1st and 2nd declension. Where they differ from the pattern is that:

most pronouns have a genitive singular ending in *–ius* and a dative singular in *–ī*;

some pronouns also have a nominative and accusative singular neuter ending in *–d*;

some pronouns also add a suffix after the case ending.

## Syntax

Pronouns are used like nouns or adjectives according to their meaning; two or more are often clustered together at the start of a sentence, with the more important coming first. Certain pronouns are used in idiomatic ways:

**1.** *alius* "different, other" when followed by *ac, atque, et, praeter, quam* or the ablative of comparison (see chapter 4 syntax §2) means "different from, other than":

vīcīnus noster est **aliō** ingeniō **atque** erus meus.
our neighbour has a **different** character **from** my master.

**2.** *īdem* "the same" when followed by *ac, atque, et* or the relative pronoun means "the same as":

> nec **eōdem** modō ille vīvit **quō** erus meus.
> nor does he live in **the same** way **as** my master.

**3.** *alius* "different, other" when repeated means "one ... another" (or in the plural "some ... others"):

> hominēs **alius aliī** prōdesse dēbent.
> men ought to help **one another**.

> nam **alius aliō** mōre vīvit.
> for **one man** lives in **one** way, **another in another**.

> sed **aliud** est maledīcere, **aliud** accūsāre.
> but it is **one thing** to speak ill of someone, **another thing** to accuse him.

**4.** *alter* "another (of two)" when repeated means "the one ... the other" (or in the plural "the one group ... the other group"):

> sunt duae sorōrēs: **altera alterī** simillima est.
> there are two sisters: **the one** is very like **the other**.

> at sorōrēs hīs hominibus **altera alterī** miseriae sunt.
> but the sisters are a cause of unhappiness to these men, **the one** sister **to the one** man, **the other to the other**.

> **alteram** ille amat sorōrem, erus **alteram**.
> he loves **the one** sister, my master **the other**.

**5.** *quisque* "each" when used with a superlative ("each most ...") means "the most ... in each case" or "all the most ...":

> sed **nōtissimum quodque** malum maximē tolerābile est.
> but **the most familiar** misfortune **in each case** is the most bearable.

**6.** *sē* "himself, herself, itself" and *suus* "his, her, its (own)" usually refer back to the subject of the clause or sentence in which they appear:

> erus **sibi** optat quod plūrimī exoptant **sibi**.
> my master wishes **for himself** what most people hanker after **for themselves**.

But they can also refer to nouns other than the subject:

> iustitia **suum cuique** distribuit.
> justice assigns **to each his own**.

**7.** *hic ... ille* "this ... that" when they refer back to nouns already mentioned can mean "the latter ... the former":

> mōs erat antīquus niveīs ātrīsque lapillīs,
> **hīs** damnāre reōs, **illīs** absolvere culpā.
> there was an ancient custom with white and black stones, to condemn defendants **with the latter**, to acquit them from guilt **with the former**.

# Metaphrasing

Pronouns are metaphrased like nouns or adjectives as appropriate, in the position their case requires:

| | |
|---|---|
| mihi | — ★s to/for me |
| tuus | your — ★s |
| ille | this — ★s *or* he ★s |

# Examples

## 1. * dīvitiās aliī praepōnunt, aliī honōrēs. (Cic. *Amic.* 20)

dīvitiae –ārum (f.pl) = riches,
   wealth

          dīvitiās   (a)  –ās
                      (b)  acc pl
                      (c)  — ★s wealth

alius –a –ud ... alius –a –ud = one
   ... another; some ... others

            aliī   (a)  –ī
                      (b)  nom pl
                      (c)  some ★ wealth

praepōnō –ōnere –osuī –ositum
   = to place in front, prefer

      praepōnunt,  (a)  –nt
                      (b)  3rd pl act
                      (c)  some prefer wealth,

alius –a –ud ... alius –a –ud = one
   ... another; some ... others

            aliī   (a)  –ī
                      (b)  nom pl
                      (c)  some prefer wealth, others ★

honor –ōris (m) = an honour,
   high public office

      honōrēs.  (a)  –ēs
                      (b)  acc pl
                      (c)  some prefer wealth, others ★ high office.

      Translation     Some prefer wealth, others high office.

## 2.   optimus quisque maximē glōriā dūcitur.
   (Cic. *Arch*. 26)

optimus –a –um = best

|         |     |                            |
| ------- | --- | -------------------------- |
| optimus | (a) | –us                        |
|         | (b) | superl, nom sing masc      |
|         | (c) | the best — ⋆s              |

quisque quaeque quidque = each
   person or thing

|         |     |                            |
| ------- | --- | -------------------------- |
| quisque | (a) | –s                         |
|         | (b) | nom sing                   |
|         | (c) | each best person ⋆s        |

maximus –a –um = greatest;
   (adv) most

|        |     |                                     |
| ------ | --- | ----------------------------------- |
| maximē | (a) | –ē                                  |
|        | (b) | superl adv                          |
|        | (c) | each best person ⋆s most greatly    |

glōria –ae (f) = glory

|        |     |                                               |
| ------ | --- | --------------------------------------------- |
| glōriā | (a) | –ā                                            |
|        | (b) | abl sing                                      |
|        | (c) | each best person ⋆s most by/with/ from glory  |

dūcō –cere –xī –ctum = to lead,
   lead on

|          |     |                                               |
| -------- | --- | --------------------------------------------- |
| dūcitur. | (a) | –tur                                          |
|          | (b) | 3rd sing pass                                 |
|          | (c) | each best person is led on most by glory.     |

|             |                                               |
| ----------- | --------------------------------------------- |
| Translation | All the best people are led on most by glory. |

## 3. *patria mihi vītā meā multō est cārior.
(Cic. *Catil*. 1.27)

patria –ae (f) = one's native land,
   country

|  |  |  |
|---|---|---|
| patria | (a) | –a |
|  | (b) | nom sing |
|  | (c) | the country ⋆s |

ego = I

|  |  |  |
|---|---|---|
| mihi | (a) | –i |
|  | (b) | dat sing |
|  | (c) | the country ⋆s to/for me |

vīta –ae (f) = life

|  |  |  |
|---|---|---|
| vītā | (a) | –ā |
|  | (b) | abl sing |
|  | (c) | the country ⋆s to/for me by/with/ from life |

meus –a –um = my (own)

|  |  |  |
|---|---|---|
| meā | (a) | –ā |
|  | (b) | abl sing fem |
|  | (c) | the country ⋆s to/for me by/with/ from my own life |

multus –a –um = much, many

|  |  |  |
|---|---|---|
| multō | (a) | –ō |
|  | (b) | dat/abl sing masc/neut |
|  | (c) | the country ⋆s to/for me by/with/ from my own life by/with/from much — |

sum esse fuī = to be

|  |  |  |
|---|---|---|
| est | (a) | –t |
|  | (b) | 3rd sing act |
|  | (c) | the country is — to/for me by/with/ from my own life by/with/from much — |

cārus –a –um = costly, dear

|  |  |  |
|---|---|---|
| cārior. | (a) | –ior |
|  | (b) | comp, nom sing fem |
|  | (c) | the country is much dearer to me than my own life. |

| Translation | My country is much dearer to me than my own life. |
|---|---|

## 4. formōsam rārō nōn sibi quisque petit.
## (Prop. 2.34.4)

formōsus –a –um = shapely,
    beautiful

                  formōsam    (a)   –am
                                    (b)   acc sing fem
                                    (c)   — ★s a beautiful —

rārō (adv) = rarely
nōn = not
sē = himself, herself, itself, etc

              rārō nōn sibi    (a)   –i
                                    (b)   dat sing
                                    (c)   rarely does — not ★ a beautiful —
                                                  to/for himself/herself/itself

quisque quaeque quidque = each
    person or thing

                     quisque    (a)   –s
                                    (b)   nom sing
                                    (c)   rarely does each person not ★ a
                                                  beautiful — to/for himself

petō –ere –īvī –ītum = to make
    for, seek to win

                      petit.    (a)   –t
                                    (b)   3rd sing act
                                    (c)   rarely does each person not seek to
                                                  win a beautiful — for himself.

                   Translation    Rarely does each man not seek to win
                                          a beautiful girl for himself.

## 5. dēnique nōn omnēs eadem mīrantur amantque. (Hor. *Ep.* 2.2.58)

dēnique (adv) = at last, in fact
nōn = not
omnis –is –e = every, all

| | | |
|---|---|---|
| dēnique nōn omnēs | (a) | –ēs |
| | (b) | nom/acc pl masc/fem |
| | (c) | in fact not all — ★ / — does not ★ all — |

īdem eadem idem = the same

| | | |
|---|---|---|
| eadem | (a) | –a |
| | (b) | nom sing fem *or* nom/acc neut pl |
| | (c) | in fact not all — ★ the same — in fact the same — does *or* do not ★ all — |

mīror –ārī –ātus = to marvel at, admire

| | | |
|---|---|---|
| mīrantur | (a) | –ntur |
| | (b) | 3rd pl pass |
| | (c) | in fact not all — admire the same — |

amō –āre –āvī –ātum = to love
–que (conj) = and

| | | |
|---|---|---|
| amantque. | (a) | –nt |
| | (b) | 3rd pl act |
| | (c) | in fact not all — admire and love the same —. |

| | |
|---|---|
| Translation | In fact not all men admire and love the same things. |

126

# Summary of Examples

1. dīvitiās aliī praepōnunt, aliī honōrēs.

2. optimus quisque maximē glōriā dūcitur.

3. patria mihi vītā meā multō est cārior.

4. formōsam rārō nōn sibi quisque petit.

5. dēnique nōn omnēs eadem mīrantur amantque.

# Exercises

Complete the following sentences on the analogy of the first:

quī illud sibi optat illō ingeniō est.
quī aliud sibi optat .......................................
quī id sibi optat .......................................
quī idem sibi optat .......................................
quī hoc sibi optat .......................................

quī aliō mōre vīvit aliīs cārus est.
quī nostrō mōre vīvit .......................................
quī vestrō mōre vīvit .......................................
quī meō mōre vīvit .......................................
quī suō mōre vīvit .......................................

# Reading

1. mīlitat omnis amans et habet sua castra Cupīdō. (Ov. *Am.* 1.9.1)

   amans –ntis (m) = a lover
   castra –ōrum (n.pl) = a fortified camp
   Cupīdō –inis (m) = Cupid (god of sexual desire)
   habeō –ēre –uī –itum = to have, possess
   mīlitō –āre –āvī –ātum (intr) = to serve as a soldier
   suus –a –um = his, her, its (own), etc.

2. glōria cuique sua est. (Tib. 1.4.77)

   glōria –ae (f) = glory
   quisque quaeque quidque = each person or thing
   suus –a –um = his, her, its (own), etc.

3. quis nisi vel mīles vel amans et frīgora noctis
   et densō mixtās perferet imbre nivēs?
   mittitur infestōs alter speculātor in hostēs:
   in rīvāle oculōs alter, ut hoste, tenet.
   ille gravēs urbēs, hic dūrae līmen amīcae
   obsidet. hic portās frangit, at ille forēs.    (Ov. *Am.* 1.9.15)

   alter –era –erum ... alter –era –erum = the one ... the other
   amans –ntis (m) = a lover
   amīca –ae (f) = a mistress
   densus –a –um = dense, heavy
   dūrus –a –um = hard, pitiless
   et ... et (conjs) = both ... and
   foris –is (f) = the door (of a building or room)
   frangō –ngere frēgī –ctum = to break (open)
   frīgus –oris (n) = cold, frost
   gravis –is –e = heavy, oppressive
   hostis –is (m) = an enemy
   imber –bris (m) = rain
   infestus –a –um = hostile, threatening
   līmen –inis (n) = the doorstep, doorway (to a building)
   mīles –itis (m) = a soldier
   mittō –ere mīsī missum = to let go, send
   mixtus –a –um = mixed, mingled (with)
   nisi (conj) = if not, except
   nix nivis (f) = snow
   nox –ctis (f) = night
   obsideō –idēre –ēdī –essum = to sit down against, besiege
   oculus –ī (m) = the eye
   perferet = will endure
   porta –ae (f) = the gate (of a city or town)
   rīvālis –is (m) = a rival
   speculātor –ōris (m) = a scout or spy
   teneō –ēre –uī –tum = to hold (fast), keep fixed
   urbs –bis (f) = a city
   ut (adv) = as, in the same way as
   vel ... vel (conjs) = either ... or

4. suum cuique decus posteritās rependit. (Tac. *Ann.* 4.35)

   decus –oris (n) = honour, glory
   posteritās –ātis (f) = future ages, posterity
   quisque quaeque quidque = each person or thing
   rependō –dere –dī –sum = to weigh out, give as due
   suus –a –um = his, her, its (own), etc.

5. nullam enim virtūs aliam mercēdem labōrum perīculōrumque
   dēsīderat praeter hanc laudis et glōriae. (Cic. *Arch.* 28)

   alius –a –ud = different, other

dēsīderō -āre -āvī -ātum = to long for, desire
enim = for
glōria -ae (f) = glory
laus -dis (f) = praise
mercēs -ēdis (f) = a payment, reward
perīculum -ī (n) = danger
praeter (prep w.acc) = beyond, except
virtūs -ūtis (f) = virtue, manly spirit, courage

6. *potest meum iūdicium nōn sōlum aliud mihi ac tibi, sed mihimet ipsī aliud aliās vidērī. (Cic. *Orat.* 237)

aliās (adv) = at another time
alius -a -ud = different, other
alius -a -ud ... alius -a -ud = one ... another
ego / egomet = I
ipse -a -um = himself, herself, itself, etc.
iūdicium -[i]ī (n) = a judgement, opinion
meus -a -um = my (own)
nōn sōlum ... sed = not only ... but
tū = you
videor vidērī vīsus (intr) = to appear, seem

7. *labor optimōs citat; senātus per tōtum diem saepe consulitur, quamquam illō tempore vīlissimus quisque aut in campō ōtium suum oblectat, aut in popīnā latet, aut tempus in aliquō circulō terit. (Sen. *Dial.* 1.5.4)

aliquī -qua -quod = some or other
aut ... aut (conjs) = either ... or
campus -ī (m) = a plain, field, the Campus Martius
circulus -ī (m) = a circle, group of people
citō -āre -āvī -ātum = to set in motion, stimulate
consulō -ere -uī -tum = to consult
diēs -ēī (m) = day
lateō -ēre -uī (intr) = to lie hidden, escape notice
oblectō -āre -āvī -ātum = to delight, beguile
optimus -a -um = best
otium -[i]ī (n) = leisure, idleness
per (prep w.acc) = through, throughout
popīna -ae (f) = a low-class eating house
quamquam = however much, although
quisque quaeque quidque = each person or thing
saepe (adv) = often
senātus -ūs (m) = the senate
suus -a -um = his, her, its (own), etc.
tempus -oris (n) = time
terō -ere trīvī trītum = to rub away, waste
tōtus -a -um = the whole, all
vīlis -is -e = cheap, of little value or importance

8. sed in magnā cōpiā rērum aliud aliī nātūra iter ostendit.
   pulchrum est bene facere reī publicae, etiam bene dīcere haud
   absurdum est. (Sall. *Cat.* 3.1)

   absurdus -a -um = discordant, inappropriate
   alius -a -ud ... alius -a -ud = one ... another
   cōpia -ae (f) = an abundance
   dīcō -cere -xī -ctum = to say, speak (of)
   etiam = also, even
   faciō -ere fēcī factum = to do, act (towards)
   haud = not
   iter -ineris (n) = a journey, path
   magnus -a -um = great
   nātūra -ae (f) = nature
   ostendō -dere -dī -tum = to hold out, offer
   pulcher -chra -chrum = beautiful, fine
   rēs reī (f) = a thing, activity
   rēs publica reī publicae (f) = affairs of state, the state

9. quis sibi rēs gestās Augustī scrībere sūmit?
   bella quis et pācēs longum diffundit in aevum?
   (Hor. *Ep.* 1.3.7)

   aevum -ī (n) = time, the past, the future
   Augustus -ī (m) = Augustus (the first emperor)
   bellum -ī (n) = warfare, a war
   diffundō -undere -ūdī -ūsum = to spread, extend
   longus -a -um = long, far distant
   pax pācis (f) = peace
   rēs gestae rērum gestārum (f.pl) = things done, achievements
   scrībō -bere -psī -ptum = to write (about)
   sē = himself, herself, itself, etc.
   sūmō -mere -mpsī -mptum = to take (upon oneself)

10. *at populō Rōmānō numquam scriptōrum cōpia fuit, quia
    optimus quisque facere quam dīcere, sua ab aliīs benefacta
    laudārī quam ipse aliōrum narrāre mālēbat. (Sall. *Cat.* 8.5)

    alius -a -ud = different, other
    benefactum -ī (n) = a good deed, service
    cōpia -ae (f) = an abundance, supply
    dīcō -cere -xī -ctum = to say, speak (of)
    faciō -ere fēcī factum = to do, act
    fuit = there has been
    ipse -a -um = himself, herself, itself, etc.
    laudō -āre -āvī -ātum = to praise
    mālēbat = preferred
    narrō -āre -āvī -ātum = to relate
    numquam (adv) = never

optimus –a –um = best
populus –ī (m) = a people, nation
quam = than, rather than
quia (conj) = because
quisque quaeque quidque = each person or thing
scriptor –ōris (m) = a writer
suus –a –um = his, her, its (own), etc.

# Vocabulary to Learn

et ... et (conjs) = both ... and
rēs reī (f) = a thing, matter
sē / sēsē = himself, herself, itself, etc
suus –a –um = his, her its (own), etc
urbs –bis (f) = a city, the city of Rome

# 11
# TENSES:
# THE IMPERFECT SYSTEM

## Morphology

In all five tenses of the imperfect system the endings for the 3rd singular active and passive are *-t* and *-tur*, and for the corresponding plurals *-nt* and *-ntur*. In the present indicative these "person" endings are added directly to the imperfect stem (with some minor phonetic adjustments); but in the other tenses and moods a "tense" ending is added first. The endings for the five tenses (numbered i-v for ease of reference throughout the chapter) are as follows:

|       |                      |                          |
|-------|----------------------|--------------------------|
| (i)   | present indicative   | stem only                |
| (ii)  | imperfect indicative | stem plus *-ba-*         |
| (iii) | future indicative    | stem plus *-b-* or *-e-* |
| (iv)  | present subjunctive  | stem plus *-a-*          |
| (v)   | imperfect subjunctive | stem plus *-re-*        |
|       |                      | (pres infin act ending)  |

The only exception is the present subjunctive of the first conjugation, which uses *-e-* instead of *-a-* in order to distinguish the subjunctive from the indicative.

# Syntax

The imperfect system makes a distinction based upon the "aspect" of the verb: it refers to action as incomplete, in contrast to the perfect system, which refers to action as completed (see chapter 17). Each system then makes further distinctions based upon the time of the action ("tense") and the attitude of the speaker towards the action ("mood").

**1.** The tenses of the imperfect system are set out below, with alternative translations to illustrate different ways of emphasising the incomplete aspect:

(i) the present indicative refers to action as incomplete in the present:

> erus meus saepe **pōtat** dē mediō diē.
> my master often **drinks / is drinking** from midday.

(ii) the imperfect indicative refers to action as incomplete in the past; it is commonly used in descriptions:

> rēgiī iuvenēs ōtium convīviīs **terēbant**.
> young men of royal blood **spent / were spending / used to spend** their leisure time at banquets.

(iii) the future indicative refers to action as incomplete in the future:

> vitia **erunt** dōnec hominēs.
> there **will be / will continue to be** vices as long as there are men.

(iv) the present subjunctive refers to action as incomplete in the future:

> quod iuvat, id semper **faciant** iuvenēs!
> **let** young men always **do** what delights them!

(v) the imperfect subjunctive refers to action as incomplete in the present:

> nōn illōs vīta **iuvāret** invīsa cīvibus.
> a life hateful to their fellow citizens **would** not **be delighting** them.

**2.** The indicative and subjunctive moods express the speaker's attitude towards what he is saying. The indicative implies that the action of the verb belongs to the world of reality:

> nōn **est** flāgitium adulescentulō scortārī neque pōtāre.
> it **is** not a disgrace for a young man to visit prostitutes nor to drink.

The subjunctive implies that the action is hypothetical in some way; it has three shades of meaning, which can lead to uncertainty unless a significant word or the context resolves the problem. Subjunctives are used to imply that an action is:

(a) possible: this "potential" use is often signalled by *forsitan* or *fortasse* "perhaps"; the negative is *nōn*:

> erus meus fortasse **iubeātur** ad amīcam venīre.
> my master **may** perhaps **be asked** to come to his mistress.

(b) desired: this "optative" use is often signalled by *ō* "oh", *utinam* or *sī* "if only!"; it is commonly used in prayers; the negative is *nē* though *utinam nōn* is also used:

> ō mihi praeteritōs **referat** sī Iuppiter annōs!
> oh, **if only** Jupiter **would bring back** for me my bygone years!

(c) commanded: this "jussive" use is grammatically identical with the optative use, but while anything may be desired, not all things can be commanded; the negative is *nē*:

> tum nē quis līminis **obseret** tabellam!
> then **let** no-one **bolt** the entrance door!

The jussive subjunctive is commonly used in questions of a "deliberative" nature, in which the present subjunctive still refers to the future but the imperfect subjunctive refers to the past; the negative is then *nōn*:

> quid **faciat** iuvenis?
> what **should** a young man **do**? / **is** a young man **to do**?

> quid **facerent** māiōrēs?
> what **should** our elders **have done**? / **were** our elders **to do**?

**3.** Verbs in main clauses referring to the future, such as the future indicative and the present subjunctive, require a future tense to be used in subordinate clauses that also refer to the future:

> hoc sī crīmen **erit**, crīmen Amōris **erit**.
> if this **is** (**will be**) a crime, it **will be** a crime of Love.

# Metaphrasing

**1.** The different tenses of the imperfect system are metaphrased as follows:

- (i)  the present indicative:  — ★s
  facit  — does —

- (ii)  the imperfect indicative:  — was ★ing
  faciēbat  — was doing —

- (iii)  the future indicative:  — will ★
  faciet  — will do —

- (iv)  the present subjunctive in three ways, corresponding to the three shades of meaning of the subjunctive (see syntax §2 above):

  faciat  (a) — may/would do —
  (b+c) may/let — do —

- (v)  the imperfect subjunctive in three ways, corresponding to the three shades of meaning of the subjunctive (see syntax §2 above):

  faceret  (a) — might/would be doing —
  (b+c) may/let — be doing —

**2.** These basic patterns can then be adapted when necessary as follows:

(a) the incomplete aspect will sometimes need to be emphasised:

faciēbat  — was doing / used to do / kept on doing —

(b) a future indicative in subordinate clauses (see syntax §3 above) will sometimes need to be translated as a present:

qui hoc faciet           (whoever will do this)
                             (whoever does this)

(c) a significant word or the context will help to identify the particular shade of meaning of a subjunctive:

forsitan faciat           — may perhaps do —

(d) in deliberative questions the present subjunctive will still refer to the future, but the imperfect subjunctive will refer to the past:

quid faciat?             what should — do / is — to do?

quid faceret?           what should — have done / was — to do?

**3.** It now becomes necessary to isolate and identify both tense and person endings:

faciēbat                 (a) –bat
                         (b) imperf indic, 3rd sing act
                         (c) — was doing —

# Examples

## 1. nox erat et biforēs intrābat lūna fenestrās.
### (Ov. *Pont.* 3.3.5)

nox –ctis (f) = night

|  | | |
|---|---|---|
| nox | (a) | –x |
|  | (b) | nom sing |
|  | (c) | night ★s |

sum esse fuī = to be

|  | | |
|---|---|---|
| erat | (a) | –rat |
|  | (b) | imperf indic, 3rd sing act |
|  | (c) | it was night |

et (conj) = and
biforis –is –e = having two leaves
    or casements, double

|  | | |
|---|---|---|
| et biforēs | (a) | –ēs |
|  | (b) | nom/acc pl masc/fem |
|  | (c) | and the double — ★ / — ★s the double — |

intrō –āre –āvī –ātum = to go into,
    enter

|  | | |
|---|---|---|
| intrābat | (a) | –bat |
|  | (b) | imperf indic, 3rd sing act |
|  | (c) | and — was entering the double — |

lūna –ae (f) = the moon

|  | | |
|---|---|---|
| lūna | (a) | –a |
|  | (b) | nom sing |
|  | (c) | and the moon was entering the double — |

fenestra –ae (f) = a window

|  | | |
|---|---|---|
| fenestrās. | (a) | –ās |
|  | (b) | acc pl |
|  | (c) | and the moon was entering the double windows. |

|  |  |
|---|---|
| Translation | It was night and the moon was entering the double windows. |

## 2. dī meliōra ferant, nec sint mihi somnia vēra! ([Tib.] 3.4.1)

deus deī (m) = a god (nom.pl: dī)

dī    (a)    –ī
       (b)    nom pl
       (c)    the gods ★

melior –ior –ius = better

meliōra    (a)    –iōra
       (b)    compar, acc pl neut
       (c)    the gods ★ better —

ferō –rre tulī latum = to carry, bring

ferant[1],    (a)    –ant
       (b)    pres subj, 3rd pl act
       (c)    the gods may bring better —
            may/let the gods bring better —!

nec (conj) = and ... not, nor
sum esse fuī = to be

nec sint[1]    (a)    –int
       (b)    pres subj, 3rd pl act
       (c)    and — may not be —
            and may/let — not be —!

ego = I

mihi    (a)    –i
       (b)    dat sing
       (c)    and — may not be — to/for me
            and may/let — not be — to/for me!

somnium –[i]ī (n) = a dream

somnia    (a)    –a
       (b)    nom pl
       (c)    and the dreams may not be — to/for me
            and may/let the dreams not be — to/for me!

vērus –a –um = real, true

vēra!    (a)    –a
       (b)    nom pl neut
       (c)    and the dreams may not be true for me.
            and may/let the dreams not be true for me!

Translation    May the gods bring better things and may the dreams not be true for me!

[1] In the original context these are optative subjunctives.

## 3. * haud facile fēmina ūna inveniētur bona. (Pac. *incert*. 35W)

haud = not
facile (adv) = easily
fēmina –ae (f) = a woman

| | | |
|---|---|---|
| haud facile fēmina | (a) | –a |
| | (b) | nom sing |
| | (c) | not easily does a woman ★ |

ūnus –a –um = one

| | | |
|---|---|---|
| ūna | (a) | –a |
| | (b) | nom sing fem |
| | (c) | not easily does one woman ★ |

inveniō –enīre –ēnī –entum = to
    come upon, find

| | | |
|---|---|---|
| inveniētur | (a) | –ētur |
| | (b) | fut indic, 3rd sing pass |
| | (c) | not easily will one woman be found |

bonus –a –um = good

| | | |
|---|---|---|
| bona. | (a) | –a |
| | (b) | nom sing fem |
| | (c) | not easily will one good woman be found. |

## 4. *quid faciant hominēs, cuive habeant fidem? (Catul. 30.6)

quis? quid? = who? what?

|  |  |
|---|---|
| quid | (a) –d |
|  | (b) nom/acc sing neut |
|  | (c) what ★s / what does — ★? |

faciō –ere fēcī factum = to make, do

|  |  |
|---|---|
| faciant | (a) –ant |
|  | (b) pres subj, 3rd pl act |
|  | (c) what would/should — do? |

homō –inis (m) = a human being, man

|  |  |
|---|---|
| hominēs, | (a) –ēs |
|  | (b) nom pl |
|  | (c) what would/should men do? |

quis? quid? = who? what?
–ve (conj) = or

|  |  |
|---|---|
| cuive | (a) –i |
|  | (b) dat sing masc/fem/neut |
|  | (c) or to/for whom/what does — ★? |

habeō –ēre –uī –itum = to have

|  |  |
|---|---|
| habeant | (a) –ant |
|  | (b) pres subj, 3rd pl act |
|  | (c) or to/for whom/what would/ should — have —? |

fidēs –ēī (f) = trust, faith

|  |  |
|---|---|
| fidem? | (a) –em |
|  | (b) acc sing |
|  | (c) or in whom/what would/should — have faith? |

| Translation | What should men do or what should they have faith in? |
|---|---|

N.B. the parallel clauses suggest that *cui* is neuter, and in the original context the subjunctives are deliberative.

## 5.   numquam erit fēlix quem torquēbit fēlīcior.
(Sen. *Dial*. 5.30.3)

numquam (adv) = never
sum esse fuī = to be

| | | |
|---|---|---|
| numquam erit | (a) | –rit |
| | (b) | fut indic, 3rd sing act |
| | (c) | there / it will never be — |
| | | — will never be — |

fēlix –īcis = fruitful, fortunate,
     happy

| | | |
|---|---|---|
| fēlix | (a) | –x |
| | (b) | nom sing masc/fem/neut |
| | (c) | there will never be a happy — |
| | | — will never be happy |

quī quae quod = who(ever),
     which, what

| | | |
|---|---|---|
| quem | (a) | –em |
| | (b) | acc sing masc |
| | (c) | (whom — ★s) |

torqueō –quēre –sī –tum = to
     twist, torture

| | | |
|---|---|---|
| torquēbit | (a) | –bit |
| | (b) | fut indic, 3rd sing act |
| | (c) | (whom — will torture) |

fēlix –īcis = fruitful, fortunate,
happy

| | | |
|---|---|---|
| fēlīcior. | (a) | –ior |
| | (b) | nom sing masc/fem |
| | (c) | (whom a happier — will torture). |

| | |
|---|---|
| Translation | He will never be happy whom a happier man tortures. |

# Summary of Examples

1. nox erat et biforēs intrābat lūna fenestrās.

2. dī meliōra ferant, nec sint mihi somnia vēra!

3. haud facile fēmina ūna inveniētur bona.

4. quid faciant hominēs, cuive habeant fidem?

5. numquam erit fēlix quem torquēbit fēlīcior.

# Exercises

Change the verb in the following sentences into each of the other tenses of the imperfect system and translate:

erus meus saepe pōtat dē mediō diē.
  (pōtō -āre -āvī -ātum = to drink)

nōn numquam iubētur ad amīcam venīre.
  (iubeō -bēre -ssī -ssum = to ask)

quid faciunt aliī?
  (faciō -ere fēcī factum = to do)

rēgiī iuvenēs ōtium convīviīs terunt.
  (terō -ere trīvī trītum = to pass)

is autem fēminam nullam invenit bonam.
  (inveniō -enīre -ēnī -entum = to find)

# Reading

1.   certa tibi ā nobīs dabitur mensūra bibendī:
       officium praestent mensque pedēsque suum.
     (Ov. *Ars.* 1.589)

     ā (prep w.abl) = from, by
     bibō -ere -ī = to drink
     certus -a -um = certain, definite
     dō dare dedī datum = to give
     mens -tis (f) = the mind
     mensūra -ae (f) = the process of measuring, a measure
     nōs = we
     officium -[i]ī (n) = a service, function
     pēs pedis (m) = the foot
     praestō -āre -itī -itum = to provide, fulfil
     -que ... -que (conjs) = both ... and
     tū = you

143

2.    Laevia sex cyathīs, septem Iustīna bibātur,
      quinque Lycas, Lȳdē quattuor, Īda tribus:
   omnis ab infūsō numerētur amīca Falernō,
      et quia nulla venit, tū mihi, Somne, venī!    (Mart. 1.71.1)

(N.B. Laevia, Iustīna, Lycas, Lȳdē and Īda are names of mistresses.)

amīca –ae (f) = a mistress
bibō –ere –ī = to drink
cyathus –ī (m) = a ladle, liquid measure
ego = I
Falernum –ī (n) = Falernian (wine)
infūsus –a –um = poured (in)
numerō –āre –āvī –ātum = to count
quattuor = four
quia (conj) = because
quinque = five
septem = seven
sex = six
Somne = Sleep
trēs trēs tria = three
tū = you
venī! = come!
veniō venīre vēnī ventum (intr) = to come

3.    utinam lex esset eadem, quae uxōrī est, virō!
   nam uxor contenta est, quae bona est, unō virō:
   quī minus vir ūnā uxōre contentus siet?    (Pl.*Mer*.823)

(N.B. siet (archaic form) = sit)

contentus –a –um = content, satisfied (with)
īdem eadem idem = the same
lex lēgis (f) = a law
minus (compar.adv) = to a smaller extent, less
nam = for
quī? = how? why?
ūnus –a –um = one, a single
utinam (particle introducing a wish) = if only!
uxor –ōris (f) = a wife

4.    ūnius hic quondam servus amōris erat.    (Prop. 2.13.36)

quondam (adv) = formerly, once
servus –ī (m) = a slave
ūnus –a –um = one, a single (gen.sing: ūnius)

5.      Eutrapelus cuicumque nocēre volēbat,
vestīmenta dabat pretiōsa: "beātus enim iam
cum pulchrīs tunicīs sūmet nova consilia et spēs:
dormiet in lūcem, scortō postpōnet honestum
officium, nummōs aliēnōs pascet".    (Hor. *Ep.* 1.18.31)

aliēnus –a –um = not one's own, borrowed from someone else
consilium –[i]ī (n) = counsel, a plan
dō dare dedī datum = to give
dormiō –īre –īvī –ītum (intr) = to sleep
enim = for
Eutrapelus –ī (m) = P.Volumnius Eutrapelus (a knight and a wit)
honestus –a –um = honourable
iam (adv) = now
lux lūcis (f) = light, daylight
noceō –ēre –uī –itum (w.dat) = to hurt, injure
novus –a –um = new
nummus –ī (m) = a coin; (pl) money, cash
officium –[i]ī (n) = a service, obligation
pascō –cere pāvī –tum = to feed, pay interest on
postpōnō –ōnere –osuī –ositum (w.dat) = to treat as inferior to
pretiōsus –a –um = costly, precious
quīcumque quaecumque quodcumque = whoever, whatever
scortum –ī (n) = a prostitute
spēs –eī (f) = an expectation, hope
sūmō –mere –mpsī –mptum = to take up, adopt
tunica –ae (f) = a tunic
vestīmentum –ī (n) = clothing; (pl) clothes
volō velle voluī = to want, wish (to)

6.   sī ventrī bene, sī laterī est pedibusque tuīs, nīl
dīvitiae poterunt rēgālēs addere māius.    (Hor. *Ep.* 1.12.5)

addō –ere –idī –itum = to add
dīvitiae –ārum (f.pl) = riches, wealth
latus –eris (n) = the side (of one's body or chest)
māior –ior –ius = greater
pēs pedis (m) = the foot
rēgālis –is –e = of or belonging to a king
tuus –a –um = your (own)
venter –tris (m) = the belly, stomach

7.  atque utinam Rōmae nēmō esset dīves, et ipse
    strāmineā posset dux habitāre casā!
    numquam vēnālēs essent ad mūnus amīcae,
    atque ūnā fieret cāna puella domō.          (Prop. 2.16.19)

    ad (prep w.acc) = to, in response to
    amīca –ae (f) = a mistress
    cānus –a –um = white, white or grey haired
    casa –ae (f) = a hut
    domus –ī (f) = a house, home
    dux –cis (m) = a leader, emperor
    fīō fierī (intr) = to become or be made
    habitō –āre –āvī –ātum (intr) = to live (in)
    ipse –a –um = himself, herself, itself, etc.
    mūnus –eris (n) = a service or favour, gift
    numquam (adv) = never
    puella –ae (f) = a girl, young woman
    strāmineus –a –um = made of straw
    ūnus –a –um = one, a single
    utinam (particle introducing a wish) = if only!
    vēnālis –is –e = able to be bought, for sale

8.  fēlix, quem Veneris certāmina mūtua perdunt:
    dī faciant, lētī causa sit ista meī!        (Ov. *Am.* 2.10.29)

    causa –ae (f) = a cause, reason
    certāmen –inis (n) = exertion, rivalry
    deus deī (m) = a god (nom.pl: dī)
    faciō –ere fēcī factum = to make, bring it about (that)
    iste –a –ud = that (of yours)
    lētum –ī (n) = death
    meus –a –um = my (own)
    mūtuus –a –um = mutual, reciprocal
    perdō –ere –idī –itum = to ruin, kill
    Venus –eris (f) = Venus (goddess of love)

9.  *prō patriā quis bonus dubitet mortem oppetere? (Cic. *Off.*
    1.57)

    dubitō –āre –āvī –ātum = to be in doubt, hesitate (to)
    mors –tis (f) = death
    oppetō –ere –īvī –ītum = to encounter, meet (prematurely)
    patria –ae (f) = one's native land, country
    prō (prep w.abl) = before, on behalf of

10.  at Catōnī studium modestiae, decoris, sed maximē sevēritātis
     erat; nōn dīvitiīs cum dīvite neque factiōne cum factiōsō, sed
     cum strēnuō virtūte, cum modestō pudōre, cum innocente
     abstinentiā certābat; esse quam vidērī bonus mālēbat; ita quō
     minus petēbat glōriam, eō magis illum assequēbātur. (Sall. *Cat.*
     54.6)

abstinentia -ae (f) = restraint, self-control
assequor -quī -cūtus = to follow after, overtake
Catō -ōnis (m) = M.Porcius Cato Uticensis (champion of the
republic)
certō -āre -āvī -ātum (intr) = to vie for superiority (with)
decus -oris (n) = honour, glory
dīvitiae -ārum (f.pl) = riches, wealth
factiō -ōnis (f) = a faction, partisanship
factiōsus -a -um = of or belonging to a faction, partisan
glōria -ae (f) = glory
innocens -ntis = innocent, virtuous
ita (adv) = so, consequently
magis (compar.adv) = to a greater extent, more
mālō mālle māluī = to prefer (to)
maximus -a -um = greatest
minus (compar.adv) = to a smaller extent, less
modestia -ae (f) = restraint, modesty
modestus -a -um = restrained, modest
petō -ere -īvī -ītum = to make for, seek to win
pudor -ōris (m) = a sense of shame, decency
quō ... eō = the (more) ... the (more)
sevēritās -ātis (f) = sternness, strictness
strēnuus -a -um = active, energetic
studium -[i]ī (n) = zeal, eagerness (for)
videor vidērī vīsus (intr) = to appear, seem

# Vocabulary to Learn

ego = I
faciō –ere fēcī factum = to make, do
meus –a –um = my (own)
nam = for
veniō venīre vēnī ventum (intr) = to come

# 12
# IMPERSONAL VERBS

## Morphology

Impersonal verbs are limited to the 3rd singular active or passive and thus end in *-t* or *-tur*. They may appear in any tense of the indicative or subjunctive, and also in the infinitive and the neuter singular of the gerundive.

## Syntax

The term "impersonal verbs" refers to verbs which are only used impersonally, and to the impersonal use of other verbs. What distinguishes them is that the *-t* or *-tur* ending does not refer to a subject noun; its function is purely formal, like "it" in the examples below. Impersonal verbs either have no subject at all, or they have a neuter pronoun such as *id* "this, it" or a subordinate clause in place of a subject noun. Consequently a literal translation is not always possible.

Impersonal verbs which are active in form include:

**1.** verbs referring to the weather or time of day such as *fulgurat* "there is a flash of lightning", *grandinat* "it is hailing", *lūcescit* "it is getting light", *ningit* "it is snowing", *pluit* "it is raining", *tonat* "there is thunder" and *vesperascit* "it is getting late":

> quārē et serēnō **tonat**?
> why **is there thunder** even from a clear sky?

**2.** verbs denoting emotion such as *miseret* "it fills with pity", *paenitet* "it fills with dissatisfaction or regret", *piget* "it fills with irritation", *pudet* "it fills with shame" and *taedet* "it fills with tiredness". These verbs of emotion take an accusative of the person affected and a genitive of the matter about which the emotion is felt (see chapter 8 syntax §§6 and 7):

> an Iovem cīvitātis mōrum **piget taedet**que?
> can it really be that Jupiter **is irritated** and **tired** (**it fills** Jupiter **with irritation** and **tiredness**) of the city's ways?

**3.** certain other verbs and phrases such as:

(a) *decet* "it becomes", *dēdecet* "it is unbecoming", *iuvat* "it delights" and *oportet* "it behoves", which take an accusative of the person affected:

> quid mē **oportet** facere?
> what **does it behove** me / **ought** I to do?

(b) *convenit* "it befits", *expedit* "it is useful", *libet* "it is pleasing", *licet* "it is permitted" and *placet* "it is pleasing" take a dative of the person concerned (see chapter 6 syntax §3):

> in tantā rē mihi neglegentī esse nōn **licet**.
> in so great a matter **it is** not **permitted** to me to be / I **can** not be heedless.

(c) *interest* and *rēfert* "it makes a difference, it matters" take a genitive or a possessive pronoun in the ablative singular feminine to refer to the person concerned (since the *rē-* of *rēfert* came to be regarded as the ablative singular of *rēs* "a thing, matter"):

> magis reīpublicae **interest** quam meā dīs supplicāre.
> **it matters** more to the state than to me to supplicate the gods.

(d) *opus est* "there is a need" takes a dative of the person concerned and an ablative of separation (see chapter 3 syntax §1):

> nōn verbīs mihi **opus est** ad erum meum excitandum.
> **there is** no **need** for me of words / I **do** not **need** words to rouse my master.

The impersonal passive stresses action rather than the agent; consequently the agent is regularly omitted. The impersonal passive is used with:

**4.** intransitive verbs:

> ad fānum ex urbe tōtā **concurritur**.
> **a rush is made** (**rushing is done**) to the temple from out of the whole city.

> nec **cessārī** potest.
> nor can **there be any hesitation** (**is hesitating** able **to be done**).

**5.** "transitive" verbs which take a "direct object" in a case other than the accusative:

> prōdigī causā deō **supplicātur**.
> because of the prodigy **supplication** of the god **is made** (**supplicating** of the god **is done**).

> lēgī mōrīque **pārendum est**.
> **obedience** to law and custom **is to be shown** (**obeying** of law and custom **is to be done**).

**6.** transitive verbs which take a direct object in the accusative; the direct object of the impersonal passive is regularly omitted:

> nec iam diēs noctēsque **estur, bibitur**.
> no longer **is there eating** and **drinking** (**is eating** and **drinking done**) day and night.

> nunc **est luendum**.
> now **atonement is to be made** (**atoning is to be done**).

This identity in form of the personal and impersonal passive can lead to uncertainty, unless the context resolves the problem.

# Metaphrasing

**1.** Impersonal verbs which are active in form are metaphrased: it ★s, according to the vocabulary; rephrasing this however will often make a better translation:

| | |
|---|---|
| taedet mē | it fills me with tiredness (of) |
| | *or* I am tired (of) |

**2.** The impersonal passive is metaphrased: ★ing is done (or if the verb is not intransitive: ★ing of — is done); rephrasing this however will often make a better translation:

| | |
|---|---|
| pārētur lēgī | obeying of the law is done |
| | *or* obedience to the law is shown |
| | *or* the law is obeyed |

**3.** These basic patterns can then be adapted when necessary as follows:

(a) a subordinate clause acting as the subject of an impersonal verb will be metaphrased in brackets after the main clause:

| | |
|---|---|
| libet mihi supplicāre | it is pleasing to me (to supplicate —) |

(b) the 3rd singular passive of transitive verbs will occasionally need an alternative metaphrase:

| | |
|---|---|
| bibitur | — is drunk |
| | *or* drinking of — is done |

# Examples

### 1. cantātur ac saltātur per omnēs gentēs aliquō modō. (Quint. *Inst.* 2.17.10)

cantō -āre -āvī -ātum = to sing

| | | |
|---|---|---|
| cantātur | (a) | -tur |
| | (b) | pres indic, 3rd sing pass |
| | (c) | — is sung / singing of — is done |

ac (conj) = and
saltō -āre -āvī -ātum (intr) = to dance

| | | |
|---|---|---|
| ac saltātur | (a) | -tur |
| | (b) | pres indic, 3rd sing pass |
| | (c) | singing and dancing is done |

per (prep w.acc) = through, throughout
omnis -is -e = every, all

| | | |
|---|---|---|
| per omnēs | (a) | -ēs |
| | (b) | acc pl masc/fem |
| | (c) | singing and dancing is done throughout all — |

gens -tis (f) = a race, nation

| | | |
|---|---|---|
| gentēs | (a) | -ēs |
| | (b) | acc pl |
| | (c) | singing and dancing is done throughout all nations |

aliquī -qua -quod = some or other

| | | |
|---|---|---|
| aliquō | (a) | -ō |
| | (b) | abl sing masc/neut |
| | (c) | singing and dancing is done throughout all nations by/with/ from some — or other |

modus -ī (m) = a manner, way

| | | |
|---|---|---|
| modō. | (a) | -ō |
| | (b) | abl sing |
| | (c) | singing and dancing is done throughout all nations in some way or other. |

| | |
|---|---|
| Translation | There is singing and dancing throughout all nations in some way or other. |

153

## 2. *ad bene vīvendum nōn magnō apparātū opus est. (Sen. *Dial.* 12.5.1)

ad (prep w.acc) = to, for
bonus −a −um = good (adv:
    bene)

|  |  |  |
|---|---|---|
| ad bene | (a) | −e |
|  | (b) | adv |
|  | (c) | — ⋆s for (⋆ well) |

vīvō −vere −xī −ctum (intr) =
    to live

|  |  |  |
|---|---|---|
| vīvendum | (a) | −ndum |
|  | (b) | gnd, acc sing |
|  | (c) | — ⋆s for (living well) |

nōn = not
magnus −a −um = great

|  |  |  |
|---|---|---|
| nōn magnō | (a) | −ō |
|  | (b) | dat/abl sing masc/neut |
|  | (c) | — ⋆s to/for/by/with/from no great — for (living well) |

apparātus −ūs (m) = pre-
    paration, lavishness

|  |  |  |
|---|---|---|
| apparātū | (a) | −ū |
|  | (b) | abl sing |
|  | (c) | — ⋆s by/with/from no great lavishness for (living well) |

opus est esse fuit (w.abl) =
    there is a need (of)

|  |  |  |
|---|---|---|
| opus est. | (a) | −t |
|  | (b) | pres indic, 3rd sing act |
|  | (c) | there is a need of no great lavishness for (living well). |

|  |  |
|---|---|
| Translation | No great lavishness is needed for living well. |

## 3.   invidētur autem praestantī flōrentīque fortūnae.
(Cic. *de Orat*. 2.210)

invideō –idēre –īdī –īsum (w.dat)
    = to envy

|  | | |
|---|---|---|
| invidētur | (a) | –tur |
| | (b) | pres indic, 3rd sing pass |
| | (c) | envying of — is done |

autem = however, but
praestans –ntis = outstanding

|  | | |
|---|---|---|
| autem praestantī | (a) | –ī |
| | (b) | dat sing masc/fem/neut |
| | (c) | but envying of outstanding — is done |

flōrens –ntis = flowering,
    flourishing
–que (conj) = and

|  | | |
|---|---|---|
| flōrentīque | (a) | –ī |
| | (b) | dat sing masc/fem/neut |
| | (c) | but envying of outstanding and flourishing — is done |

fortūna –ae (f) = fortune,
    prosperity

|  | | |
|---|---|---|
| fortūnae. | (a) | –ae |
| | (b) | dat sing |
| | (c) | but envying of outstanding and flourishing prosperity is done. |

| | |
|---|---|
| Translation | But outstanding and flourishing prosperity is envied. |

155

## 4.  *aliquōs libīdinis infāmiaeque suae neque pudet neque taedet. (Cic. *Ver.* 35)

aliquis –qua –quid = someone,
  something

aliquōs   (a)  –ōs
          (b)  acc pl masc
          (c)  — ★s some people

libīdō –inis (f) = desire,
  wantonness

libīdinis  (a)  –is
          (b)  gen sing
          (c)  — ★s some people of wantonness

infāmia –ae (f) = ill-fame,
  dishonour
–que (conj) = and

infāmiaeque  (a)  –ae
            (b)  gen sing
            (c)  — ★s some people of wantonness
                 and dishonour

suus –a –um = his, her, its
  (own), etc.

suae     (a)  –ae
         (b)  gen sing fem
         (c)  — ★s some people of their wanton-
              ness and dishonour

neque ... neque (conjs) =
  neither ... nor
pudet –ēre –uit = it fills with
  shame (at)

neque pudet  (a)  –t
            (b)  pres indic, 3rd sing act
            (c)  it fills some people neither with
                 shame at their wantonness and dis-
                 honour

neque ... neque (conjs) =
  neither ... nor
taedet –dēre –sum est = it fills
  with tiredness (of)

neque taedet.  (a)  –t
              (b)  pres indic, 3rd sing act
              (c)  it fills some people neither with
                   shame at nor with tiredness of their
                   wantonness and dishonour.

Translation   Some people are neither ashamed at
              nor tired of their wantonness and
              dishonour.

## 5.  at bene nōn poterat sine pūrō pectore vīvī.
(Lucr. 5.18)

at (conj) = but
bonus -a -um = good (adv: bene)

| | | |
|---|---|---|
| at bene | (a) | -e |
| | (b) | adv |
| | (c) | but — ★s well |

nōn = not
possum posse potuī = to be able
    (to)

| | | |
|---|---|---|
| nōn poterat | (a) | -rat |
| | (b) | imperf indic, 3rd sing act |
| | (c) | but — was not able (to ★ well) |

sine (prep w.abl) = without
pūrus -a -um = clean, pure

| | | |
|---|---|---|
| sine pūrō | (a) | -ō |
| | (b) | abl sing masc/neut |
| | (c) | but — was not able (to ★ well without a pure —) |

pectus -oris (n) = the breast, heart

| | | |
|---|---|---|
| pectore | (a) | -e |
| | (b) | abl sing |
| | (c) | but — was not able (to ★ well without a pure heart) |

vīvō -vere -xī -ctum (intr) = to live

| | | |
|---|---|---|
| vīvī. | (a) | -ī |
| | (b) | pres infin pass |
| | (c) | but (living well without a pure heart) was not able (to be done). |

| | |
|---|---|
| Translation | But a good life could not be lived without a pure heart. |

# Summary of Examples

1. cantātur ac saltātur per omnēs gentēs aliquō modō.

2. ad bene vīvendum nōn magnō apparātū opus est.

3. invidētur autem praestantī flōrentīque fortūnae.

4. aliquōs libīdinis infāmiaeque suae neque pudet neque taedet.

5. at bene nōn poterat sine pūrō pectore vīvī.

# Exercises

Complete the following sentences on the analogy of the first:

sī libet bene vīvere, bene vīvitur.
sī libet saepe pōtāre . . . . . . . . . . .
sī libet semper amāre  . . . . . . . .
sī libet fortūnae invidēre  . . . . . .
sī libet libīdinī servīre . . . . . . . . .
sī libet lēgibus pārēre  . . . . . . . .

# Reading

1.  *quem Rōmānōrum pudet uxōrem dūcere in convīvium? (Nep. *pr.* 6)

    convīvium –[i]ī (n) = a dinner-party, banquet
    dūcō –cere –xī –ctum = to lead, take
    pudet –ēre –uit = it fills with shame (to)
    uxor –ōris (f) = a wife

2.  anteā stolātae ībant nūdīs pedibus in clīvum, passīs capillīs, mentibus pūrīs, et Iovem aquam exōrābant. itaque statim urceātim plovēbat; aut tunc aut numquam; et omnēs redībant ūdī tamquam mūrēs. (Petr. 44.18)

    (N.B. plovēbat (vulgar form) = pluēbat)

    anteā (adv) = in the past
    aqua –ae (f) = water, rain

aut ... aut (conjs) = either ... or
capillus -ī (m) = the hair of the head; (pl) one's hair
clīvus -ī (m) = a hill, the Capitoline Hill
eō īre iī itum (intr) = to go
exōrō -āre -āvī -ātum = to pray to, beseech (for)
itaque (adv) = and so, accordingly
Iuppiter Iovis (m) = Jupiter (god of the sky)
mens -tis (f) = the mind
mūs mūris (m) = a mouse
nūdus -a -um = naked, bare
numquam (adv) = never
passus -a -um = spread out, let loose
pēs pedis (m) = the foot
pluit -ere -uit (intr) = it is raining
pūrus -a -um = clean, pure
redeō -īre -iī -itum (intr) = to come back, return
statim (adv) = immediately, at once
stolātus -a -um = wearing a long white dress
tamquam (conj) = in the same way as, like
tunc (adv) = then
ūdus -a -um = wet, soaked
urceātim (adv) = in jugfuls


3.  carendum nōn sōlum crīmine turpitūdinis vērum etiam sus-
    pīciōne. (Quint.*Inst*.2.2.14)

    careō -ēre -uī -itum (w.abl) = to be without, free from
    crīmen -inis (n) = an accusation, ground for reproach
    nōn sōlum ... vērum etiam = not only ... but also
    suspīciō -ōnis (f) = a suspicion
    turpitūdō -inis (f) = ugliness, indecency


4.  at quam multōs diēs in eā villā turpissimē es perbacchātus! ab
    hōrā tertiā bibēbātur lūdēbātur vomēbātur. (Cic. *Phil.* 2.104)

    bibō -ere -ī = to drink
    diēs -ēī (m) = a day
    es perbacchātus = you spent (time) in bacchanalian orgies
    hōra -ae (f) = an hour
    lūdō -dere -sī -sum (intr) = to play, gamble
    quam! = to what an extent! how much! how!
    tertius -a -um = third
    turpis -is -e = ugly, disgusting, shameful
    villa -ae (f) = a country dwelling
    vomō -ere -uī -itum (intr) = to be sick, vomit

5. *quid tum? omniane bonīs virīs quae facere possunt facienda sunt, etiamne sī turpia, sī perniciōsa erunt, sī facere omnīnō nōn licēbit? licet autem quod lēgibus, quod mōre māiōrum institūtīsque concēditur. neque enim quod quisque potest id eī licet, nec sī nōn obstātur proptereā etiam permittitur. (Cic. *Phil.* 13.14)

concēdō –dere –ssī –ssum = to concede, allow
enim = for
etiam = also, even
institūtum –ī (n) = an established practice, habit
lex lēgis (f) = a law
licet –ēre –uit (w.dat) = it is permitted (to)
māior –ior –ius = greater, older; (m.pl) ancestors
mōs mōris (m) = an established practice, custom
–ne? (interrogative particle) = can it be that ...?
neque ... nec (conjs) = neither ... nor
obstō –āre –itī –ātum (w.dat) = to stand in the way of
omnīnō (adv) = entirely, altogether
permittō –ittere –īsī –issum = to permit, allow
perniciōsus –a –um = destructive, pernicious
proptereā (adv) = because of that, for that reason
quisque quaeque quidque = each person or thing
tum (adv) = then
turpis –is –e = ugly, disgusting, shameful

6. *sileātur dē nocturnīs ēius bacchātiōnibus ac vigiliīs; lēnōnum, āleātōrum, perductōrum nulla mentiō fiat; damna, dēdecora praetereantur. (Cic. *Ver.* 1.33)

āleātor –ōris (m) = one who plays a game of chance, gambler
bacchātiō –ōnis (f) = a bacchanalian orgy
damnum –ī (n) = a financial loss
dē (prep w.abl) = from, about
dēdecus –oris (n) = dishonour, disgrace; (pl) disgraceful acts
fīō fierī (intr) = to become or be made
lēnō –ōnis (m) = a brothel-keeper, pimp
mentiō –ōnis (f) = mention
nocturnus –a –um = of or belonging to the night
perductor –ōris (m) = one who leads or misleads, a seducer
praetereō –īre –iī –itum = to pass by or over, omit
sileō –ēre –uī (intr) = to be silent, say nothing
vigilia –ae (f) = keeping watch, staying awake

7.  vīvitur parvō bene, cui paternum
    splendet in mensā tenuī salīnum
    nec levēs somnōs timor aut cupīdō
          sordidus aufert.       (Hor. *Carm.* 2.16.13)

auferō –rre abstulī ablātum = to carry away, carry off
aut (conj) = or
cupīdō –inis (m) = desire, greed
levis –is –e = light, gentle
mensa –ae (f) = a table
parvus –a –um = small; (neut.sing) little (wealth)
paternus –a –um = of one's father or forefathers
salīnum –ī (n) = a salt-cellar
somnus –ī (m) = sleep
sordidus –a –um = dirty, sordid
splendeō –ēre (intr) = to shine
tenuis –is –e = slender, poor
timor –ōris (m) = fear
vīvō –vere –xī –ctum (intr) = to live

8.  *hūius institūtī patrēs nostrōs nōn paenitēbat. (Cic. *Div. Caec.*
    69)

institūtum –ī (n) = an established practice, habit
noster –tra –trum = our (own)
paenitet –ēre –uit = it fills with dissatisfaction or regret
pater –tris (m) = a father, forefather

9.  ad supervacua sūdātur; illa sunt quae togam conterunt, quae nōs
    senescere sub tentōriō cōgunt, quae in aliēna lītora inpingunt: ad
    manum est quod sat est. cui cum paupertāte bene convenit,
    dīves est. (Sen. *Ep.* 4.11)

ad (prep w.acc) = to, towards the attainment of
aliēnus –a –um = belonging to others, foreign
cōgō –ere coēgī coactum = to drive together, force
conterō –terere –trīvī –trītum = to grind down, wear out
convenit –enīre –ēnit –entum (w.dat) = it is agreed (by)
inpingō –ingere –ēgī –actum = to dash (upon), drive (on to)
lītus –oris (n) = a coast, shore
manus –ūs (f) = the hand
nōs = we
paupertās –ātis (f) = poverty
sat (n.indecl) = sufficient, enough
senescō –escere –uī (intr) = to grow old
sub (prep w.acc/abl) = under, beneath
sūdō –āre –āvī –ātum (intr) = to sweat
supervacuus –a –um = superfluous, unnecessary
tentōrium –iī (n) = a tent
toga –ae (f) = a toga (formal outer garment)

10. quippe ex voluntāte perversā facta est libīdō, et dum servītur libīdinī, facta est consuētūdō, et dum consuētūdinī nōn resistitur, facta est necessitās. (August. *Conf.* 8.10)

consuētūdō –inis (f) = a custom, habit
dum (conj) = as long as, while
facta est = is created
libīdō –inis (f) = desire, wantonness
necessitās –ātis (f) = necessity, a need
perversus –a –um = facing the wrong way, misguided
quippe = the reason is that, for
resistō –istere –titī (w.dat) = to stand up (to), resist
serviō –īre –īvī –ītum (w.dat) = to serve, be a slave (to)
voluntās –ātis (f) = one's will, choice

# Vocabulary to Learn

enim = for
eō īre iī itum (intr) = to go
nōs = we
noster –tra –trum = our (own)
vīvō –vere –xī –ctum (intr) = to live

# 13
# *UT* AND THE SUBJUNCTIVE

## Morphology

The use of *ut* with the subjunctive does not introduce any new forms.

## Syntax

The conjunctions *ut/utī* "that" and *nē* "that ... not" are used to introduce subordinate clauses containing a verb in the subjunctive; they stand in place of a subject or object noun or in place of an adverb in relation to the main clause. Advance warning of the subordinate clause is often given by a neuter pronoun such as *id* "this, it" or by some other significant word. The use of the subjunctive in these clauses is an automatic consequence of subordination: in some its original meaning is still felt, but in others it came to be used like an indicative to refer to real, not hypothetical events.

*Ut* is used with the subjunctive in:

**1.** noun clauses dependent on verbs such as *accidere* "to happen", *efficere* "to cause", *esse* "to be" and *fierī* "to happen":

> sōl efficit **ut** arbusta **flōreant**.
> the sun brings it about **that** the trees **flourish**.

In this use of the subjunctive to refer to real events the potential sense is suppressed but its original negative *non* is retained:

> sed haec pestilentia id efficit **ut** arbusta **nōn flōreant**.
> but this plague brings it about **that** the trees **do not flourish**.

**2.** noun clauses dependent on verbs of wishing and commanding:

> senectūtem **ut adipiscantur** omnēs optant.
> all men pray **that they may reach / to reach** old age.

In this use of the subjunctive the optative or jussive sense is exploited and its original negative *nē* is used:

> **nē** iuvenis **moriātur** erus meus optat.
> my master prays **that he may not die / not to die** young.

**3.** noun clauses dependent on verbs of fearing:

> cautus vīcīnum metuet **nē trahat** inde malum.
> a cautious man will fear his neighbour, **that he may catch** the plague from him.

In this use of the subjunctive the optative sense is exploited: the fear that something may happen is expressed as a wish that it may not; the opposite fear, that something may not happen, is expressed as a wish that it may. Thus the negative is *ut* or *nē nōn*:

> cautus metuet **ut careat / nē nōn careat** ipse malō.
> a cautious man will fear **that he may not escape** the plague himself.

**4.** adverbial clauses of purpose:

> at erus meus medicāmentum vīcīnō nostrō dabat **ut** eum **cūrāret.**
> but my master was giving our neighbour medicine **to cure / in order to cure** him.

In this use of the subjunctive the optative sense is exploited and its original negative *nē* is used:

> isque hoc bibēbat **nē** morbus **ingravesceret.**
> and he was drinking this **so that / in order that** the disease **might not grow worse.**

The main clause often gives advance warning of the purpose clause with words such as *ideō, idcircō, proptereā* "for this reason" and *eō animō, eō consiliō, eā mente* "with this intention".

**5.** adverbial clauses of result:

> medicāmentī erat vīs tanta **ut** eum **sānāret.**
> the strength of the medicine was so great **that it might / could cure** him.

This use of the subjunctive can also refer to real as well as to hypothetical events, suppressing the potential sense of the subjunctive while retaining its original negative *nōn*:

> medicāmentī erat vīs tanta **ut** morbus **nōn ingravesceret**.
> the strength of the medicine was so great **that** the disease **did not grow worse**.

The main clause often gives advance warning of the result clause with words such as *adeō* "to such an extent", *ita* or *sīc* "in such a way", *tālis* "such", *tam* (with adjectives and adverbs) "so", *tantus* "so great" and *tot* "so many".

**6.** adverbial clauses of result dependent upon comparative adjectives and adverbs:

> vīcīnus noster **rōbustior** est **quam ut** morbō **pereat**.
> our neighbour is **stronger than that he should die** / **too strong to die** of the disease.

**7.** the impersonal idiom *tantum abest ut ... ut* "it is so far from the case that ... that". The first *ut* introduces a noun clause (see note 1 above), the second an adverb clause (see note 5 above):

> **tantum abest ut** ille morbō **pereat ut** iam **convalescat**.
> **it is so far from the case that he is dying** / **he is so far from dying** of the disease, **that he is** now **recovering**.

**8.** an ordered sequence of tenses, which governs the relationship between the tense of the verb in the main clause and that of the subjunctive in the subordinate clause. When the main verb is a "primary" tense such as the present or future indicative, then a "primary" tense of the subjunctive such as the present is used (see notes 1-3 above): but when the main verb is a "historic" tense such as the imperfect indicative, then a "historic" tense of the subjunctive such as the imperfect is used (see notes 4-5 above). But the rule is not rigidly applied to result clauses; a historic main verb can be followed by a primary subjunctive when the result of the past action continues into the present:

> tanta **erat** vīs medicāmentī ut ille iam **convalescat**.
> so great **was** the strength of the medicine that **he is** now **recovering**.

# Metaphrasing

**1.** The conjunction *ut* introducing a subordinate clause with the subjunctive is metaphrased: that — ★s (and *nē*: that — does not ★), in brackets:

ut bibat                      (that — drinks —)

It is left thus suspended until it becomes clear how it fits into the whole sentence.

**2.** This basic pattern can then be adapted when necessary as follows:

(a) the type of clause will determine the precise translation; some clauses will need "may/could/should" to be used as appropriate:

ut bibat rogat               — asks (that — may drink —)

or an alternative metaphrase: so that / in order that — ★s

ut bibat venit               — comes (so that — may drink —)

or yet another alternative: so as to / in order to / to ★

ut bibat venit               — comes (to drink —)

(b) when *ut* is dependent on a verb of fearing (see note 3 above), it is metaphrased like *nē*, and vice versa:

ut bibat metuit             — fears (that — may not drink —)

(c) when a comparative is followed by *quam ut* and the subjunctive, it is metaphrased: too — to ★

sevērior est quam ut bibat     — is too stern (to drink —)

(d) when *nē* begins a sentence with the subjunctive, it is not immediately clear whether it is the main clause or a subordinate clause, so that an alternative metaphrase is needed:

nē bibat                       may/let — not drink — <br>                                 *or* (that — does not drink —)

# Examples

## 1. clārior rēs erat quam ut tegī ac dissimulārī posset. (Liv. 26.51.11)

clārus –a –um = bright, clear (to
    see)

|  |  |  |
|---|---|---|
| clārior | (a) | –ior |
|  | (b) | compar, nom sing masc/fem |
|  | (c) | a clearer — ★s |

rēs reī (f) = a thing, matter

|  |  |  |
|---|---|---|
| rēs | (a) | –s |
|  | (b) | nom sing |
|  | (c) | a clearer matter ★s |

sum esse fuī = to be

|  |  |  |
|---|---|---|
| erat | (a) | –rat |
|  | (b) | imperf indic, 3rd sing act |
|  | (c) | the matter was clearer |

quam = than
ut (conj) = that
tegō –gere –xī –ctum = to cover,
    hide

|  |  |  |
|---|---|---|
| quam ut tegī | (a) | –ī |
|  | (b) | pres infin pass |
|  | (c) | than (that — ★s to be hidden) |

ac (conj) = and
dissimulō –āre –āvī –ātum = to
    conceal, disguise

|  |  |  |
|---|---|---|
| ac dissimularī | (a) | –rī |
|  | (b) | pres infin pass |
|  | (c) | (that — ★s to be hidden and disguised) |

possum posse potuī = to be
    able (to)

|  |  |  |
|---|---|---|
| posset. | (a) | –set |
|  | (b) | imperf subj, 3rd sing act |
|  | (c) | (that — was able to be hidden and disguised). |

| Translation | The matter was too clear to be able to be hidden and disguised. |
|---|---|

## 2. est miserōrum ut malevolentēs sint atque invideant bonīs. (Pl. *Capt.* 583)

sum esse fuī = to be

|       |     |                                    |
|-------|-----|------------------------------------|
| est   | (a) | –t                                 |
|       | (b) | pres indic, 3rd sing act           |
|       | (c) | there / it is — *or* — is —        |

miser –era –erum = pitiable,
   wretched, unhappy

|          |     |                                    |
|----------|-----|------------------------------------|
| miserōrum | (a) | –ōrum                             |
|          | (b) | gen pl masc/neut                   |
|          | (c) | it is typical of unhappy —         |
|          |     | — is — of unhappy —                |

ut (conj) = that
malevolens –ntis = ill-disposed,
   spiteful

|                |     |                                         |
|----------------|-----|-----------------------------------------|
| ut malevolentēs | (a) | –ēs                                    |
|                | (b) | nom/acc pl masc/fem                      |
|                | (c) | (that spiteful — ★s / — ★s spiteful —) |

sum esse fuī = to be

|      |     |                          |
|------|-----|--------------------------|
| sint | (a) | –int                     |
|      | (b) | pres subj, 3rd pl act     |
|      | (c) | (that — are spiteful)     |

atque (conj) = and
invideō –idēre –īdī –īsum (w.dat)
   = to envy

|                 |     |                                         |
|-----------------|-----|-----------------------------------------|
| atque invideant | (a) | –ant                                    |
|                 | (b) | pres subj, 3rd pl act                    |
|                 | (c) | (that — are spiteful and envy —)         |

bonus –a –um = good; (m.pl)
   the well-off

|        |     |                                         |
|--------|-----|-----------------------------------------|
| bonīs. | (a) | –īs                                     |
|        | (b) | dat pl masc                             |
|        | (c) | (that — are spiteful and envy the       |
|        |     | well-off).                              |

|             |                                                                            |
|-------------|----------------------------------------------------------------------------|
| Translation | It is typical of the unhappy that they are spiteful and envy the well-off. |

## 3. *dēcrētum erat utī consul vidēret nē quid rēs publica dētrīmentī caperet. (Cic. *Catil*. 1.4)

dēcrētus –a –um = decided,
    decreed

<table>
<tr><td>dēcrētum</td><td>(a)</td><td>–um</td></tr>
<tr><td></td><td>(b)</td><td>nom/acc sing neut or acc sing masc</td></tr>
<tr><td></td><td>(c)</td><td>a decreed — ★s / it is decreed<br>or — ★s a decreed —</td></tr>
</table>

sum esse fuī = to be

<table>
<tr><td>erat</td><td>(a)</td><td>–rat</td></tr>
<tr><td></td><td>(b)</td><td>imperf indic, 3rd sing act</td></tr>
<tr><td></td><td>(c)</td><td>— was decreed / it was decreed</td></tr>
</table>

utī (conj) = that
consul –lis (m) = a consul (the
    highest magistrate)

<table>
<tr><td>utī consul</td><td>(a)</td><td>–l</td></tr>
<tr><td></td><td>(b)</td><td>nom sing</td></tr>
<tr><td></td><td>(c)</td><td>(that the consul ★s)</td></tr>
</table>

videō vidēre vīdī vīsum = to
    see, see to it (that)

<table>
<tr><td>vidēret</td><td>(a)</td><td>–ret</td></tr>
<tr><td></td><td>(b)</td><td>imperf subj, 3rd sing act</td></tr>
<tr><td></td><td>(c)</td><td>(that the consul should see to it)</td></tr>
</table>

nē (conj) = that ... not
quis qua quid = anyone, anything

<table>
<tr><td>nē quid</td><td>(a)</td><td>–d</td></tr>
<tr><td></td><td>(b)</td><td>nom/acc sing neut</td></tr>
<tr><td></td><td>(c)</td><td>(that not anything ★s / — does not ★ anything)</td></tr>
</table>

rēs publica reī publicae (f) =
    affairs of state, the state

<table>
<tr><td>rēs publica</td><td>(a)</td><td>–s and –a</td></tr>
<tr><td></td><td>(b)</td><td>nom sing</td></tr>
<tr><td></td><td>(c)</td><td>(that the state does not ★ anything)</td></tr>
</table>

dētrīmentum –ī (n) = dimi-
    nishment, harm

<table>
<tr><td>dētrīmentī</td><td>(a)</td><td>–ī</td></tr>
<tr><td></td><td>(b)</td><td>gen sing</td></tr>
<tr><td></td><td>(c)</td><td>(that the state does not ★ any harm)</td></tr>
</table>

capiō –ere cēpī –tum = to take
    (hold of), suffer

<table>
<tr><td>caperet.</td><td>(a)</td><td>–ret</td></tr>
<tr><td></td><td>(b)</td><td>imperf subj, 3rd sing act</td></tr>
<tr><td></td><td>(c)</td><td>(that the state should not suffer any harm).</td></tr>
</table>

<table>
<tr><td>Translation</td><td>It was decreed that the consul should see to it that the state should not suffer any harm.</td></tr>
</table>

## 4. *nōn ita cīvitās aegra est ut consuētīs remediīs sistī possit. (Liv. 3.20.8)

nōn = not
ita (adv) = so, in such a way
cīvitās –ātis (f) = a city, state

|  | nōn ita cīvitās | (a) | –s |
|  |  | (b) | nom sing |
|  |  | (c) | the state ★s not in such a way |

aeger –gra –grum = ill, ailing

|  | aegra | (a) | –a |
|  |  | (b) | nom sing fem |
|  |  | (c) | the ailing state ★s not in such a way |

sum esse fuī = to be

|  | est | (a) | –t |
|  |  | (b) | pres indic, 3rd sing act |
|  |  | (c) | the state is not ailing in such a way |

ut (conj) = that
consuētus –a –um = customary, usual

|  | ut consuētīs | (a) | –īs |
|  |  | (b) | dat/abl pl masc/fem/neut |
|  |  | (c) | (that — ★s to/for/by/with/from the usual —) |

remedium –[i]ī (n) = a remedy

|  | remediīs | (a) | –īs |
|  |  | (b) | dat/abl pl |
|  |  | (c) | (that — ★s to/for/by/with/from the usual remedies) |

sistō –ere stetī statum = to cause to stand, check

|  | sistī | (a) | –ī |
|  |  | (b) | pres infin pass |
|  |  | (c) | (that — ★s to be checked with the usual remedies) |

possum posse potuī = to be able (to)

|  | possit. | (a) | –sit |
|  |  | (b) | pres subj, 3rd sing act |
|  |  | (c) | (that — is able to be checked with the usual remedies). |

Translation    The state is not ailing in such a way that it can be checked with the usual remedies.

## 5. ōrandum est ut sit mens sāna in corpore sānō.
(Juv. 10.356)

ōrō –āre –āvī –ātum = to pray to,
    pray for

| | | |
|---|---|---|
| ōrandum | (a) | –ndum |
| | (b) | gndv, nom sing neut |
| | (c) | — ★s to be prayed to / for |

sum esse fuī = to be

| | | |
|---|---|---|
| est | (a) | –t |
| | (b) | pres indic, 3rd sing act |
| | (c) | — is to be prayed to / for |

ut (conj) = that
sum esse fuī = to be

| | | |
|---|---|---|
| ut sit | (a) | –it |
| | (b) | pres subj, 3rd sing act |
| | (c) | (that there is — / that — is —) |

mens –tis (f) = the mind

| | | |
|---|---|---|
| mens | (a) | –s |
| | (b) | nom sing |
| | (c) | (that there is a mind / the mind is —) |

sānus –a –um = healthy, sound

| | | |
|---|---|---|
| sāna | (a) | –a |
| | (b) | nom sing fem |
| | (c) | (that there is a sound mind) |

in (prep w.acc/abl) = into / in,
    on
corpus –oris (n) = the body

| | | |
|---|---|---|
| in corpore | (a) | –e |
| | (b) | abl sing |
| | (c) | (that there is a sound mind in the body) |

sānus –a –um = healthy, sound

| | | |
|---|---|---|
| sānō. | (a) | –ō |
| | (b) | abl sing neut |
| | (c) | (that there is a sound mind in a sound body). |

| | |
|---|---|
| Translation | It is to be prayed for that there is a sound mind in a sound body. |

# Summary of Examples

1. clārior rēs erat quam ut tegī ac dissimularī posset.

2. est miserōrum ut malevolentēs sint atque invideant bonīs.

3. dēcrētum erat utī consul vidēret nē quid rēs publica dētrīmentī caperet.

4. nōn ita cīvitās aegra est ut consuētīs remediīs sistī possit.

5. ōrandum est ut sit mens sāna in corpore sānō.

# Exercises

Complete the following sentences on the analogy of the first:

sī omnia flōrent, sōl efficit ut flōreant.
sī miserī invident bonīs, cupiditās efficit ut . . . . . . . . .
sī omnēs moriuntur, pestilentia efficit ut . . . . . . . . . . .
sī rēs publica aegra est, luxuria efficit ut . . . . . . . . . . .
sī vīcīnus sānātur, medicāmentum efficit ut . . . . . . . .

sī omnia flōrēbant, sōl efficiēbat ut flōrērent.
sī miserī invidēbant bonīs, cupiditās efficiēbat ut . . . .
sī omnēs moriēbantur, pestilentia efficiēbat ut . . . . . .
sī rēs publica aegra erat, luxuria efficiēbat ut . . . . . . .
sī vīcīnus sānābātur, medicāmentum efficiēbat ut . . .

# Reading

1.  est ut virō vir lātius ordinet
    arbusta sulcīs.                           (Hor. *Carm.* 3.1.9)

    arbustum –ī (n) = a wood, plantation
    lātus –a –um = broad, extensive
    ordinō –āre –āvī –ātum = to set out in rows, dispose
    sulcus –ī (m) = a furrow


2.  *Chabrias et vīvēbat lautē et indulgēbat sibi līberālius quam ut
    invidiam vulgī posset effugere. (Nep.*Cha*.3.2)

    Chabrias –ae (m) = Chabrias (a distinguished Athenian general)
    effugiō –ugere –ūgī = to escape from, avoid
    indulgeō –gēre –sī –tum (w.dat) = to indulge
    invidia –ae (f) = ill-will, envy
    lautus –a –um = well-washed, luxurious, "posh"
    līberālis –is –e = of or relating to free men, lavish
    vulgus –ī (n) = the common people, general public


3.  Vmmidius quīdam (nōn longa est fābula) dīves
    ut mētīrētur nummōs; ita sordidus ut sē
    nōn umquam servō melius vestīret; adusque
    suprēmum tempus nē sē pēnūria victūs
    opprimeret metuēbat.                      (Hor. *Serm.* 1.1.95)

    adusque (prep w.acc) = all the way to, right up to
    fābula –ae (f) = talk, a tale
    ita (adv) = so, in such a way
    longus –a –um = long
    melior –ior –ius = better
    mētior –īrī mensus = to measure (by size or volume)
    metuō –ere –ī metūtum = to fear
    nummus –ī (m) = a coin; (pl) money, cash
    opprimō –imere –essī –essum = to press upon, overtake
    pēnūria –ae (f) = scarcity, lack (of)
    quīdam quaedam quoddam = a certain (person or thing)
    servus –ī (m) = a slave
    sordidus –a –um = dirty, squalid, mean
    suprēmus –a –um = highest, last
    tempus –oris (n) = time, a moment or period of time
    umquam (adv) = at any time, ever
    vestiō –īre –īvī –ītum = to clothe, dress
    victus –ūs (m)= food
    Vmmidius –[i]ī (m) = Ummidius (a typical miser)

173

4. nēmō istōrum dissimulat, nēmō labōrat ut obscūra sua cupiditās esse videātur. (Cic. *Ver*. 5.126)

cupiditās –ātis (f) = desire, greed
dissimulō –āre –āvī –ātum = to conceal, disguise
iste –a –ud = that (of yours)
labōrō –āre –āvī –ātum (intr) = to labour, take pains
obscurus –a –um = dim, obscure
videor vidērī vīsus (intr) = to appear, seem

5. *ac philosophia quidem tantum abest ut laudētur ut ā plērīsque neglecta, ā multīs etiam vituperētur. (Cic. *Tusc*. 5.6)

etiam = also, even
laudō –āre –āvī –ātum = to praise
neglectus –a –um = neglected, ignored
philosophia –ae (f) = philosophy
plērusque –aque –umque = most of; (m.pl) most people
quidem = indeed
tantum abest abesse (intr) = it is so far from the case (that)
vituperō –āre –āvī –ātum = to criticise adversely

6. *nē nimis laetae rēs essent, pestilentia coēgit senātum imperāre decemvirīs ut librōs Sibyllīnōs inspicerent; eōrumque monitū lectisternium fuit. (Liv. 7.27.1)

coēgit = compelled, forced
decemvir –rī (m) = a member of a commission of ten men
fuit = there was
imperō –āre –āvī –ātum (w.dat) = to order, command
inspiciō –icere –exī –ectum = to look at, consult
laetus –a –um = flourishing, prosperous
lectisternium –[i]ī (n) = a feast in honour of the gods
liber –brī (m) = the inner bark of a tree, a book
monitus –ūs (m) = warning, advice
nimis (adv) = excessively, too
pestilentia –ae (f) = a plague
senatus –ūs (m) = the senate
Sibyllīnus –a –um = of or connected with a Sibyl

7. sī rēs publica corruptior est quam ut adiuvārī possit, sī occupāta est malīs, nōn nītētur sapiens in supervacuum. (Sen. *Dial*. 8.3.3)

adiuvō –iuvāre –iuvī –iutum = to help
corruptus –a –um = rotten, corrupt
malum –ī (n) = something bad, a misfortune
nītor –tī –xus (intr) = to lean (upon), strive (towards)
occupātus –a –um = taken over, occupied
rēs publica reī publicae (f) = affairs of state, the state
supervacuus –a –um = superfluous, unnecessary

8.   *Sēricae vestēs ingentī summā ab ignōtīs etiam ad commercium gentibus accersuntur, ut mātrōnae nostrae nē adulterīs quidem plūs suī in cubiculō quam in pūblicō ostendant. (Sen. *Ben.* 7.9.5)

accersō –ere –īvī –ītum = to send for, import
adulter –erī (m) = an adulterer, lover
commercium –[i]ī (n) = trade, commerce
cubiculum –ī (n) = a bedroom
etiam = also, even
gens –tis (f) = a race, nation
ignōtus –a –um = unknown
ingens –tis = huge, vast
matrōna –ae (f) = a married woman, wife
nē ... quidem = not even
ostendō –dere –dī –tum = to hold out, reveal
plūs –ris (n) = a greater amount, more
publicum –ī (n) = public property, the public domain
Sēricus –a –um = of or belonging to the Chinese, silken
summa –ae (f) = the total (of something), a sum (of money)
vestis –is (f) = clothing, clothes

9.   sociī nōn argentum, nōn aurum, nōn vestem, nōn mancipia repetunt, nōn ornāmenta quae ex urbibus fānīsque ērepta sunt; metuunt hominēs imperītī nē iam haec populus Rōmānus concēdat et ita velit fierī. (Cic. *Ver.* 5.126)

argentum –ī (n) = silver
aurum –ī (n) = gold
concēdō –dere –ssī –ssum = to concede, allow
ēreptus –a –um = seized, stolen
fānum –ī (n) = a shrine, temple
fīō fierī (intr) = to happen or be done
iam (adv) = now
imperītus –a –um = inexperienced, ignorant
ita (adv) = so, in this way
mancipium –[i]ī (n) = ownership, a slave
metuō –ere –ī metutum = to fear
ornāmentum –ī (n) = an ornament, adornment
populus –ī (m) = a people, nation
repetō –ere –īvī –ītum = to seek to recover, claim back
socius –[i]ī (m) = a companion, ally
vestis –is (f) = clothing, clothes
volō velle voluī = to want, wish (to)

10. *pestilentia in agrīs forīsque et conciliābulīs et in urbe tanta erat ut Libitīna fūneribus vix sufficeret. dēcrētum erat ut et consulēs hostiīs māiōribus sacrificārent et decemvirī librōs adīrent. eōrum dēcrētō supplicātiō circā omnia pulvīnāria Rōmae in diem ūnum indicta est. (Liv. 40.19.3)

adeō –īre –iī –itum = to go to, consult
circā (prep w.acc) = round
conciliābulum –ī (n) = a district administrative centre
consul –lis (m) = a consul (the highest magistrate)
decemvir –rī (m) = a member of a commission of ten men
dēcrētum –ī (n) = a decision, decree
dēcrētus –a –um = decided, decreed
diēs –ēī (m) = a day
forum –ī (n) = a public square, "assize town"
fūnus –eris (n) = a funeral
hostia –ae (f) = a sacrificial victim
in (prep w.acc/abl) = into, for / in, on
indicta est = was proclaimed
liber –brī (m) = the inner bark of a tree, a book
Libitīna –ae (f) = Libitina (goddess of funerals)
māior –ior –ius = greater, older, full-grown
pestilentia –ae (f) = a plague
pulvīnar –āris (n) = a cushioned couch (for the image of a god)
sacrificō –āre –āvī –ātum (intr) = to sacrifice
sufficiō –icere –ēcī –ectum (intr) = to be sufficient (for)
supplicātiō –ōnis (f) = supplication (of a god)
tantus –a –um = so great
ūnus –a –um = one
vix (adv) = with difficulty, hardly

# Vocabulary to Learn

dō dare dedī datum = to give, grant
etiam = also, even
nē = not; (conj) that ... not
ut (conj) = that
videō vidēre vīdī vīsum = to see

# 14
# PRESENT PARTICIPLES

## Morphology

The present participle (active) is formed from the imperfect stem and ends in –ns or –nt– followed by 3rd declension case endings; there is no corresponding passive participle, the gerundive being used instead (see chapter 7 syntax §2). The ablative singular exhibits the only variation, ending in –ī when the participle is used as an adjective, but in –e when it is used in place of a noun or in the "ablative absolute" construction (see below).

## Syntax

The present participle is a verbal adjective. As a verb it is active in meaning (deponents included) and can take a direct object in the appropriate case; as an adjective it agrees in gender, number and case with the noun it modifies. The precise relation of the noun and participle to the main clause (temporal, causal, concessive, etc) is usually not defined but left to the understanding of the reader.

**1.** The present participle is used to refer to action contemporaneous with that of the main verb:

> Ōceanum intereā **surgens** Aurōra relinquit.
> Dawn meanwhile **getting up** leaves the ocean behind.

**2.** A noun and participle are often used in place of two nouns:

> **sōl oriens** et **occidens** (i.e. **sōlis ortus** et **occāsus**) diem noctemque conficit.
> **the sun rising** and **setting** (i.e. **the sunrise** and **sunset**) causes day and night.

A participle can also be used on its own without a noun to modify:

> diēs longus vidētur opus **dēbentibus**.
> the day seems long **to those obliged to do** work.

**3.** The "ablative absolute" construction is an example of the ablative of accompaniment (see chapter 3 syntax §3). It expresses action logically connected with that of the main clause but grammatically independent. Most often it consists of a noun in the ablative and a participle in agreement with it:

> omnia **Sāturnō** tellūs **regnante** ferēbat.
> the earth used to produce everything **with Saturn reigning** / **when Saturn was reigning**.

However an ablative absolute can also consist of a noun in the ablative and a second noun or adjective in the ablative in apposition to it:

> quam bene **Sāturnō** vīvēbant **rēge** priōrēs!
> how well our predecessors used to live **with Saturn as king** / **when Saturn was king**!

An ablative absolute of this type is often used to identify the year by the names of the two consuls elected for that year:

> aedēs Monētae dēdicātur **C.Marciō Rutulō T.Manliō Torquātō consulibus**.
> a temple is dedicated to Moneta **with C.Marcius Rutulus and T.Manlius Torquatus as consuls** / **in the consulship of C.Marcius Rutulus and T.Manlius Torquatus** (i.e. in 344 B.C.).

# Metaphrasing

**1.** A present participle is metaphrased: ★ing (or if the verb is not intransitive: ★ing —), in brackets, after the noun it modifies:

occidentem                — ★s — (setting)

**2.** An ablative is metaphrased in the usual way:

sōle                    — ★s by/with/from the sun

**3.** These basic patterns can then be adapted when necessary as follows:

(a) a noun and participle in agreement with it will sometimes need to be rephrased as a clause (temporal, causal, concessive, etc. as appropriate) or as two nouns:

sōl occidens           the sun (setting) ★s
                             *or* the sun (when it sets) ★s
                             *or* the sunset ★s

(b) a second ablative will often form an ablative absolute construction with the first, and the whole phrase is then enclosed in brackets:

sōle occidente         (with the sun setting)

The phrase is left thus suspended until it becomes clear how it relates to the rest of the sentence, when it can be rephrased if necessary:

sōle occidente         (with the sun setting)
                             *or* when the sun sets
                             *or* at sunset

# Examples

## 1. *lucra petens habilī taurōs adiungit arātrō rusticus. (Tib. 1.9.7)

lucrum –ī (n) = material gain,
    profit

| | | |
|---|---|---|
| lucra | (a) | –a |
| | (b) | nom/acc pl |
| | (c) | profits ★ / — ★s profits |

petō –ere –īvī –ītum = to make
    for, seek (to win)

| | | |
|---|---|---|
| petens | (a) | –ns |
| | (b) | pres part, nom sing masc/fem/neut |
| | | *or* acc sing neut |
| | (c) | — (seeking profits) ★s |
| | | *or* — ★s — (seeking profits) |

habilis –is –e = easy to handle,
    wieldy

| | | |
|---|---|---|
| habilī | (a) | –ī |
| | (b) | dat/abl sing masc/fem/neut |
| | (c) | — (seeking profits) ★s *or* — ★s — (seeking profits) to/for/by/with/ from the wieldy — |

taurus –ī (m) = a bull

| | | |
|---|---|---|
| taurōs | (a) | –ōs |
| | (b) | acc pl |
| | (c) | — (seeking profits) ★s bulls to/for/ by/with/from the wieldy — |

adiungō –gere –xī –ctum = to
    attach, yoke

| | | |
|---|---|---|
| adiungit | (a) | –t |
| | (b) | pres indic, 3rd sing act |
| | (c) | — (seeking profits) yokes bulls to the wieldy — |

arātrum –ī (n) = a plough

| | | |
|---|---|---|
| arātrō | (a) | –ō |
| | (b) | dat sing |
| | (c) | — (seeking profits) yokes bulls to the wieldy plough |

rusticus –a –um = connected
    with a farm or the country

| | | |
|---|---|---|
| rusticus. | (a) | –us |
| | (b) | nom sing masc |
| | (c) | a country — (seeking profits) yokes bulls to the wieldy plough. |

| | |
|---|---|
| Translation | The countryman, seeking profits, yokes his bulls to the wieldy plough. |

## 2.  *omnia prospera ēveniunt sequentibus deōs, adversa spernentibus. (Liv. 5.51.5)

omnis –is –e = every, all

|  | | |
|---|---|---|
| omnia | (a) | –a |
|  | (b) | nom/acc pl neut |
|  | (c) | all — ★ / — ★s all — |

prosperus –a –um = pros-
perous, successful

|  | | |
|---|---|---|
| prospera | (a) | –a |
|  | (b) | nom/acc pl neut |
|  | (c) | all successful — ★ / — ★s all successful — |

ēveniō –enīre –ēnī –entum
(intr) = to come out, turn out

|  | | |
|---|---|---|
| ēveniunt | (a) | –nt |
|  | (b) | pres indic, 3rd pl act |
|  | (c) | all — turn out successful |

sequor –quī –cūtus = to follow
(the precepts of), obey

|  | | |
|---|---|---|
| sequentibus | (a) | –ntibus |
|  | (b) | pres part, dat/abl pl masc/fem/neut |
|  | (c) | all — turn out successful to/for/by/with/from — (obeying —) |

deus deī (m) = a god

|  | | |
|---|---|---|
| deōs, | (a) | –ōs |
|  | (b) | acc pl |
|  | (c) | all — turn out successful for — (obeying the gods), |

adversus –a –um = turned
towards or against, un-
favourable

|  | | |
|---|---|---|
| adversa | (a) | –a |
|  | (b) | nom pl neut |
|  | (c) | — ★ unfavourable |

spernō –ere sprēvī sprētum =
to reject, spurn

|  | | |
|---|---|---|
| spernentibus. | (a) | –ntibus |
|  | (b) | pres part, dat pl masc/fem/neut |
|  | (c) | — ★ unfavourable for — (spurning —). |

| Translation | All things turn out successful for those obeying the gods, but un-favourable for those spurning them. |
|---|---|

## 3.   *impiger extrēmōs currit mercātor ad Indōs, per mare pauperiem fugiens.  (Hor. *Ep.* 1.1.45)

impiger –gra –grum = active,
    energetic

                   impiger    (a)   –r
                                      (b)   nom sing masc
                                      (c)   the energetic — ★s

extrēmus –a –um = uttermost,
    farthest

                  extrēmōs   (a)   –ōs
                                      (b)   acc pl masc
                                      (c)   the energetic — ★s the farthest —

currō –rere cucurrī –sum (intr)
    = to run, rush

                      currit    (a)   –t
                                      (b)   pres indic, 3rd sing act
                                      (c)   the energetic — rushes the farthest
                                              —

mercātor –ōris (m) = a
    merchant, trader

                  mercātor   (a)   –r
                                        (b)   nom sing
                                      (c)   the energetic merchant rushes the
                                              farthest —

ad (prep w.acc) = to
Indus –ī (m) = an Indian

                  ad Indōs,   (a)   –ōs
                                        (b)   acc pl
                                      (c)   the energetic merchant rushes to the
                                              farthest Indians,

per (prep w.acc) = through,
    across
mare –is (n) = the sea

                  per mare   (a)   –e
                                        (b)   acc sing
                                      (c)   — ★s across the sea

pauperiēs –ēī (f) = poverty

                 pauperiem   (a)   –em
                                        (b)   acc sing
                                      (c)   — ★s poverty across the sea

fugiō –ere fūgī = to run away
from

|         |     |                                      |
| ------- | --- | ------------------------------------ |
| fugiens. | (a) | –ns                                 |
|         | (b) | pres part, nom sing masc            |
|         | (c) | the energetic merchant (running away from poverty across the sea) rushes to the farthest Indians. |

Translation     The energetic merchant rushes to the farthest Indians, as he runs away from poverty across the sea.

## 4.   grassārī et transeuntēs percutere quaestus est. (Sen. *Ben.* 4.17.4)

grassor –ārī –ātus (intr) = to
advance, prowl about (for
victims)

|           |     |                   |
| --------- | --- | ----------------- |
| grassārī  | (a) | –rī               |
|           | (b) | pres infin pass   |
|           | (c) | (to prowl about)  |

et (conj) = and

transeō –īre –iī –itum (intr) = to
go through or over, pass by

|                 |     |                                               |
| --------------- | --- | --------------------------------------------- |
| et transeuntēs  | (a) | –ntēs                                         |
|                 | (b) | pres part, nom/acc pl masc/fem                |
|                 | (c) | and — (passing by) ★ / — ★s — (passing by)    |

percutiō –tere –ssī –ssum = to
hit, kill

|            |     |                               |
| ---------- | --- | ----------------------------- |
| percutere  | (a) | –re                           |
|            | (b) | pres infin act                |
|            | (c) | (and to kill — passing by)    |

quaestus –ūs (m) = the acquisition of wealth, a way
of making money

|           |     |                                                        |
| --------- | --- | ------------------------------------------------------ |
| quaestus  | (a) | –us                                                    |
|           | (b) | nom sing                                               |
|           | (c) | (to kill — passing by) ★s a way of making money        |

sum esse fuī = to be

|      |     |                                                        |
| ---- | --- | ------------------------------------------------------ |
| est. | (a) | –t                                                     |
|      | (b) | pres indic, 3rd sing act                               |
|      | (c) | (to kill — passing by) is a way of making money.       |

Translation     To prowl about and kill passers-by is a way of making money.

## 5.   custōde rērum Caesare nōn furor cīvīlis aut vīs exiget ōtium. (Hor. *Carm*. 4.15.17)

custōs –ōdis (m) = a guardian

| | | |
|---|---|---|
| custōde | (a) | –e |
| | (b) | abl sing |
| | (c) | — ⋆s by/with/from the guardian |

rēs reī (f) = a thing, matter; (pl) public affairs

| | | |
|---|---|---|
| rērum | (a) | –ērum |
| | (b) | gen pl |
| | (c) | — ⋆s by/with/from the guardian of public affairs |

Caesar –aris (m) = G.Octavius Caesar Augustus (the first emperor)

| | | |
|---|---|---|
| Caesare | (a) | –e |
| | (b) | abl sing |
| | (c) | (with Caesar as the guardian of public affairs) |

nōn = not

furor –ōris (m) = madness, frenzy

| | | |
|---|---|---|
| nōn furor | (a) | –r |
| | (b) | nom sing |
| | (c) | frenzy does not ⋆ |

cīvīlis –is –e = connected with one's fellow citizens, civil

| | | |
|---|---|---|
| cīvīlis | (a) | –is |
| | (b) | nom sing masc |
| | (c) | civil frenzy does not ⋆ |

aut (conj) = or

vīs vis (f) = physical strength, violence

| | | |
|---|---|---|
| aut vīs | (a) | –s |
| | (b) | nom sing |
| | (c) | civil frenzy or violence does not ⋆ |

exigō –igere –ēgī –actum = to drive out

| | | |
|---|---|---|
| exiget | (a) | –et |
| | (b) | fut indic, 3rd sing act |
| | (c) | civil frenzy or violence will not drive out — |

ōtium –[i]ī (n) = leisure, peace

| | | |
|---|---|---|
| ōtium. | (a) | –um |
| | (b) | acc sing |
| | (c) | civil frenzy or violence will not drive out peace. |

Translation        While Caesar is guardian of public affairs, no civil frenzy or violence will drive out peace.

# Summary of Examples

1. lucra petens habilī taurōs adiungit arātrō rusticus.

2. omnia prospera ēveniunt sequentibus deōs, adversa spernentibus.

3. impiger extrēmōs currit mercātor ad Indōs,
   per mare pauperiem fugiens.

4. grassārī et transeuntēs percutere quaestus est.

5. custōde rērum Caesare nōn furor
   cīvīlis aut vīs exiget ōtium.

# Exercises

Complete the following sentences on the analogy of the first:

quī lucra petit, omnia eī prospera ēveniunt lucra petentī.
quī bene vīvit, omnia eī prospera ēveniunt ..........
quī pauperiem fugit, omnia eī prospera ēveniunt ......
quī bene regnat, omnia eī prospera ēveniunt ..........
quī deōs sequitur, omnia eī prospera ēveniunt ........

sī Sāturnus regnābat, tellūs omnia ferēbat Sāturnō regnante.
sī priōrēs bene vīvēbant, tellūs omnia ferēbat .............
sī rusticus deōs sequēbātur, tellūs omnia ferēbat ..........
sī hominēs agrōs colent, tellūs omnia feret ...............
sī dī volent, tellūs omnia feret ..........................

# Reading

1.  Aurōra intereā miserīs mortālibus almam
    extulerat lūcem referens opera atque labōrēs.
    (Verg. *Aen.* 11.182)

    almus –a –um = life-giving, kindly
    aurōra –ae (f) = the dawn
    extulerat = had brought out, revealed
    intereā (adv) = meanwhile
    lux lūcis (f) = light, daylight
    mortālis –is (m) = a human being, mortal
    opus –eris (n) = work, a task
    referō –rre rettulī relātum = to bring back, bring round again

2.  ibi L.Cotta pugnans interficitur cum maximā parte mīlitum.
    (Caes. *B.G.* 5.37.4)

    Cotta –ae (m) = L.Aurunculeius Cotta (a legate of Caesar)
    ibi (adv) = there, there and then
    interficiō –ficere –fēcī –fectum = to kill
    maximus –a –um = greatest, very great
    mīles –itis (m) = a soldier
    pars –tis (f) = a part
    pugnō –āre –āvī –ātum (intr) = to fight

3.  luctantem Īcariīs fluctibus Africum
    mercātor metuens ōtium et oppidī
    laudat rūra suī; mox reficit ratīs
    quassās, indocilis pauperiem patī.      (Hor. *Carm.* 1.1.15)

    Africus –ī (m) = a south-west wind
    fluctus –ūs (m) = a wave (of the sea)
    Īcarius –a –um = of Icarus or the Icarian Sea
    indocilis –is –e = unable to be taught (to)
    laudō –āre –āvī –ātum = to praise
    luctor –ārī –ātus (intr) = to wrestle, struggle
    mercātor –ōris (m) = a merchant, trader
    metuō –ere –ī metūtum = to fear
    mox (adv) = soon, soon after
    oppidum –ī (n) = a town
    ōtium –[i]ī (n) = leisure, peace
    patior –tī –ssus = to undergo, tolerate
    pauperiēs –ēī (f) = poverty
    quassus –a –um = battered
    ratis –is (f) = a raft, ship
    reficiō –icere –ēcī –ectum = to restore, repair
    rūs rūris (n) = the country, a country estate

4.  *vītem serpentem multiplicī lapsū et errāticō, ferrō amputans
    coercet ars agricolārum, nē silvescat sarmentīs et in omnīs partīs
    nimia fundātur. (Cic. *Sen.* 52)

    agricola -ae (m) = a farmer
    amputō -āre -āvī -ātum = to cut off, prune back
    ars –tis (f) = an art, craft, skill
    coerceō -ēre -uī -itum = to keep within bounds, restrict
    errāticus -a -um = wandering
    ferrum -ī (n) = iron, an iron implement or blade
    fundō –dere fūdī fūsum = to pour out, spread
    lapsus -ūs (m) = the act of slipping, creeping
    multiplex -icis = having many twists or turns
    nimius -a -um = excessive, too much
    pars –tis (f) = a part, direction
    sarmentum -ī (n) = a shoot, branch
    serpō -ere -sī (intr) = to crawl, wind
    silvescō -ere (intr) = to run to wood
    vītis –is (f) = a vine

5.              alius sit fortis in armīs,
        sternat et adversōs Marte favente ducēs,
    ut mihi pōtantī possit sua dīcere facta
        mīles et in mensā pingere castra merō.     (Tib. 1.10.29)

    adversus -a -um = turned towards or against, hostile
    alius -a -ud = different, other
    arma -ōrum (n.pl) = weapons, arms
    castra -ōrum (n.pl) = a fortified camp
    dīcō -cere -xī -ctum = to say, speak (of)
    dux -cis (m) = a leader, commander
    factum -ī (n) = a deed, exploit
    faveō -ēre fāvī fautum (w.dat) = to favour, be propitious (to)
    Mars -tis (m) = Mars (god of war)
    mensa -ae (f) = a table
    merum -ī (n) = neat wine (unmixed with water)
    mīles –itis (m) = a soldier
    pingō -ngere -nxī -ctum = to paint, depict
    pōtō -āre -āvī -ātum (intr) = to drink
    sternō -ere strāvī strātum = to lay out, strike down

6.  quem vocet dīvum populus ruentis
    imperī rēbus? prece quā fatīgent
    virginēs sanctae minus audientem
    carmina Vestam?                          (Hor. *Carm.* 1.2.25)

    audiō –īre –īvī –ītum = to hear, listen to
    carmen –inis (n) = a hymn, chant
    dīvus –ī (m) = a god
    fatīgō –āre –āvī –ātum = to tire out, weary
    imperium –[i]ī (n) = authority, an empire
    minus (compar.adv) = to a smaller extent, less
    populus –ī (m) = a people, nation
    prex –ecis (f) = a prayer
    quī? quae? quod? = what?
    rēs reī (f) = a thing, matter; (pl) public affairs
    ruō –ere –ī (intr) = to rush (downwards), fall
    sanctus –a –um = sacrosanct, holy
    Vesta –ae (f) = Vesta (goddess of the hearth)
    virgō –inis (f) = a girl, Vestal virgin
    vocō –āre –āvī –ātum = to call upon, invoke


7.  inde L.Genuciō et Q.Servīliō consulibus et ab sēditiōne et ā
    bellō quiētīs rēbus, nē quandō ā metū ac perīculīs vacārent,
    pestilentia ingens orta. (Liv. 7.1.7)

    (N.B. L.Genucius and Q.Servīlius were consuls in 365 B.C.)

    bellum –ī (n) = warfare, a war
    consul –lis (m) = a consul (the highest magistrate)
    inde (adv) = from there or then, then
    ingens –ntis = huge, vast
    metus –ūs (m) = fear
    orta (est) = arose, broke out
    perīculum –ī (n) = danger
    pestilentia –ae (f) = a plague
    quandō = at any time, ever
    quiētus –a –um = at rest, at peace
    sēditiō –ōnis (f) = civil strife or discord
    vacō –āre –āvī –ātum (intr) = to be empty, free (from)

8. ecce autem dūrō fūmans sub vōmere taurus
   concidit et mixtum spūmīs vomit ōre cruōrem
   extrēmōsque ciet gemitūs. it tristis arātor
   maerentem abiungens frāternā morte iuvencum,
   atque opere in mediō dēfixa relinquit arātra.
   (Verg. *Georg.* 3.515)

   abiungō -gere -xī -ctum = to detach, unyoke
   arātor -ōris (m) = a ploughman
   arātrum -ī (n) = a plough
   cieō ciēre cīvī citum = to stir up, raise
   concidō -ere -ī (intr) = to fall down, collapse
   cruor -ōris (m) = blood
   dēfixus -a -um = fixed, planted
   dūrus -a -um = hard, unfeeling
   ecce (interjection) = behold! look!
   extrēmus -a -um = uttermost, last
   frāternus -a -um = of or belonging to a brother
   fūmō -āre -āvī (intr) = to smoke, steam
   gemitus -ūs (m) = a groan
   iuvencus -ī (m) = a bullock
   maereō -ēre (intr) = to mourn, grieve
   medius -a -um = middle, the middle of
   mixtus -a -um = mixed, mingled (with)
   mors -tis (f) = death
   opus -eris (n) = work, a task
   ōs ōris (n) = the mouth
   relinquō -inquere -īquī -ictum = to leave (behind), abandon
   spūma -ae (f) = foam, froth
   sub (prep w.acc/abl) = under, beneath
   taurus -ī (m) = a bull
   tristis -is -e = gloomy, sad
   vōmer -eris (m) = a ploughshare
   vomō -ere -uī -itum = to vomit

9. M.Minūciō deinde et A.Semprōniō consulibus magna vīs
   frumentī ex Siciliā advecta. (Liv. 2.34.7)

   (N.B. M.Minūcius and A.Semprōnius were consuls in 491 B.C.)

   advecta (est) = was brought, imported
   consul -lis (m) = a consul (the highest magistrate)
   deinde (adv) = from there or then, then
   frūmentum -ī (n) = corn
   magnus -a -um = great
   vīs vis (f) = physical strength, amount

10. dēsīderantem quod satis est neque
    tumultuōsum sollicitat mare
       nec saevus Arctūrī cadentis
        impetus aut orientis Haedī,
    nōn verberātae grandine vīneae
    fundusque mendax, arbore nunc aquās
        culpante, nunc torrentia agrōs
        sīdera, nunc hiemēs inīquas.          (Hor.*Carm*.3.1.25)

aqua –ae (f) = water, rain
arbor –oris (f) = a tree
Arctūrus –ī (m) = Arcturus (the star or constellation)
aut (conj) = or
cadō –ere cecidī cāsum (intr) = to fall, set
culpō –āre –āvī –ātum = to blame, find fault with
dēsīderō –āre –āvī –ātum = to long for, desire
fundus –ī (m) = a country estate, farm
grandō –inis (f) = hail
haedus –ī (m) = a young goat, the Kid (the star)
hiems –mis (f) = winter, a storm
impetus –ūs (m) = onrush, onset
inīquus –a –um = unequal, adverse
mare –is (n) = the sea
mendax –ācis = prone to lie, deceptive
nunc (adv) = now
orior –īrī –tus (intr) = to rise
saevus –a –um = savage, violent
satis (n.indecl) = sufficient, enough
sīdus –eris (n) = a star, constellation
sollicitō –āre –āvī –ātum = to harass, worry
torreō –rrēre –rruī –stum = to scorch, bake
tumultuōsus –a –um = turbulent, tempestuous
verberātus –a –um = lashed, beaten down
vīnea –ae (f) = a vine

# Vocabulary to Learn

audiō –īre –īvī –ītum = to hear
aut (conj) = or
diēs –ēī (m) = day
ferō –rre tulī lātum = to carry, bear, bring
nox –ctis (f) = night

# 15
# PERSON ENDINGS: THE IMPERFECT SYSTEM

## Morphology

The full set of person endings for the five tenses of the imperfect system is set out below. In all but one the ending *-r* or *-r-* distinguishes the passive from the active form:

|  |  | ACTIVE | PASSIVE |
|---|---|---|---|
| Singular | 1. | *-ō / -m* | *-r* |
|  | 2. | *-s* | *-ris / -re* |
|  | 3. | *-t* | *-tur* |
| Plural | 1. | *-mus* | *-mur* |
|  | 2. | *-tis* | *-minī* |
|  | 3. | *-nt* | *-ntur* |

The 1st singular active endings *-ō* and *-m* are mutually exclusive, but the 2nd singular passive endings *-ris* and *-re* are true alternatives.

These person endings are added (with some minor phonetic adjustments) to the imperfect stem and tense endings of the imperfect system (see chapter 11). The only exception is the future indicative of 3rd and 4th conjugation verbs, the 1st singular of which ends in *-am* or *-ar* like the present subjunctive.

# Syntax

**1.** Person endings show whether the subject of the verb is 1st person "I" or "we", 2nd person "you" singular or plural, or 3rd person "he, she, it" or "they":

> homō **sum**: hūmānī nīl ā mē aliēnum **putō**.
> **I am** a human being: **I consider** nothing human to be alien to me.

Personal pronouns are used to emphasise the subject rhetorically and in lively, colloquial speech:

> rūre **ego** vīventem, **tū** dīcis in urbe beātum.
> **I** call someone living in the country, **you** call someone living in the town happy.

Even when the subject is not expressed by a pronoun, it can still be modified by an adjective or noun in the nominative:

> nunc urbem et lūdōs et balnea **vīlicus** optās.
> now you **a farm bailiff** wish for the city and its games and baths.

**2.** Certain endings can also be used without referring to a specific subject. The 2nd singular of the present indicative or subjunctive (potential) can refer to anyone in general:

> at quis virtūtem amplectitur ipsam, praemia sī **tollās**?
> but who embraces virtue itself, if **you remove / one removes** its rewards?

The 3rd singular of impersonal verbs does not refer to a subject noun at all (see chapter 12). The 3rd plural can refer to people in general, especially as the authority for a proverb or report:

> caecīs hoc, ut **āiunt**, satis clārum est.
> this is clear enough, as **they say**, for the blind to see.

# Metaphrasing

**1.** A 1st or 2nd person verb allows both subject and verb to be metaphrased together:

> facis                              you do —

**2.** A nominative in agreement with the subject of a 1st or 2nd person verb is metaphrased after the subject pronoun:

vīlicus facis                     you a bailiff do —

Rephrasing this will often make a better translation:

vīlicus facis                     as bailiff you do —


**3.** A 1st or 2nd person subjunctive is metaphrased in three ways, corresponding to the three shades of meaning of the subjunctive (see chapter 11 syntax §2):

faciās                            (a) you may/would do —
                                   (b) may you do —
                                   (c) you should do —

But a 2nd person subjunctive referring to no specific person may need an alternative translation:

faciās                            you do / one does —


**4.** A 3rd plural verb will occasionally need an alternative translation:

āiunt                              — say —
                              *or* they / people say —


**5.** These basic patterns can then be adapted when necessary as follows:

(a) a 3rd or 4th conjugation verb with the 1st singular ending *–am* or *–ar* (future indicative or present subjunctive?) will occasionally need metaphrasing in alternative ways:

faciam                        I will do —
                           *or* I may / may I / I should
                           do —

(b) a verb with the ending *–re* (present infinitive active or present indicative, 2nd singular passive?) will occasionally need an alternative metaphrase:

amāre                        (to love —)
                        *or* you are loved

# Examples

## 1. rūre meō possum quidvīs perferre patīque. (Hor. *Ep.* 1.15.17)

rūs rūris (n) = the country, a
    country estate

|  | | |
|---|---|---|
| rūre | (a) | –e |
| | (b) | abl sing |
| | (c) | — ⋆s by/with/from/on an estate |

meus –a –um = my (own)

|  | | |
|---|---|---|
| meō | (a) | –ō |
| | (b) | abl sing neut |
| | (c) | — ⋆s by/with/from/on my estate |

possum posse potuī = to be
    able (to)

|  | | |
|---|---|---|
| possum | (a) | –m |
| | (b) | pres indic, 1st sing act |
| | (c) | I am able (to ⋆ by/with/from/on my estate) |

quīvīs quaevīs quidvīs =
    anyone or anything (you
    please)

|  | | |
|---|---|---|
| quidvīs | (a) | –d |
| | (b) | acc sing neut |
| | (c) | (to ⋆ anything by/with/from/on my estate) |

perferō –rre pertulī perlātum =
    to carry through, endure

|  | | |
|---|---|---|
| perferre | (a) | –re |
| | (b) | pres infin act |
| | (c) | (to endure anything on my estate) |

patior –tī –ssus = to undergo,
    tolerate
–que (conj) = and

|  | | |
|---|---|---|
| patīque. | (a) | –ī |
| | (b) | pres infin pass |
| | (c) | (to endure and tolerate anything on my estate). |

| | |
|---|---|
| Translation | On my estate I can endure and tolerate anything. |

## 2. \*nātūram sī sequēmur ducem, numquam aberrābimus. (Cic. *Off.* 1.100)

nātūra –ae (f) = nature

|  |  |  |
|---|---|---|
| nātūram | (a) | –am |
|  | (b) | acc sing |
|  | (c) | — ⋆s nature |

sī (conj) = if
sequor –quī –cūtus = to follow

|  |  |  |
|---|---|---|
| sī sequēmur | (a) | –ēmur |
|  | (b) | fut indic, 1st pl pass |
|  | (c) | if we will follow nature |

dux –cis (m) = a leader, guide

|  |  |  |
|---|---|---|
| ducem, | (a) | –em |
|  | (b) | acc sing |
|  | (c) | if we will follow nature as a guide, |

numquam (adv) = never
aberrō –āre –āvī –ātum (intr) =
to wander away, go wrong

|  |  |  |
|---|---|---|
| numquam aberrābimus. | (a) | –bimus |
|  | (b) | fut indic, 1st pl act |
|  | (c) | we will never go wrong. |

|  |  |
|---|---|
| Translation | If we follow nature as a guide, we will never go wrong. |

## 3. sed quia semper avēs quod abest, praesentia temnis. (Lucr.3.957)

sed (conj) = but
quia (conj) = because
semper (adv) = always
aveō –ēre = to be avid for, crave

| sed quia semper avēs | (a) | –s |
| | (b) | pres indic, 2nd sing act |
| | (c) | but because you always crave — |

quī quae quod = who(ever), which, what

| quod | (a) | –d |
| | (b) | nom/acc sing neut |
| | (c) | (what ★s / what — ★s) |

absum abesse āfuī (intr) = to be absent, be missing

| abest, | (a) | –t |
| | (b) | pres indic, 3rd sing act |
| | (c) | (what is missing), |

praesens –tis = present, readily available

| praesentia | (a) | –ia |
| | (b) | nom/acc pl neut |
| | (c) | available — ★s / — ★s available — |

temnō –ere = to scorn, despise

| temnis. | (a) | –s |
| | (b) | pres indic, 2nd sing act |
| | (c) | you despise available —. |

| Translation | But because you always crave what is missing, you despise things readily available. |

## 4.  *at mihi fēlīcem vītam fingēbam dēmens.
(Tib. 1.5.19)

at (conj) = but
ego = I

|  | | |
|---|---|---|
| at mihi | (a) | –i |
|  | (b) | dat sing |
|  | (c) | but — *s to/for me |

fēlix –īcis = fruitful, fortunate,
      happy

|  | | |
|---|---|---|
| fēlīcem | (a) | –em |
|  | (b) | acc sing masc/fem |
|  | (c) | but — *s a happy — to/for me |

vīta –ae (f) = life

|  | | |
|---|---|---|
| vītam | (a) | –am |
|  | (b) | acc sing |
|  | (c) | but — *s a happy life to/for me |

fingō –ngere –nxī –ctum = to
      form, imagine

|  | | |
|---|---|---|
| fingēbam | (a) | –bam |
|  | (b) | imperf indic, 1st sing act |
|  | (c) | but I was imagining a happy life for myself |

dēmens –ntis = out of one's
      mind, mad

|  | | |
|---|---|---|
| dēmens. | (a) | –ns |
|  | (b) | nom sing masc |
|  | (c) | but I mad was imagining a happy life for myself. |

|  | |
|---|---|
| Translation | But like a madman I was imagining a happy life for myself. |

## 5. videō meliōra probōque, dēteriōra sequor.
### (Ov. Met. 7.20)

videō vidēre vīdī vīsum = to see

| | | |
|---|---|---|
| videō | (a) | -ō |
| | (b) | pres indic, 1st sing act |
| | (c) | I see — |

melior -ior -ius = better

| | | |
|---|---|---|
| meliōra | (a) | -iōra |
| | (b) | compar, acc pl neut |
| | (c) | I see the better — |

probō -āre -āvī -ātum = to
    approve of
-que (conj) = and

| | | |
|---|---|---|
| probōque, | (a) | -ō |
| | (b) | pres indic, 1st sing act |
| | (c) | I see and approve of the better —, |

dēterior -ior -ius = more
    unpleasant, worse

| | | |
|---|---|---|
| dēteriōra | (a) | -iōra |
| | (b) | compar, nom/acc pl neut |
| | (c) | the worse — ★s / — ★s the worse — |

sequor -quī -cūtus = to follow

| | | |
|---|---|---|
| sequor. | (a) | -or |
| | (b) | pres indic, 1st sing pass |
| | (c) | I follow the worse —. |

| | |
|---|---|
| Translation | I see the better course of action and approve of it, but I follow the worse. |

N.B. in the original context the connotations of *meliōra* "the better things" and *dēteriōra* "the worse things" are made clear.

# Summary of Examples

1. rūre meō possum quidvīs perferre patīque.

2. nātūram sī sequēmur ducem, numquam aberrābimus.

3. sed quia semper avēs quod abest, praesentia temnis.

4. at mihi fēlīcem vītam fingēbam dēmens.

5. videō meliōra probōque, dēteriōra sequor.

# Exercises

Change the verb in the following sentences into the other persons,
singular and plural, and translate:

fēlīcem vītam fingēbam.
praesentia temnō.
videō meliōra probōque.
numquam aberrābō.
deteriōra sequor.

# Reading

1. urbis amātōrem Fuscum salvēre iubēmus
   rūris amātōrēs, hāc in rē scīlicet ūnā
   multum dissimilēs, at cētera paene gemellī.
   (Hor. *Ep*. 1.10.1)

   amātor -ōris (m) = a lover
   cēterus -a -um = the rest of; (n.pl.as adv) in all other respects
   dissimilis -is -e = unlike, different
   Fuscus -ī (m) = Aristius Fuscus (a schoolmaster and a writer)
   gemellus -a -um = twin, like twins
   paene (adv) = almost, practically
   rūs rūris (n) = the country, a country estate
   salvēre iubeō -bēre -ssī -ssum = to bid good day, greet
   scīlicet = naturally, of course
   ūnus -a -um = one

2. haec sit prōpositī nostrī summa: quod sentīmus loquāmur, quod
   loquimur sentiāmus; concordet sermō cum vītā. (Sen. *Ep*. 75.4)

   concordō -āre -āvī -ātum (intr) = to agree, be in harmony
   loquor -ī locūtus = to say, speak (of)
   prōpositum -ī (n) = something set before one, a proposition
   sentiō -tīre -sī -sum = to perceive, feel
   sermō -ōnis (m) = one's speech, talk
   summa -ae (f) = the total (of something), the gist

3. strēnua nōs exercet inertia: nāvibus atque
quadrīgīs petimus bene vīvere. quod petis hīc est,
est Vlubrīs, animus sī tē nōn dēficit aequus.
(Hor. *Ep.* 1.11.28)

aequus –a –um = level, calm
deficiō –icere –ēcī –ectum = to fail, let down
exerceō –ēre –uī –itum = to exercise, keep busy
hīc (adv) = in this place, here
inertia –ae (f) = idleness, inactivity
nāvis –is (f) = a ship
petō –ere –īvī –ītum = to make for, seek (to)
quadrīga –ae (f) = a four-horse chariot
strēnuus –a –um = active, restless
tū = you
Vlubrae –ārum (f.pl) = Ulubrae (a small town in Latium)

4. est ergō ulla rēs tantī aut commodum ullum tam expetendum, ut
virī bonī et splendōrem et nōmen āmittās? (Cic. *Off.* 3.82)

āmittō –ittere –īsī –issum = to send away, lose
commodum –ī (n) = an advantage, benefit
ergō = therefore
expetō –ere –īvī –ītum = to seek out, seek after
nōmen –inis (n) = one's name, reputation
splendor –ōris (m) = brightness, splendour
tam (adv) = to such a degree, so
tantus –a –um = so great; (gen.sing.neut) of such great value
ullus –a –um = any

5. tū nīdum servās, ego laudō rūris amoenī
rīvōs et muscō circumlita saxa nemusque.
(Hor. *Ep.* 1.10.6)

amoenus –a –um = beautiful, charming
circumlitus –a –um = smeared over, decorated (with)
laudō –āre –āvī –ātum = to praise
muscus –ī (m) = moss
nemus –oris (n) = a wood, forest
nīdus –ī (m) = a nest, eyrie
rīvus –ī (m) = a stream
rūs rūris (n) = the country, a country estate
saxum –ī (n) = a rock, boulder
servō –āre –āvī –ātum = to watch over, keep (to)
tū = you

6. ipse seram tenerās mātūrō tempore vītēs
   rusticus et facilī grandia pōma manū:
   nec Spēs dēstituat sed frūgum semper acervōs
   praebeat et plēnō pinguia musta lacū.
   nam veneror, seu stīpes habet dēsertus in agrīs
   seu vetus in triviō flōrida serta lapis.
   (Tib. 1.1.7)

   acervus -ī (m) = a heap, pile
   dēsertus -a -um = deserted, solitary
   dēstituō -uere -uī -ūtum = to leave stranded, fail
   facilis -is -e = easy, easily moving, deft
   flōridus -a -um = abounding in or made of flowers
   frux -ūgis (f) = a fruit, crop
   grandis -is -e = large, tall
   habeō -ēre -uī -itum = to have, possess
   ipse -a -um = himself, herself, itself, etc.
   lacus -ūs (m) = a lake, vat
   lapis -idis (m) = a stone
   manus -ūs (f) = the hand
   mātūrus -a -um = ripe
   mustum -ī (n) = unfermented grape-juice, must
   pinguis -is -e = fat, full-bodied
   plēnus -a -um = full
   pōmum -ī (n) = a fruit tree
   praebeō -ēre -uī -itum = to put forward, provide
   rusticus -a -um = connected with a farm or the country
   semper (adv) = always
   serō -ere sēvī satum = to plant, sow
   serta -ōrum (n.pl) = chains of flowers, garlands
   seu ... seu (conjs) = whether ... or
   spēs -eī (f) = hope
   stīpes -itis (m) = a tree-trunk, tree-stump
   tempus -oris (n) = time, a moment or period of time
   tener -era -erum = tender, young
   trivium -[i]ī (n) = the meeting-place of three roads
   veneror -ārī -ātus = to worship, revere
   vetus -eris = old
   vītis -is (f) = a vine

7. *nōn potestis voluptāte omnia dērigentēs aut tuērī aut retinēre
   virtūtem. (Cic. *Fin.* 2.71)

   aut ... aut (conjs) = either ... or
   dērigō -igere -exī -ectum = to make straight, regulate
   retineō -ēre -uī retentum = to hold back, retain
   tueor -ērī tuitus = to look at, preserve
   voluptās -ātis (f) = pleasure

8. sī potes āvellī circensibus, optima Sōrae
   aut Fabrāteriae domus aut Frusinōne parātur,
   quantī nunc tenebrās ūnum condūcis in annum. (Juv. 3.223)

   (N.B. Sōra, Fabrāteria and Frusinō are small towns in Latium.)

   annus -ī (m) = a year
   āvellō -ellere -ellī -olsum = to pluck off, tear away
   circensēs -ium (m.pl) = games (in the Circus Maximus)
   condūcō -cere -xī -ctum = to bring together, rent
   domus -ūs (f) = a house, home
   nunc (adv) = now
   optimus -a -um = best
   parō -āre -āvī -ātum = to provide, obtain
   quantus -a -um = as great as; (gen.sing.neut) at as great a price as
   tenebrae -ārum (f.pl) = darkness, a dark place or den
   ūnus -a -um = one

9. facilius est currentem, ut āiunt, incitāre quam commovēre
   languentem. (Cic. de Orat. 2.186)

   āiō (defective) = to say
   commoveō -ovēre -ōvī -ōtum = to move vigorously, rouse to action
   currō -rere cucurrī -sum (intr) = to run, rush
   facilis -is -e = easy
   incitō -āre -āvī -ātum = to speed up, spur on
   langueō -ēre (intr) = to be sluggish or idle
   ut (adv) = as

10. sit mihi quod nunc est, etiam minus, et mihi vīvam
    quod superest aevī, sī quid superesse volunt dī;
    sit bona librōrum et prōvīsae frūgis in annum
    cōpia, neu fluitem dubiae spē pendulus hōrae.
    sed satis est ōrāre Iovem quī pōnit et aufert,
    det vītam, det opēs: aequum mī animum ipse parābō.
    (Hor. Ep. 1.18.107)

    (N.B. mī = mihi)

    aequus -a -um = level, calm
    aevum -ī (n) = time, life
    annus -ī (m) = a year
    auferō -rre abstulī ablātum = to carry away, carry off
    cōpia -ae (f) = an abundance, plenty
    deus deī (m) = a god (nom.pl: dī)
    dubius -a -um = uncertain, doubtful
    fluitō -āre -āvī (intr) = to flow, drift
    frux -ūgis (f) = a fruit, crop
    hōra -ae (f) = an hour
    ipse -a -um = himself, herself, itself, etc.

Iuppiter Iovis (m) = Jupiter (the supreme being)
liber -brī (m) = the inner bark of a tree, a book
minus -ōris (n) = a smaller amount, less
neu (conj) = and ... not, nor
nunc (adv) = now
opēs opum (f.pl) = resources, riches
ōrō -āre -āvī -ātum = to pray to, pray for
parō -āre -āvī -ātum = to provide, obtain
pendulus -a -um = hanging (from)
pōnō pōnere posuī positum = to place, put (before one)
prōvīsus -a -um = made available in advance, ready provided
quis qua quid = anyone, anything
satis (n.indecl) = sufficient, enough
spēs -eī (f) = hope
supersum -esse -fuī (intr) = to be above, remain
volō velle voluī = to want, wish (to)

# Vocabulary to Learn

aut ... aut (conjs) = either ... or
habeō -ēre -uī -itum = to have, possess, consider (to be)
tū = you
tuus -a -um = your (own)
volō velle voluī = to want, wish (to)

# 16
# IMPERATIVES AND EXCLAMATIONS

## Morphology

The endings for the present and future imperatives are added to the imperfect stem (with some minor phonetic adjustments) as follows:

| | |
|---|---|
| 2nd sing act | stem only (plus $-e$) (plus $-t\bar{o}$) |
| 2nd pl act | stem plus $-te$ (or $-t\bar{o}te$) |
| 2nd sing pass | stem plus $-re$ |
| 2nd pl pass | stem plus $-min\bar{\imath}$ |

In the 2nd singular active, only 3rd conjugation verbs add $-e$ to the consonant stem: but *dīc* "say!", *dūc* "lead!", *fer* "carry!" and *fac* "do!" end in the bare stem. The alternative endings in $-t\bar{o}$ and $-t\bar{o}te$ are used for the future imperative. The passive endings are used mostly with deponent verbs; thus further ambiguity for the already ambiguous $-re$ ending is infrequent.

The commonest ending for the vocative singular is the same as for the corresponding nominative singular. Exceptions are:

2nd declension nouns and adjectives in $-us$, which end in $-e$;

2nd declension nouns and adjectives in $-ius$, which end in $-\bar{\imath}$;

*meus*, which has the unique form *mī*.

The ending for the vocative plural is the same as for the corresponding nominative plural. This identity of nominative and vocative endings seldom leads to uncertainty, since the vocative is an exclamation independent of the sentence structure.

# Syntax

**1.** The imperative is, like the indicative and subjunctive, a mood expressing the speaker's attitude towards what he is saying. It is similar to the jussive and optative uses of the subjunctive in that it expresses a command, request or entreaty:

> **abī** in malam rem! = **go** to hell!
>
> **ignosce** mihi! = **forgive** me!

It is often prefaced, less often followed, by the imperative *age* or *agite* (or: *agedum* or *agitedum*) "come!":

> **age**, dā veniam servō!
> **come**, grant forgiveness to your slave!

The negative is *nē* with the imperative or subjunctive (see chapter 11 syntax §2c; chapter 20 syntax §3). Alternatively *nōlī* or *nōlīte* "be unwilling, don't!" followed by the infinitive is used:

> sed abī intrō! **nōlī stāre!**
> but go inside! **don't stand** there!

**2.** The present imperative normally commands instant obedience; the future imperative expects a less immediate response. Both imperatives however refer to the future. Consequently:

(a) a future tense is used in subordinate clauses that also refer to the future (see chapter 11 syntax §3):

> vērum sī quid **agēs**, statim **iubētō!**
> but if **you do** (**are going to do**) anything, **give orders** at once!

(b) a primary tense of the subjunctive is used in subordinate clauses dependent on an imperative (see chapter 13 syntax §8):

> vāde, valē, **cave nē titubēs!**
> go, goodbye, **take care** that **you do** not **stumble!**

**3.** The subject of the imperative is *tū* or *vōs* "you". Even when the subject is not expressed by a personal pronoun, it can still be modified by an adjective or noun in the nominative (see chapter 15 syntax §1):

> tū nē cēde malīs sed contrā **audentior** ītō!
> don't **you** give in to misfortunes but go to face them **more boldly!**

**4.** Exclamations are independent of the sentence structure. Different exclamations use different cases, the commonest of which is the vocative:

> cēnābis bene, **mī Fabulle**, apud mē.
> you will dine well, **my Fabullus**, at my house.

The nominative and accusative are also used:

> ō **faustum** et **fēlīcem diem**!
> oh, **what a lucky** and **happy day**!

# Metaphrasing

**1.** An imperative is metaphrased: ★! (or if the verb is not intransitive: ★ —!):

> ignosce                              forgive —!

**2.** A deponent verb ending in the stem plus *–re* or *–minī* (present indicative or imperative?) will occasionally need an alternative metaphrase:

> sequiminī                            you follow —
>                                      *or* follow —!

**3.** A nominative in agreement with the subject of an imperative is metaphrased after, or in place of, the subject pronoun:

> audentior ītō                        more bold go!

Rephrasing this will often make a better translation:

> audentior ītō                        go more boldly!

**4.** An exclamation is at first metaphrased in the position its case requires:

> fēlīcem diem                         — ★s a happy day

When it becomes clear that it is an exclamation, the translation can then be adapted accordingly and introduced into the English sentence at an appropriate point:

> fēlīcem diem!                        what a happy day!

# Examples

## 1. nunc dum tibi libet licetque, pōtā, perde rem! (Pl. *Mos.* 20)

nunc (adv) = now
dum (conj) = while
tū = you

| | | |
|---|---|---|
| nunc dum tibi | (a) | –i |
| | (b) | dat sing |
| | (c) | now while — ★s to/for you |

libet –ēre –uit (w.dat) = it is
    pleasing (to)

| | | |
|---|---|---|
| libet | (a) | –t |
| | (b) | pres indic, 3rd sing act |
| | (c) | now while it is pleasing to you |

licet –ēre –uit (w.dat) = it is
    permitted (to)
–que (conj) = and

| | | |
|---|---|---|
| licetque, | (a) | –t |
| | (b) | pres indic, 3rd sing act |
| | (c) | now while it is pleasing and permitted to you, |

pōtō –āre –āvī –ātum = to drink

| | | |
|---|---|---|
| pōtā, | (a) | –ā |
| | (b) | pres imper, 2nd sing act |
| | (c) | drink —! |

perdō –ere –idī –itum = to ruin,
    dissipate, waste

| | | |
|---|---|---|
| perde | (a) | –e |
| | (b) | pres imper, 2nd sing act |
| | (c) | waste —! |

rēs reī (f) = property, wealth

| | | |
|---|---|---|
| rem! | (a) | –em |
| | (b) | acc sing |
| | (c) | waste your wealth! |

| | |
|---|---|
| Translation | Now while it is pleasing and permitted to you, drink! waste your wealth! |

## 2. capāciōrēs affer hūc, puer, scyphōs!
(Hor. *Epod.* 9.33)

capax -ācis = capacious, large

              capāciōrēs   (a)   -iōrēs
                                   (b)   compar, nom/acc pl masc/fem
                                   (c)   larger — ★ / — ★s larger —

afferō -rre attulī allātum = to
    carry to, bring
hūc (adv) = hither, here

                 affer hūc,   (a)   -r
                                   (b)   pres imper, 2nd sing act
                                   (c)   bring larger — here!

puer -erī (m) = a boy, slave

                      puer,   (a)   -r
                                     (b)   voc sing
                                   (c)   bring larger — here, boy!

scyphus -ī (m) = a large two-
    handled drinking vessel,
    goblet

                scyphōs!   (a)   -ōs
                                   (b)   acc pl
                                   (c)   Bring larger goblets here, boy!

## 3.  sed sī sapis, omnia hūmānā condiciōne mētīre! (Sen. *Ep.* 110.4)

sed (conj) = but
sī (conj) = if
sapiō –ere –īvī (intr) = to have a
    taste, be wise

|  |  |  |
|---|---|---|
| sed sī sapis, | (a) | –s |
|  | (b) | pres indic, 2nd sing act |
|  | (c) | but if you are wise, |

omnis –is –e = every, all

|  |  |  |
|---|---|---|
| omnia | (a) | –ia |
|  | (b) | nom/acc pl neut |
|  | (c) | all — ★ / — ★s all — |

hūmānus –a –um = human

|  |  |  |
|---|---|---|
| hūmānā | (a) | –ā |
|  | (b) | abl sing fem |
|  | (c) | all — ★ / — ★s all — by/with/from |
|  | th | the human — |

condiciō –ōnis (f) = a contract,
    condition

|  |  |  |
|---|---|---|
| condiciōne | (a) | –e |
|  | (b) | abl sing |
|  | (c) | all — ★ / — ★s all — by/with/from the human condition |

mētior –īrī mensus = to measure

|  |  |  |
|---|---|---|
| mētīre! | (a) | –re |
|  | (b) | pres indic *or* pres imper, 2nd sing pass |
|  | (c) | you measure all — by the human condition. |
|  |  | *or* measure all — by the human condition! |

|  |  |
|---|---|
| Translation | But if you are wise, measure every- thing by the human condition! |

N.B. In the original context *mētīre* is imperative.

# 4. dōna praesentis cape laetus hōrae ac linque sevēra! (Hor. *Carm.* 3.8.27)

dōnum –ī (n) = a gift

|  |  |  |
|---|---|---|
| dōna | (a) | –a |
|  | (b) | nom/acc pl |
|  | (c) | gifts ★ / — ★s gifts |

praesens –ntis = present

|  |  |  |
|---|---|---|
| praesentis | (a) | –is |
|  | (b) | gen sing masc/fem/neut |
|  | (c) | the gifts of the present — ★ / — ★s the gifts of the present — |

capiō –ere cēpī –tum = to take (hold of), seize

|  |  |  |
|---|---|---|
| cape | (a) | –e |
|  | (b) | pres imper, 2nd sing act |
|  | (c) | seize the gifts of the present —! |

laetus –a –um = flourishing, happy

|  |  |  |
|---|---|---|
| laetus | (a) | –us |
|  | (b) | nom sing masc |
|  | (c) | happy seize the gifts of the present —! |

hōra –ae (f) = an hour

|  |  |  |
|---|---|---|
| hōrae | (a) | –ae |
|  | (b) | gen sing |
|  | (c) | happy seize the gifts of the present hour! |

ac (conj) = and

linquō –ere līquī = to leave, abandon

|  |  |  |
|---|---|---|
| ac linque | (a) | –e |
|  | (b) | pres imper, 2nd sing act |
|  | (c) | and abandon —! |

sevērus –a –um = stern, serious

|  |  |  |
|---|---|---|
| sevēra! | (a) | –a |
|  | (b) | acc pl neut |
|  | (c) | and abandon serious —! |

| Translation | Seize the gifts of the present hour and be happy, and abandon serious matters! |
|---|---|

## 5.  quidquid faciēs, respice ad mortem!
(Sen. *Ep.* 114.27)

quisquis quidquid = whoever,
   whatever

| | | |
|---|---|---|
| quidquid | (a) | –d |
| | (b) | nom/acc sing neut |
| | (c) | whatever ★s / whatever — ★s |

faciō –ere fēcī factum = to make,
   do

| | | |
|---|---|---|
| faciēs, | (a) | –ēs |
| | (b) | fut indic, 2nd sing act |
| | (c) | whatever you will do, |

respiciō –icere –exī –ectum
   (intr) = to look round, have
   regard

| | | |
|---|---|---|
| respice | (a) | –e |
| | (b) | pres imper, 2nd sing act |
| | (c) | have regard! |

ad (prep w.acc) = to
mors –tis (f) = death

| | | |
|---|---|---|
| ad mortem! | (a) | –em |
| | (b) | acc sing |
| | (c) | have regard to death! |
| Translation | | Whatever you do, have regard to death! |

# Summary of Examples

1. nunc dum tibi libet licetque, pōtā, perde rem!

2. capāciōrēs affer hūc, puer, scyphōs!

3. sed sī sapis, omnia hūmānā condiciōne mētīre!

4. dōna praesentis cape laetus hōrae ac
   linque sevēra!

5. quidquid faciēs, respice ad mortem!

# Exercises

Complete the following sentences on the analogy of the first:

tū, cui libet pōtāre, pōtā!
tū, cui libet cavēre .................................
tū, cui libet linquere sevēra ........................
tū, cui libet abīre intrō ...........................
tū, cui libet omnia hūmānā condiciōne mētīrī ..........

vōs, quibus libet pōtāre, pōtāte!
vōs, quibus libet cavēre ...........................
vōs, quibus libet linquere sevēra ...................
vōs, quibus libet abīre intrō .......................
vōs, quibus libet omnia hūmānā condiciōne mētīrī .....

# Reading

1.  pōne merum et tālōs; pereat quī crastina cūrat:
        mors aurem vellens "vīvite!" āit "veniō".
    ([Verg.] *Copa* 38)

    auris –is (f) = the ear
    āiō (defective) = to say
    crastinus –a –um = of tomorrow
    cūrō –āre –āvī –ātum = to care for, care about
    merum –ī (n) = neat wine (unmixed with water)
    mors –tis (f) = death
    pereō –īre –iī –itum (intr) = to vanish, die
    pōnō pōnere posuī positum = to place, put (before one)
    talus –ī (m) = the ankle-bone, knuckle-bone (used for gaming)
    vellō –ere –ī vulsum = to pull or pluck out, tug at

2.  adulescens, quaesō hercle, ēloquere tuum mihi nōmen, nisi
    piget! (Pl. *Men.* 1066)

    adulescens –ntis (m) = a young man
    ēloquor –quī –cūtus = to speak out, tell
    hercle = by Hercules, in the name of Hercules
    nisi (conj) = if not, unless
    nōmen –inis (n) = one's name
    piget –ēre –uit = it fills with irritation
    quaesō –ere = to ask, beg

213

3. vīve pius: moriēre; pius cole sacra: colentem
   mors gravis ā templīs in cava busta trahet.(Ov. *Am.* 3.9.37)

bustum -ī (n) = a funeral pyre, tomb
cavus -a -um = hollow
colō -ere -uī cultum = to worship, practise (religion)
gravis -is -e = heavy, overpowering
morior -ī -tuus (intr) = to die
mors -tis (f) = death
pius -a -um = faithful to moral obligations, reverent
sacer -cra -crum = holy, sacred
templum -ī (n) = a shrine, temple
trahō -here -xī -ctum = to drag, haul

4. nōlīte ā mē commonērī velle: vōsmet ipsī vōbīscum recordāminī!
   (Cic. *Mur.* 50)

commoneō -ēre -uī -itum = to remind
-cum (prep w.abl) = with
ipse -a -um = himself, herself, itself, etc.
nōlō -lle -luī = to be unwilling, not to want (to)
recordor -ārī -ātus = to call to mind, recollect
vōs / vōsmet = you

5. ō formōse puer, nimium nē crēde colōrī!
   alba ligustra cadunt, vaccīnia nigra leguntur.
   (Verg. *Ecl.* 2.17)

albus -a -um = white
cadō -ere cecidī cāsum (intr) = to fall
color -ōris (m) = colour, complexion
crēdō -ere -idī -itum (w.dat) = to trust, rely on
formōsus -a -um = shapely, beautiful
legō -ere lēgī lectum = to gather, pick
ligustrum -ī (n) = a white-flowered shrub, probably privet
niger -gra -grum = black, dark
nimium (adv) = excessively, too much
ō = oh
puer -erī (m) = a boy, slave
vaccīnium -[i]ī (n) = bilberry

6.    \*colligere incertōs et in ordine pōnere crīnēs
        docta neque ancillās inter habenda Napē,
      accipe et ad dominam perarātās māne tabellās
        perfer et obstantēs sēdula pelle morās.    (Ov. *Am.* 1.11.1)

accipiō –ipere –ēpī –eptum = to take (hold of), receive
ancilla –ae (f) = a slave girl, maidservant
colligō –igere –ēgī –ectum = to gather together
crīnis –is (m) = a lock of hair
doctus –a –um (w.infin) = well taught (to), expert (at)
domina –ae (f) = a mistress
incertus –a –um = uncertain, wayward
inter (prep w.acc) = among, in the class of
māne (adv) = in the morning
mora –ae (f) = a delay, obstacle
Napē –ēs (f) = Nape (a maidservant of Ovid's mistress)
obstō –āre –itī –ātum (intr) = to stand in the way
ordō –inis (m) = a line, row
pellō –ere pepulī pulsum = to beat against, fend off
perarātus –a –um = furrowed, inscribed
perferō –rre pertulī perlātum = to carry through, deliver
pōnō pōnere posuī positum = to place, put
sēdulus –a –um = attentive, painstaking
tabella –ae (f) = a (writing) tablet

7.    amābō, mea dulcis Ipsitilla,
      meae dēliciae, meī lepōrēs,
      iubē ad tē veniam merīdiātum!    (Catul. 32.1)

amō –āre –āvī –ātum = to love, be grateful to
dēliciae –ārum (f.pl) = pleasure, delight
dulcis –is –e = sweet, charming
Ipsitilla –ae (f) = Ipsitilla (? a girl-friend of Catullus)
iubeō –bēre –ssī –ssum = to order, ask (that)
lepos –ōris (m) = charm; (pl) a "charmer"
merīdiātum = to take a siesta

8.    tū quoque nē timidē custōdēs, Dēlia, falle!
        audendum est: fortēs adiuvat ipsa Venus.    (Tib. 1.2.15)

adiuvō –iuvāre –iūvī –iūtum = to help
audeō –dēre –sus = to have the courage, dare (to)
custōs –ōdis (m) = a guardian, guard
Dēlia –ae (f) = Delia (a mistress of Tibullus)
fallō –lere fefellī –sum = to deceive, elude
ipse –a –um = himself, herself, itself, etc.
quoque (adv) = as well, also
timidus –a –um = timid, fearful
Venus –eris (f) = Venus (goddess of love)

215

9. "pōne seram, cohibē!" sed quis custōdiet ipsōs
   custōdēs, quī nunc lascīvae furta puellae
   hāc mercēde silent? crīmen commūne tacētur.
   prospicit hoc prūdens et ab illīs incipit uxor.     (Juv. 6.O31)

   cohibeō -ēre -uī -itum = to contain, confine
   commūnis -is -e = common, shared
   crīmen -inis (n) = an accusation, crime
   custōdiō -īre -īvī -ītum = to guard
   custōs -ōdis (m) = a guardian, guard
   furtum -ī (n) = stealing, stolen pleasure
   incipiō -ipere -ēpī -eptum = to take in hand, begin
   ipse -a -um = himself, herself, itself, etc.
   lascīvus -a -um = playful, "sexy"
   mercēs -ēdis (f) = a payment, reward
   nunc (adv) = now
   pōnō pōnere posuī positum = to place, put (in position)
   prospiciō -icere -exī -ectum = to see before one, anticipate
   prūdens -ntis = looking ahead, prudent
   puella -ae (f) = a girl, young woman
   sera -ae (f) = a bar (to fasten a door)
   sileō -ēre -uī = to be silent, keep quiet about
   taceō -ēre -uī -itum = to be silent, say nothing about
   uxor -ōris (f) = a wife

10. ō mē fēlīcem! ō nox mihi candida! et ō tū
    lectule dēliciīs facte beāte meīs!                 (Prop. 2.15.1)

    candidus -a -um = bright, white, lucky
    dēliciae -ārum (f.pl) = pleasure, delight
    factus -a -um = made
    lectulus -ī (m) = a couch, bed
    ō = oh

# Vocabulary to Learn

amō -āre -āvī -ātum = to love
ipse -a -um = himself, herself, itself, etc.
nunc (adv) = now
pōnō pōnere posuī positum = to place, put
puer -erī (m) = a boy

# 17
# TENSES:
# THE PERFECT SYSTEM

## Morphology

In all five tenses of the perfect system, it is the perfect stem, not the person ending, which distinguishes between active and passive, and so the ending for all 3rd singulars is *-t* and for all 3rd plurals *-nt*. In the perfect indicative these person endings are added (with some minor phonetic adjustments) directly to the active stem, and in the passive to the stem of the auxiliary verb *esse* "to be". In the other tenses and moods of the active a tense ending is added first; in the passive the person endings are added to the appropriate stem of the auxiliary verb *esse*. The active tense endings and, for the passive, the stems of the auxiliary verb *esse* (numbered i-v for ease of reference throughout the chapter) are as follows:

|  |  | ACTIVE | PASSIVE |
|---|---|---|---|
| (i) | perf indic | stem only | stem plus *(e)s–* |
| (ii) | pluperf indic | stem plus *–era–* | stem plus *era–* |
| (iii) | fut perf indic | stem plus *–eri–* | stem plus *er–* |
| (iv) | perf subj | stem plus *–eri–* | stem plus *si–* |
| (v) | pluperf subj | stem plus *–isse–* | stem plus *esse–* |
|  |  | (perf infin act) | (perf infin pass) |

Exceptions are:

the perfect indicative, 3rd plural active, which may end in *–ērunt* or alternatively *–ēre*;

the perfect active tenses in *–v–*, which may drop the *–v–* and contract, such as *amāvērunt* and *amārunt*.

# Syntax

The perfect system makes a distinction based upon the "aspect" of the verb: in contrast to the imperfect system, which refers to action as incomplete (see chapter 11), the perfect system refers to action as completed or to the state resulting from completed action:

> nox **erat** et dominae **vēnit** epistula ad erum meum.
> it **was** night and a letter **came** to my master from his mistress.

**1.** The perfect system like the imperfect system then makes further distinctions of tense and mood:

(i) the perfect indicative is used as a "present" perfect to refer to action as completed in the present or to the state that results from completed action:

> suus cuique **attribūtus est** error.
> to each man his own aberration **has been** / **is allotted**.

It is also used as an "aorist" perfect to refer to action in the past:

> dein longō nox ūna et altera lūsū **consumpta est**.
> then one night and another **was spent** in a long game of love.

(ii) the pluperfect indicative refers to action as completed in the past or to the state that resulted from completed action; it often refers to the earlier of two past actions:

> haec iuventūtem, ubi familiārēs opēs **dēfēcerant**, ad facinora incendēbant.
> these things incited young men, when their family resources **had run out**, to deeds of crime.

(iii) the future perfect indicative refers to action as completed in the future or to the state that will result from completed action; it often refers to the earlier of two future actions:

> actiō recta nōn erit nisi recta **fuerit** voluntās.
> an action will not be right unless the intention **was** (**will have been**) right.

(iv) the perfect subjunctive normally refers to action as completed in the future:

> utinam mūnus nōn **poposcerit** illa!
> if only **it may be that she has** not **asked** for a present!

Occasionally however it refers to action as incomplete in the future (see chapter 20 syntax §3).

(v) the pluperfect subjunctive refers to action as completed in the past:

> utinam illam cupiditātem hominibus deī nē **dedissent**!
> if only the gods **had not given** men that greed!

**2.** The tenses of the perfect system are also subject to the sequence of tenses rule (see chapter 13 syntax §8 on the "sequence of tenses"). When the main verb is a primary tense such as the "present" perfect or future perfect indicative, then a primary tense of the subjunctive such as the present is used:

> hoc **effēcit** ut nēmō contentus **vīvat**.
> this **has brought** it about that no-one **lives** content.

When the main verb is a historic tense such as the "aorist" perfect or pluperfect indicative, then a historic tense of the subjunctive such as the imperfect is used:

> hoc **effēcit** ut erus meus Rōmam venīre **iubērētur**.
> this **brought** it about that my master **was asked** to come to Rome.

But the perfect and pluperfect subjunctive are also used in subordinate clauses, the perfect in primary sequence, the pluperfect in historic sequence. The perfect subjunctive then refers to action as completed in the present:

> verētur ille nē domina sē absente **corrupta sit**.
> **he is afraid** that his mistress **has been seduced** in his absence.

The pluperfect subjunctive still refers to action as completed in the past:

> verēbātur ille nē domina sē absente **corrupta esset**.
> **he was afraid** that his mistress **had been seduced** in his absence.

# Metaphrasing

**1.** The different tenses of the perfect system are metaphrased as follows:

(i) the perfect indicative: — has ★ed

fēcit                           — has done —

(ii) the pluperfect indicative: — had ★ed

fēcerat                       — had done —

(iii) the future perfect indicative: — will have ★ed

fēcerit                       — will have done —

(iv) the perfect subjunctive in three ways, corresponding to the three shades of meaning of the subjunctive (see chapter 11 syntax §2):

fēcerit                  (a) it may be that — has done —

                         (b) may it be that — has done —

                         (c) let it be that — has done —

(v) the pluperfect subjunctive in three ways, corresponding to the three shades of meaning of the subjunctive (see chapter 11 syntax §2):

fēcisset                (a) — might/would have done —

                         (b) if only — had done —

                         (c) — should have done —

**2.** These basic patterns can then be adapted when necessary as follows:

(a) any perfect tense will sometimes need an alternative translation for the state resulting from completed action:

hoc factum est             this — has been done
                              *or* this — is done

(b) a perfect indicative will sometimes need an alternative translation for the "aorist" perfect:

hoc factum est             this — has been done
                              *or* this — was done

(c) a future perfect indicative in subordinate clauses (see syntax §1(iii) above) will sometimes need to be translated by another tense:

| | |
|---|---|
| sī hoc fēcerit | if — will have done this — / if — does this — |

(d) a verb ending in -eri- (future perfect indicative or perfect subjunctive?) will occasionally need metaphrasing in alternative ways:

| | |
|---|---|
| fēcerit | — will have done — or it may be / may it be / let it be that — has done — |

(e) a significant word or the context will help to identify the particular shade of meaning of a subjunctive:

| | |
|---|---|
| forsitan fēcerit | it may perhaps be that — has done — |

# Examples

## 1. fēlix quī propriīs aevum transēgit in agrīs.
(Claud. *Carm. Min.* 20.1)

fēlix –īcis = fruitful, fortunate,
    happy

| | | |
|---|---|---|
| fēlix | (a) | –x |
| | (b) | nom sing masc/fem/neut *or* acc sing neut |
| | (c) | a happy — ★s *or* — ★s a happy — |

quī quae quod = who(ever),
    which, what

| | | |
|---|---|---|
| quī | (a) | –ī |
| | (b) | nom sing masc |
| | (c) | a happy — ★s (whoever ★s) |

proprius –a –um = his, her, its
    own, etc.

| | | |
|---|---|---|
| propriīs | (a) | –īs |
| | (b) | dat/abl pl masc/fem/neut |
| | (c) | (whoever ★s to/for/by/with/from his own —) |

aevum –ī (n) = time, life

| | | |
|---|---|---|
| aevum | (a) | –um |
| | (b) | acc sing |
| | (c) | (whoever ★s his life to/for/by/ with/from his own —) |

transigō –igere –ēgī –actum = to
    drive through, pass

| | | |
|---|---|---|
| transēgit | (a) | –it |
| | (b) | perf indic, 3rd sing act |
| | (c) | (whoever has passed his life to/for/ by/with/from his own —) |

in (prep w.acc/abl) = into / in,
    on
ager agrī (m) = land, a field

| | | |
|---|---|---|
| in agrīs. | (a) | –īs |
| | (b) | abl pl |
| | (c) | (whoever has passed his life on his own lands). |

| | |
|---|---|
| Translation | Happy (is) the man who has passed his life on his own lands. |

## 2.   quam quisque nōrit artem, in hāc sē exerceat.
   (Cic. *Tusc.* 1.41)

quī quae quod = who(ever),
   which, what

|  |  |  |
|---|---|---|
| quam | (a) | –am |
|  | (b) | acc sing fem |
|  | (c) | (whomever/whatever — ★s) |

quisque quaeque quidque = each
   person or thing

|  |  |  |
|---|---|---|
| quisque | (a) | –s |
|  | (b) | nom sing masc |
|  | (c) | (whomever/whatever each person ★s) |

noscō –scere nōvī nōtum = to get
   to know; (perf tenses) to
   know

|  |  |  |
|---|---|---|
| nōrit (nōverit) | (a) | –erit |
|  | (b) | fut perf indic, 3rd sing act |
|  | (c) | (whomever/whatever each person will have got to know) |

ars –tis (f) = an art, craft, skill

|  |  |  |
|---|---|---|
| artem, | (a) | –em |
|  | (b) | acc sing |
|  | (c) | (whatever skill each person will have got to know), |

in (prep w.acc/abl) = into / in,
   on
hic haec hoc = this

|  |  |  |
|---|---|---|
| in hāc | (a) | –āc |
|  | (b) | abl sing fem |
|  | (c) | — ★s in this — |

sē = himself, herself, itself, etc.

|  |  |  |
|---|---|---|
| sē | (a) | –ē |
|  | (b) | acc sing |
|  | (c) | — ★s himself in this — |

exerceō –ēre –uī –itum = to
   exercise, occupy

|  |  |  |
|---|---|---|
| exerceat. | (a) | –at |
|  | (b) | pres subj, 3rd sing act |
|  | (c) | may/let — occupy himself in this —. |

| Translation | Whatever skill each person knows, in this let him occupy himself. |
|---|---|

## 3. ex dīvitiīs iuventūtem luxuria atque avāritia cum superbiā invāsēre. (Sall. *Cat.* 12.2)

ex (prep w.abl) = from, as a
   result of
dīvitiae -ārum (f.pl) = riches,
   wealth

| | | |
|---|---|---|
| ex dīvitiīs | (a) | -īs |
| | (b) | abl pl |
| | (c) | — ★s as a result of wealth |

iuventūs -ūtis (f) = the youth,
   young men

| | | |
|---|---|---|
| iuventūtem | (a) | -em |
| | (b) | acc sing |
| | (c) | — ★s young men as a result of wealth |

luxuria -ae (f) = luxury, extravagance

| | | |
|---|---|---|
| luxuria | (a) | -a |
| | (b) | nom sing |
| | (c) | extravagance ★s young men as a result of wealth |

atque (conj) = and
avāritia -ae (f) = avarice, greed

| | | |
|---|---|---|
| atque avāritia | (a) | -a |
| | (b) | nom sing |
| | (c) | extravagance and greed ★ young men as a result of wealth |

cum (prep w.abl) = with,
   together with
superbia -ae (f) = pride,
   arrogance

| | | |
|---|---|---|
| cum superbiā | (a) | -ā |
| | (b) | abl sing |
| | (c) | extravagance and greed ★ young men together with arrogance as a result of wealth |

invādō -dere -sī -sum = to enter,
   invade

| | | |
|---|---|---|
| invāsēre. | (a) | -ēre |
| | (b) | perf indic, 3rd pl act |
| | (c) | extravagance and greed have invaded young men together with arrogance as a result of wealth. |

| | |
|---|---|
| Translation | As a result of wealth, extravagance and greed invaded young men together with arrogance. |

## 4. illud, quod paupertātem nōbīs gravem fēcerat, et dīvitiās gravēs fēcit. (Sen. *Ep.* 17.12)

ille –a –ud = that, this

|   |   |   |
|---|---|---|
| illud, | (a) | –d |
|   | (b) | nom/acc sing neut |
|   | (c) | that — ★s / — ★s that —, |

quī quae quod = who(ever),
    which, what

|   |   |   |
|---|---|---|
| quod | (a) | –d |
|   | (b) | nom/acc sing neut |
|   | (c) | (which ★s / which — ★s) |

paupertās –ātis (f) = poverty

|   |   |   |
|---|---|---|
| paupertātem | (a) | –em |
|   | (b) | acc sing |
|   | (c) | (which ★s poverty) |

nōs = we

|   |   |   |
|---|---|---|
| nōbīs | (a) | –īs |
|   | (b) | dat/abl pl |
|   | (c) | (which ★s poverty to/for/by/with/ from us) |

gravis –is –e = heavy, oppressive

|   |   |   |
|---|---|---|
| gravem | (a) | –em |
|   | (b) | acc sing fem |
|   | (c) | (which ★s oppressive poverty to/ for/by/with/from us) |

faciō –ere fēcī factum = to make

|   |   |   |
|---|---|---|
| fēcerat, | (a) | –erat |
|   | (b) | pluperf indic, 3rd sing act |
|   | (c) | (which had made poverty oppressive for us), |

et = also
dīvitiae –ārum (f.pl) = riches,
    wealth

|   |   |   |
|---|---|---|
| et dīvitiās | (a) | –ās |
|   | (b) | acc pl |
|   | (c) | that — also ★s wealth |

gravis –is –e = heavy, oppressive

|   |   |   |
|---|---|---|
| gravēs | (a) | –ēs |
|   | (b) | acc pl fem |
|   | (c) | that — also ★s wealth oppressive |

faciō –ere fēcī factum = to make

|   |   |   |
|---|---|---|
| fēcit. | (a) | –it |
|   | (b) | perf indic, 3rd sing act |
|   | (c) | that — also made wealth oppressive. |

Translation    That which had made poverty
oppressive for us also made wealth
oppressive.

N.B. in the original context *illud* refers to an attitude of mind towards wealth.

## 5.  in virtūte posita est vēra fēlīcitās.
### (Sen. *Dial.* 7.16.1)

in (prep w.acc/abl) = into / in, on
virtūs –ūtis (f) = virtue

| | | |
|---|---|---|
| in virtūte | (a) | –e |
| | (b) | abl sing |
| | (c) | — ★s in/on virtue |

pōnō pōnere posuī positum = to
place, base (on)

| | | |
|---|---|---|
| posita est | (a) | est |
| | (b) | perf indic, 3rd sing pass |
| | (c) | — is based on virtue |

vērus –a –um = real, true

| | | |
|---|---|---|
| vēra | (a) | –a |
| | (b) | nom sing fem |
| | (c) | real — is based on virtue |

fēlīcitās –ātis (f) = good fortune,
happiness

| | | |
|---|---|---|
| fēlīcitās. | (a) | –s |
| | (b) | nom sing |
| | (c) | real happiness is based on virtue. |

# Summary of Examples

1. fēlix quī propriīs aevum transēgit in agrīs.

2. quam quisque nōrit artem, in hāc sē exerceat.

3. ex dīvitiīs iuventūtem luxuria atque avāritia cum superbiā invāsēre.

4. illud, quod paupertātem nōbīs gravem fēcerat, et dīvitiās gravēs
fēcit.

5. in virtūte posita est vēra fēlīcitās.

# Exercises

Change the verb in the following sentences into each of the tenses of the perfect system and translate:

luxuria atque avāritia iuventūtem invādunt.
(invādō –dere –sī –sum = to invade)

nēmō contentus vīvit.
(vīvō –vere –xī –ctum (intr) = to live)

familiārēs opēs dēficiunt.
(dēficiō –icere –ēcī –ectum (intr) = to run out)

nēmō artem agrī colendī noscit.
(noscō –scere nōvī nōtum = to get to know)

ad dominam suam quisque abit.
(abeō –īre –iī –itum (intr) = to go off)

# Reading

1.  ō fortūnātōs nimium, sua sī bona nōrint,
    agricolās! quibus ipsa procul discordibus armīs
    fundit humō facilem victum iustissima tellūs.
    (Verg. *Georg.* 2.458)

    agricola –ae (m) = a farmer
    arma –ōrum (n.pl) = weapons, arms
    bonum –ī (n) = something good, a blessing
    discors –rdis = at variance (with each other)
    facilis –is –e = easy, easily obtained, readily available
    fortūnātus –a –um = fortunate, blessed
    fundō –ere fūdī fūsum = to pour out
    humus –ī (f) = the earth, soil
    iustus –a –um = fair, just
    nimium (adv) = excessively, extremely
    noscō –scere nōvī nōtum = to get to know; (perf) to know
    procul (adv) = apart, far away (from)
    sī (conj) = if, if only
    tellūs –ūris (f) = the earth
    victus –ūs (m) = food, sustenance

2. quī labōrēs, perīcula, dubiās atque asperās rēs facile tolerāverant,
   iīs ōtium dīvitiaeque (optanda aliās) onerī miseriaeque fuēre.
   (Sall. *Cat.* 10.2)

   aliās (adv) = at another time, in other circumstances
   asper −era −erum = rough, adverse
   dīvitiae −ārum (f.pl) = riches, wealth
   dubius −a −um = uncertain, doubtful
   facile (adv) = easily
   miseria −ae (f) = a pitiful condition, unhappiness
   onus −eris (n) = a burden, nuisance
   optō −āre −āvī −ātum = to wish, pray for
   ōtium −[i]ī (n) = leisure, idleness
   perīculum −ī (n) = danger
   rēs reī (f) = a thing, circumstance
   sum esse fuī = to be
   tolerō −āre −āvī −ātum = to support, withstand

3. prīma peregrīnōs obscēna pecūnia mōrēs
   intulit, et turpī frēgērunt saecula luxū
   dīvitiae mollēs. quid enim Venus ēbria cūrat?
   (Juv. 6.298)

   cūrō −āre −āvī −ātum = to care for, care about
   dīvitiae −ārum (f.pl) = riches, wealth
   ēbrius −a −um = drunk, drunken
   frangō −ngere frēgī −ctum = to break (down), weaken
   inferō −rre intulī illātum = to carry into, introduce
   luxus −ūs (m) = luxury, extravagance
   mollis −is −e = soft, effeminate
   mōs mōris (m) = an established practice; (pl) habits, morals
   obscēnus −a −um = boding ill, filthy
   pecūnia −ae (f) = wealth, money
   peregrīnus −a −um = foreign
   prīmus −a −um = first
   saeculum −ī (n) = a generation
   turpis −is −e = ugly, disgusting, shameful
   Venus −eris (f) = Venus (goddess of love)

4. ō utinam tum, cum Lacedaemona classe petēbat,
   obrutus īnsānīs esset adulter aquīs!          (Ov. *Her.* 1.5)

   (N.B. obrutus ... esset = obrutus esset)

   adulter −erī (m) = an adulterer
   aqua −ae (f) = water
   classis −is (f) = a fleet
   cum (conj) = when
   īnsānus −a −um = demented, raging
   Lacedaemō −onis (f) = Sparta (acc.sing: Lacedaemona)

obruō -ere -ī -tum = to smother, overwhelm
petō -ere -īvī -ītum = to make for
tum (adv) = then
utinam (particle introducing a wish) = if only!

5. *L.Sulla exercitum, quem in Asiā ductāverat, contrā mōrem māiōrum luxuriōsē nimisque līberāliter habuerat. loca amoena, voluptāria facile in ōtiō ferōcīs mīlitum animōs mollīverant: ibi prīmum insuēvit exercitus populī Rōmānī amāre, pōtāre, signa, tabulās pictās, vāsa caelāta mīrārī. (Sall. *Cat.* 11.5)

amō -āre -āvī -ātum = to love, fornicate
amoenus -a -um = beautiful, charming
caelātus -a -um = embossed or engraved in relief
contrā (prep w.acc) = opposite, contrary to
ductō -āre -āvī -ātum = to conduct, lead
exercitus -ūs (m) = an army
facile (adv) = easily
ferox -ōcis = fierce, warlike
habeō -ēre -uī -itum = to have, treat (in such and such a way)
ibi (adv) = there, there and then
insuescō -escere -ēvī -ētum = to become accustomed (to)
līberālis -is -e = of or relating to free men, generous
locus -ī (m) = a place (loca: n.pl ending)
luxuriōsus -a -um = luxurious, extravagant
māior -ior -ius = greater, older; (m.pl) ancestors
mīles -itis (m) = a soldier
mīror -ārī -ātus = to be surprised (at), admire
molliō -īre -īvī -ītum = to soften, weaken
mōs mōris (m) = an established practice
nimis (adv) = excessively, extremely
ōtium -[i]ī (n) = leisure, idleness
populus -ī (m) = a people, nation
pōtō -āre -āvī -ātum = to drink
prīmum (adv) = first, for the first time
signum -ī (n) = a mark (of identity), image, statue
Sulla -ae (m) = L.Cornelius Sulla Felix (the dictator)
tabula picta tabulae pictae (f) = a painted tablet, painting
vāsum -ī (n) = a vessel (for food or drink), dish
voluptārius -a -um = pleasurable

6. fortūna omnia ea victōribus praemia posuit. (Sall. *Cat.* 20.15)

fortūna -ae (f) = fortune, success
praemium -[i]ī (n) = payment, prize
victor -ōris (m) = a victor, conqueror

7.  *voluptātibus itaque illī sē mergunt quibus carēre nōn possunt,
    et ob hoc miserrimī sunt, quod eō pervēnērunt ut illīs quae
    supervacua fuerant facta sint necessāria. (Sen. *Ep.* 39.6)

    careō –ēre –uī –itum (w.abl) = to be without, go without
    eō ... ut = to such a point that
    itaque (adv) = and so, accordingly
    mergō –gere –sī –sum = to immerse
    necessārius –a –um = necessary, essential
    ob (prep w.acc) = because of
    perveniō –enīre –ēnī –entum (intr) = to come (to)
    quod (conj) = because
    supervacuus –a –um = superfluous, unnecessary
    voluptās –ātis (f) = pleasure

8.  ōtium, Catulle, tibī molestum est:
    ōtiō exsultās nimiumque gestīs:
    ōtium et rēgēs prius et beātas
        perdidit urbēs.                                    (Catul. 51.13)

    Catullus –ī (m) = C.Valerius Catullus (the love poet)
    exsultō –āre –āvī (intr) = to leap up, exult
    gestiō –īre –īvī (intr) = to act with abandon, be elated
    molestus –a –um = troublesome
    nimium (adv) = excessively, extremely
    ōtium –[i]ī (n) = leisure, idleness
    perdō –ere –idī –itum = to ruin, destroy
    prius (adv) = before (now)
    rex rēgis (m) = a king

9.  forsitan immundae Tatiō regnante Sabīnae
        nōluerint habilēs plūribus esse virīs:
    nunc Mars externīs animōs exercet in armīs,
        at Venus Aenēae regnat in urbe suī.
    lūdunt formōsae: casta est quam nēmo rogāvit;
        aut, sī rusticitās nōn vetat, ipsa rogat.    (Ov. *Am.* 1.8.39)

    Aenēās –ae (m) = Aeneas (son of Venus and founder of Rome)
    animus –ī (m) = the mind, spirit; (pl) anger
    arma –ōrum (n.pl) = weapons, arms
    castus –a –um = free from taint, chaste
    exerceō –ēre –uī –itum = to exercise, indulge
    externus –a –um = external, foreign
    formōsus –a –um = shapely, beautiful
    forsitan (adv) = perhaps
    habilis –is –e = easy to handle, readily available
    immundus –a –um = unclean, slovenly
    lūdō –dere –sī –sum (intr) = to play (the game of love)
    Mars –tis (m) = Mars (god of war and father of Romulus)

nōlō -lle -luī = to be unwilling, not to want (to)
plūrēs -ēs -a = more (than one), several
regnō -āre -āvī -ātum (intr) = to reign
rogō -āre -āvī -ātum = to ask, sollicit
rusticitās -ātis (f) = country ways, lack of sophistication
Sabīna -ae (f) = a Sabine woman
Tatius -[i]ī (m) = Tatius (an early Sabine king)
Venus -eris (f) = Venus (goddess of love)
vetō -āre -uī -itum = to forbid

10. *sī quae nōn nupta mulier domum suam patefēcerit omnium
cupiditātī palamque sēsē in meretrīciā vītā collocārit, virōrum
aliēnissimōrum convīviīs ūtī instituerit: cum hāc sī quī adulescens forte fuerit, utrum hic adulter an amātor, expugnāre
pudīcitiam an explēre libīdinem voluisse videātur? (Cic. *Cael.*
49)

adulescens -ntis (m) = a young man
adulter -erī (m) = an adulterer
aliēnus -a -um = belonging to others, unfamiliar
amātor -ōris (m) = a lover
collocō -āre -āvī -ātum = to put (in place), involve (in)
convīvium -[i]ī (n) = a dinner-party, banquet
cupiditās -ātis (f) = desire, lust
domus -ūs (f) = a house, home
expleō -ēre -ēvī -ētum = to fill up, satisfy
expugnō -āre -āvī -ātum = to take by storm, break down
forte (adv) = by chance
instituō -uere -uī -ūtum = to set up, make it a habit (to)
libīdō -inis (f) = desire, lust
meretrīcius -a -um = of or belonging to a courtesan
mulier -eris (m) = a woman
nuptus -a -um = married
palam (adv) = openly
patefaciō -facere -fēcī -factum = to reveal, open up
pudīcitia -ae (f) = chastity
quī quae quod = any
sēsē = himself, herself, itself, etc.
ūtor -ī ūsus (w.abl) = to use, spend one's time in
utrum ... an? (interrogatives) = is it that ... or that ...?
videor vidērī vīsus (intr) = to appear, seem (to)
voluisse = to have wanted, wished (to)

# Vocabulary to Learn

domina –ae (f) = a mistress
domus –ī/–ūs (f) = a house, home
petō –ere –īvī –ītum = to make for, seek
quisque quaeque quidque = each person or thing
videor vidērī vīsus (intr) = to appear, seem (to)

# 18
# PAST AND FUTURE PARTICIPLES

## Morphology

The past participle and the future participle are formed from the perfect passive stem, which ends in –t– or –s–. The past participle (passive) then adds 1st and 2nd declension case endings; there is no corresponding active participle. The future participle (active) first adds –ūr– and then adds 1st and 2nd declension case endings; there is no corresponding passive participle, the gerundive being used instead (see chapter 7 syntax §2).

## Syntax

The past participle and the future participle are verbal adjectives and agree in gender, number and case with the nouns they modify. The precise relation of the noun and participle to the main clause (temporal, causal, concessive, etc.) is usually not defined but left to the understanding of the reader.

**1.** The past participle is passive in meaning (deponents excepted) and can be modified by an ablative of the agent or instrument (see chapter 3 syntax §§ 1 and 2) or by a dative of the agent (see chapter 6 syntax §7). It is used to refer to action preceding that of the main verb:

> vīcīnus noster spē praedae **adductus** in Asiam īre parat.
> our neighbour **led on** by the hope of plunder is preparing to go to Asia.

**2.** The future participle is active in meaning (deponents included) and can take a direct object in the appropriate case. It is used to refer to action following, or likely to follow, that of the main verb:

> iam iamque **itūrus** lēgit comitēs.
> **about to go** at any time now, he has chosen his companions.

**3.** A noun and participle are often used in place of two nouns:

> nēminī **terra mūtāta** (i.e. **terrae mūtātiō**) mūtāvit genus aut mōrēs.
> a **country changed** (i.e. **change of country**) has not changed anyone's race or habits.

Both participles can also be used on their own without a noun to modify:

> nītimur in **vetitum** semper cupimusque **negāta**.
> we always strive towards **the forbidden thing** and want **things denied** us.

> nōs caeca cupiditās in **nocitūra**, certē numquam **satiātūra** praecipitat.
> blind greed drives us into things **likely to harm** us, certainly never **likely to satisfy** us.

**4.** An ablative absolute construction can be formed using either participle (see chapter 14 syntax §3):

> aurum omnēs **victā** iam **pietāte** colunt.
> all men **with their scruples** now **overcome** / **having** now **overcome their scruples** worship gold.

# Metaphrasing

**1.** A past participle is metaphrased: ★ed, in brackets, after the noun it modifies:

adductus — (led on) ★s

**2.** A future participle is metaphrased: about to ★ / going to ★ / likely to ★, in brackets, after the noun it modifies:

itūrus — (about to go) ★s

**3.** These basic patterns can then be adapted when necessary as follows:

(a) a noun and participle in agreement with it will sometimes need to be rephrased as a clause (temporal, causal, concessive, etc. as appropriate) or as two nouns:

terra mūtāta
a country (changed) ★s
*or* a country (when changed) ★s
*or* a change of country ★s

(b) what appears to be a past participle in the nominative may prove to be a perfect tense from which the auxiliary verb *esse* "to be" has been separated or omitted:

adductus — (led on) ★s
adductus homō est the man has been led on

If *esse* does not appear (and the sentence ends without a main verb), it must be supplied at the end of the metaphrasing process and the translation adjusted:

adductus homō. the man (led on) ★s
the man has been led on.

(c) a dative which has been metaphrased in the usual way may prove to be the agent of a past participle, so that the prepositions "to/for" will need to be replaced with "by":

tibi — ★s to/for you
tibi adductus — (led on by you) ★s

(d) an ablative which has been metaphrased in the usual way will often form an ablative absolute construction with a second ablative, and the whole phrase is then enclosed in brackets:

pietāte                               — ★s by/with/from scruples
pietāte victā                    (with scruples overcome)

The phrase is left thus suspended until it becomes clear how it relates to the rest of the sentence, when it can be rephrased if necessary:

pietāte victā                    (with scruples overcome)
                                         *or* when scruples are overcome
                                         *or* after overcoming one's
                                         scruples

# Examples

## 1.  accipimus peritūra peritūrī. (Sen. *Dial*. 1.5.7)

accipiō –ipere –ēpī –eptum = to
    take (hold of), inherit
                          accipimus  (a)  –mus
                                     (b)  pres indic, 1st pl act
                                     (c)  we inherit —

pereō –īre –iī –itum (intr) = to
    vanish, perish
                           peritūra  (a)  –tūra
                                     (b)  fut part, acc pl neut
                                     (c)  we inherit — (going to perish)

pereō –īre –iī –itum (intr) = to
    vanish, perish
                           peritūrī.  (a)  –tūrī
                                      (b)  fut part, nom pl masc
                                      (c)  we (going to perish) inherit —
                                           (going to perish).

                          Translation   We who are going to perish inherit
                                        things which are going to perish.

## 2.   imperat aut servit collecta pecūnia cuique.
(Hor. *Ep.* 1.10.47)

imperō –āre –āvī –ātum (w.dat)
   = to order, rule

|  |  |  |
|---|---|---|
| imperat | (a) | –t |
|  | (b) | pres indic, 3rd sing act |
|  | (c) | — rules — |

aut (conj) = or
serviō –īre –īvī –ītum (w.dat) =
   to serve, be a slave (to)

|  |  |  |
|---|---|---|
| aut servit | (a) | –t |
|  | (b) | pres indic, 3rd sing act |
|  | (c) | — rules or serves — |

colligō –igere –ēgī –ectum = to
   gather together, accumulate

|  |  |  |
|---|---|---|
| collecta | (a) | –ta |
|  | (b) | past part, nom sing fem |
|  | (c) | — (accumulated) rules or serves — |

pecūnia –ae (f) = wealth, money

|  |  |  |
|---|---|---|
| pecūnia | (a) | –a |
|  | (b) | nom sing |
|  | (c) | wealth (accumulated) rules or serves — |

quisque quaeque quidque = each
   person or thing

|  |  |  |
|---|---|---|
| cuique. | (a) | –i |
|  | (b) | dat sing masc/fem/neut |
|  | (c) | wealth (accumulated) rules or serves each person. |

|  |  |
|---|---|
| Translation | Accumulated wealth rules or serves each individual. |

## 3.   captā urbe nihil fit reliquī victīs. (Sall. *Cat.* 52.4)

capiō –ere cēpī –tum = to take
  (hold of), capture

|       | | |
|-------|---|---|
| captā | (a) | –tā |
|       | (b) | past part, abl sing fem |
|       | (c) | — *s by/with/from — (captured) |

urbs –bis (f) = a city

|      | | |
|------|---|---|
| urbe | (a) | –e |
|      | (b) | abl sing |
|      | (c) | (with a city captured) |

nihil (n.indecl) = nothing

|       | | |
|-------|---|---|
| nihil | (a) | –l |
|       | (b) | nom/acc sing |
|       | (c) | nothing *s *or* — *s nothing / not at all |

fīō fierī = to become or be made

|     | | |
|-----|---|---|
| fit | (a) | –t |
|     | (b) | pres indic, 3rd sing act |
|     | (c) | nothing becomes — *or* there becomes nothing |

reliquus –a –um = remaining,
  left

|         | | |
|---------|---|---|
| reliquī | (a) | –ī |
|         | (b) | gen sing neut |
|         | (c) | there becomes nothing left |

vincō –ere vīcī victum = to
  conquer, defeat

|         | | |
|---------|---|---|
| victīs. | (a) | –tīs |
|         | (b) | past part, dat pl masc//fem/neut |
|         | (c) | there becomes nothing left for — (defeated). |

|             | |
|-------------|---|
| Translation | When a city is captured there is nothing left for the defeated. |

## 4.   *rogātiōnem prōmulgāvērunt tribūnī plēbis ut ager ex hostibus captus virītim dīviderētur. (Liv. 4.48.2)

rogātiō –ōnis (f) = a request,
  (formal) proposal

|            | | |
|------------|---|---|
| rogātiōnem | (a) | –em |
|            | (b) | acc sing |
|            | (c) | — *s a proposal |

prōmulgō –āre –āvī –ātum = to
   proclaim, promulgate
        prōmulgāvērunt  (a)  –ērunt
                    (b)  perf indic, 3rd pl act
                    (c)  — promulgated a proposal

tribūnus –ī (m) = a tribune (a
   senior magistrate)
               tribūnī  (a)  –ī
                    (b)  nom pl
                    (c)  the tribunes promulgated a proposal

plebs –ēbis (f) = the general
   body of citizens, the people
               plēbis  (a)  –is
                    (b)  gen sing
                    (c)  the tribunes of the people pro-
                           mulgated a proposal

ut (conj) = that
ager agrī (m) = land
              ut ager  (a)  –r
                    (b)  nom sing
                    (c)  (that the land ⋆s)

ex (prep w.abl) = from
hostis –is (m) = an enemy
        ex hostibus  (a)  –ibus
                    (b)  abl pl
                    (c)  (that the land ⋆s from the enemy)

capiō –ere cēpī –tum = to take
   (hold of), capture
              captus  (a)  –tus
                    (b)  past part, nom sing masc
                    (c)  (that the land captured from the
                         enemy ⋆s)

virītim (adv) = man by man, on
   an individual basis
dividō –idere –īsī –īsum = to
   divide, share out
    virītim dīviderētur.  (a)  –rētur
                    (b)  imperf subj, 3rd sing pass
                    (c)  (that the land captured from the
                         enemy should be shared out on an
                         individual basis).

          Translation     The tribunes of the people pro-
                         mulgated a proposal that the land
                         captured from the enemy should be
                         shared out on an individual basis.

## 5. Graecia capta ferum victōrem cēpit et artēs intulit agrestī Latiō. (Hor. *Ep*. 2.1.156)

Graecia -ae (f) = Greece

|  | Graecia | (a) | -a |
|---|---|---|---|
|  |  | (b) | nom sing |
|  |  | (c) | Greece ★s |

capiō -ere cēpī -tum = to take (hold of), capture

|  | capta | (a) | -ta |
|---|---|---|---|
|  |  | (b) | past part, nom sing fem |
|  |  | (c) | Greece (captured) ★s |

ferus -a -um = wild, savage

|  | ferum | (a) | -um |
|---|---|---|---|
|  |  | (b) | nom/acc sing neut *or* acc sing masc |
|  |  | (c) | Greece (captured) ★s the savage — |

victor -ōris (m) = a victor, conqueror

|  | victōrem | (a) | -em |
|---|---|---|---|
|  |  | (b) | acc sing |
|  |  | (c) | Greece (captured) ★s her savage conqueror |

capiō -ere cēpī -tum = to take (hold of), capture

|  | cēpit | (a) | -it |
|---|---|---|---|
|  |  | (b) | perf indic, 3rd sing act |
|  |  | (c) | Greece (captured) captured her savage conqueror |

et (conj) = and
ars -tis (f) = an art

|  | et artēs | (a) | -ēs |
|---|---|---|---|
|  |  | (b) | nom/acc pl |
|  |  | (c) | and arts ★ / — ★s arts |

inferō -rre intulī illātum = to carry into, introduce

|  | intulit | (a) | -it |
|---|---|---|---|
|  |  | (b) | perf indic, 3rd sing act |
|  |  | (c) | and — introduced the arts |

agrestis -is -e = of or connected with the fields, uncivilised

|  | agrestī | (a) | -ī |
|---|---|---|---|
|  |  | (b) | dat sing masc/fem/neut |
|  |  | (c) | and — introduced the arts to an uncivilised — |

Latium –[i]ī (n) = Latium (the
area of central Italy around
Rome)

| | | |
|---|---|---|
| Latiō. | (a) | –ō |
| | (b) | dat sing |
| | (c) | and — introduced the arts to an uncivilised Latium. |
| Translation | | Captured Greece captured her savage conqueror and introduced the arts to an uncivilised Latium. |

# Summary of Examples

1. accipimus peritūra peritūrī.

2. imperat aut servit collecta pecūnia cuique.

3. captā urbe nihil fit reliquī victīs.

4. rogātiōnem prōmulgāvērunt tribūnī plēbis ut ager ex hostibus captus virītim dīviderētur.

5. Graecia capta ferum victōrem cēpit et artēs intulit agrestī Latiō.

# Exercises

Complete the following sentences on the analogy of the first:

hoc tū vetās: hoc vetitum nōbīs placet.
hoc tū negās: hoc . . . . . . . . . . . . . . . . . .
agrum tū dīvidis: ager . . . . . . . . . . . . . .
urbem vōs capitis: urbs . . . . . . . . . . . .
terram nōs mūtāmus: terra . . . . . . . . . . .

hoc tū vetās: hōc vetitō nōs beātī sumus.
hoc tū negās: hōc . . . . . . . . . . . . . . . . . .
agrum tū dīvidis: agrō . . . . . . . . . . . . . .
urbem vōs capitis: urbe . . . . . . . . . . . . .
terram nōs mūtāmus: terrā . . . . . . . . . . .

hic in Asiam īre parat: multa facit in Asiam itūrus.
hic terram mūtāre parat: multa facit . . . . . . . . . . . .
hic urbem capere parat: multa facit . . . . . . . . . . . .
hic agrum dīvidere parat: multa facit . . . . . . . . . . .
hic rem facere parat: multa facit . . . . . . . . . . . . . .

# Reading

1.  *quid flēs, Asteriē, quem tibi candidī
    prīmō restituent vēre Favōniī
    Thynā merce beātum Gȳgēn?                (Hor. *Carm.* 3.7.1)

    Asteriē -ēs (f) = Asterie (beloved of Gyges)
    beō -āre -āvī -ātum = to make happy, enrich
    candidus -a -um = bright, cloudless
    Favōnius -[i]ī (m) = the west wind, zephyr
    fleō -ēre -ēvī -ētum = to weep, cry for
    Gȳgēs -is (m) = Gyges (acc.sing: Gȳgēn; a merchant)
    merx -cis (f) = merchandise, goods
    prīmus -a -um = first, the beginning of
    quis? quid? = who? what? (acc.sing.neut) why?
    restituō -uere -uī -ūtum = to set up again, restore
    Thȳnus -a -um = of the Thyni, Bithynian
    vēr -ris (n) = spring

2.  ad mercēdem piī sumus, ad mercēdem impiī, et honesta
    quamdiū aliqua illīs spēs inest sequimur, in contrārium transi-
    tūrī sī plūs scelera prōmittent. (Sen. *Ep.* 115.10)

    ad (prep w.acc) = to, towards (the attainment of)
    aliquī -qua -quod = some or other
    contrārius -a -um = opposite
    honestus -a -um = honourable
    impius -a -um = unfaithful to moral obligations, dishonest
    insum inesse infuī (intr) = to be in, be attached (to)
    mercēs -ēdis (f) = a payment, reward
    pius -a -um = faithful to moral obligations, honest
    plūs -ris (n) = a greater amount, more
    prōmittō -ittere -īsī -issum = to promise
    quamdiū = as long as
    scelus -eris (n) = a crime
    sequor -quī -cūtus = to follow, strive after
    spēs -eī (f) = an expectation, hope
    transeō -īre -iī -itum (intr) = to go through or over

3.  cēterum oppidum incensum, Numidae pūberēs interfectī, aliī omnēs vēnumdatī, praeda mīlitibus dīvīsa. (Sall. *Jug.* 91.6)

alius –a –ud = diffferent, other
cēterus –a –um = the rest of; (acc.sing.neut) for the rest
dīvidō –idere –īsī –īsum = to divide, share out
incendō –dere –dī –sum = to set on fire
interficiō –ficere –fēcī –fectum = to kill
mīles –itis (m) = a soldier
Numida –ae (m) = a Numidian
oppidum –ī (n) = a town
praeda –ae (f) = plunder
pūbēs –eris = grown up, adult
vēnumdō –dare –dedī –datum = to put up for sale


4.  raptāturque comīs per vim nova nupta prehensīs. (Ov. *Met.* 12.223)

coma –ae (f) = the hair of the head, one's hair
novus –a –um = new
nupta –ae (f) = a wife, bride
per (prep w.acc) = through, through the use of
prehendō –dere –dī –sum = to take hold of, grasp
raptō –āre –āvī –ātum = to carry away, drag off
vīs vis (f) = physical strength, force


5.  placent agrī, postquam tuī factī sunt? rārum id quidem: nihil enim aequē grātum est adeptīs quam concupiscentibus. (Plin. *Ep.* 2.15.1)

adipiscor –ipiscī –eptus = to overtake, obtain
aequus –a –um = level, equal
concupiscō –iscere –īvī –itum = to desire ardently, long for
grātus –a –um (w.dat) = appreciative or appreciated, pleasing to
placeō –ēre –uī (w.dat) = to please
postquam (conj) = after
quam = than, as
quidem = indeed
rārus –a –um = rare

6. *illīc nostrīs ē prōvinciīs lixae ac negōtiātōrēs repertī, quōs iūs commerciī, dein cupīdō augendī pecūniam, postrēmō oblīviō patriae suīs quemque ab sēdibus hostīlem in agrum transtulerat. (Tac. *Ann.* 2.62)

augeō –gēre –xī –ctum = to increase
commercium –[i]ī (n) = trade, commerce
cupīdō –inis (f) = desire, greed
dein (adv) = from there or then, then
hostīlis –is –e = of or belonging to an enemy, hostile
illīc (adv) = in that place, there
iūs iuris (n) = law, the right
lixa –ae (f) = a camp-follower
negōtiātor –ōris (m) = a trader
oblīviō –ōnis (f) = forgetfulness
patria –ae (f) = one's native land, country
pecūnia –ae (f) = wealth, money
postrēmō (adv) = lastly, finally
prōvincia –ae (f) = a province
reperiō –īre repperī –tum = to discover, find
sēdēs –is (f) = a seat, one's home
transferō –ferre –tulī –lātum = to carry, bring

7. iam prīdem Syrus in Tiberim dēfluxit Orontēs
et linguam et mōrēs et cum tībīcine chordās
oblīquās nec nōn gentīlia tympana sēcum
vexit et ad circum iussās prostāre puellās.     (Juv. 3.62)

ad (prep w.acc) = to, at
chorda –ae (f) = gut, a string (of a musical instrument)
circus –ī (m) = a circle, the Circus Maximus
–cum (prep w.abl) = with, together with
dēfluō –ere –xī –xum (intr) = to flow (down)
gentīlis –is –e = of one's family, tribe or nation
iam prīdem (advs) = for a long time now
iubeō –bēre –ssī –ssum = to order
lingua –ae (f) = the tongue, a language
mōs mōris (m) = an established practice; (pl) habits, morals
nec nōn (conj) = and also, and furthermore
oblīquus –a –um = set at an angle, oblique
Orontēs –is (m) = the river Orontes
prostō –āre –itī –itum (intr) = to offer oneself for sale
puella –ae (f) = a girl, young woman
Syrus –a –um = Syrian
Tiberis –is (m) = the river Tiber
tībīcen –inis (m) = a flute-player
tympanum –ī (n) = a drum
vehō –here –xī –ctum = to carry

8.  Iccī, beātīs nunc Arabum invidēs
    gāzīs, et ācrem mīlitiam parās
        nōn ante dēvictīs Sabaeae
        rēgibus, horribilīque Mēdō

    nectis catēnās? quae tibi virginum
    sponsō necatō barbara serviet?
        puer quis ex aulā capillīs
        ad cyathum statuētur unctīs?        (Hor. *Carm.* 1.29.1)

ācer ācris ācre = sharp, fierce
ad (prep w.acc) = to, at
ante (adv) = before, previously
Arabs -is (m) = an Arab
aula -ae (f) = a courtyard, palace
barbarus -a -um = foreign
beātus -a -um = happy, rich
capillus -ī (m) = the hair of the head; (pl) one's hair
catēna -ae (f) = a chain, fetter
cyathus -ī (m) = a ladle (used for serving wine)
dēvincō -incere -īcī -ictum = to defeat decisively, subdue
gāza -ae (f) = treasure
horribilis -is -e = terrifying
Iccius -[i]ī (m) = Iccius (a philosophy student turned soldier)
invideō -idēre -īdī -īsum (w.dat) = to envy
Mēdus -a -um = Median or Persian
mīlitia -ae (f) = military service, a military campaign
necō -āre -āvī -ātum = to kill
nectō -ere nexī nexum = to weave, link together
parō -āre -āvī -ātum = to provide, prepare
quī? quae? quod? = what? which?
rex rēgis (m) = a king
Sabaea -ae (f) = Sabaea (a region in S.W.Arabia)
serviō -īre -īvī -ītum (w.dat) = to serve, be a slave (to)
sponsus -ī (m) = a betrothed man, bridegroom
statuō -uere -uī -ūtum = to set (in place), station
unguō -guere -xī -ctum = to anoint with oil or unguents
virgō -inis (f) = a girl, virgin

9. admīrātiōnem nōbīs parentēs aurī argentīque fēcērunt, et tenerīs
infūsa cupiditās altius sēdit crēvitque nōbīscum. (Sen. *Ep.*
115.11)

admīrātiō –ōnis (f) = wonder (at), admiration (for)
altus –a –um = high, deep
argentum –ī (n) = silver
aurum –ī (n) = gold
crescō –ere crēvī crētum (intr) = to grow
–cum (prep w.abl) = with, together with
cupiditās –ātis (f) = desire, greed
infundō –undere –ūdī –ūsum = to pour in, instil
parens –ntis (m/f) = a parent
sedeō –ēre sēdī sessum (intr) = to sit, settle
tener –era –erum = tender, young

10. damnōsa quid nōn imminuit diēs?
aetās parentum pēior avīs tulit
    nōs nēquiōrēs, mox datūrōs
    prōgeniem vitiōsiōrem. (Hor. *Carm.* 3.6.45)

aetās –ātis (f) = one's age, an age or era
avus –ī (m) = a grandfather
damnōsus –a –um = ruinous, destructive
diēs –ēī (f) = a day, the lapse of time
dō dare dedī datum = to give (birth to)
imminuō –uere –uī –ūtum = to make smaller, diminish
mox (adv) = soon, next
nēquam (indecl.adj) = bad, worthless (compar: nēquior –ior –ius)
parens –ntis (m/f) = a parent
pēior –ior –ius = more harmful, worse
prōgeniēs –ēī (f) = an offspring, progeny
vitiōsus –a –um = faulty, corrupt

# Vocabulary to Learn

capiō –ere cēpī captum = to take (hold of), seize, capture
iam (adv) = now, already
(n)umquam (adv) = (n)ever
puella –ae (f) = a girl
vincō –ere vīcī victum = to conquer, defeat

# 19
# SUPINES AND DEFECTIVE VERBS

## Morphology

The supine is formed from the perfect passive stem, which ends in –*t*– or –*s*–; it then adds two 4th declension case endings, the accusative singular in –*um*, and the ablative singular in –*ū*.

The perfect infinitive active is formed from the perfect active stem plus –*isse*; the only exception is an alternative form for regular verbs with stems in –*v*–, which may drop the –*v*– and contract, such as *amāvisse* and *amāsse*.

Defective verbs are verbs which lack various forms. Those which have only perfect forms have a perfect infinitive active like regular verbs.

## Syntax

**1.** The supine is a verbal noun. As a verb it is active in meaning (deponents included) and can take a direct object in the appropriate case; as a noun it is always singular and only appears in the accusative and ablative.

**2.** Supines are used:

(a) in the accusative with verbs of motion to express purpose (see chapter 2 syntax §4b):

> pater hūc mē mīsit ad tē **ōrātum** tuus.
> your father sent me here to you **to implore** you.

(b) in the ablative with various adjectives to express the respect in which the adjective is applied (see chapter 3 syntax §4):

> forsitan hoc mīrābile **audītū** esse videātur.
> perhaps this may seem to be strange **to hear** (**in the hearing**).

Only supines in the accusative take a direct object; a supine in the ablative never does.

**3.** Defective verbs lack various forms:

(a) some, such as *volō velle voluī* "to want", lack the perfect passive forms;

(b) some, such as *gaudeō gaudēre gāvīsus* "to rejoice", lack the perfect active forms and use the corresponding passive forms like deponent verbs to provide a full range of active tenses;

(c) three verbs have only perfect forms: *coepī coepisse coeptum* "to have begun" refers to action as completed:

> dīmidium factī quī **coepit** habet.
> whoever **has begun** has half the deed done.

But *meminī meminisse* "to remember" and *ōdī ōdisse ōsum* "to hate" though perfect in form refer, like the imperfect system, to action as incomplete (see chapter 11):

> caveant intemperantiam, **meminerint** verēcundiae adulescentēs.
> young men should beware of licentiousness, **they should remember** modesty.

Only *meminī* shows traces of an imperfect stem in having the future imperative forms *mementō* and *mementōte* (see chapter 16).

**4.** The perfect infinitive is a verbal noun. As a verb it expresses the bare action of the perfect stem; as a noun it is used like the present infinitive in the nominative and accusative singular only (see chapter 1 syntax §§ 3 and 4; chapter 2 syntax §§ 1 and 2):

> est virtūs placitīs **abstinuisse** bonīs.
> it is a virtue **to have refrained** from (someone's) appealing charms.

# Metaphrasing

**1.** A supine is metaphrased: to ★ (or: to ★ —, as appropriate), in brackets:

> audītū                          (to hear)

It is left thus suspended until it becomes clear how it fits into the whole sentence:

> audītū mīrābile est            it is strange (to hear)

**2.** An ambiguous form having the same ending for the past participle and the supine may need an alternative metaphrase:

> audītum                         — (heard) ★s / — ★s — (heard)
>                                  *or* (to hear —)

**3.** A perfect infinitive is metaphrased: to have ★ed (or: to have ★ed —), in brackets:

> abstinuisse                     (to have refrained)

# Examples

## 1. ōdērunt peccāre bonī virtūtis amōre.
(Hor. *Ep*. 1.16.52)

ōdī –isse ōsum = to hate, hate (to)

| | | |
|---|---|---|
| ōdērunt | (a) | –ērunt |
| | (b) | perf indic, 3rd pl act |
| | (c) | — hate — |

peccō –āre –āvī –ātum (intr) = to
make a mistake, do wrong

| | | |
|---|---|---|
| peccāre | (a) | –re |
| | (b) | pres infin act |
| | (c) | — hate (to do wrong) |

bonus –a –um = good

| | | |
|---|---|---|
| bonī | (a) | –ī |
| | (b) | nom pl masc |
| | (c) | good — hate (to do wrong) |

virtūs –ūtis (f) = virtue

| | | |
|---|---|---|
| virtūtis | (a) | –is |
| | (b) | gen sing |
| | (c) | good — hate (to do wrong) of virtue |

amor –ōris (m) = love

| | | |
|---|---|---|
| amōre. | (a) | –e |
| | (b) | abl sing |
| | (c) | good — hate (to do wrong) from love of virtue. |

| | |
|---|---|
| Translation | Good men hate to do wrong from their love of virtue. |

## 2. quod optimum factū vidēbitur, faciēs.
(Cic. *Att.* 7.22.2)

quī quae quod = who(ever),
    which, what

|  |  |  |
|---|---|---|
| quod | (a) | –d |
|  | (b) | nom/acc sing neut |
|  | (c) | (whatever ★s / whatever — ★s) |

optimus –a –um = best

|  |  |  |
|---|---|---|
| optimum | (a) | –um |
|  | (b) | superl, nom/acc sing neut *or* acc sing masc |
|  | (c) | (whatever ★s the best — / whatever the best — ★s) |

faciō –ere fēcī factum = to make,
    do

|  |  |  |
|---|---|---|
| factū | (a) | –tū |
|  | (b) | supine, abl sing |
|  | (c) | (whatever ★s the best — to do / whatever the best — to do ★s) |

videor vidērī vīsus (intr) = to
    appear, seem

|  |  |  |
|---|---|---|
| vidēbitur, | (a) | –bitur |
|  | (b) | fut indic, 3rd sing pass |
|  | (c) | (whatever will seem the best — to do), |

faciō –ere fēcī factum = to make,
    do

|  |  |  |
|---|---|---|
| faciēs. | (a) | –ēs |
|  | (b) | fut indic, 2nd sing act |
|  | (c) | you will do —. |

|  |  |
|---|---|
| Translation | You will do whatever seems best to do. |

## 3.  missus mercātum ab suō adulescens patre emit mulierem.  (Pl. *Mer. Arg.* 1.1)

mittō –ere mīsī missum = to let
 go, send

| | | |
|---|---|---|
| missus | (a) | –sus |
| | (b) | past part, nom sing masc |
| | (c) | — (sent) ★s |

mercor –ārī –ātus = to buy,
 engage in trade

| | | |
|---|---|---|
| mercātum | (a) | –tum |
| | (b) | supine, acc sing |
| | (c) | — (sent to engage in trade) ★s |

ab (prep w.abl) = from, by
suus –a –um = his, her, its (own),
 etc.

| | | |
|---|---|---|
| ab suō | (a) | –ō |
| | (b) | abl sing masc/neut |
| | (c) | — (sent to engage in trade by his —) ★s |

adulescens –ntis (m) = a young
 man

| | | |
|---|---|---|
| adulescens | (a) | –s |
| | (b) | nom sing |
| | (c) | a young man (sent to engage in trade by his —) ★s |

pater –tris (m) = a father

| | | |
|---|---|---|
| patre | (a) | –e |
| | (b) | abl sing |
| | (c) | a young man (sent to engage in trade by his father) ★s |

emō emere ēmī emptum = to
 buy

| | | |
|---|---|---|
| emit | (a) | –t |
| | (b) | pres indic, 3rd sing act |
| | (c) | a young man (sent to engage in trade by his father) buys — |

mulier –eris (m) = a woman

| | | |
|---|---|---|
| mulierem. | (a) | –em |
| | (b) | acc sing |
| | (c) | a young man (sent to engage in trade by his father) buys a woman. |

| | |
|---|---|
| Translation | A young man, sent to engage in trade by his father, buys a woman. |

# 4.  infēlix, properās ultima nōsse mala. (Prop. 1.5.4)

infēlix –īcis = unfruitful, unfortunate, unhappy

|  |  |  |
|---|---|---|
| infēlix, | (a) | –x |
|  | (b) | voc sing masc/fem/neut |
|  | (c) | unhappy —, |

properō –āre –āvī –ātum = to
   hurry (to)

|  |  |  |
|---|---|---|
| properās | (a) | –s |
|  | (b) | pres indic, 2nd sing act |
|  | (c) | you hurry (to ★) |

ultimus –a –um = most distant,
   utmost

|  |  |  |
|---|---|---|
| ultima | (a) | –a |
|  | (b) | acc pl neut |
|  | (c) | you hurry (to ★ the utmost —) |

noscō –scere nōvī nōtum = to get
   to know; (perf tenses) to
   know

|  |  |  |
|---|---|---|
| nōsse (nōvisse) | (a) | –isse |
|  | (b) | perf infin act |
|  | (c) | you hurry (to know the utmost —) |

malum –ī (n) = something bad, a
   misfortune

|  |  |  |
|---|---|---|
| mala. | (a) | –a |
|  | (b) | acc pl |
|  | (c) | you hurry (to know the utmost misfortunes). |

|  |  |
|---|---|
| Translation | Unhappy man, you are hurrying to know the utmost misfortunes. |

N.B. in the original context it is clear who is being is addressed.

## 5.    forsan et haec ōlim meminisse iuvābit.
(Verg. *Aen.* 1.203)

forsan (adv) = perhaps
et (adv) = even
hic haec hoc = this

| forsan et haec | (a) | –aec |
| | (b) | nom sing fem *or* nom/acc pl neut |
| | (c) | perhaps even this *or* these — ★ / — ★s even these — |

ōlim (adv) = at some time (in the past or future), one day
meminī –inisse = to remember

| ōlim meminisse | (a) | –isse |
| | (b) | perf infin act |
| | (c) | perhaps even this *or* these — ★ (to remember — one day) (perhaps to remember even these — one day) |

iuvat –āre –iūvit iūtum = it delights

| iuvābit. | (a) | –bit |
| | (b) | fut indic, 3rd sing act |
| | (c) | perhaps it will delight — (to remember even these — one day). |

| Translation | Perhaps it will be a delight to remember even these things one day. |

# Summary of Examples

1. ōdērunt peccāre bonī virtūtis amōre.

2. quod optimum factū vidēbitur, faciēs.

3. missus mercātum ab suō adulescens patre emit mulierem.

4. infēlix, properās ultima nōsse mala.

5. forsan et haec ōlim meminisse iuvābit.

# Exercises

Complete the following sentences on the analogy of the first:

quī tē ōrāvit, is ā tuō patre missus est ad tē ōrātum.
quī tē rogāvit, is ā tuō patre missus est ad tē ........
quī tē revocāvit, is a tuō patre missus est ad tē ......
quī nōs vīdit, is ā nostrō patre missus est ad nōs .....
quī nōs petīvit, is ā nostrō patre missus est ad nōs ...
quī nōs invēnit, is ā nostrō patre missus est ad nōs ...

# Reading

1. cito nēquitia subrēpit; virtūs difficilis inventū est, rectōrem
   ducemque dēsīderat: etiam sine magistrō vitia discuntur. (Sen.
   Q.N. 3.30.8)

   cito (adv) = quickly, soon
   dēsīderō -āre -āvī -ātum = to long for, need
   difficilis -is -e = difficult
   discō –ere didicī = to learn
   dux –cis (m) = a leader, guide
   inveniō -enīre -ēnī -entum = to come upon, find
   magister -trī (m) = a master, teacher
   nēquitia -ae (f) = badness, worthlessness
   rector –ōris (m) = a helmsman, tutor
   sine (prep w.abl) = without
   subrēpō –ere –sī –tum (intr) = to creep up (to, on)

2. stultitia est, pater, vēnātum dūcere invītās canēs. (Pl. St. 139)

   canis –is (m/f) = a dog
   dūcō –cere –xī –ctum = to lead, take
   invītus -a -um = unwilling, reluctant
   pater –tris (m) = a father
   stultitia -ae (f) = stupidity, folly
   vēnor -ārī -ātus (intr) = to go hunting

3. virtūs est vitium fugere, et sapientia prīma
   stultitiā caruisse.                            (Hor. Ep. 1.1.41)

   careō –ēre –uī –itum (w.abl) = to be without, be free from
   fugiō –ere fūgī = to run away from
   prīmus -a -um = first, the beginning of
   sapientia -ae (f) = wisdom
   stultitia -ae (f) = stupidity, folly

4.  \*mandēmus memoriae quod vir mītissimus et ob hoc quoque maximus Thrasea crēbrō dīcere solēbat: quī vitia ōdit, hominēs ōdit. (Plin. *Ep.* 8.22.3)

crēbrō (adv) = frequently, repeatedly
dīcō –cere –xī –ctum = to say
mandō –āre –āvī –ātum = to hand over, commit
maximus –a –um = greatest
memoria –ae (f) = memory
mītis –is –e = soft, gentle
ob (prep w.acc) = because of
ōdī –isse ōsum = to hate
quoque (adv) = as well, also
soleō –ēre –itus = to be accustomed (to)
Thrasea –ae (m) = P.Thrasea Paetus (the Stoic philosopher)

5.  \*Hannibal invictus patriam dēfensum revocātus bellum gessit adversus P.Scīpiōnem. (Nep. *Han.* 6.1)

adversus (prep w.acc) = opposite, against
bellum –ī (n) = warfare, a war
dēfendō –dere –dī –sum = to fend off, defend
gerō –rere –ssī –stum = to bear, carry on
Hannibal –alis (m) = Hannibal (the Carthaginian general)
invictus –a –um = unconquered
patria –ae (f) = one's native land, country
revocō –āre –āvī –ātum = to call back, recall
Scīpiō –ōnis (m) = P.Cornelius Scipio (conqueror of Carthage)

6.  nōn est autem prūdentis errantīs ōdisse; aliōquī ipse sibi odiō erit. (Sen. *Dial.* 3.14.2)

aliōquī (adv) = otherwise
errō –āre –āvī –ātum (intr) = to wander, err
ōdī –isse ōsum = to hate
odium –[i]ī (n) = hatred, an object of hatred
prūdens –ntis = looking ahead, intelligent

7.  \*sed ubi Carthāgō, aemula imperī Rōmānī, ab stirpe interiit, cuncta maria terraeque patēbant, saevīre fortūna ac miscēre omnia coepit. (Sall. *Cat.* 10.1)

aemulus –a –um (w.gen) = emulous, rival (of)
Carthāgō –inis (f) = Carthage
coepī –isse –tum = to have begun (to)
cunctus –a –um = the whole of; (pl) all
fortūna –ae (f) = fortune
imperium –[i]ī (n) = authority, an empire
intereō –īre –iī –itum (intr) = to die, be destroyed
mare –is (n) = the sea

misceō -ēre -uī mixtum = to mix (up), throw into confusion
pateō -ēre -uī (intr) = to be open
saeviō -īre -iī -ītum (intr) = to behave savagely, rage
stirps -pis (f) = the stem or stock (of a tree)
terra -ae (f) = the earth, land
ubi = where, when

8.  sīc ruit ad celebrēs cultissima fēmina lūdōs;
      cōpia iūdicium saepe morāta meum est.
    spectātum veniunt, veniunt spectentur ut ipsae;
      ille locus castī damna pudōris habet.
    (Ov. *Ars.* 1.97)

castus -a -um = free from taint, chaste
celeber -bris -bre = busy, crowded
cōpia -ae (f) = an abundance, multitude
cultus -a -um = cultivated, sophisticated
damnum -ī (n) = a (financial or other) loss
fēmina -ae (f) = a woman
habeō -ēre -uī -itum = to have, hold out
iūdicium -[i]ī (n) = a judgement, decision
locus -ī (m) = a place
lūdus -ī (m) = play, a game; (pl) public games
moror -ārī -ātus = to delay, hold up
pudor -ōris (m) = a sense of shame, restraint
ruō -ere -ī (intr) = to rush
saepe (adv) = often
sīc (adv) = thus
spectō -āre -āvī -ātum = to look at, watch

9.  *omnia praeterībō quae mihi turpia dictū vidēbuntur. vōs,
    quaesō, date hoc et concēdite pudōrī meō ut aliquam partem dē
    istius impudentiā reticēre possim. (Cic. *Ver.* 1.32)

aliquī -qua -quod = some or other
concēdō -dere -ssī -ssum = to concede, grant
dē (prep w.abl) = from, about
dīcō -cere -xī -ctum = to say, speak (of)
impudentia -ae (f) = shamelessness (in sexual matters)
iste -a -ud = that (of yours)
pars -tis (f) = a part
praetereō -īre -iī -itum = to pass by or over, omit
pudor -ōris (m) = a sense of shame, decency
quaesō -ere = to ask, beg
reticeō -ēre -uī (intr) = to keep silent
turpis -is -e = ugly, disgusting, shameful
vōs = you

10. quam iuvat immītēs ventōs audīre cubantem
    et dominam tenerō continuisse sinū!          (Tib. 1.1.45)

contineō –inēre –inuī –entum = to hold, confine, enfold
cubō –āre –uī –itum (intr) = to lie down (in bed)
immītis –is –e = harsh, merciless
iuvāt –āre iūvit iūtum = it delights
quam! = to what an extent! how much! how!
sinus –ūs (m) = a fold (of clothing), embrace
tener –era –erum = tender, gentle
ventus –ī (m) = the wind

# Vocabulary to Learn

dīcō –cere –xī –ctum = to say, speak of, call
mittō –ere mīsī missum = to let go, send
pater –tris (m) = a father
vōs = you
vester –tra –trum = your (own)

# 20
# PERSON ENDINGS: THE PERFECT SYSTEM

## Morphology

The full set of person endings for the five tenses of the perfect system is set out below:

|  |  | PERF INDIC ACT | OTHER TENSES |
|---|---|---|---|
| Singular | 1. | $-\bar{\imath}$ | $-\bar{o}$ / $-m$ |
|  | 2. | $-ist\bar{\imath}$ | $-s$ |
|  | 3. | $-it$ | $-t$ |
| Plural | 1. | $-imus$ | $-mus$ |
|  | 2. | $-istis$ | $-tis$ |
|  | 3. | $-\bar{e}runt$ / $-\bar{e}re$ | $-nt$ |

The 1st singular endings $-\bar{o}$ and $-m$ are mutually exclusive, but the perfect indicative, 3rd plural active endings $-\bar{e}runt$ and $-\bar{e}re$ are true alternatives.

These person endings are added (with some minor phonetic adjustments) to the stems and tense endings of the perfect system (see chapter 17). Exceptions are:

the future indicative, 1st singular active, which ends in $-er\bar{o}$;

the perfect subjunctive, 2nd singular active, which ends in $-er\bar{\imath}s$; 1st and 2nd plural, which end in $-er\bar{\imath}mus$ and $-er\bar{\imath}tis$;

alternative forms of the perfect active tenses in $-v-$, which may drop the $-v-$ and contract, such as $am\bar{a}ver\bar{o}$ and $am\bar{a}r\bar{o}$.

# Syntax

**1.** Person endings are used as in the imperfect system to identify the subject (see chapter 15 syntax §1):

> perfer, ere, obdūrā! multō graviōra **tulistī**.
> hold on, master, endure! **you have borne** much heavier troubles.

Personal pronouns are not strictly necessary. Even when the subject is not expressed by a pronoun, it can still be modified by an adjective or noun in the nominative:

> frustrā sum igitur gāvīsus **miser**.
> So I **wretched man** have rejoiced in vain.

**2.** Certain endings can also be used as in the imperfect system without referring to a specific subject (see chapter 15 syntax §2):

> ut sēmentem **fēceris**, ita metēs.
> as **you sow** (**will have done your sowing**), so you will reap.

**3.** The jussive use of the perfect subjunctive, 2nd singular and plural is restricted to negative commands, in which it refers like the present subjunctive to action as incomplete in the future (see chapter 11 syntax §1(iv)):

> hoc facitō! hoc **nē fēcerīs**!
> do this! **don't do** this!

# Metaphrasing

**1.** A 1st or 2nd person verb allows both subject and verb to be metaphrased together:

> fēcī            I have done —

**2.** A nominative in agreement with the subject of a 1st or 2nd person verb is metaphrased after the subject pronoun:

> fēcī miser          I wretched have done —

Rephrasing this will often make a better translation:

> fēcī miser          I wretched man have done —

**3.** A 1st or 2nd person subjunctive is metaphrased in three ways, corresponding to the three shades of meaning of the subjunctive (see chapter 11 syntax §2):

fēcerīs

(a) it may be that you have done —

(b) may it be that you have done —

nē fēcerīs

(c) you should not do — / don't do —

# Examples

## 1.  vēnistīne domum ad tuōs penātēs? (Catul. 9.3)

veniō venīre vēnī ventum (intr)
   = to come

-ne? (interrogative particle) =
   can it be that ...?

| | | |
|---|---|---|
| vēnistīne | (a) | –istī |
| | (b) | perf indic, 2nd sing act |
| | (c) | have you come? |

domus –ūs (f) = a house, home

| | | |
|---|---|---|
| domum | (a) | –um |
| | (b) | acc sing |
| | (c) | have you come home? |

ad (prep w.acc) = to

tuus –a –um = your (own)

| | | |
|---|---|---|
| ad tuōs | (a) | –ōs |
| | (b) | acc pl masc |
| | (c) | have you come home to your —? |

penātēs –ium (m.pl) = the
   penates (gods of the house-
   hold)

| | | |
|---|---|---|
| penātēs? | (a) | –ēs |
| | (b) | acc pl |
| | (c) | have you come home to your penates? |

261

## 2. *Rhodum vēnimus ubi, quās mercīs vexeram, omnīs vendidī. (Pl. *Mer.* 93)

Rhodus –ī (f) = the island of
Rhodes

| | | |
|---|---|---|
| Rhodum | (a) | –um |
| | (b) | acc sing |
| | (c) | — ★s Rhodes |

veniō venīre vēnī ventum (intr)
= to come
ubi = where, when

| | | |
|---|---|---|
| vēnimus ubi, | (a) | –imus |
| | (b) | perf indic, 1st pl act |
| | (c) | we came to Rhodes where, |

quī quae quod = who(ever),
which, what

| | | |
|---|---|---|
| quās | (a) | –ās |
| | (b) | acc pl fem |
| | (c) | (whatever — ★s) |

merx –cis (f) = merchandise,
goods

| | | |
|---|---|---|
| mercīs | (a) | –īs |
| | (b) | acc pl |
| | (c) | (whatever goods — ★s) |

vehō –here –xī –ctum = to carry,
bring

| | | |
|---|---|---|
| vexeram, | (a) | –eram |
| | (b) | pluperf indic, 1st sing act |
| | (c) | (whatever goods I had brought), |

omnis –is –e = every, all

| | | |
|---|---|---|
| omnīs | (a) | –īs |
| | (b) | acc pl masc/fem |
| | (c) | where — ★s all the — |

vendō –ere –idī –itum = to sell

| | | |
|---|---|---|
| vendidī. | (a) | –ī |
| | (b) | perf indic, 1st sing act |
| | (c) | where I sold all the —. |

| | |
|---|---|
| Translation | We came to Rhodes, where I sold all the goods which I had brought. |

## 3. sequentur tē quōcumque pervēneris vitia. (Sen. *Ep.* 28.1)

sequor –quī –cūtus = to follow

                                       sequentur
(a) –entur
(b) fut indic, 3rd pl pass
(c) — will follow —

tū = you

                                       tē
(a) –ē
(b) acc sing
(c) — will follow you

quōcumque = to any place to which, wherever

perveniō –enīre –ēnī –entum (intr) = to come (to), get (to)

         quōcumque pervēneris
(a) –eris
(b) fut perf, 2nd sing act
(c) — will follow you wherever you will have got to

vitium –[i]ī (n) = a fault, vice

                                   vitia.
(a) –a
(b) nom pl
(c) vices will follow you wherever you will have got to.

                           Translation
Your vices will follow you wherever you get to.

263

## 4.          mihi dulcēs
### ignoscent, sī quid peccārō stultus, amīcī.
### (Hor. *Serm.* 1.3.140)

ego = I

| | | |
|---|---|---|
| mihi | (a) | –i |
| | (b) | dat sing |
| | (c) | — ⋆s to/for me |

dulcis –is –e = sweet, kind

| | | |
|---|---|---|
| dulcēs | (a) | –ēs |
| | (b) | nom/acc pl masc/fem |
| | (c) | kind — ⋆ / — ⋆s kind — to/for me |

ignoscō –oscere –ōvī –ōtum
(w.dat) = to forgive

| | | |
|---|---|---|
| ignoscent, | (a) | –ent |
| | (b) | fut indic, 3rd pl act |
| | (c) | kind — will forgive me, |

sī (conj) = if
quis qua quid = anyone, anything

| | | |
|---|---|---|
| sī quid | (a) | –d |
| | (b) | nom/acc sing neut |
| | (c) | if anything ⋆s / — ⋆s anything |

peccō –āre –āvī –ātum (intr) = to
make a mistake, do wrong

| | | |
|---|---|---|
| peccārō (peccāverō) | (a) | –erō |
| | (b) | fut perf, 1st sing act |
| | (c) | if I will have done wrong in any way |

stultus –a –um = foolish

| | | |
|---|---|---|
| stultus, | (a) | –us |
| | (b) | nom sing masc |
| | (c) | if I foolish will have done wrong in any way, |

amīcus –ī (m) = a friend

| | | |
|---|---|---|
| amīcī. | (a) | –ī |
| | (b) | nom pl |
| | (c) | kind friends will forgive me. |

| | |
|---|---|
| Translation | Kind friends will forgive me, if I do wrong in any way. |

# 5. utinam ante vīdissēs neque tōtum animum tuum maerōrī dedissēs! (Cic. *Att.* 3.8.4)

utinam (particle introducing a
    wish) = if only!
ante (adv) = before, beforehand
videō vidēre vīdī vīsum = to see

| | | |
|---|---|---|
| utinam ante vīdissēs | (a) | –issēs |
| | (b) | pluperf subj, 2nd sing act |
| | (c) | if only you had seen — beforehand! |

neque (conj) = and ... not, nor
tōtus –a –um = the whole, all

| | | |
|---|---|---|
| neque tōtum | (a) | –um |
| | (b) | nom/acc sing neut *or* acc sing masc |
| | (c) | and the whole — not ★ / — not ★ the whole —! |

animus –ī (m) = the mind, spirit

| | | |
|---|---|---|
| animum | (a) | –um |
| | (b) | acc sing |
| | (c) | and — not ★ the whole mind! |

tuus –a –um = your (own)

| | | |
|---|---|---|
| tuum | (a) | –um |
| | (b) | acc sing masc |
| | (c) | and — not ★ your whole mind! |

maeror –ōris (m) = grief

| | | |
|---|---|---|
| maerōrī | (a) | –ī |
| | (b) | dat sing |
| | (c) | and — not ★ your whole mind to/for grief! |

dō dare dedī datum = to give,
    give over

| | | |
|---|---|---|
| dedissēs! | (a) | –issēs |
| | (b) | pluperf subj, 2nd sing act |
| | (c) | and you had not given over your whole mind to grief! |

| | |
|---|---|
| Translation | If only you had seen beforehand and had not given over your whole mind to grief! |

# Summary of Examples

1. vēnistīne domum ad tuōs penātēs?

2. Rhodum vēnimus ubi, quās mercīs vexeram,
   omnīs vendidī.

3. sequentur tē quōcumque pervēneris vitia.

4. mihi dulcēs ignoscent, sī quid peccārō stultus, amīcī.

5. utinam ante vīdissēs neque tōtum animum tuum maerōrī dedissēs!

# Exercises

Change the verb in the following sentences into the other persons, singular and plural, and translate:

Rhodum pervēnī.
multās mercīs vexeram.
omnīs hās mercīs vendidī.
paucīs diēbus domum vēnerō.
sed frustrā sum gāvīsus.

# Reading

1. pater ad mercātum hinc mē meus mīsit Rhodum;
   biennium iam factum est postquam abiī domō.
   ibi amāre occēpī formā eximiā mulierem.
   (Pl. *Mer.* 11)

   abeō –īre –iī –itum (intr) = to go away
   biennium –[i]ī (n) = a period of two years
   eximius –a –um = outstanding, exceptionally fine
   forma –ae (f) = form, shape, beauty
   hinc (adv) = hence, from here
   ibi (adv) = there, there and then
   mercātus –ūs (m) = a market, fair
   mulier –eris (f) = a woman
   occipiō –ipere –ēpī –eptum = to take up, begin
   postquam (conj) = after, since
   Rhodus –ī (f) = the island of Rhodes

2. tū modo, dum lūcet, fructum nē dēsere vītae!
   omnia sī dederis oscula, pauca dabis.
   (Prop. 2.15.49)

   dēserō –ere –uī –tum = to forsake, abandon, give up
   dum (conj) = as long as, while
   fructus –ūs (m) = the enjoyment (of something), fruit
   lūcet –ēre luxit (intr) = it is light, there is life
   modo (adv) = just, only
   osculum –ī (n) = a kiss
   paucī –ae –a = few

3. sed vidēn? fortūna hūmāna fingit artatque ut libet:
   mē quī līber fueram servum fēcit, ē summō infimum;
   quī imperāre insuēram, nunc alterius imperiō obsequor.
   (Pl. *Capt.* 304)

   (N.B. vidēn? = vidēsne?)

   alter –era –erum = another (of two)
   artō –āre –āvī –ātum = to fix tightly, restrict
   ē (prep w.abl) = from, from being
   fingō –ngere –nxī –ctum = to form, shape
   fortūna –ae (f) = fortune
   hūmānus –a –um = human
   imperō –āre –āvī –ātum (w.dat) = to order, command
   imperium –[i]ī (n) = authority, command
   infimus –a –um = lowest
   insuescō –escere –ēvī –ētum = to become accustomed (to)
   līber –era –erum = free
   libet –ēre –uit (w.dat) = it is pleasing (to)
   –ne? (interrogative particle) = can it be that ... ?
   obsequor –quī –cūtus (w.dat) = to follow, submit (to)
   servus –ī (m) = a slave
   summus –a –um = highest
   ut = as

4.  *omnēs nātiōnēs servitūtem ferre possunt: nostra cīvitās nōn potest, nec ullam aliam ob causam, nisi quod nōs ita ā māioribus institūtī atque imbūtī sumus, ut omnia consilia atque facta ad dignitātem et ad virtūtem referrēmus. (Cic. *Phil.* 10.20)

ad (prep w.acc) = to, by reference to
alius -a -ud = different, other
causa -ae (f) = a cause, reason
cīvitās -ātis (f) = a city, state
consilium -[i]ī (n) = counsel, a plan
dignitās -ātis (f) = worthiness, excellence
factum -ī (n) = a deed, action
imbuō -uere -uī -ūtum = to moisten, permeate
instituō -uere -uī -ūtum = to set up, instruct
ita (adv) = so, in such a way
māior -ior -ius = greater, older; (m.pl) ancestors
nātiō -ōnis (f) = a people, nation
nisi (conj) = if not, except
ob (prep w.acc) = because of
quod (conj) = because
referō -rre rettulī relātum = to bring back, refer, judge
servitūs -ūtis (f) = slavery, enslavement
ullus -a -um = any

5.  hīc mihi servitium videō dominamque parātam:
    iam mihi, lībertās illa paterna, valē!
    servitium sed triste datur, teneorque catēnīs,
      et numquam miserō vincla remittit Amor,
    et seu quid meruī seu nīl peccāvimus, ūrit.
      ūror, iō, removē, saeva puella, facēs! (Tib. 2.4.1)

catēna -ae (f) = a chain, fetter
fax -cis (f) = a torch, firebrand
hīc (adv) = here
iō (interjection) = ah!
lībertās -ātis (f) = freedom
mereō -ēre -uī -itum = to earn, deserve
parō -āre -āvī -ātum = to provide, prepare
paternus -a -um = of one's father or forefathers
peccō -āre -āvī -ātum (intr) = to make a mistake, do wrong
quis qua quid = anyone, anything
remittō -ittere -īsī -issum = to let go back, slacken
removeō -ovēre -ōvī -ōtum = to move back, take away
saevus -a -um = savage, cruel
servitium -[i]ī (n) = slavery, enslavement
seu ... seu (conjs) = whether ... or
teneō -ēre -uī -tum = to hold (fast), keep in check
tristis -is -e = gloomy, grim

ūrō –ere ussī ustum = to heat by fire, burn
valē! = goodbye!
vinclum –ī (n) = a chain, fetter

6.  numquam virtūtis molle documentum est. verberat nōs et
    lacerat fortūna: patiāmur. nōn est saevitia, certāmen est, quod
    quō saepius adierimus, fortiōrēs erimus: solidissima corporis
    pars est quam frequens ūsus agitāvit. (Sen. *Dial.* 1.4.12)

    adeō –īre –iī –itum = to go to, engage in
    agitō –āre –āvī –ātum = to set in motion, exercise
    certāmen –inis (n) = exertion, struggle
    corpus –oris (n) = the body
    documentum –ī (n) = teaching, an example
    fortūna –ae (f) = fortune
    frequens –ntis = repeated, frequent
    lacerō –āre –āvī –ātum = to tear, torture
    mollis –is –e = soft, gentle
    pars –tis (f) = a part
    patior –tī –ssus = to undergo, tolerate
    quō ... (eō) = the (more) ... the (more)
    saepe (adv) = often
    saevitia –ae (f) = savageness, cruelty
    solidus –a –um = solid, firm
    ūsus –ūs (m) = use
    verberō –āre –āvī –ātum = to flog, batter

7.  atque utinam dominae mītī quoque praeda fuissem,
        formōsae quoniam praeda futūrus eram!   (Ov. *Am.* 2.17.5)

    formōsus –a –um = shapely, beautiful
    mītis –is –e = soft, gentle
    praeda –ae (f) = plunder, prey
    quoniam (conj) = since, because
    quoque (adv) = as well, also
    utinam (particle introducing a wish) = if only!

8.  imbēcillī fluvidīque inter vāna constitimus: ad illa mittāmus
    animum quae aeterna sunt. (Sen. *Ep.* 58.27)

    aeternus –a –um = eternal, everlasting
    constō –āre –itī (intr) = to take up a position, stand (still)
    fluvidus –a –um = flowing, impermanent
    imbēcillus –a –um = weak, feeble
    inter (prep w.acc) = among, in the midst of
    vānus –a –um = empty, illusory

9.  o dī, sī vestrum est miserērī, aut sī quibus umquam
        extrēmam iam ipsā in morte tulistis opem,
    mē miserum aspicite et, sī vītam pūriter ēgī,
        ēripite hanc pestem perniciemque mihi!          (Catul. 76.17)

    agō agere ēgī actum = to drive, live
    aspiciō –icere –exī –ectum = to catch sight of, look at
    deus deī (m) = a god (nom.pl: dī)
    ēripiō –ipere –ipuī –eptum = to tear away
    extrēmus –a –um = uttermost, last-minute
    misereor –ērī –itus (w.gen) = to pity
    mors –tis (f) = death
    ops opis (f) = resource, help
    perniciēs –ēī (f) = death, a bane
    pestis –is (f) = death, a plague
    pūrus –a –um = clean, innocent (adv: pūriter)
    quis qua quid = anyone, anything

10. *nihil ignōverīs! nihil grātiae causā fēcerīs! misericordiā com-
    mōtus nē sīs! in sententiā permanētō! (Cic. *Mur.* 65)

    causā (prep w.gen) = for the sake of, because of
    commoveō –overe –ōvī –ōtum = to move vigorously, stir
    grātia –ae (f) = favour, kindness
    ignoscō –oscere –ōvī –ōtum = to forgive
    misericordia –ae (f) = pity
    permaneō –ēre –sī –sum (intr) = to remain, persist
    sententia –ae (f) = an opinion, intention

# Vocabulary to Learn

deus deī (m) = a god
imperō –āre –āvī –ātum (w.dat) = to order, command
māior –ior –ius = greater, older, elder
quis qua quid = anyone, anything
sequor –quī –cūtus = to follow

# 21
# CONDITIONAL CLAUSES

## Morphology

Conditional clauses do not introduce any new forms.

## Syntax

Conditional clauses are introduced by conjunctions such as *sī* "if", *nisi* "if not, unless", and *sīve / seu ... sīve / seu* "whether ... or". They express the condition under which the statement, question or command of the main clause is true, but different types of conditional clause imply different things about the likelihood of the condition's being fulfilled.

**1.** Clauses with the indicative express an "open" condition, i.e. one which implies nothing about its fulfilment:

> nullī **negō**, sī quis mē essum **vocat**.
> **I refuse** no-one, if anyone **invites** me to eat.

The verbs in the two clauses may be in any tense of the indicative, often though not necessarily the same:

> nullī **negāvī**, sī quis mē essum **vocāvit**.
> **I have refused** no-one, if anyone **has invited** me to eat.

> nullī **negābō**, sī quis mē essum **vocābit**.
> **I will refuse** no-one, if anyone **invites** (**will invite**) me to eat.

nullī **negābō**, sī quis mē essum **vocāverit**.
**I will refuse** no-one, if anyone **invites** (**will have invited**)
me to eat.

The main clause may be a question or command:

**num** tū negās, sī quis tē essum vocat?
**surely** you do **not** refuse, if anyone invites you to eat?

**nōlī negāre**, sī quis tē essum vocābit!
**don't refuse**, if anyone invites you to eat!

The conditional clause may have a 2nd singular present subjunctive
(see chapter 15 syntax §2) in place of the indicative:

nēmō negat, sī quem essum **vocēs**.
no-one refuses, if **you invite** / **one invites** someone to eat.

**2.** Clauses with the present or perfect subjunctive express a "hypothetical" condition, i.e. one which is granted only as an assumption
and may or may not be fulfilled:

nullī **negem**, sī quis mē essum **vocet**.
**I would refuse** no-one, if anyone **were to invite** / **invited**
me to eat.

nullī **negem**, sī quis mē essum **vocāverit**.
**I would refuse** no-one, if anyone **were to have invited** /
**invited** me to eat.

**3.** Clauses with the imperfect or pluperfect subjunctive express an
"unreal" condition, i.e. one which is contrary to fact and cannot be
fulfilled:

nullī **negārem**, sī quis mē essum **vocāret**.
**I would be refusing** no-one, if anyone **were inviting** /
**invited** me to eat.

nullī **negāvissem**, sī quis mē essum **vocāvisset**.
**I would have refused** no-one, if anyone **had invited** me to
eat.

**4.** In clauses with the subjunctive, an optative or jussive subjunctive is
normally used in the conditional clause and a potential subjunctive in
the main clause: but certain verbs or verb phrases remain in the
indicative since their own meaning approximates to the force of the
subjunctive:

(a) verbs of duty or possibility such as *dēbēre* "ought" and *posse* "to be able":

> nēmō negāre **poterat**, sī quem essum vocāret erus meus.
> no-one **was able to** / **could** refuse, if my master were inviting someone to eat.

(b) *esse* "to be", especially with future participles and gerundives:

> nēmō **negātūrus fuit**, sī quis essum vocāvisset erus meus.
> no-one **was going to refuse** / **would have refused**, if my master had invited someone to eat.

# Metaphrasing

The different tenses of the indicative and subjunctive are metaphrased in the usual way, but a subjunctive in a conditional clause will need an alternative metaphrase:

| | |
|---|---|
| sī vocet | if — were to invite / invited — |
| sī vocāret | if — were inviting / invited — |
| sī vocāvisset | if — had invited — |

# Examples

## 1. sī sunt dī, beneficī in hominēs sunt.
## (Cic. *Div*. 2.104)

sī (conj) = if
sum esse fuī = to be

| | | |
|---|---|---|
| sī sunt | (a) | –nt |
| | (b) | pres indic, 3rd pl act |
| | (c) | if there are — / — are — |

deus deī (m) = a god (nom.pl: dī)

| | | |
|---|---|---|
| dī, | (a) | –ī |
| | (b) | nom pl |
| | (c) | if there are gods, |

beneficus –a –um = beneficent, kind

| | | |
|---|---|---|
| beneficī | (a) | –ī |
| | (b) | nom pl masc *or* gen sing masc/neut |
| | (c) | kind — ★ *or* of a kind — |

in (prep w.acc/abl) = into, towards / in, on
homō –inis (m) = a human being, man

| | | |
|---|---|---|
| in hominēs | (a) | –ēs |
| | (b) | acc pl |
| | (c) | kind — ★ towards men *or* of a kind — towards men |

sum esse fuī = to be

| | | |
|---|---|---|
| sunt. | (a) | –nt |
| | (b) | pres indic, 3rd pl act |
| | (c) | — are kind towards men. |

| | |
|---|---|
| Translation | If there are gods, they are kind towards men. |

## 2.   vocem tē ad cēnam, nisi egomet cēnem forīs.
(Pl. *St.* 190)

vocō –āre –āvī –ātum = to call,
    invite

| | | |
|---|---|---|
| vocem | (a) | –em |
| | (b) | pres subj, 1st sing act |
| | (c) | I would/should invite — |

tū = you

| | | |
|---|---|---|
| tē | (a) | –ē |
| | (b) | acc sing |
| | (c) | I would/should invite you |

ad (prep w.acc) = to
cēna –ae (f) = dinner

| | | |
|---|---|---|
| ad cēnam, | (a) | –am |
| | (b) | acc sing |
| | (c) | I would/should invite you to dinner, |

nisi (conj) = if not
egomet = I myself

| | | |
|---|---|---|
| nisi egomet | (a) | –o |
| | (b) | nom sing |
| | (c) | if I myself not ★ |

cēnō –āre –āvī –ātum (intr) = to
    dine
forīs (adv) = out of doors, away
    from home, out

| | | |
|---|---|---|
| cēnem forīs. | (a) | –em |
| | (b) | pres subj, 1st sing act |
| | (c) | if I myself were not to dine out. |

| | |
|---|---|
| Translation | I would invite you to dinner, if I myself were not (going) to dine out. |

## 3. *sī acum quaererēs, acum invēnissēs iam diū. (Pl. *Men.* 238)

sī (conj) = if
acus –ūs (f) = a pin, needle

| | | |
|---|---|---|
| sī acum | (a) | –um |
| | (b) | acc sing |
| | (c) | if — *s a needle |

quaerō –rere –sīvī –sītum = to
    look for

| | | |
|---|---|---|
| quaererēs, | (a) | –rēs |
| | (b) | imperf subj, 2nd sing act |
| | (c) | if you were looking for a needle, |

acus –ūs (f) = a pin, needle

| | | |
|---|---|---|
| acum | (a) | –um |
| | (b) | acc sing |
| | (c) | — *s a needle |

inveniō –enīre –ēnī –entum = to
    come upon, find
iam diū (advs) = for a long time
    now, long ago

| | | |
|---|---|---|
| invēnissēs iam diū. | (a) | –issēs |
| | (b) | pluperf subj, 2nd sing act |
| | (c) | you would have found a needle long ago. |

| | |
|---|---|
| Translation | If you were looking for a needle, you would have found a needle long ago. |

## 4.  ferreus essem, sī tē nōn amārem.
(Cic. *Fam*. 15.21.3)

ferreus –a –um = made of iron,
    hard-hearted

|  | ferreus | (a) | –us |
|---|---|---|---|
|  |  | (b) | nom sing masc |
|  |  | (c) | a hard-hearted — ★s |

sum esse fuī = to be

|  | essem, | (a) | –sem |
|---|---|---|---|
|  |  | (b) | imperf subj, 1st sing act |
|  |  | (c) | I would/should be hard-hearted, |

sī (conj) = if
tū = you

|  | sī tē | (a) | –ē |
|---|---|---|---|
|  |  | (b) | acc/abl sing |
|  |  | (c) | if — ★s you / — ★s by/with/from you |

nōn = not
amō –āre –āvī –ātum = to love

|  | nōn amārem. | (a) | –rem |
|---|---|---|---|
|  |  | (b) | imperf subj, 1st sing act |
|  |  | (c) | if I were not loving you. |

|  | Translation | I would be hard-hearted, if I did not love you. |
|---|---|---|

## 5. vīna parant animum Venerī, nisi plūrima sūmās. (Ov. *Rem.* 805)

vīnum –ī (n) = wine; (pl)
    draughts of wine

| | | |
|---|---|---|
| vīna | (a) | –a |
| | (b) | nom/acc pl |
| | (c) | draughts of wine ★ / — ★s draughts of wine |

parō –āre –āvī –ātum = to pro-
    vide, prepare

| | | |
|---|---|---|
| parant | (a) | –nt |
| | (b) | pres indic, 3rd pl act |
| | (c) | draughts of wine prepare — / — prepare draughts of wine |

animus –ī (m) = the mind, spirit

| | | |
|---|---|---|
| animum | (a) | –um |
| | (b) | acc sing |
| | (c) | draughts of wine prepare the mind |

Venus –eris (f) = Venus (goddess
    of love), sex

| | | |
|---|---|---|
| Venerī, | (a) | –ī |
| | (b) | dat sing |
| | (c) | draughts of wine prepare the mind for love, |

nisi (conj) = if not, unless
plūrimī –ae –a = very many

| | | |
|---|---|---|
| nisi plūrima | (a) | –a |
| | (b) | nom/acc pl neut |
| | (c) | unless very many — ★ / — ★s very many — |

sūmō –mere –mpsī –mptum = to
    take up, take

| | | |
|---|---|---|
| sūmās. | (a) | –ās |
| | (b) | pres subj, 2nd sing act |
| | (c) | unless you take very many —. |

| | |
|---|---|
| Translation | Draughts of wine prepare the mind for love, unless you take very many. |

# Summary of Examples

1. sī sunt dī, beneficī in hominēs sunt.

2. vocem tē ad cēnam, nisi egomet cēnem forīs.

3. sī acum quaererēs, acum invēnissēs iam diū.

4. ferreus essem, sī tē nōn amārem.

5. vīna parant animum Venerī, nisi plūrima sūmās.

# Exercises

Change the verb in the following sentences from the indicative to the corresponding tense of the subjunctive and translate:

sī quis mē essum vocat, beneficus est.
sī quis ferreus erat, nēminem ad cēnam vocābat.
sī quis bonam cēnam dederat, multum vīnī parāverat.
sī quis nimium vīnī biberat, ēbrius erat.
sī quis nōn nulla vīna sumpsit, Venerī parātus est.

# Reading

1.  nihil est tam fallax quam vīta hūmāna, nihil tam insidiōsum: nōn meherculēs quisquam illam accēpisset, nisi darētur ignōrantibus. (Sen. *Dial.* 6.22.3)

    accipiō –ipere –ēpī –eptum = to take (hold of), accept
    fallax –ācis = deceitful, treacherous
    hūmānus –a –um = human
    ignōrō –āre –āvī –ātum = to have no knowledge of
    insidiōsus –a –um = full of hidden dangers, hazardous
    meherculēs (interjection) = by Hercules
    nisi (conj) = if not, unless
    quisquam quicquam = anyone, anything
    tam ... quam = to such a degree ... as, so ... as

2. *et sī quis deus mihi largiātur ut ex hāc aetāte repuerascam et in
   cūnīs vāgiam, valdē recūsem. quid habet enim vīta commodī?
   quid nōn potius labōris? (Cic. *Sen.* 83)

   aetās –ātis (f) = one's age
   commodum –ī (n) = an advantage, benefit
   cūnae –ārum (f.pl) = a cradle
   largior –īrī –ītus = to bestow, grant
   potius (compar.adv) = rather, instead
   recūsō –āre –āvī –ātum = to demur, protest
   repuerascō –ere (intr) = to become a boy again
   vāgiō –īre –īvī (intr) = to wail, cry
   valdē (adv) = vigorously, strongly

3. sī in aliquā dēsertissimā sōlitūdine ad saxa et ad scopulōs haec
   conquerī ac dēplōrāre vellem, tamen omnia mūta atque inanima
   tantā et tam indignā rērum acerbitāte commovērentur. (Cic.
   *Ver.* 5.171)

   acerbitās –ātis (f) = harshness, cruelty
   aliquī –qua –quod = some or other
   commoveō –ovēre –ōvī –ōtum = to move vigorously, stir
   conqueror –rī –stus = to complain of, bewail
   dēplōrō –āre –āvī –ātum = to lament
   dēsertus –a –um = deserted, uninhabited
   inanimus –a –um = lifeless, inanimate
   indignus –a –um = undeserving, undeserved
   mūtus –a –um = dumb, silent
   saxum –ī (n) = a rock, boulder
   scopulus –ī (m) = a crag, cliff
   sōlitūdō –inis (f) = solitude
   tam (adv) = to such a degree, so
   tamen (adv) = nevertheless, yet
   tantus –a –um = so great

4. cēnābis bene, mī Fabulle, apud mē
   paucīs, sī tibi dī favent, diēbus,
   sī tēcum attuleris bonam atque magnam
   cēnam, non sine candidā puellā
   et vīnō et sale et omnibus cachinnīs.          (Catul. 13.1)

   afferō –rre attulī allātum = to carry to, bring
   apud (prep w.acc) = at, at the house of
   cachinnus –ī (m) = a laugh, guffaw
   candidus –a –um = bright, white, fair-skinned
   cēna –ae (f) = dinner
   cēnō –āre –āvī –ātum (intr) = to dine
   –cum (prep w.abl) = with

Fabullus -ī (m) = Fabullus (a friend of Catullus)
faveō -ēre fāvī fautum (w.dat) = to favour
magnus -a -um = great, big
meus -a -um = my (own) (voc.sing: mī)
paucī -ae -a = few
sāl salis (m) = salt, wit
sine (prep w.abl) = without
vīnum -ī (n) = wine

5. nihil enim est tam angustī animī tamque parvī quam amāre
dīvitiās, nihil honestius magnificentiusque quam pecūniam
contemnere, sī nōn habeās, sī habeās, ad beneficentiam līberā-
litātemque conferre. (Cic. *Off*. 1.68)

angustus -a -um = narrow, limited
beneficentia -ae (f) = beneficence, kindness
conferō -rre contulī collātum = to carry, apply
contemnō -nere -psī -ptum = to despise, disregard
dīvitiae -ārum (f.pl) = riches, wealth
honestus -a -um = honourable
līberālitās -ātis (f) = generosity
magnificus -a -um = splendid (compar: magnificentior -ior -ius)
parvus -a -um = small, petty
pecūnia -ae (f) = wealth, money
tam ... quam = to such a degree ... as, so ... as

6. neque enim bonitās nec līberālitās nec cōmitās esse potest, nōn
plūs quam amīcitia, sī haec nōn per sē expetantur sed ad
voluptātem ūtilitātemve referantur. (Cic. *Off*. 3.118)

ad (prep w.acc) = to, by reference to
amīcitia -ae (f) = friendship
bonitās -ātis (f) = goodness, kindness
cōmitās -ātis (f) = friendliness, courtesy
expetō -ere -īvī -ītum = to seek out, seek after
līberālitās -ātis (f) = generosity
neque ... nec (conjs) = neither ... nor
per sē = for his, her, its, etc. (own) sake
plūs (compar.adv) = to a greater extent, more
referō -rre rettulī relātum = to bring back, refer, judge
ūtilitās -ātis (f) = utility, expediency
-ve (conj) = or
voluptās -ātis (f) = pleasure

7. ō nāta mēcum consule Manliō,
   seu tū querēlās sīve geris iocōs
   seu rixam et insānōs amōrēs
   seu facilem, pia testa, somnum,

   quōcumque lectum nōmine Massicum
   servās, movērī digna bonō diē,
   dēscende, Corvīnō iubente
   prōmere languidiōra vīna.          (Hor. *Carm.* 3.21.1)

consul -lis (m) = a consul (the highest magistrate)
Corvīnus -ī (m) = M.Valerius Messalla Corvinus (a distinguished
    friend of Horace)
-cum (prep w.abl) = with, at the same time as
dēscendō -dere -dī -sum (intr) = to come down, descend
dignus -a -um = worthy, deserving (to)
facilis -is -e = easy, easeful
gerō -rere -ssī -stum = to bear, contain
insānus -a -um = demented, crazy
iocus -ī (m) = a joke
iubeō -bēre -ssī -ssum = to order, ask (to)
languidus -a -um = enfeebled, mellow
lectus -a -um = choice, select
Manlius -[i]ī (m) = L.Manlius Torquatus (consul in 65 BC)
Massicum -ī (n) = Massic wine
moveō -ēre mōvī mōtum = to move, disturb
nascor -ī nātus (intr) = to be born
nōmen -inis (n) = a name, heading, account
ō (interjection) = oh
pius -a -um = faithful to moral obligations, dutiful
prōmō -mere -mpsī -mptum = to bring forth, fetch out
querēla -ae (f) = a complaint
quīcumque quaecumque quodcumque = whoever, whatever
rixa -ae (f) = a quarrel, brawl
servō -āre -āvī -ātum = to watch over, preserve
seu ... sīve / seu (conjs) = whether ... or
somnus -ī (m) = sleep
testa -ae (f) = an earthenware jar, wine-jar
vīnum -ī (n) = wine; (pl) bowls of wine

8. in ipsā enim Graeciā philosophia tantō in honōre numquam
   fuisset, nisi doctissimōrum contentiōnibus dissensiōnibusque
   viguisset. (Cic. *Tusc.* 2.4)

   contentiō –ōnis (f) = exertion, a dispute
   dissensiō –ōnis (f) = a disagreement
   doctus –a –um = learned, wise
   Graecia –ae (f) = Greece
   honōs –ōris (m) = honour
   nisi (conj) = if not
   philosophia –ae (f) = philosophy
   tantus –a –um = so great
   vigeō –ēre –uī (intr) = to be active or lively, flourish

9. mors ad tē venit; timenda erat, sī tēcum esse posset: necesse est
   aut nōn perveniat aut transeat. (Sen. *Ep.* 4.3)

   –cum (prep w.abl) = with
   mors –tis (f) = death
   necesse (adv) = necessary, inevitable
   perveniō –enīre –ēnī –entum (intr) = to come (to), get (to)
   timeō –ēre –uī = to be afraid of, fear
   transeō –īre –īvī –itum = to go through or over, pass by

10. mellītōs oculōs tuōs, Iuventī,
    sī quis mē sinat usque bāsiāre,
    usque ad mīlia bāsiem trecenta
    nec numquam videar satur futūrus,
    nōn sī densior āridīs aristīs
    sit nostrae seges osculātiōnis.                    (Catul. 48.1)

    āridus –a –um = dry, parched
    arista –ae (f) = an ear of corn
    bāsiō –āre –āvī –ātum = to kiss
    densus –a –um = dense, closely packed together
    futūrus –a –um (esse) = to be going to be, likely to be
    Iuventius –[i]ī (m) = Juventius (son of a distinguished family)
    mellītus –a –um = containing honey, honey-sweet
    mille (indecl.adj) = a thousand; (pl.neut: mīlia)
    oculus –ī (m) = the eye
    osculātiō –ōnis (f) = kissing
    satur –ra –rum = well-fed, replete
    seges –etis (f) = a field or crop of standing corn
    sinō sinere sīvī situm = to let, allow
    trecentī –ae –a = three hundred
    usque (adv) = all the way (to), up (to), continually

# Vocabulary to Learn

dīvitiae –ārum (f.pl) = riches, wealth
neque/nec ... neque/nec (conjs) = neither ... nor
nisi (conj) = if not
vocō –āre –āvī –ātum = to call, invite
voluptās –ātis (f) = pleasure

# 22
# INFINITIVES

## Morphology

The ending for the present infinitive active and passive is the imperfect stem plus *-re* and *-(r)ī*. The ending for the perfect infinitive active is the perfect active stem plus *-isse*: for the perfect infinitive passive the past participle ending in *-tus* or *-sus* plus *esse* is used. The future infinitive active is formed from the future participle ending in *-tūrus* or *-sūrus* plus *esse*: the future infinitive passive is formed from the accusative of the supine ending in *-tum* or *-sum* plus *īrī* (an impersonal passive use of *īre* "to go").

## Syntax

**1.** Present infinitives are used:

(a) as the subject, object or complement of the main verb (see chapter 1 syntax §§ 3 and 4; chapter 2 syntax §§ 1 and 2):

> illud est dulce, **esse** et **bibere**.
> this is sweet, **to eat** and **drink**.

(b) in place of a past tense of the indicative. A series of "historic" infinitives is used by historians to paint a scene in bold strokes. The subject, if expressed, remains in the nominative:

> hesternā nocte omnēs **pōtāre**, multī **cantāre**, nonnullī **saltāre**.
> last night all **drank**, many **sang**, some **danced**.

(c) with certain adjectives to express the respect in which the adjective is applied:

> et puer ipse fuit **cantārī** dignus.
> and the boy himself was worthy **to be sung about.**

This use of the infinitive however is extremely rare.

**2.** Present, perfect and future infinitives are used to turn a main clause into a subordinate clause, especially to represent an original statement in reported speech. The original subject is expressed by an accusative, the original verb by an infinitive:

> **puer** puellam **amat** → **puerum** puellam **amāre**
> **the boy loves** the girl → that **the boy loves** the girl

This "accusative and infinitive" construction is used:

(a) as the subject or complement of copulative verbs such as *esse* "to be" and *vidērī* "to seem":

> clārum est **puerum** puellam **amāre**.
> it is clear that **the boy loves** the girl.

(b) as the subject or object of verbs of saying, thinking, perceiving, etc.:

> quis nescit **puerum** puellam **amāre**?
> who does not know that **the boy loves** the girl?

**3.** The accusative and infinitive construction thus involves:

(a) an appropriate noun or pronoun for the "subject" accusative. When it is a different 3rd person "subject" from that in the main clause, pronouns such as *is* "this; he, she, it" or *ille* "that; he, she, it" are used:

> erus meus dīcit **eum** puellam amāre.
> my master says that **he** (i.e. **the boy**) loves the girl.

But when it is the same 3rd person "subject" as that in the main clause, the reflexive pronoun *sē* or *sēsē* "himself, herself, itself, themselves" is used:

et puer ipse dīcit **sē** puellam amāre.
and the boy himself says that **he** (i.e. **he himself**) loves the girl.

(b) an appropriate tense for the infinitive. The present infinitive is used for action contemporaneous with that of the main verb, the perfect infinitive for action preceding it, the future infinitive or *fore ut* plus the present or imperfect subjunctive according to the sequence of tenses rule (see chapter 13 syntax §8) for action following it:

negō: puella fidēlis **est**.
I deny: the girl **is** faithful.
negō puellam fidēlem **esse**.

negō: puella fidēlis **erat** / **fuit** / **fuerat**.
I deny: the girl **was** / **has been** / **had been** faithful.
negō puellam fidēlem **fuisse**.

negō: puella fidēlis **erit**.
I deny: the girl **will be** faithful.
negō puellam fidēlem **futūram esse** / **fore**.
negō **fore ut** puella fidēlis **sit**.

(c) the agreement of participles used in the future infinitive active and perfect infinitive passive with the "subject" accusative:

puer dīcit **sē** puellam semper **amātūrum esse**.
the boy says that **he will** always **love** the girl.

puer dīcit sē **puellam** semper **amātūram esse**.
the boy says that **the girl will** always **love** him.

(d) some danger of ambiguity with transitive verbs between the "subject" accusative and direct object accusative:

puer ipse dīcit **eam dīvitem** amāre.
the boy himself says that **she** loves **a rich man** / **a rich man** loves **her**.

Usually the context resolves the problem unless the speaker is being deliberately ambiguous.

**4.** An alternative construction is often used to avoid an impersonal passive main verb. The "subject" accusative is made the subject of the main verb with consequential changes in the agreement of adjectives and participles:

> dīcitur **illum** voluptātī **dēditum esse**.
> it is said that **he is devoted** to pleasure.

> dīcitur **ille** voluptātī **dēditus esse**.
> **he** is said **to be devoted** to pleasure.

**5.** When a subordinate clause forms part of the original statement, its verb is changed from indicative to subjunctive as an automatic consequence of the change to reported speech, the tense of the subjunctive being determined by the sequence of tenses rule (see chapter 13 syntax §8):

> ille dīxit, quī **invēnisset** novam voluptātem, eī sē praemium datūrum esse.
> he said that he would give a reward to the man who **invented** a new pleasure.

Even when there is no verb of saying, the change is still made if the subordinate clause is virtually reported speech:

> ille praemium prōposuit, quī **invēnisset** novam voluptātem.
> he offered a reward "to the man who **invented** a new pleasure".

This use of the subjunctive, like the inverted commas, indicates that the subordinate clause is part of what was originally said.

# Metaphrasing

**1.** The different tenses of the infinitive are metaphrased as follows:

(a) the present infinitive: to ★ (or: to be ★ed):

amāre                        (to love —)

(b) the perfect infinitive: to have ★ed (or: to have been ★ed):

amāvisse                     (to have loved —)

(c) the future infinitive: to be going to ★ (or: to be going to be ★ed):

amātūrum esse               (to be going to love —)

**2.** An accusative and an infinitive may need metaphrasing in one or more ways as appropriate:

(a) as a unit:

| | |
|---|---|
| eum amāre | (to love him) |

(b) as two separate elements:

| | |
|---|---|
| eum amāre | (to love —) ★s him |
| | *or* — ★s him (to love —) |

(c) as an accusative and infinitive construction:

| | |
|---|---|
| eum amāre | (that he loves — / — loves him) |

**3.** The verb of a subordinate clause in reported speech (or virtually reported speech), though subjunctive, will need to be translated by the indicative:

| | |
|---|---|
| eum quem amēs adesse | (that he whom you love is here) |

**4.** These basic patterns can then be adapted when necessary as follows:

(a) what appears to be a past or future participle in the accusative may prove to be a perfect or future infinitive from which the auxiliary verb *esse* "to be" has been separated or omitted:

| | |
|---|---|
| is sē amātum | he ★s himself (loved) |

If *esse* does not appear, it must be supplied at the end of the metaphrasing process and the translation adjusted:

| | |
|---|---|
| is sē amātum dīcit. | he says that he has been loved. |

(b) a series of present infinitives is metaphrased in the usual way; but if they prove to be historic infinitives, they will need an alternative translation:

| | |
|---|---|
| esse, bibere, cantāre | (to eat —, drink —, sing —) |
| | *or* — ate —, drank —, sang — |

# Examples

## 1. ego vērō et gaudeō et gaudēre mē dīcō.
(Plin. *Ep.* 9.23.5)

ego = I
vērō (adv) = in truth, in fact

| | | |
|---|---|---|
| ego vērō | (a) | –o˙ |
| | (b) | nom sing |
| | (c) | I in fact ★ |

et ... et (conjs) = both ... and
gaudeō –dēre gāvīsus (intr) = to
    rejoice

| | | |
|---|---|---|
| et gaudeō | (a) | –ō |
| | (b) | pres indic, 1st sing act |
| | (c) | I in fact both rejoice |

et ... et (conjs) = both ... and
gaudeō –dēre gāvīsus (intr) = to
    rejoice

| | | |
|---|---|---|
| et gaudēre | (a) | –re |
| | (b) | pres infin act |
| | (c) | I in fact both rejoice and (to rejoice) |

ego = I

| | | |
|---|---|---|
| mē | (a) | –ē |
| | (b) | acc sing |
| | (c) | and (to rejoice) ★s me / — ★s me (to rejoice) <br> *or* (that I rejoice) |

dīcō –cere –xī –ctum = to say

| | | |
|---|---|---|
| dīcō. | (a) | –ō |
| | (b) | pres indic, 1st sing act |
| | (c) | and I say (that I rejoice). |

| | |
|---|---|
| Translation | I in fact both rejoice and say that I rejoice. |

## 2. omnēs id faciunt, cum sē amārī intellegunt. (Pl. *Truc.* 17)

omnis –is –e = every, all

                    omnēs    (a)  –ēs
                                  (b)  nom/acc pl masc/fem
                                  (c)  all — ★ / — ★s all —

is ea id = this, that

                        id    (a)  –d
                                  (b)  nom/acc sing neut
                                  (c)  all — ★ this — / this — ★s all —

faciō –ere fēcī factum = to make, do

                  faciunt,    (a)  –nt
                                  (b)  pres indic, 3rd pl act
                                  (c)  all — do this —,

cum (conj) = when
sē = himself, herself, itself, etc.

                  cum sē    (a)  –ē
                                  (b)  acc/abl sing
                                  (c)  when — ★s themselves / — ★s by/
                                            with/from themselves

amō –āre –āvī –ātum = to love

                  amārī    (a)  –rī
                                  (b)  pres infin pass
                                  (c)  when — ★s themselves (to be loved) /
                                          (to be loved) ★s themselves
                                          *or* (that they are loved)

intellegō –gere –xī –ctum = to understand, realise

              intellegunt.    (a)  –nt
                                  (b)  pres indic, 3rd pl act
                                  (c)  when — realise (that they are loved).

                  Translation    They all do this, when they realise that they are loved.

## 3. *prōmittō tibi tē magnam voluptātem esse cap-tūrum. (Cic. *Fam.* 13.77.2)

prōmittō –ittere –īsī –issum = to
  promise

| | | | |
|---|---|---|---|
| | prōmittō | (a) | –ō |
| | | (b) | pres indic, 1st sing act |
| | | (c) | I promise — |

tū = you

| | | | |
|---|---|---|---|
| | tibi | (a) | –i |
| | | (b) | dat sing |
| | | (c) | I promise — to you |

tū = you

| | | | |
|---|---|---|---|
| | tē | (a) | –ē |
| | | (b) | acc sing |
| | | (c) | (that you ★ / — ★s you) |

magnus –a –um = great

| | | | |
|---|---|---|---|
| | magnam | (a) | –am |
| | | (b) | acc sing fem |
| | | (c) | (that you ★ great — / great — ★s you) |

voluptās –ātis (f) = pleasure

| | | | |
|---|---|---|---|
| | voluptātem | (a) | –em |
| | | (b) | acc sing |
| | | (c) | (that you ★ great pleasure / great pleasure ★s you) |

capiō –ere cēpī –tum = to take
  (hold of), gain

| | | | |
|---|---|---|---|
| | esse captūrum. | (a) | –tūrum esse |
| | | (b) | fut infin act |
| | | (c) | (that you will gain great pleasure). |

| | | |
|---|---|---|
| Translation | | I promise you that you will gain great pleasure. |

## 4. *mementō prōmīsisse tē mihi omne argentum redditum īrī! (Pl. *Cur.* 490)

meminī –inisse = to remember

mementō   (a)  –tō
   (b)  fut imper, 2nd sing act
   (c)  remember —!

prōmittō –ittere –īsī –issum = to promise

prōmīsisse   (a)  –isse
   (b)  perf infin act
   (c)  (that — promised —)!

tū = you

tē   (a)  –ē
   (b)  acc sing
   (c)  (that you promised — / — promised you)!

ego = I

mihi   (a)  –i
   (b)  dat sing
   (c)  (that you promised — to me / — promised you to me)!

omnis –is –e = every, all

omne   (a)  –e
   (b)  acc sing neut
   (c)  (that you promised all the — to me / all the — promised you to me)!

argentum –ī (n) = silver, money

argentum   (a)  –um
   (b)  acc sing
   (c)  (that you promised all the money to me)!

reddō –ere –idī –itum = to give back, repay

redditum īrī!   (a)  –tum īrī
   (b)  fut infin pass
   (c)  (that you promised that all the money would be repaid to me)!

Translation   Remember that you promised that all the money would be repaid to me!

## 5. negat Epicūrus iūcundē posse vīvī nisi cum virtūte vīvātur. (Cic. *Tusc.* 3.49)

negō –āre –āvī –ātum = to say no,
   deny

| | | |
|---|---|---|
| negat | (a) | –t |
| | (b) | pres indic, 3rd sing act |
| | (c) | — denies — |

Epicūrus –ī (m) = Epicurus (the
   Greek philosopher)

| | | |
|---|---|---|
| Epicūrus | (a) | –us |
| | (b) | nom sing |
| | (c) | Epicurus denies — |

iūcundus –a –um = pleasant

| | | |
|---|---|---|
| iūcundē | (a) | –ē |
| | (b) | adv |
| | (c) | Epicurus denies — pleasantly |

possum posse potuī = to be able
   (to)

| | | |
|---|---|---|
| posse | (a) | –se |
| | (b) | pres infin act |
| | (c) | (that — is able to ★ pleasantly) |

vīvō –vere –xī –ctum (intr) = to
   live

| | | |
|---|---|---|
| vīvī | (a) | –ī |
| | (b) | pres infin pass |
| | (c) | (that living is able to be done pleasantly) |

nisi (conj) = if not, unless
cum (prep w.abl) = with
virtūs –ūtis (f) = virtue

| | | |
|---|---|---|
| nisi cum virtūte | (a) | –e |
| | (b) | abl sing |
| | (c) | (unless — ★s with virtue) |

vīvō –vere –xī –ctum (intr) = to
   live

| | | |
|---|---|---|
| vīvātur. | (a) | –ātur |
| | (b) | pres subj, 3rd sing pass |
| | (c) | (unless living is done with virtue). |

| | |
|---|---|
| Translation | Epicurus denies that a pleasant life can be lived unless life is lived with virtue. |

# Summary of Examples

1. ego vērō et gaudeō et gaudēre mē dīcō.

2. omnēs id faciunt, cum sē amārī intellegunt.

3. prōmittō tibi tē magnam voluptātem esse captūrum.

4. mementō prōmīsisse tē mihi omne argentum redditum īrī!

5. negat Epicūrus iūcundē posse vīvī nisi cum virtūte vīvātur.

# Exercises

Complete the following sentences on the analogy of the first:

ego gaudeō et dīcō mē gaudēre.
ego tē videō et dīcō . . . . . . . . . . . . . . . . . . .
ego tē audiō et dīcō . . . . . . . . . . . . . . . . . . .
ego tē amō et dīcō . . . . . . . . . . . . . . . . . .
ego beātus sum et dīcō . . . . . . . . . . . . . . . . .

ego vēnī et dīcō mē vēnisse.
ego vīdī et dīcō . . . . . . . . . . . . . . . . . . . . . .
ego vīcī et dīcō . . . . . . . . . . . . . . . . . . . . . .
ego amāvī et dīcō . . . . . . . . . . . . . . . . . . . .
ego beātus eram et dīcō . . . . . . . . . . . . . . .

nōs gaudēbimus et dīcō nōs gāvīsūrōs esse.
nōs iūcundē vīvēmus et dīcō . . . . . . . . . . .
nōs voluptātem capiēmus et dīcō . . . . . . . .
nōs omnia ferēmus et dīcō . . . . . . . . . . . . .
nōs beātī erimus et dīcō . . . . . . . . . . . . . . .

# Reading

1. ille mī pār esse deō vidētur,
   ille, sī fās est, superāre dīvōs,
   quī sedens adversus identidem tē
       spectat et audit.               (Catul. 51.1)

   (N.B. mī = mihi)

   adversus (prep w.acc) = opposite
   dīvus -ī (m) = a god
   fās (n.indecl) = what is right (by divine law)
   identidem (adv) = repeatedly, continually
   pār paris (w.dat) = equal (to)
   sedeō -ēre sēdī sessum (intr) = to sit
   spectō -āre -āvī -ātum = to look at, watch
   superō -āre -āvī -ātum = to get above, surpass

2. maximās vērō virtūtes iacēre omnēs necesse est voluptāte
   dominante. (Cic. *Fin.* 2.117)

   dominor -ārī -ātus = to rule (as a despot), dominate
   iaceō -ēre -uī -itum (intr) = to lie, be overthrown
   maximus -a -um = greatest
   necesse (adv) = necessary, inevitable
   vērō (adv) = in truth, in fact

3. iūcundum, mea vīta, mihi prōpōnis amōrem
       hunc nostrum inter nōs perpetuumque fore.
   dī magnī, facite ut vērē prōmittere possit,
       atque id sincērē dīcat et ex animō,
   ut liceat nōbīs tōtā perdūcere vītā
       aeternum hoc sanctae foedus amīcitiae.    (Catul. 109.1)

   aeternus -a -um = eternal, unending
   amīcitia -ae (f) = friendship
   animus -ī (m) = the mind, heart
   faciō -ere fēcī factum = to make, bring it about (that)
   foedus -eris (n) = a treaty, agreement
   inter (prep w.acc) = among, between
   iūcundus -a -um = pleasant
   licet -ēre -uit (w.dat) = it is permitted
   magnus -a -um = great
   perdūcō -cere -xī -ctum = to lead through, continue
   perpetuus -a -um = unbroken, lasting
   prōmitto -ittere -īsī -issum = to promise
   prōpōnō -ōnere -osuī -ositum = to put before one, propose
   sanctus -a -um = sacrosanct, inviolable
   sincērus -a -um = pure, genuine
   tōtus -a -um = the whole of, all

verus -a -um = real, true
vīta -ae (f) = life (as a term of endearment)

4.  quī autem ita fruī volunt voluptātibus, ut nullī propter eās
    consequantur dolōrēs, et quī suum iūdicium retinent, nē
    voluptāte victī faciant id, quod sentiant nōn esse faciendum, iī
    voluptātem maximam adipiscuntur praetermittendā voluptāte.
    (Cic. *Fin.* 1.48)

adipiscor -ipiscī -eptus = to overtake, achieve
consequor -quī -cūtus = to follow (as a consequence)
dolor -ōris (m) = pain, distress
fruor -ī -ctus (w.abl) = to enjoy
ita (adv) = so, in such a way
iūdicium -[i]ī (n) = judgement
maximus -a -um = greatest
praetermittō -ittere -īsī -issum = to let go by, let slip
propter (prep w.acc) = because of
retineō -ēre -uī retentum = to hold back, hold on to
sentiō -tīre -sī -sum = to perceive, feel

5.  nullī sē dīcit mulier mea nūbere mālle
        quam mihi, nōn sī sē Iuppiter ipse petat.
    dīcit: sed mulier cupidō quod dīcit amantī
        in ventō et rapidā scrībere oportet aquā.      (Catul. 70.1)

amans -ntis (m) = a lover
aqua -ae (f) = water
cupidus -a -um = desirous, wanton
Iuppiter Iovis (m) = Jupiter (the supreme being)
mālō mālle māluī = to want or wish more, prefer (to)
mulier -eris (f) = a woman
nūbō -bere -psī -ptum (w.dat) = to marry
oportet -ēre -uit = it behoves, one ought
quam = than, rather than
rapidus -a -um = rushing
scrībō -bere -psī -ptum = to write
ventus -ī (m) = wind

6.  animī autem voluptātēs et dolōrēs nascī fatēmur ē corporis
    voluptātibus et dolōribus. (Cic. *Fin.* 1.55)

corpus -oris (n) = the body
dolor -ōris (m) = pain, distress
fateor -ērī fassus = to admit, declare
nascor -ī nātus (intr) = to be born

7. dīcēbās quondam sōlum tē nōsse Catullum,
   Lesbia, nec prae mē velle tenēre Iovem.
   dīlexī tum tē nōn tantum ut vulgus amīcam,
   sed pater ut gnātōs diligit et generōs.    (Catul. 72.1)

(N.B. nōsse = nōvisse)

amīca -ae (f) = a mistress
Catullus -ī (m) = C.Valerius Catullus (the love poet)
dīligō –igere –exī –ectum = to love
gener -rī (m) = a son in law
gnātus -ī (m) = a son
Iuppiter Iovis (m) = Jupiter (the supreme being)
Lesbia -ae (f) = Lesbia (the mistress of Catullus)
noscō –scere nōvī nōtum = to get to know (carnally)
prae (prep w.abl) = before, in comparison with
quondam (adv) = formerly, once
sōlus -a –um = alone
tantum (adv) = so much, merely
teneō –ēre –uī –tum = to hold, embrace
tum (adv) = then
ut = as
vulgus -ī (n) = the common people, general public

8. numquam putāvī fore ut supplex ad tē venīrem. (Cic. *Att.*
   16.16c.10)

putō –āre –āvī –ātum = to think
supplex –icis = suppliant

9. nulla potest mulier tantum sē dīcere amātam
   vērē, quantum ā mē Lesbia amāta mea est.
   nulla fidēs ullō fuit umquam foedere tanta,
   quanta in amōre tuō ex parte reperta meā est. (Catul. 87.1)

fidēs -ēī (f) = trust, good faith
foedus -eris (n) = a treaty, agreement
Lesbia -ae (f) = Lesbia (the mistress of Catullus)
mulier -eris (f) = a woman
pars -tis (f) = a part, side
reperiō -īre repperī -tum = to find (to be)
tantus -a –um ... quantus -a –um = so great as, so much as
tuus -a –um = your (own), of you
ullus -a –um = any
vērus -a –um = real, true

10. stultus et improbus hic amor est dignusque notārī. (Hor. *Serm.* 1.3.24)

dignus –a –um = worthy (to)
improbus –a –um = unprincipled, shameless
notō –āre –āvī =ātum = to mark, brand (as a sign of disgrace)
stultus –a –um = foolish

# Vocabulary to Learn

gaudeō –dēre gāvīsus (intr) = to rejoice
magnus –a –um = great
mulier –eris (f) = a woman
negō –āre –āvī –ātum = to say no, refuse, deny
semper (adv) = always

# 23
# CAUSAL, CONCESSIVE
# AND TEMPORAL CLAUSES

## Morphology

The clauses which follow do not introduce any new forms.

## Syntax

**1.** Causal clauses give a reason for the action of the main clause. They
are introduced by conjunctions such as *quia, quod* "because" and
*quandōquidem, quoniam, sīquidem* "since". The indicative is used by
the speaker to give a reason on his own authority:

> Rōmae erus meus arguitur **quod rusticus est.**
> in Rome my master is criticised **because he is unsophisti-
> cated.**

The subjunctive is used to give a reason on someone else's authority; it
is virtually a subordinate clause in reported speech (see chapter 22
syntax §5):

> Rōmae erus meus arguitur **quod rusticus sit.**
> in Rome my master is criticised **"because he is unsophisti-
> cated".**

This use of the subjunctive, like the inverted commas, indicates that the speaker is quoting someone else's reason. The same contrast of indicative and subjunctive is found when one reason is rejected in favour of another:

> Rōmae erus meus arguitur **nōn quod** improbus **sit, sed quia** rusticus **est**.
> in Rome my master is criticised **not because he is** unprincipled, **but because he is** unsophisticated.

**2.** Concessive clauses admit the existence of something in spite of which the action of the main clause takes place. They are introduced by conjunctions such as:

(a) *etsī, etiamsī, tametsī* "even if, although". As in conditional clauses (see chapter 21) the indicative is used to concede something as a fact:

> **etsī tacet** ille, palam id quidem est.
> **although he says nothing**, this is indeed evident.

The subjunctive is used to concede something as an assumption:

> **etsī taceat** ille, palam id quidem est.
> **although he may say nothing**, this is indeed evident.

(b) *licet* "granted that", *quamvīs* "as ... as you like, no matter how ...", *ut* "although", which are normally used with the subjunctive to concede not only an assumption but also a fact:

> **quamvīs** ēlegantēs illī sibi **videantur**, errant.
> **no matter how** refined **they may appear** to themselves, they are making a mistake.

(c) *quamquam* "however much, although", which is normally used with the indicative to concede a fact:

> **quamquam** ēlegantēs illī sibi **videntur**, errant.
> **however** refined **they appear** to themselves, they are making a mistake.

**3.** Temporal clauses relate the action of the main clause to the time of some other action. They are introduced by conjunctions such as:

(a) *cum* "when", *postquam* "after", *quotiens* "whenever", *simul atque / ac* "as soon as", and *ubi* "when", to refer to action earlier than that of the main clause;

(b) *dōnec*, *dum*, *quoad* "while, until", *dummodo* "so long as, provided that", and *quamdiū* "as long as", to refer to action contemporaneous with that of the main clause;

(c) *antequam / ante ... quam* and *priusquam / prius ... quam* "sooner than, before", to refer to action later than that of the main clause.

The indicative is normally used to refer to action as fact:

> exīre ex urbe **priusquam lūcescit** soleō.
> I am accustomed to get out of the city **before it gets light**.

The subjunctive is used to refer to action as wished or willed:

> exīre ex urbe **priusquam lūcescat** volō.
> I want to get out of the city **before it can get light**.

This use of the subjunctive expresses the intention of the speaker. But the logic of this is not always observed; the subjunctive comes to be used with little justification:

> tempestās minātur **antequam surgat**.
> a storm threatens **before it rises**.

# Metaphrasing

**1.** Verbs in causal clauses, whether indicative or subjunctive, are normally metaphrased by the indicative:

quia surgat                    because — rises

But when the speaker is reporting a reason on someone else's authority, it will sometimes be necessary to show this by inverted commas and/or phrases such as "it is claimed, it is said":

quia surgat                    "because — rises"
                               *or* because, it is said, — rises


**2.** Verbs in concessive clauses are normally metaphrased by the same mood in English as in Latin:

etsī surgit                    although — rises

etsī surgat                    although — may rise


**3.** Verbs in temporal clauses, whether indicative or subjunctive, are normally metaphrased by the indicative:

antequam surgat                before — rises

But when the subjunctive expresses intention, it will sometimes be necessary to show this by "can/could/should" as appropriate:

antequam surgat                before — can rise

# Examples

## 1. *gubernātōrēs, cum exsultantēs lollīginēs vīdērunt, tempestātem significārī putant. (Cic. *Div.* 2.145)

gubernātor –ōris (m) = a helmsman, pilot

| | | gubernātōrēs, | (a) | –ēs |
| | | | (b) | nom/acc pl |
| | | | (c) | helmsmen ★ / — ★s helmsmen, |

cum (conj) = when
exsultō –āre –āvī (intr) = to leap
up

| | | cum exsultantēs | (a) | –ntēs |
| | | | (b) | pres part, nom/acc pl masc/fem |
| | | | (c) | when — (leaping up) ★ / — ★s — (leaping up) |

lollīgō –inis (f) = a squid

| | | lollīginēs | (a) | –ēs |
| | | | (b) | nom/acc pl |
| | | | (c) | when squids (leaping up) ★ / — ★s squids (leaping up) |

videō vidēre vīdī vīsum = to see

| | | vīdērunt, | (a) | –ērunt |
| | | | (b) | perf indic, 3rd pl act |
| | | | (c) | when — have seen squids (leaping up), |

tempestās –ātis (f) = a portion of
time, a storm

| | | tempestātem | (a) | –em |
| | | | (b) | acc sing |
| | | | (c) | helmsmen ★ a storm |

significō –āre –āvī –ātum = to
indicate, signify

| | | significārī | (a) | –rī |
| | | | (b) | pres infin pass |
| | | | (c) | helmsmen ★ a storm (to be signified) |

putō –āre –āvī –ātum = to think

| | | putant. | (a) | –nt |
| | | | (b) | pres indic, 3rd pl act |
| | | | (c) | helmsmen think (that a storm is signified). |

Translation

Helmsmen, when they have seen squids leaping up, think that a storm is signified.

## 2.     mea māter īrāta est mihi, quia nōn redierim domum.
(Pl. *Cist*. 101)

meus –a –um = my (own)

| | | |
|---|---|---|
| mea | (a) | –a |
| | (b) | nom sing fem *or* nom/acc pl neut |
| | (c) | my — ★s *or* — ★s my — |

māter –tris (f) = a mother

| | | |
|---|---|---|
| māter | (a) | –r |
| | (b) | nom sing |
| | (c) | my mother ★s |

īrātus –a –um (w.dat) = angry (with)

| | | |
|---|---|---|
| īrāta | (a) | –a |
| | (b) | nom sing fem |
| | (c) | my angry mother ★s |

sum esse fuī = to be

| | | |
|---|---|---|
| est | (a) | –t |
| | (b) | pres indic, 3rd sing act |
| | (c) | my mother is angry |

ego = I

| | | |
|---|---|---|
| mihi, | (a) | –i |
| | (b) | dat sing |
| | (c) | my mother is angry with me, |

quia (conj) = because
nōn = not
redeō –īre –iī –itum (intr) = to come back, return

| | | |
|---|---|---|
| quia nōn redierim | (a) | –erim |
| | (b) | perf subj, 1st sing act |
| | (c) | because I have not returned |

domus –ī (f) = a house, home

| | | |
|---|---|---|
| domum. | (a) | –um |
| | (b) | acc sing |
| | (c) | because I have not returned home. |

| | |
|---|---|
| Translation | My mother is angry with me, because I have not returned home. |

## 3. ante autem vidēmus fulgōrem quam sonum audiāmus. (Sen. *Q.N.* 2.12.6)

ante ... quam (conj) = before
autem = however, but
videō vidēre vīdī vīsum = to see

| | | |
|---|---|---|
| ante autem vidēmus | (a) | –mus |
| | (b) | pres indic, 1st pl act |
| | (c) | but we see — before |

fulgor –ōris (m) = brightness, a
    flash of lightning

| | | |
|---|---|---|
| fulgōrem | (a) | –em |
| | (b) | acc sing |
| | (c) | but we see a flash of lightning before |

ante ... quam (conj) = before
sonus –ī (m) = a noise

| | | |
|---|---|---|
| quam sonum | (a) | –um |
| | (b) | acc sing |
| | (c) | before — ★s the noise |

audiō –īre –īvī –ītum = to hear

| | | |
|---|---|---|
| audiāmus. | (a) | –āmus |
| | (b) | pres subj, 1st pl act |
| | (c) | before we can hear the noise. |

| | |
|---|---|
| Translation | But we see a flash of lightning before we can hear the noise. |

## 4. manē, etsī properās! (Pl. *Per.* 272)

maneō –ere –sī –sum (intr) = to
    remain, not to go away

| | | |
|---|---|---|
| manē, | (a) | –ē |
| | (b) | pres imper, 2nd sing act |
| | (c) | don't go away! |

etsī (conj) = even if, although
properō –āre –āvī –ātum (intr) =
    to hurry, be in a hurry

| | | |
|---|---|---|
| etsī properās! | (a) | –s |
| | (b) | pres indic, 2nd sing act |
| | (c) | don't go away, even if you are in a hurry! |

## 5. cum feriant ūnum, nōn ūnum fulmina terrent.
### (Ov. *Pont.* 3.2.9)

cum (conj) = when, although
feriō –īre = to strike

|  |  |  |
|---|---|---|
| cum feriant | (a) | –ant |
|  | (b) | pres subj, 3rd pl act |
|  | (c) | although — may strike — |

ūnus –a –um = one, only one

|  |  |  |
|---|---|---|
| ūnum, | (a) | –um |
|  | (b) | acc sing masc/neut |
|  | (c) | although — may strike only one —, |

nōn = not
ūnus –a –um = one, only one

|  |  |  |
|---|---|---|
| nōn ūnum | (a) | –um |
|  | (b) | nom/acc sing neut *or* acc sing masc |
|  | (c) | not only one — ★s / — ★s not only one — |

fulmen –inis (n) = a thunderbolt

|  |  |  |
|---|---|---|
| fulmina | (a) | –a |
|  | (b) | nom/acc pl |
|  | (c) | not only one — ★s thunderbolts / thunderbolts ★ not only one — |

terreō –ēre –uī –itum = to terrify

|  |  |  |
|---|---|---|
| terrent. | (a) | –nt |
|  | (b) | pres indic, 3rd pl act |
|  | (c) | thunderbolts terrify not only one —. |

|  |  |
|---|---|
| Translation | Although thunderbolts may strike only one person, it is not only one person that they terrify. |

# Summary of Examples

1. gubernātōrēs, cum exsultantēs lollīgīnēs vīdērunt, tempestātem significārī putant.

2.　　　　　mea māter īrāta est mihi,
quia nōn redierim domum.

3. ante autem vidēmus fulgōrem quam sonum audiāmus.

4. manē, etsī properās!

5. cum feriant ūnum, nōn ūnum fulmina terrent.


# Exercises

Complete the following sentences on the analogy of the first:

quī beātē vīvit, is gaudet quod beātē vīvat.
quī honestus dīcitur, is gaudet quod honestus . . . . . . . . . . . . .
quī ēlegans vidētur, is gaudet quod ēlegans . . . . . . . . . . . . . . .
quī dīves vocātur, is gaudet quod dīves . . . . . . . . . . . . . . . . . .
quī rusticus est, is gaudet quod rusticus . . . . . . . . . . . . . . . . . .

quī beātē vīvēbat, is gaudēbat quod beātē vīveret.
quī honestus dīcēbātur, is gaudēbat quod honestus . . . . . . . . . .
quī ēlegans vidēbātur, is gaudēbat quod ēlegans . . . . . . . . . . . .
quī dīves vocābātur, is gaudēbat quod dīves . . . . . . . . . . . . . . .
quī rusticus erat, is gaudēbat quod rusticus . . . . . . . . . . . . . . .

# Reading

1. urbem princeps lustrāvit ex responsō haruspicum, quod Iovis ac Minervae aedēs dē caelō tactae erant. (Tac. *Ann.* 13.24)

   aedēs –is (f) = a temple
   caelum –ī (n) = the sky, heaven
   dē (prep w.abl) = from, about
   ex (prep w.abl) = from, in accordance with
   haruspex –icis (m) = a soothsayer
   Iuppiter Iovis (m) = Jupiter (the supreme being)
   lustrō –āre –āvī –ātum = to purify ceremonially
   Minerva –ae (f) = Minerva (goddess of wisdom and crafts)
   princeps –ipis (m) = the first man, emperor
   quod (conj) = because
   responsum –ī (n) = an answer, reply
   tangō –ere tetigī tactum = to touch, strike (with lightning)

2. vetus autem illud Catōnis admodum scītum est, quī mīrārī sē āiēbat quod nōn rīdēret haruspex haruspicem cum vīdisset. quota enim quaeque rēs ēvenit praedicta ab istīs? (Cic. *Div.* 2.51)

   admodum (adv) = very
   āiō (defective) = to say
   Catō –ōnis (m) = M.Porcius Cato (censor 184 BC)
   cum (conj) = when
   ēveniō –īre –ēvī –entum (intr) = to come out, happen
   haruspex –icis (m) = a soothsayer
   iste –a –ud = that (of yours)
   mīror –ārī –ātus = to be surprised (at), admire
   praedīcō –cere –xī –ctum = to foretell
   quisque quaeque quodque = each
   quod (conj) = because
   quotus –a –um? = as what fraction of the total?
   rīdeō –dēre –sī –sum (intr) = to laugh
   scītus –a –um = clever, knowing
   vetus –eris = old

3. ut sit magna, tamen certē lenta īra deōrum est;
   sī cūrant igitur cunctōs pūnīre nocentēs,
   quandō ad mē venient?                                 (Juv. 13.100)

   certus –a –um = certain, assured
   cunctus –a –um = the whole of; (pl) all
   cūrō –āre –āvī –ātum = to care (to)
   igitur (conj) = therefore
   īra –ae (f) = anger
   lentus –a –um = yielding, slow
   nocens –ntis = injurious, guilty
   pūniō –īre –īvī –ītum = to punish

quandō? = when?
tamen (adv) = nevertheless, yet
ut (conj) = although

4. nēmō enim ipsam voluptātem, quia voluptās sit, aspernātur aut
   ōdit aut fugit, sed quia consequuntur magnī dolōrēs eōs, quī
   ratiōne voluptātem sequī nesciunt. (Cic. *Fin.* 1.32)

   aspernor -ārī -ātus = to push away, spurn
   consequor -quī -cutus = to follow, attend on
   dolor -ōris (m) = pain, distress
   fugiō -ere fūgī = to run away from, shun
   nesciō -īre -īvī -ītum = not to know (how to)
   ōdī -isse ōsum = to hate, dislike
   quia (conj) = because
   ratiō -ōnis (f) = reason

5. est alius metuens nē crīmen poena sequātur;
   hic putat esse deōs et pēierat, atque ita sēcum:
   "dēcernat quodcumque volet dē corpore nostrō
   Īsis et īrātō feriat mea lūmina sīstrō,
   dummodo vel caecus teneam quōs abnego nummōs".
   (Juv. 13.90)

   abnegō -āre -āvī -ātum = to refuse, disavow
   alius -a -ud = different, other
   caecus -a -um = blind
   corpus -oris (n) = the body
   crīmen -inis (n) = an accusation, crime
   -cum (prep w.abl) = with
   dē (prep w.abl) = from, about
   dēcernō -ernere -rēvī -rētum = to decide, decree
   dummodo (conj) = provided that, as long as
   feriō -īre = to strike
   īrātus -a -um = angry
   Īsis -idis (f) = Isis (an Egyptian goddess)
   ita (adv) = so, in this way, as follows
   lūmen -inis (n) = light, an eye
   metuō -ere -ī metūtum = to fear
   nummus -ī (m) = a coin; (pl) money, cash
   pēierō -āre -āvī -ātum (intr) = to perjure oneself
   poena -ae (f) = penalty, punishment
   putō -āre -āvī -ātum = to think, consider
   quīcumque quaecumque quodcumque = whoever, whatever
   sīstrum -ī (n) = a rattle (used in the worship of Isis)
   teneō -ēre -uī -tum = to hold (fast), keep
   vel (adv) = even

6. sed meherculēs extrā iocum valdē mihi tuae litterae facētae ēlegantēsque vīsae sunt. illa, quamvīs rīdicula essent, sīcut erant, mihi tamen rīsum nōn mōvērunt. (Cic. *Fam.* 7.32.3)

ēlegans –ntis = tasteful, felicitous
extrā (prep w.acc) = outside, apart from
facētus –a –um = clever, witty
iocus –ī (m) = a joke, joking
littera –ae (f) = a letter of the alphabet; (pl) letter, epistle
meherculēs (interjection) = by Hercules
moveō –ēre mōvī mōtum = to move, provoke
quamvīs = as ... as you like, no matter how ...
rīdiculus –a –um = laughable, amusing
rīsus –ūs (m) = laughter
sīcut (conj) = in the same way as, just as
tamen (adv) = nevertheless, yet
valdē (adv) = vigorously, extremely

7. fēcēre tamen et aliī tālia, etsī vōs ignōrātis. (Apul. *Apol.* 9)

alius –a –ud = different, other
etsī (conj) = even if, although
ignōrō –āre –āvī –ātum = to be ignorant of, not to know
tālis –is –e = such
tamen (adv) = nevertheless, yet

8. postquam dīvitiae honōrī esse coepēre et eās glōria, imperium, potentia sequēbatur, hebescere virtūs, paupertās probrō habērī, innocentia prō malevolentiā dūcī coepit. (Sall. *Cat.* 12.1)

coepī –isse –tum = to have begun (to)
dūco –cere –xī –ctum = to lead, take (for)
glōria –ae (f) = glory
hebescō –ere (intr) = to grow blunt or sluggish
honōs –ōris (m) = honour
imperium –[i]ī (n) = authority, command
innocentia –ae (f) = innocence, blamelessness
malevolentia –ae (f) = ill will, malevolence
paupertās –ātis (f) = poverty
postquam (conj) = after
potentia –ae (f) = power, influence
prō (prep w.abl) = before, in place of, as
probrum –ī (n) = a reproach, disgrace

9.  dēlicta māiōrum immeritus luēs,
    Rōmāne, dōnec templa refēceris
    aedēsque lābentīs deōrum et
    foeda nigrō simulācra fūmō.
    (Hor. *Carm.* 3.6.1)

    aedēs –is (f) = a temple
    dēlictum –ī (n) = an offence, misdeed
    dōnec (conj) = until
    foedus –a –um = foul, dirty
    fūmus –ī (m) = smoke
    immeritus –a –um = undeserving
    lābor –bī –psus (intr) = to glide (down), collapse
    luō –ere –ī = to atone for, expiate
    niger –gra –grum = black
    reficiō –icere –ēcī –ectum = to restore, repair
    Rōmānus –ī (m) = a Roman
    simulācrum –ī (n) = a likeness, statue
    templum –ī (n) = a shrine, temple

10. incipe! quī rectē vīvendī prōrogat hōram,
    rusticus exspectat dum dēfluat amnis: at ille
    lābitur et lābētur in omne volūbilis aevum.
    (Hor. *Ep.* 1.2.41)

    aevum –ī (n) = time, eternity
    amnis –is (m) = a river
    dēfluō –ere –xī –xum (intr) = to flow downwards, flow away
    dum (conj) = while, until
    exspectō –āre –āvī –ātum (intr) = to wait
    hōra –ae (f) = an hour, the (proper) time
    incipiō –ipere –ēpī –eptum = to take in hand, begin
    lābor –bī –psus (intr) = to glide, flow
    prōrogō –āre –āvī –ātum = to prolong, postpone
    rectus –a –um = straight, right
    rusticus –ī (m) = a countryman, yokel
    volūbilis –is –e = rolling onwards

# Vocabulary to Learn

alius –a –ud = different, other
fugiō –ere fūgī = to run away from
ita (adv) = so, in this way
paupertās –ātis (f) = poverty
tamen (adv) = nevertheless, yet

# 24
# QUESTIONS

## Morphology

The future subjunctive is introduced in this chapter to complement the subjunctive tenses of the imperfect and perfect systems (see chapters 11 and 17). The future subjunctive active is formed from the future participle ending in *-tūrus* or *-sūrus* plus the present or imperfect subjunctive of *esse*; there is no corresponding passive subjunctive.

## Syntax

**1.** Direct questions are asked:

(a) by a change in the tone of voice;

(b) by a specific question word such as:

> quis? quid? = who? what?
> quī? quae? quod? = what? which?
> uter? = which of two?
> quālis? = what sort of?
> quantus? = how great?
> quot? = how many?
> quam? (with adjectives and adverbs) = how?
> quōmodo? (with verbs) = how?
> quandō? = when?
> quārē? = why?
> unde? = from where? from whom?
> ubi? = where (at)? when?
> quō? = where to?

> heu, Fortūna, **quis** est crūdēlior in nōs tē deus?
> alas, Fortune, **what** god is crueller to us than you?

(c) by an interrogative particle for which there is no simple English equivalent. The particle *-ne* is used to indicate a question, *an* to indicate surprise, disbelief or indignation:

> est**ne** hoc vērum?
> **can it be that** this is true / is this true?

> **an** hoc vērum est?
> **can it really be that** this is true / is this **really** true?

*Utrum* or *utrumne* is used to indicate that the first of two questions is being asked, *an* or *anne* (negative: *an nōn*) to indicate the second (and any subsequent) question:

> **utrum** hoc vērum est **an nōn**?
> **is it that** this is true **or is it that** it is not / is this true **or not**?

*Nōnne* is used to indicate that a positive answer is expected such as *ita* or *etiam* "yes":

> **nōnne** deōrum crūdēlissimus Fortūna est? **ita** vērō.
> Fortune **is** the cruellest of the gods, **isn't she**? **Yes** indeed.

*Num* or *numquid* is used to indicate that a negative answer is expected such as *nōn ita* "no" or *minimē* "not at all":

> **num** hoc negare potes? **minimē**.
> you **can't** deny this, **can you**? **Not at all**.

**2.** In direct questions the indicative and subjunctive are used in the usual way, the indicative for questions of fact as in the examples above, the subjunctive for questions of possibility or intention (see chapter 11 syntax §2):

> quid **censeās**? quid hominēs **crēdant**?
> what **would you advise**? what **are** men **to believe**?

**3.** Indirect questions are derived from direct questions. They are introduced by the same question words and by the interrogative particles *an*, *-ne*, *num* (its negative implication now lost) "whether" and *utrum ... an* (its negative now *necne*) "whether ... or". Indirect questions are used as the subject or object of verbs of asking, knowing, telling, etc.:

> at ego quaerō sint**ne** dī **necne** sint.
> but I ask **whether** there are **or** there are **not** gods.

**4.** In indirect questions the subjunctive is used as an automatic consequence of subordination. The choice of tense for the subjunctive is governed by the sequence of tenses rule (see chapter 13 syntax §8) and the time to which the question refers. In primary sequence the present, perfect and future subjunctive formed with *sim* are used:

## PRIMARY SEQUENCE

| | **Tense of Main Verb** | | **Tense of Subordinate Verb** |
|---|---|---|---|
| | Present | *with* | |
| *any* | "Present" Perfect | *any* | Present Time: pres subj: *sim* |
| *one* | Future | *one* | Past Time: perf subj: *fuerim* |
| *of* | Future Perfect | *of* | Future Time: fut subj: *futūrus sim* |
| | Imperative | | |

> sapientēs **rogō** quid dē hāc rē **sentiant**.
> **I ask** wise men what **they think** about this matter.

In historic sequence the imperfect, pluperfect and future subjunctive formed with *essem* are used:

## HISTORIC SEQUENCE

| | **Tense of Main Verb** | | **Tense of Subordinate Verb** |
|---|---|---|---|
| *any* | Imperfect | *with* | Present Time: imperf subj: *essem* |
| *one* | "Aorist" Perfect | *any* *one* | Past Time: pluperf subj: *fuissem* |
| *of* | Pluperfect | *of* | Future Time: fut subj: *futūrus essem* |

> sapientēs **rogābam** quid dē hāc rē **sentīrent**.
> **I asked** wise men what **they thought** about this matter.

Indirect questions with a passive verb follow the same pattern; but with no future subjunctive passive, Latin either avoids the need for it or uses the present or imperfect subjunctive with adverbs such as *mox* "presently", *brevī* "shortly" and *posteā* "afterwards" to introduce a reference to the future.

**5.** The original potential or jussive sense of the subjunctive can be retained in indirect questions:

> nē sapientēs quidem sciunt quid **respondeant**.
> not even wise men know what **they would / should reply**.

But the potential sense of the subjunctive in direct questions is normally expressed in indirect questions by the future subjunctive or the infinitive with *posse* "to be able":

> nesciunt quid **responsūrī sint / respondēre possint**.
> they do not know what **they would / could reply**.

The jussive sense of the subjunctive in direct questions is expressed in indirect questions by the gerundive of obligation (see chapter 7 syntax §2a) or the infinitive with a verb of obligation:

> nesciunt quid **respondendum sit / respondēre dēbeant**.
> they do not know what **they should reply**.

# Metaphrasing

**1.** Direct questions are metaphrased with the usual order of subject and verb inverted:

    quaeritne?               does — ask —?

Specific question words are placed at the start of the sentence:

    quid quaerit?           what does — ask?

**2.** Indirect questions are metaphrased in brackets with the usual order of subject and verb retained:

    quaeratne            (whether — asks —)

Specific question words are placed at the start of the question:

    quid quaerat         (what — asks)

**3.** A sentence beginning with a question word is metaphrased at first as a direct question. A verb in the indicative will confirm this; a verb in the subjunctive will suggest an indirect question as one of three possible alternatives, which a main verb of asking, etc. will confirm:

    quid quaerat         what would/should — ask?
                           *or* (what — asks)

**4.** These basic patterns can then be adapted when necessary as follows:

(a) on rare occasions the subjunctive in an indirect question will need an alternative metaphrase to show that in the original question was a potential or jussive subjunctive:

    quid quaerat         (what — asks)
                           *or* (what — would/should ask)

(b) on rare occasions a present or imperfect passive subjunctive with an adverb of time will need an alternative metaphrase to show that the original question referred to the future:

    quid posteā quaerātur    (what is asked afterwards)
                              (what will be asked afterwards)

# Examples

1. *videāmus prīmum deōrumne prōvidentiā mundus regātur, deinde consulantne dī rēbus hūmānīs. (Cic. *N.D.* 3.65)

videō vidēre vīdī vīsum = to see

|  |  |  |
|---|---|---|
| videāmus | (a) | –āmus |
|  | (b) | pres subj, 1st pl act |
|  | (c) | we may/would see — *or* let us see — |

prīmum (adv) = first
deus deī (m) = a god
–ne (interrogative particle) = whether

|  |  |  |
|---|---|---|
| prīmum deōrumne | (a) | –ōrum |
|  | (b) | gen pl |
|  | (c) | let us see first (whether of the gods) |

prōvidentia –ae (f) = foresight, providence

|  |  |  |
|---|---|---|
| prōvidentiā | (a) | –ā |
|  | (b) | abl sing |
|  | (c) | (whether — ★s by/with/from the providence of the gods) |

mundus –ī (m) = the firmament, the world

|  |  |  |
|---|---|---|
| mundus | (a) | –us |
|  | (b) | nom sing |
|  | (c) | (whether the world ★s by/with/from the providence of the gods) |

regō –gere –xī –ctum = to make straight, rule

|  |  |  |
|---|---|---|
| regātur, | (a) | –ātur |
|  | (b) | pres subj, 3rd sing pass |
|  | (c) | (whether the world is ruled by the providence of the gods), |

deinde = from there or then, then
consulō –ere –uī –ltum (w.dat) = to consult (the interests of), look after
–ne (interrogative particle) = whether

|  |  |  |
|---|---|---|
| deinde consulantne | (a) | –ant |
|  | (b) | pres subj, 3rd pl act |
|  | (c) | (then whether — look after —) |

deus deī (m) = a god (nom.pl: dī)

|  |  |  |
|---|---|---|
| dī | (a) | –ī |
|  | (b) | nom pl |
|  | (c) | (then whether the gods look after —) |

rēs reī (f) = a thing, affair

| | | |
|---|---|---|
| rēbus | (a) | –bus |
| | (b) | dat pl |
| | (c) | (then whether the gods look after affairs) |

hūmānus -a –um = human

| | | |
|---|---|---|
| hūmānīs. | (a) | –īs |
| | (b) | dat pl fem |
| | (c) | (then whether the gods look after human affairs). |

| | |
|---|---|
| Translation | Let us see first whether the world is ruled by the providence of the gods, then whether the gods look after human affairs. |

## 2. *quid paulō ante dīxerim nōnne meministī? (Cic. *Fin.* 2.10)

quis? quid? = who? what?

| | | |
|---|---|---|
| quid | (a) | –d |
| | (b) | nom/acc sing |
| | (c) | what ⋆s / what does — ⋆? |

paulus -a –um = small, little
  (adv: paulō)
ante (adv) = before, earlier

| | | |
|---|---|---|
| paulō ante | (a) | –ō |
| | (b) | adv |
| | (c) | what ⋆s / what does — ⋆ a little earlier? |

dīcō –cere –xī –ctum = to say

| | | |
|---|---|---|
| dīxerim | (a) | –erim |
| | (b) | perf subj, 1st sing act |
| | (c) | (what I said a little earlier) |

nōnne? (interrogative particle) = surely?
meminī –inisse = to remember

| | | |
|---|---|---|
| nōnne meministī? | (a) | –istī |
| | (b) | perf indic, 2nd sing act |
| | (c) | surely you remember (what I said a little earlier)? |

| | |
|---|---|
| Translation | Surely you remember what I said a little earlier? |

# LEARNING LATIN

## 3.  *Athēniensēs mīsērunt Delphōs consultum quidnam facerent dē rēbus suīs. (Nep. *Them.* 2.6)

Athēniensis –is –e = Athenian;
   (m.pl) the Athenians

Athēniensēs  (a)  –ēs
      (b)  nom/acc pl masc
      (c)  the Athenians ★ / — ★s the
           Athenians

mittō –ere mīsī missum = to let
   go, send

mīsērunt  (a)  –ērunt
      (b)  perf indic, 3rd pl act
      (c)  the Athenians sent — / — sent the
           Athenians

Delphī –ōrum (m.pl) = Delphi
   (a town famous for the
   oracle of Apollo)

Delphōs  (a)  –ōs
      (b)  acc pl
      (c)  the Athenians sent — to Delphi

consulō –ere –uī –ltum = to
   consult, ask

consultum  (a)  –tum
      (b)  supine, acc sing
      (c)  the Athenians sent — to Delphi to
           ask —

quisnam? quaenam? quidnam? =
   who? what?

quidnam  (a)  –d
      (b)  nom/acc sing neut
      (c)  (what ★s / what — ★s)

faciō –ere fēcī factum = to make,
   do

facerent  (a)  –rent
      (b)  imperf subj, 3rd pl act
      (c)  (what — were doing)
          *or* (what — would/should do)

dē (prep w.abl) = from, about
rēs reī (f) = a thing, affair

dē rēbus  (a)  –bus
      (b)  abl pl
      (c)  (what — were doing about affairs)
          *or* (what — would/should do about
          affairs)

suus –a –um = his, her, its (own),
    etc.

suīs.   (a)   –īs
        (b)   abl pl fem
        (c)   (what — were doing about their affairs).
              *or* (what — would/should do about their affairs).

Translation        The Athenians sent to Delphi to ask what they should do about their affairs.

N.B. in the original context it is clear that *facerent* has a jussive sense.

## 4. quid sit futūrum crās fuge quaerere!
(Hor. *Carm.* 1.9.13)

quis? quid? = who? what?

quid    (a)   –d
          (b)   nom/acc sing
          (c)   what ⋆s / what does — ⋆?

sum esse fuī = to be

sit    (a)   –it
          (b)   pres subj, 3rd sing act
          (c)   what may/should be —?
              *or* (what is —)

sum esse fuī = to be
crās (adv) = tomorrow

futūrum crās    (a)   –tūrum
          (b)   fut part, nom sing neut
          (c)   what may/should be going to be —
               tomorrow?
              *or* (what is going to be — tomorrow)

fugiō –ere fūgī = to run away
     from, forbear

fuge    (a)   –e
          (b)   pres imper, 2nd sing act
          (c)   forbear (what is going to be —
              tomorrow)!

quaerō –rere –sīvī –sītum = to
     look for, ask

quaerere!    (a)   –re
          (b)   pres infin act
          (c)   forbear (to ask what is going to be —
              tomorrow)!

Translation    Forbear to ask what is going to be
              tomorrow!

## 5. *dīcī nōn potest quam sim disputātiōne dēlectātus. (Cic. *Tusc.* 2.10)

dīcō –cere –xī –ctum = to say

|                | dīcī | (a) | –ī |
|---|---|---|---|
|  |  | (b) | pres infin pass |
|  |  | (c) | (to be said) |

nōn = not

possum posse potuī = to be able (to)

|                | nōn potest | (a) | –t |
|---|---|---|---|
|  |  | (b) | pres indic, 3rd sing act |
|  |  | (c) | — is not able (to be said) |

quam! = to what an extent! how much!

sum esse fuī = to be

|                | quam sim | (a) | –im |
|---|---|---|---|
|  |  | (b) | pres subj, 1st sing act |
|  |  | (c) | (how much I am —) |

disputātiō –ōnis (f) = a discussion

|                | disputātiōne | (a) | –e |
|---|---|---|---|
|  |  | (b) | abl sing |
|  |  | (c) | (how much I am — by/with/from the discussion) |

delectō –āre –āvī –ātum = to delight

|                | delectātus. | (a) | –tus *or* –tus sim |
|---|---|---|---|
|  |  | (b) | past part, nom sing masc *or* perf subj, 1st sing pass |
|  |  | (c) | (how much I am delighted *or* I have been delighted by the discussion). |

Translation — It cannot be said how much I am delighted by the discussion.

# Summary of Examples

1. videāmus prīmum deōrumne prōvidentiā mundus regātur, deinde consulantne dī rēbus hūmānīs.

2. quid paulō ante dīxerim nōnne meministī?

3. Athēniēnsēs mīsērunt Delphōs consultum quidnam facerent dē rēbus suīs.

4. quid sit futūrum crās fuge quaerere.

5. dīcī nōn potest quam sim disputātiōne delectātus.

# Exercises

Complete the following sentences on the analogy of the first:

suntne dī? quaerō sintne dī.
quid censēs? quaerō quid ................................
an deōs esse negās? quaerō an deōs esse ......................
quid dīcis? quaerō quid ................................
num fortūnā mundus regitur? quaerō num fortūnā mundus .....

quid dīxistī? quaerō quid dīxerīs.
an sapientēs rogāvistī? quaerō an sapientēs ...................
num sapientēs rogābis? quaerō num sapientēs .................
an deōs esse negāvērunt? quaerō an deōs esse ..................
num deōs esse negābunt? quaerō num deōs esse ...............

suntne dī? quaerēbam essentne dī?
quid dīcis? quaerēbam quid ................................
an sapientēs rogāvistī? quaerēbam an sapientēs ................
sapientēsne rogābis? quaerēbam sapientēsne ..................
num fortūnā mundus regitur? quaerēbam num fortūnā mundus ..

# Reading

1.  nesciō an ullum iūcundius tempus exēgerim, quam quō nūper apud Spurinnam fuī. (Plin. *Ep.* 3.1.1)

    an? (interrogative particle) = whether?
    apud (prep w.acc) = at, at the house of

exigō –ere –ēgī –actum = to pass (time)
iūcundus –a –um = pleasant
nesciō –īre –īvī –ītum = not to know
nūper (adv) = lately, recently
Spūrinna –ae (m) = Vestricius Spurinna (a lyric poet)
tempus –oris (n) = time
ullus –a –um = any

2. hūc ut vēnimus, incidēre nōbīs
sermōnēs variī, in quibus, quid esset
iam Bīthȳnia, quō modō sē habēret,
et quōnam mihi prōfuisset aere.          (Catul. 10.5)

aes aeris (n) = bronze, money
Bīthȳnia –ae (f) = Bithynia (a fruitful province in Asia Minor)
habeō –ēre –uī –itum (w.advbs) = to have, be (in such and such a
    way)
hūc (adv) = hither, to this place
incidō –ere –ī incasum (intr) = to fall (into), occur
modus –ī (m) = a manner, way
prōsum prōdesse prōfuī (intr) = to be useful, advantageous
quīnam? quaenam? quodnam? = what?
sermō –ōnis (m) = talk, a topic of conversation
ut (conj) = when, as soon as
varius –a –um = varied, different

3. unde habeās quaerit nēmō, sed oportet habēre. (Juv. 14.207)

oportet –ēre –uit = it behoves, one ought
quaerō –rere –sīvī –sītum = to look for, ask
unde? = whence? from where?

4. num tibi cum faucēs ūrit sitis, aurea quaeris
pōcula? num ēsuriens fastīdīs omnia praeter
pāvōnem rhombumque?          (Hor. Serm. 1.2.114)

aureus –a –um = golden, gilded
cum (conj) = when
ēsuriens –ntis = hungry
fastīdiō –īre –īvī –ītum = to disdain, scorn
faucēs –ium (f.pl) = the upper throat, pharynx
num? (interrogative particle) = surely ... not?
pāvō –ōnis (m) = a peacock
pōculum –ī (n) = a cup, goblet
praeter (prep w.acc) = beyond, except
quaerō –rere –sīvī –sītum = to look for, ask for
rhombus –ī (m) = a turbot
sitis –is (f) = thirst
ūro –ere ussī ustum = to burn, parch

5.  hoc nōs pessimōs facit, quod nēmō vītam suam respicit; quid
    factūrī sīmus cōgitāmus, et id rārō, quid fēcerimus nōn cogitā-
    mus; atquī consilium futūrī ex praeteritō venit. (Sen. *Ep.* 83.2)

    atquī (conj) = and yet
    cōgitō –āre –āvī –ātum = to ponder, consider
    consilium –[i]ī (n) = a counsel, plan
    futūrus –a –um = future
    pessimus –a –um = very bad
    praeteritus –a –um = past
    quod (conj) = because, that
    rārō (adv) = rarely, seldom
    respiciō –icere –exī –ectum = to look round, look back upon

6.  * isne tibi melius suādet quī, rem faciās, rem,
       sī possīs rectē, sī nōn, quōcumque modō rem,
       an quī Fortūnae tē responsāre superbae
       liberum et ērectum praesens hortātur et aptat?
       (Hor. *Ep.* 1.1.65)

    aptō –āre –āvī –ātum = to fit, get ready
    ērectus –a –um = upright, not cowed
    Fortūna –ae (f) = Fortune (goddess of luck)
    hortor –ārī –ātus = to encourage
    līber –era –erum = free, independent
    melior –ior –ius = better
    modus –ī (m) = a manner, way
    –ne ... an? (interrog.particles) = can it be that ... or that ...?
    praesens –tis = present, ready to help
    quīcumque quaecumque quodcumque = whoever, whatever
    rectus –a –um = straight, right
    rēs reī (f) = property, wealth
    responsō –āre (w.dat) = to answer, answer back defiantly
    suādeō –dēre –sī –sum (w.dat) = to advise
    superbus –a –um = proud, haughty

7.  * duplex est enim vīs animōrum atque nātūra; ūna pars in appetītū
    posita est, quae hominem hūc et illūc rapit, altera in ratiōne,
    quae docet et explānat, quid faciendum fugiendumve sit. ita fit
    ut ratiō praesit, appetītus obtemperet. (Cic. *Off.* 1.101)

    alter –era –erum = the other (of two)
    appetītus –ūs (m) = a desire, appetite
    doceō –ēre –uī –tum = to teach
    duplex –icis = double, dual
    explānō –āre –āvī –ātum = to explain, expound
    fīō fierī (intr) = to happen, come about
    hūc (adv) = hither, to this place
    illūc (adv) = thither, to that place

nātūra -ae (f) = nature, character
obtemperō -āre -āvī -ātum (w.dat) = to be submissive to, obey
pars -tis (f) = a part
praesum -esse -fuī (w.dat) = to be in charge, in command (of)
rapiō -ere -uī -tum = to seize, carry off
ratiō -ōnis (f) = reason, rationality
ūnus -a -um = one
-ve (conj) = or
vīs vis (f) = physical strength, force

8.  sī quis dēspoliātus āmissā ūnicā tunicā complōrāre sē mālit,
    quam circumspicere quōmodo frīgus effugiat et aliquid inveniat
    quō tegat scapulās, nōnne tibi videātur stultissimus? (Sen. *Ep.*
    63.11)

aliquis -qua -quid = someone, something
āmittō -ittere -īsī -issum — to send away, lose
circumspiciō -ere -exī -ectum = to look around, consider
complōrō -āre -āvī -ātum = to lament, weep for
dēspoliō -āre -āvī -ātum = to rob, strip
effugiō -ere -fūgī = to escape (from), avoid
frīgus -oris (n) = cold
inveniō -īre -ēnī -entum = to come upon, find
mālō mālle māluī = to want or wish more, prefer (to)
nōnne? (interrogative particle) = surely ...?
quam = than, rather than
quōmodo? = in what way? how?
scapulae -ārum (f.pl) = the shoulder-blades
stultus -a -um = foolish
tegō -gere -xī -ctum = to cover
tunica -ae (f) = a tunic
ūnicus -a -um = one and only

9.  sī sunt dī neque ante dēclārant hominibus quae futūra sint, aut
    nōn dīligunt hominēs aut quid ēventūrum sit ignōrant. (Cic.
    *Div.* 2.101)

ante (adv) = before, beforehand
dēclārō -āre -āvī -ātum = to make known, reveal
dīligō -igere -exī -ectum = to love, have regard for
ēveniō -īre -ēnī -entum (intr) = to happen
ignōrō -āre -āvī -ātum = to be ignorant of, not to know

329

10.  sermō oritur, nōn dē villīs domibusve aliēnīs,
     nec male necne Lepōs saltet; sed quod magis ad nōs
     pertinet et nescīre malum est agitāmus: utrumne
     dīvitiīs hominēs an sint virtūte beātī;
     quidve ad amīcitiās, ūsus rectumne, trahat nōs;
     et quae sit nātūra bonī summumque quid ēius.
     (Hor.*Serm*.2.6.71)

agitō -āre -āvī -ātum = to set in motion, discuss
aliēnus -a -um = belonging to others
amīcitia -ae (f) = friendship
bonum -ī (n) = something good, the good
dē (prep w.abl) = from, about
Lepōs -ōris (m) = "Charmer" (a star dancer)
magis (compar.adv) = to a greater extent, more
malus -a -um = bad
nātūra -ae (f) = nature, character
-ne (interrogative particle) = whether, or
necne? (interrogative particle) = (whether) ... or not?
nesciō -īre -īvī -ītum = not to know
orior -īrī -tus (intr) = to arise, begin
pertineō -ēre -uī (intr) = to extend, relate (to)
rectus -a -um = straight, right; (n.sing) what is right
saltō -āre -āvī -ātum (intr) = to dance
sermō -ōnis (m) = talk, a topic of conversation
summus -a -um = highest; (n.sing) the highest degree or form
trahō -ere -xī -ctum = to drag, draw
ūsus -ūs (m) = use, usefulness
utrumne ... an? (interrogative particles) = whether ... or?
-ve (conj) = or
villa -ae (f) = a country dwelling

# Vocabulary to Learn

dē (prep w.abl) = from, about
pars -tis (f) = a part
quaerō -rere -sīvī -sītum = to look for, ask
ratiō -ōnis (f) = reason
ūnus -a -um = one, a single

# 25
# *QUI* AND THE SUBJUNCTIVE

## Morphology

The use of *quī* and the subjunctive does not introduce any new forms.

## Syntax

*Quī* is used in various cases with the subjunctive; in some clauses the potential sense is strongly felt, in others the optative or jussive sense. The tense of the subjunctive is governed by the sequence of tenses rule (see chapter 13 syntax §8).

**1.** *Quī* and the subjunctive is used attributively to express:

(a) cause (and occasionally concession):

> ō fortūnāte adulescens, **quī** fictilibus **ūtāris**!
> oh fortunate young man, **who use / to use** earthenware!

The causal sense is often signalled by *quippe* "since", *ut* "as" or *utpote* "inasmuch as":

> ō fortūnāte adulescens, **quippe quī** fictilibus **ūtāris**!
> oh fortunate young man, **since you use** earthenware!

(b) purpose:

> nulla Corinthia habēs ex **quibus bibās**.
> you have no Corinthian bronzes from **which you may drink / to drink** from.

**2.** *Quī* and the subjunctive is used predicatively to express tendency or result in clauses dependent on:

(a) demonstrative pronouns:

> vīcīnus noster **is** est **quī** Corinthia **habeat**.
> our neighbour is **that (sort of) man who would have / the sort of man to have** Corinthian bronzes.

(b) indefinite and interrogative pronouns, *nēmō* "no-one", *nihil* "nothing", *nullus* "not any, no", *sōlus* "the only one" and *ūnus* "one":

> nec **sōlus** ille est **quī** Corinthia **habeat**.
> and he is not **the only one who would have / the only one to have** Corinthian bronzes.

(c) *est quī* "there is the (sort of) person who" and *sunt quī* "there are (the sort of) people who":

> **sunt quī** vīcīnō nostrō **invideant**.
> **there are (the sort of) people who would envy** our neighbour / **people who envy** our neighbour.

(d) comparatives with *quam*:

> **cupidior** ille est **quam quī** beātē **vīvat**.
> he is **more greedy than the (sort of) man who would live / too greedy to live** happily.

(e) adjectives such as *dignus* "worthy", *indignus* "unworthy" and *idōneus* "suitable":

> nōn **dignus** ille est **cui invideātur**.
> he is not **(the sort of man) worthy of whom envy may be felt / worthy to be envied**.

**3.** *Quō* "whereby, so that" (ablative singular neuter) and the subjunctive is used to introduce purpose clauses with a comparative adjective or adverb:

> erus meus fictilibus ūtitur **quō solūtiōre** animō **bibat**.
> my master uses earthenware **so that he may drink / to drink with a more relaxed** mind.

**4.** *Quōminus* "so that ... not" (*quō* "whereby" and *minus* "less") and the subjunctive is used to introduce purpose clauses dependent on verbs of hindering, preventing and forbidding:

> vīcīnus dīves nihil obstat erō meō **quōminus** beātus **sit**.
> a rich neighbour does not hinder my master at all **so that he may not be / from being** happy.

**5.** *Quīn* "but that" (nominative *quī* "who" or instrumental *quī* "how" and *nē* "not") and the subjunctive is used to introduce various clauses dependent on a negative or interrogative main verb:

(a) adjectival clauses expressing tendency or result:

> quis est **quīn censeat** in virtūte dīvitiās esse?
> who is there **but that he would think / who does not think** that riches consist in virtue?

(b) noun clauses dependent on verbs of hindering, preventing and forbidding:

> nihil mihi obstat **quīn censeam** in virtūte dīvitiās esse.
> nothing hinders me **but that I should think / from thinking** that riches consist in virtue.

(c) noun clauses dependent on verbs of doubting:

> numquid dubitās **quīn** in virtūte dīvitiae **sint**?
> surely you do not doubt **but that** riches **consist / that** riches **consist** in virtue?

(d) noun clauses dependent on expressions such as *nōn multum abest* "it is not far from the case" and *fierī nōn potest* "it cannot be the case":

> fierī nōn potest **quīn** in virtūte dīvitiae **sint**.
> it cannot be the case **but that / it must be the case that** riches **consist** in virtue.

# Metaphrasing

**1.** *Quī* with the subjunctive is metaphrased: who/which ★s (or: to ★), in brackets:

| | |
|---|---|
| quī habeat | (who has —) *or* (to have —) |

**2.** *Quō* with a comparative and the subjunctive is metaphrased: so that — ★s (or: so as to / in order to / to ★), in brackets:

| | |
|---|---|
| quō plūs habeat | (so that — has more) *or* (to have more) |

**3.** *Quōminus* with the subjunctive is metaphrased: so that — not ★s (or: from ★ing), in brackets:

| | |
|---|---|
| quōminus habeat | (so that — does not have —) *or* (from having —) |

**4.** *Quīn* with the subjunctive is metaphrased: but that — ★s (or: who/which not ★s, or: from/without ★ing, as appropriate), in brackets:

| | |
|---|---|
| quīn habeat | (but that — has —) *or* (who/which does not have —) *or* (from/without having —) |

**5.** These basic patterns can then be adapted when necessary; some clauses will need "may/can/should/would" to be used as appropriate:

| | |
|---|---|
| quōminus habeat | (so that — does not have —) *or* (so that — should not have —) |

# Examples

### 1. sōlus sum quī vēra Corinthia habeam.
(Petr. 50.2)

sōlus –a –um = alone, the only
    (one)

|  | sōlus | (a) | –us |
|---|---|---|---|
|  |  | (b) | nom sing masc |
|  |  | (c) | the only — ★s |

sum esse fuī = to be

|  | sum | (a) | –m |
|---|---|---|---|
|  |  | (b) | pres indic, 1st sing act |
|  |  | (c) | I am the only — |

quī quae quod = who(ever),
    which, what

|  | quī | (a) | –ī |
|---|---|---|---|
|  |  | (b) | nom sing masc |
|  |  | (c) | (who ★s) |

vērus –a –um = real, genuine

|  | vēra | (a) | –a |
|---|---|---|---|
|  |  | (b) | acc pl neut |
|  |  | (c) | (who ★s real —) |

Corinthius –a –um = Corinthian;
    (n.pl) Corinthian bronzes

|  | Corinthia | (a) | –a |
|---|---|---|---|
|  |  | (b) | acc pl neut |
|  |  | (c) | (who ★s real Corinthian bronzes) |

habeō –ēre –uī –itum = to have,
    possess

|  | habeam. | (a) | –am |
|---|---|---|---|
|  |  | (b) | pres subj, 1st sing act |
|  |  | (c) | (who has real Corinthian bronzes). |

|  |  |  |
|---|---|---|
| Translation | | I am the only one to have real Corinthian bronzes. |

## 2. *negō in Siciliā tōtā ullum vās fuisse quīn Verrēs abstulerit. (Cic. *Ver.* 4.1)

negō -āre -āvī -ātum = to say no,
    deny

|  |  |  |
|---|---|---|
| negō | (a) | -ō |
|  | (b) | pres indic, 1st sing act |
|  | (c) | I deny — |

in (prep w.acc/abl) = into / in,
    on
Sicilia -ae (f) = the island of Sicily

|  |  |  |
|---|---|---|
| in Siciliā | (a) | -ā |
|  | (b) | abl sing |
|  | (c) | I deny — in Sicily |

tōtus -a -um = the whole of, all

|  |  |  |
|---|---|---|
| tōtā | (a) | -ā |
|  | (b) | abl sing fem |
|  | (c) | I deny — in the whole of Sicily |

ullus -a -um = any

|  |  |  |
|---|---|---|
| ullum | (a) | -um |
|  | (b) | acc sing masc/neut |
|  | (c) | I deny any — in the whole of Sicily |

vās vāsis (n) = a vessel for food or
    drink, (precious) plate

|  |  |  |
|---|---|---|
| vās | (a) | -s |
|  | (b) | acc sing |
|  | (c) | I deny any plate in the whole of Sicily |

sum esse fuī = to be

|  |  |  |
|---|---|---|
| fuisse | (a) | -isse |
|  | (b) | perf infin act |
|  | (c) | I deny (that there was any plate in the whole of Sicily) |

quīn (conj) = but that
Verrēs -is (m) = C.Verres (the
    corrupt governor of Sicily)

|  |  |  |
|---|---|---|
| quīn Verrēs | (a) | -s |
|  | (b) | nom sing |
|  | (c) | (but that Verres ★s) |

auferō -rrc abstulī ablātum = to
    carry away, take away

|  |  |  |
|---|---|---|
| abstulerit. | (a) | -erit |
|  | (b) | perf subj, 3rd sing act |
|  | (c) | (but that Verres took — away). |

|  |  |
|---|---|
| Translation | I deny that there was any plate in the whole of Sicily which Verres did not take away. |

## 3. sānus tū nōn es quī fūrem mē vocēs. (Pl. *Aul.* 769)

sānus –a –um = healthy, sane

|  | sānus | (a) | –us |
|--|--|--|--|
|  |  | (b) | nom sing masc |
|  |  | (c) | a sane — ★s |

tū = you

|  | tū | (a) | –ū |
|--|--|--|--|
|  |  | (b) | nom sing |
|  |  | (c) | you sane ★ |

nōn = not
sum esse fuī = to be

|  | nōn es | (a) | –s |
|--|--|--|--|
|  |  | (b) | pres indic, 2nd sing act |
|  |  | (c) | you are not sane |

quī = who(ever), which, what

|  | quī | (a) | –ī |
|--|--|--|--|
|  |  | (b) | nom sing masc |
|  |  | (c) | (who ★s) |

fūr –ris (m) = a thief

|  | fūrem | (a) | –em |
|--|--|--|--|
|  |  | (b) | acc sing |
|  |  | (c) | (who ★s a thief) |

ego = I

|  | mē | (a) | –ē |
|--|--|--|--|
|  |  | (b) | acc/abl sing |
|  |  | (c) | (who ★s a thief me / by/with/from me) |

vocō –āre –āvī –ātum = to call

|  | vocēs. | (a) | –ēs |
|--|--|--|--|
|  |  | (b) | pres subj, 2nd sing act |
|  |  | (c) | (who call me a thief). |

|  | Translation | You are insane to call me a thief. |
|--|--|--|

## 4. *nātūra hominī addidit ratiōnem, quā regerentur animī appetītūs. (Cic. *N.D.* 2.34)

nātūra –ae (f) = nature

|  | nātūra | (a) | –a |
| --- | --- | --- | --- |
|  |  | (b) | nom sing |
|  |  | (c) | nature ★s |

homō –inis (m) = a human being, man

|  | hominī | (a) | –ī |
| --- | --- | --- | --- |
|  |  | (b) | dat sing |
|  |  | (c) | nature ★s to/for man |

addō –ere –idī –itum = to add (to)

|  | addidit | (a) | –it |
| --- | --- | --- | --- |
|  |  | (b) | perf indic, 3rd sing act |
|  |  | (c)* | nature added — to man |

ratiō –ōnis (f) = reason

|  | ratiōnem, | (a) | –em |
| --- | --- | --- | --- |
|  |  | (b) | acc sing |
|  |  | (c) | nature added reason to man, |

quī quae quod = who(ever), which, what

|  | quā | (a) | –ā |
| --- | --- | --- | --- |
|  |  | (b) | abl sing fem |
|  |  | (c) | (by which — ★s) |

regō –gere –xī –ctum = to make straight, rule

|  | regerentur | (a) | –rentur |
| --- | --- | --- | --- |
|  |  | (b) | imperf subj, 3rd pl pass |
|  |  | (c) | (by which — could be ruled) |

animus –ī (m) = the mind, spirit

|  | animī | (a) | –ī |
| --- | --- | --- | --- |
|  |  | (b) | nom pl / gen sing |
|  |  | (c) | (by which the minds / the — of the mind could be ruled) |

appetītus –ūs (m) = a desire, appetite

|  | appetītūs. | (a) | –ūs |
| --- | --- | --- | --- |
|  |  | (b) | nom pl |
|  |  | (c) | (by which the appetites of the mind could be ruled). |

|  |  |
| --- | --- |
| Translation | Nature added reason to man, by which the appetites of the mind could be ruled. |

## 5. *non deterret sapientem mors, quominus in omne tempus rei publicae suisque consulat.* (Cic. *Tusc.* 1.91)

non = not
deterreo –ere –ui –itum = to
    deter, discourage

| | | |
|---|---|---|
| non deterret | (a) | –t |
| | (b) | pres indic, 3rd sing act |
| | (c) | — does not discourage — |

sapiens –ntis = wise

| | | |
|---|---|---|
| sapientem | (a) | –em |
| | (b) | acc sing |
| | (c) | — does not discourage a wise — |

mors –tis (f) = death

| | | |
|---|---|---|
| mors, | (a) | –s |
| | (b) | nom sing |
| | (c) | death does not discourage a wise —, |

quominus (conj) = so that ... not
in (prep w.acc/abl) = into, for /
    in, on
omnis –is –e = every, all

| | | |
|---|---|---|
| quominus in omne | (a) | –e |
| | (b) | acc sing neut |
| | (c) | (so that — does not ★ for all —) |

tempus –oris (n) = time

| | | |
|---|---|---|
| tempus | (a) | –s |
| | (b) | acc sing |
| | (c) | (so that — does not ★ for all time) |

res publica rei publicae (f) =
    affairs of state, the state

| | | |
|---|---|---|
| rei publicae | (a) | –i –ae |
| | (b) | dat sing |
| | (c) | (so that — does not ★ to/for the state for all time) |

suus –a –um = his, her, its (own),
    etc.
-que (conj) = and

| | | |
|---|---|---|
| suisque | (a) | –is |
| | (b) | dat pl masc/fem/neut |
| | (c) | (so that — does not ★ to/for the state and his own — for all time) |

consulō –ere –uī –tum (w.dat) =
    to consult the interests of,
    look after

|  |  |  |
|---|---|---|
| consulat. | (a) | –at |
|  | (b) | pres subj, 3rd sing act |
|  | (c) | (so that — does not look after the state and his own — for all time). |

|  |  |
|---|---|
| Translation | Death does not discourage a wise man from looking after the state and his own family for all time. |

# Summary of Examples

1. sōlus sum quī vēra Corinthia habeam.

2. negō in Siciliā tōtā ullum vās fuisse quīn Verrēs abstulerit.

3. sānus tū nōn es quī fūrem mē vocēs.

4. nātūra hominī addidit ratiōnem, quā regerentur animī appetītūs.

5. nōn dēterret sapientem mors, quōminus in omne tempus reī publicae suīsque consulat.

# Exercises

Complete the following sentences on the analogy of the first, using the appropriate form of *quī* and the subjunctive, and translate:

quis Corinthia habet? quis est quī Corinthia habeat?
quis fictilibus ūtitur? quis est ................ .....?
egone sōlus fictilibus ūtor? egone sōlus sum .....?
an rusticum mē vocās? an sānus ēs ............ .....?
num beātior vīvis? num Corinthia habēs ... .. .....?
ego nōnne beātissimus sum? quid obstat ... .. .....?

# Reading

1. ⋆post autem apparātū rēgiō acceptī sermōnem in multam noctem
   prōdūximus. deinde ut cubitum discessimus, mē et dē viā
   fessum et quī ad multam noctem vigilāssem artior quam solēbat
   somnus complexus est. (Cic. *Rep.* 6.10)

   accipiō –ipere –ēpī –eptum = to receive, entertain
   apparātus –ūs (m) = preparation, lavishness
   artus –a –um = tight, deep (of sleep)
   complector –ctī –xus = to embrace
   cubō –āre –uī –itum (intr) = to lie down
   deinde (adv) = from there or then, then
   discēdō –dere –ssī –ssum (intr) = to go away, part company
   fessus –a –um = tired
   multus –a –um = much, late
   post (adv) = afterwards
   prōdūcō –cere –xī –ctum = to draw out, continue
   rēgius –a –um = royal, kingly
   sermō –ōnis (m) = talk, conversation
   soleō –ēre –itus = to be accustomed (to)
   somnus –ī (m) = sleep
   ut (conj) = when, as soon as
   via –ae (f) = a road, journey
   vigilō –āre –āvī –ātum (intr) = to be or stay awake

2. nīl admīrārī prope rēs est ūna, Numīcī,
   sōlaque quae possit facere et servāre beātum.
   (Hor. *Ep.* 1.6.1)

   admīror –ārī –ātus = to wonder at, be impressed by, covet
   Numīcius –[i]ī (m) = Numicius (? a friend of Horace)
   prope (adv) = almost, about
   servō –āre –āvī –ātum = to keep
   sōlus –a –um = alone, only

3. nequeō mihi temperāre quōminus ūnum exemplum antīquitātis
   afferam. (Plin. *Nat.* 18.41)

   afferō –rre attulī allātum = to bring to, adduce
   antīquitās –ātis (f) = antiquity, ancient times
   exemplum –ī (n) = an example, precedent
   nequeō –īre –iī = to be unable (to)
   quōminus (conj) = so that ... not
   temperō –āre –āvī –ātum (w.dat) = to restrain, hold back

4. * Caelius, cum domus patris ā forō longē abesset, quō facilius et
nostrās domūs obīre et ipse a suīs colī posset, condūxit in Palātiō
nōn magnō domum. (Cic. *Cael.* 18)

absum –esse āfuī (intr) = to be away (from), distant (from)
Caelius –[i]ī (m) = M.Caelius Rufus (involved in a notorious
    scandal)
colō –ere –uī cultum = to cultivate, frequent
condūcō –ere –xī –ctum = to hire, rent
cum (conj) = since
facilis –is –e = easy (adv: facile)
forum –ī (n) = a market-place, forum
longus –a –um = long, long-distant; (adv) far
magnus –a –um = great; (abl.sing.neut) at a great price
obeō –īre –iī –itum = to visit
Palātium –[i]ī (n) = the Palatine hill
quō (w.compar) = in order that, so that

5. gemmās, marmor, ebur, Tyrrhēna sigilla, tabellās,
argentum, vestīs Gaetūlō mūrice tinctās,
sunt quī nōn habeant, est quī nōn cūrat habēre.
(Hor. *Ep.* 2.2.180)

argentum –ī (n) = silver
cūrō –āre –āvī –atum = to care (to)
ebur eboris (n) = ivory
Gaetūlus –a –um = Gaetulian (from N.W. Africa)
gemma –ae (f) = a gem, jewel
marmor –oris (n) = marble
mūrex –icis (m) = a shell fish, purple dye
sigillum –ī (n) = a statuette, figurine
tabella –ae (f) = a painted panel, picture
tingō –gere –xī –ctum = to soak, dye
Tyrrhēnus –a –um = Etruscan, Tuscan
vestis –is (f) = clothing, clothes

6. observā tē itaque, numquid vestis tua domusque dissentiant,
numquid in tē līberālis sīs, in tuōs sordidus, numquid cēnēs
frūgāliter, aedificēs luxuriōse; ūnam semel ad quam vīvās
rēgulam prende et ad hanc omnem vītam tuam exaequā. (Sen.
*Ep.* 20.3)

ad (prep w.acc) = to, in accordance with
aedificō –āre –āvī –ātum = to build
cēnō –āre –āvī –ātum (intr) = to dine

dissentiō –tīre –sī –sum (intr) = to disagree, differ
exaequō –āre –āvī –ātum = to make level or equal
frūgālis –is –e = frugal, economical
in (prep w.acc) = to, towards
itaque (adv) = and so
līberālis –is –e = of or relating to free men, lavish
luxuriōsus –a –um = luxurious, extravagant
numquid (interrogative particle) = whether
observō –āre –āvī –ātum = to watch, take notice of
prendō –dere –dī –sum = to take hold of, adopt
rēgula –ae (f) = a ruler, rule, standard
semel (adv) = once for all
sordidus –a –um = dirty, mean
vestis –is (f) = clothing, clothes

7.  vix tamen ēripiam positō pāvōne, velīs quīn
    hōc potius quam gallīnā tergēre palātum,
    corruptus vānīs rērum, quia vēneat aurō
    rāra avis et pictā pandat spectācula caudā.
    (Hor. *Serm.* 2.2.23)

aurum –ī (n) = gold
avis –is (f) = a bird
cauda –ae (f) = the tail (of an animal or bird)
corrumpō –ere –ūpī –uptum = to spoil, entice
ēripiō –ipere –ipuī –eptum = to snatch away
gallīna –ae (f) = a hen
palātum –ī (n) = the palate
pandō –ere passum = to spread out, unfold
pāvō –ōnis (m) = a peacock
pingō –ngere –nxī –ctum = to adorn with colours, paint
potius (compar.adv) = rather
quia (conj) = because
quīn (conj) = but that
rārus –a –um = uncommon, rare
spectāculum –ī (n) = a show
tergeō –gēre –sī –sum = to rub clean, "tickle"
vānus –a –um = empty; (neut) vanity, illusion
vēneō –īre –iī (intr) = to be sold
vix (adv) = with difficulty, hardly

8. brevis ā nātūrā nōbīs vīta data est, at memoria bene redditae vītae sempiterna. quae sī nōn esset longior quam haec vīta, quis esset tam āmens quī maximīs labōribus et perīculīs ad summam laudem glōriamque contenderet? (Cic. *Phil.* 14.32)

āmens –ntis = mad, frantic
brevis –is –e = short
contendō –dere –dī –tum (intr) = to strain or exert oneself
glōria –ae (f) = glory
laus –dis (f) = praise
longus –a –um = long, longlasting
maximus –a –um = greatest
memoria –ae (f) = memory, remembrance
nātūra –ae (f) = nature
perīculum –ī (n) = danger
reddō –ere –idī –itum = to give back, surrender
sempiternus –a –um = everlasting, imperishable
summus –a –um = highest
tam (adv) = to such a degree, so

9. nam saepe ego audīvī Q.Maximum, P.Scīpiōnem, praetereā cīvitātis nostrae praeclārōs virōs solitōs ita dīcere, cum māiōrum imāginēs intuerentur, vehementissimē sibi animum ad virtūtem accendī. at contrā quis est omnium hīs mōribus, quīn dīvitiīs et sumptibus, nōn probitāte neque industriā cum māiōribus suīs contendat? (Sall. *Jug.* 4.5)

accendō –dere –dī –sum = to set on fire, inflame
cīvitās –ātis (f) = a state, city
contendō –dere –dī –tum (intr) = to contend, vie (with)
contrā (adv) = on the other hand, in contrast
cum (conj) = when
imāgō –inis (f) = a likeness, mask
industria –ae (f) = diligence, industry
intueor –ērī –itus = to contemplate, look on as a model
mōs mōris (m) = an established practice; (pl) habits, morals
praeclārus –a –um = famous, celebrated
praetereā (adv) = besides
probitās –ātis (f) = honesty, integrity
P.Scīpiō –ōnis (m) = P.Cornelius Scipio (conqueror of Hannibal)
quīn (conj) = but that
Q.Maximus –ī (m) = Q.Fabius Maximus Cunctator ("the Delayer")
saepe (adv) = often
soleō –ēre –itus = to be accustomed (to)
sumptus –ūs (m) = the spending of money, lavish expenditure
vehemens –tis = violent, powerful, ardent

10.   multaque praetereā tibi possum commemorandō
      argūmenta fidem dictīs corrādere nostrīs.
      vērum animō satis haec vestīgia parva sagācī
      sunt per quae possīs cognoscere cētera tūte.      (Lucr. 1.400)

argumentum –ī (n) = a proof
cēterus –a –um = the rest (of)
cognoscō –ere cognōvī –itum = to get to know
commemorō –āre –āvī –ātum = to mention
corrādō –dere –sī –sum = to rake together
dictum –ī (n) = something said, a word, utterance
fidēs –ēī (f) = trust, credibility
parvus –a –um = small, little
per (prep w.acc) = through, by means of
praetereā (adv) = besides
sagax –ācis = keen scented, intellectually quick
satis (n.indecl) = sufficient, enough
tūte (emphatic form) = you yourself
vērum (adv) = but in truth
vestīgium –[i]ī (n) = a footprint, track

# Vocabulary to Learn

cognoscō –ere cognōvī –itum = to get to know
itaque (adv) = and so
saepe (adv) = often
tempus –oris (n) = time
vērus –a –um = real, true; (adv: vērō) in truth, in fact;
      (adv: vērum) but in truth

# TABLES

The following pages contain paradigms of all the different types of nouns, adjectives, pronouns and verbs dealt with in this course. These tables should be studied carefully in conjunction with the Morphology and Syntax sections of each chapter, and may be referred to while kernelling.

Some adjectives and pronouns have the same form for all genders in the genitive, dative and ablative cases. Where this occurs, the forms are entered only in the central column (i.e. under *f.*).

The abbreviations for grammatical terms used in this course are set out below:

abl: ablative
acc: accusative
act: active
adj: adjective
adv: adverb
compar: comparative
conj: conjunction
dat: dative
f/fem: feminine
fut: future
gen: genitive
gnd: gerund
gndv: gerundive
imper: imperative
imperf: imperfect
indecl: indeclinable
indic: indicative

infin: infinitive
intr: intransitive
m/masc: masculine
n/neut: neuter
nom: nominative
part: participle
pass: passive
perf: perfect
pl: plural
pluperf: pluperfect
prep: preposition
pres: present
sing: singular
subj: subjunctive
superl: superlative
voc: vocative
w.: with

# NOUNS

## First Declension

|  | Sing. | Pl. |
|------|-------|--------|
| Nom. | vīta | vītae |
| Acc. | vītam | vītās |
| Gen. | vītae | vītārum |
| Dat. | vītae | vītīs |
| Abl. | vītā | vītīs |

## Second Declension

|  | Sing. | Pl. | Sing. | Pl. | Sing. | Pl. |
|------|-------|--------|-------|----------|-------|---------|
| Nom. | erus | erī | puer | puerī | ager | agrī | vīnum | vīna |
| Acc. | erum | erōs | puerum | puerōs | agrum | agrōs | vīnum | vīna |
| Gen. | erī | erōrum | puerī | puerōrum | agrī | agrōrum | vīnī | vīnōrum |
| Dat. | erō | erīs | puerō | puerīs | agrō | agrīs | vīnō | vīnīs |
| Abl. | erō | erīs | puerō | puerīs | agrō | agrīs | vīnō | vīnīs |

## Third Declension Consonant Stems

|  | Sing. | Pl. | Sing. | Pl. | Sing. | Pl. | Sing. | Pl. |
|------|-------|--------|-------|--------|---------|-----------|-------|-----------|
| Nom. | rex | rēgēs | amor | amōrēs | homō | hominēs | genus | genera |
| Acc. | rēgem | rēgēs | amōrem | amōrēs | hominem | hominēs | genus | genera |
| Gen. | rēgis | rēgum | amōris | amōrum | hominis | hominum | generis | generum |
| Dat. | rēgī | rēgibus | amōrī | amōribus | hominī | hominibus | generī | generibus |
| Abl. | rēge | rēgibus | amōre | amōribus | homine | hominibus | genere | generibus |

## Third Declension –i Stems

| | Sing. | Pl. | | Sing. | Pl. | | Sing. | Pl. |
|---|---|---|---|---|---|---|---|---|
| Nom. | cīvis | cīvēs | | nūbēs | nūbēs | | urbs | urbēs |
| Acc. | cīvem | cīvēs (–īs) | | nūbem | nūbēs (–īs) | | urbem | urbēs (–īs) |
| Gen. | cīvis | cīvium | | nūbis | nūbium | | urbis | urbium |
| Dat. | cīvī | cīvibus | | nūbī | nūbibus | | urbī | urbibus |
| Abl. | cīve (–ī) | civibus | | nūbe | nūbibus | | urbe | urbibus |

| | Sing. | Pl. |
|---|---|---|
| Nom. | animal | animālia |
| Acc. | animal | animālia |
| Gen. | animālis | animālium |
| Dat. | animālī | animālibus |
| Abl. | animālī | animālibus |

## Fourth Declension

| | Sing. | Pl. | | Sing. | Pl. |
|---|---|---|---|---|---|
| Nom. | manus | manūs | | cornū | cornua |
| Acc. | manum | manūs | | cornū | cornua |
| Gen. | manūs | manuum | | cornūs | cornuum |
| Dat. | manuī | manibus | | cornū | cornibus |
| Abl. | manū | manibus | | cornū | cornibus |

## Fifth Declension

| | Sing. | Pl. | | Sing. | Pl. |
|---|---|---|---|---|---|
| Nom. | diēs | diēs | | rēs | rēs |
| Acc. | diem | diēs | | rem | rēs |
| Gen. | diēī | diērum | | reī | rērum |
| Dat. | diēī | diēbus | | reī | rēbus |
| Abl. | diē | diēbus | | rē | rēbus |

# ADJECTIVES

## First and Second Declension

### Sing.

|      | m.      | f.       | n.       |
|------|---------|----------|----------|
| Nom. | bonus   | bona     | bonum    |
| Acc. | bonum   | bonam    | bonum    |
| Gen. | bonī    | bonae    | bonī     |
| Dat. | bonō    | bonae    | bonō     |
| Abl. | bonō    | bonā     | bonō     |
| Nom. | miser   | misera   | miserum  |
| Acc. | miserum | miseram  | miserum  |
| Gen. | miserī  | miserae  | miserī   |
| Dat. | miserō  | miserae  | miserō   |
| Abl. | miserō  | miserā   | miserō   |
| Nom. | pulcher | pulchra  | pulchrum |
| Acc. | pulchrum| pulchram | pulchrum |
| Gen. | pulchrī | pulchrae | pulchrī  |
| Dat. | pulchrō | pulchrae | pulchrī  |
| Abl. | pulchrō | pulchrā  | pulchrō  |

### Pl.

|      | m.         | f.         | n.         |
|------|------------|------------|------------|
| Nom. | bonī       | bonae      | bona       |
| Acc. | bonōs      | bonas      | bona       |
| Gen. | bonōrum    | bonārum    | bonōrum    |
| Dat. | bonīs      | bonīs      | bonīs      |
| Abl. | bonīs      | bonīs      | bonīs      |
| Nom. | miserī     | miserae    | misera     |
| Acc. | miserōs    | miseras    | misera     |
| Gen. | miserōrum  | miserārum  | miserōrum  |
| Dat. | miserīs    | miserīs    | miserīs    |
| Abl. | miserīs    | miserīs    | miserīs    |
| Nom. | pulchrī    | pulchrae   | pulchra    |
| Acc. | pulchrōs   | pulchras   | pulchra    |
| Gen. | pulchrōrum | pulchrārum | pulchrōrum |
| Dat. | pulchrīs   | pulchrīs   | pulchrīs   |
| Abl. | pulchrīs   | pulchrīs   | pulchrīs   |

# Third Declension –i Stems

| | Sing. | | | Pl. | | |
|---|---|---|---|---|---|---|
| | *m.* | *f.* | *n.* | *m.* | *f.* | *n.* |
| *Nom.* | fortis | fortis | forte | fortēs | fortēs | fortia |
| *Acc.* | fortem | fortem | forte | fortēs (-īs) | fortēs (-īs) | fortia |
| *Gen.* | | fortis | | | fortium | |
| *Dat.* | | fortī | | | fortibus | |
| *Abl.* | | fortī | | | fortibus | |
| *Nom.* | sapiens | sapiens | sapiens | sapientēs | sapientēs | sapientia |
| *Acc.* | sapientem | sapientem | sapiens | sapientēs (-īs) | sapientēs (-īs) | sapientia |
| *Gen.* | | sapientis | | | sapientium | |
| *Dat.* | | sapientī | | | sapientibus | |
| *Abl.* | | sapientī (–e) | | | sapientibus | |
| *Nom.* | ācer | ācris | ācre | ācrēs | ācrēs | ācria |
| *Acc.* | ācrem | ācrem | ācre | ācrēs (-īs) | ācrēs (-īs) | ācria |
| *Gen.* | | ācris | | | ācrium | |
| *Dat.* | | ācrī | | | ācribus | |
| *Abl.* | | ācrī | | | ācribus | |

# ADJECTIVES (cont.)

## Third Declension Consonant Stems

### Sing.

|      | m.        | f.        | n.      |
|------|-----------|-----------|---------|
| Nom. | vetus     | vetus     | vetus   |
| Acc. | veterem   | veterem   | vetus   |
| Gen. |           | veteris   |         |
| Dat. |           | veterī    |         |
| Abl. |           | vetere    |         |

|      | m.          | f.          | n.        |
|------|-------------|-------------|-----------|
| Nom. | tristior    | tristior    | tristius  |
| Acc. | tristiōrem  | tristiōrem  | tristius  |
| Gen. |             | tristiōris  |           |
| Dat. |             | tristiōrī   |           |
| Abl. |             | tristiōre   |           |

### Pl.

|      | m.           | f.           | n.       |
|------|--------------|--------------|----------|
| Nom. | veterēs      | veterēs      | vetera   |
| Acc. | veterēs      | veterēs      | vetera   |
| Gen. |              | veterum      |          |
| Dat. |              | veteribus    |          |
| Abl. |              | veteribus    |          |

|      | m.            | f.            | n.         |
|------|---------------|---------------|------------|
| Nom. | tristiōrēs    | tristiōrēs    | tristiōra  |
| Acc. | tristiōrēs    | tristiōrēs    | tristiōra  |
| Gen. |               | tristiōrum    |            |
| Dat. |               | tristiōribus  |            |
| Abl. |               | tristiōribus  |            |

## Comparison of Adjectives

### Regular

| Positive | Comparative | Superlative   |
|----------|-------------|---------------|
| dūrus    | dūrior      | dūrissimus    |
| tristis  | tristior    | tristissimus  |
| fēlix    | fēlīcior    | fēlīcissimus  |
| miser    | miserior    | miserrimus    |
| facilis  | facilior    | facillimus    |

### Irregular

| Positive | Comparative | Superlative |
|----------|-------------|-------------|
| bonus    | melior      | optimus     |
| malus    | pēior       | pessimus    |
| parvus   | minor       | minimus     |
| multus   | plūs        | plūrimus    |
| magnus   | māior       | maximus     |

# PRONOUNS

| | Sing. | | | Pl. | | |
|---|---|---|---|---|---|---|
| | *m.* | *f.* | *n.* | *m.* | *f.* | *n.* |
| *Nom.* | is | ea | id | eī (iī) | eae | ea |
| *Acc.* | eum | eam | id | eōs | eās | ea |
| *Gen.* | ēius | ēius | ēius | eōrum | eārum | eōrum |
| *Dat.* | eī | eī | eī | | eīs (iīs) | |
| *Abl.* | eō | eā | eō | | eīs (iīs) | |
| *Nom.* | hic | haec | hoc | hī | hae | haec |
| *Acc.* | hunc | hanc | hoc | hōs | hās | haec |
| *Gen.* | hūius | hūius | hūius | hōrum | hārum | hōrum |
| *Dat.* | huic | huic | huic | hīs | hīs | |
| *Abl.* | hōc | hāc | hōc | hīs | hīs | |
| *Nom.* | ille | illa | illud | illī | illae | illa |
| *Acc.* | illum | illam | illud | illōs | illās | illa |
| *Gen.* | illius | illius | illius | illōrum | illārum | illōrum |
| *Dat.* | illī | illī | illī | illīs | illīs | |
| *Abl.* | illō | illā | illō | illīs | illīs | |
| *Nom.* | īdem | eadem | idem | eīdem (īdem) | eaedem | eadem |
| *Acc.* | eundem | eandem | idem | eōsdem | eāsdem | eadem |
| *Gen.* | ēiusdem | ēiusdem | ēiusdem | eōrundem | eārundem | eōrundem |
| *Dat.* | eīdem | eīdem | eīdem | | eīsdem (īsdem) | |
| *Abl.* | eōdem | eādem | eōdem | | eīsdem (īsdem) | |

The following 1st and 2nd declension adjectives have a genitive and dative singular in *-ius* and *-ī* like pronouns: *nullus* "not any, no", *sōlus* "alone, only", *tōtus* "the whole of, all", *ūnus* "one, a single".

353

# PRONOUNS (cont.)

Sing.

| | m. | f. | n. |
|---|---|---|---|
| Nom. | quī | quae | quod |
| Acc. | quem | quam | quod |
| Gen. | cūius | cūius | cūius |
| Dat. | cui | cui | cui |
| Abl. | quō | quā | quō |

Pl.

| | m. | f. | n. |
|---|---|---|---|
| Nom. | quī | quae | quae |
| Acc. | quōs | quās | quae |
| Gen. | quōrum | quārum | quōrum |
| Dat. | quibus (quīs) | quibus (quīs) | |
| Abl. | quibus (quīs) | quibus (quīs) | |

Like *quī* are:

(a) interrogative pronouns:

| | | | |
|---|---|---|---|
| Nom. | quis? | | quid? |
| | quī? | | quod? |
| Acc. | quem? | | quid? |
| | quem? | | quod? |
| | *etc.* | | |

(b) indefinite pronouns:

| | m. | n. | f. | n. |
|---|---|---|---|---|
| Nom. | quis | quid | qua | quid |
| | quī | quod | quae | quod |
| Acc. | quem | quid | quam | quid |
| | quem | quod | quam | quod |

(c) compounds of *quī*

## Personal Pronouns

| | Sing. | Pl. |
|---|---|---|
| Nom. | ego | nōs |
| Acc. | mē | nōs |
| Gen. | meī | nostrī (–um) |
| Dat. | mihi | nōbīs |
| Abl. | mē | nōbīs |

| | Sing. | Pl. |
|---|---|---|
| Nom. | tū | vōs |
| Acc. | tē | vōs |
| Gen. | tuī | vestrī (–um) |
| Dat. | tibi | vōbīs |
| Abl. | tē | vōbīs |

| | Sing. and Pl. |
|---|---|
| Nom. | – |
| Acc. | sē (sēsē) |
| Gen. | suī |
| Dat. | sibi |
| Abl. | sē (sēsē) |

The following suffixes are sometimes added to personal pronouns:

(a) –*met* to add emphasis, e.g. *egomet* "I myself";

(b) –*cum* (prep w.abl), e.g. *mēcum* "with me".

# VERBS: THE IMPERFECT SYSTEM

| | 1 Act. | 1 Pass. | 2 Act. | 2 Pass. | 3 Act. | 3 Pass. | 4 Act. | 4 Pass. |
|---|---|---|---|---|---|---|---|---|
| **Present Indicative** | | | | | | | | |
| Sing. 1 | amō | amor | habeō | habeor | dīcō | dīcor | audiō | audior |
| 2 | amās | amāris (–re) | habēs | habēris (–re) | dīcis | dīceris (–re) | audīs | audīris (–re) |
| 3 | amat | amātur | habet | habētur | dīcit | dīcitur | audit | audītur |
| Pl. 1 | amāmus | amāmur | habēmus | habēmur | dīcimus | dīcimur | audīmus | audīmur |
| 2 | amātis | amāminī | habētis | habēminī | dīcitis | dīciminī | audītis | audīminī |
| 3 | amant | amantur | habent | habentur | dīcunt | dīcuntur | audiunt | audiuntur |
| **Imperfect Indicative** | | | | | | | | |
| Sing. 1 | amābam | amābar | habēbam | habēbar | dīcēbam | dīcēbar | audiēbam | audiēbar |
| 2 | amābās | amābāris (–re) | habēbās | habēbāris (–re) | dīcēbās | dīcēbāris (–re) | audiēbās | audiēbāris (–re) |
| 3 | amābat | amābātur | habēbat | habēbātur | dīcēbat | dīcēbātur | audiēbat | audiēbātur |
| Pl. 1 | amābāmus | amābāmur | habēbāmus | habēbāmur | dīcēbāmus | dīcēbāmur | audiēbāmus | audiēbāmur |
| 2 | amābātis | amābāminī | habēbātis | habēbāminī | dīcēbātis | dīcēbāminī | audiēbātis | audiēbāminī |
| 3 | amābant | amābantur | habēbant | habēbantur | dīcēbant | dīcēbantur | audiēbant | audiēbantur |
| **Future Indicative** | | | | | | | | |
| Sing. 1 | amābō | amābor | habēbō | habēbor | dīcam | dīcar | audiam | audiar |
| 2 | amābis | amāberis (–re) | habēbis | habēberis (–re) | dīcēs | dīcēris (–re) | audiēs | audiēris (–re) |
| 3 | amābit | amābitur | habēbit | habēbitur | dīcet | dīcetur | audiet | audiētur |
| Pl. 1 | amābimus | amābimur | habēbimus | habēbimur | dīcēmus | dīcēmur | audiēmus | audiēmur |
| 2 | amābitis | amābiminī | habēbitis | habēbiminī | dīcētis | dīceminī | audiētis | audiēminī |
| 3 | amābunt | amābuntur | habēbunt | habēbuntur | dīcent | dīcentur | audient | audientur |

## VERBS: THE IMPERFECT SYSTEM (cont.)

### Present Subjunctive

| | | 1 Act. | 1 Pass. | 2 Act. | 2 Pass. | 3 Act. | 3 Pass. | 4 Act. | 4 Pass. |
|---|---|---|---|---|---|---|---|---|---|
| Sing. | 1 | amem | amer | habeam | habear | dīcam | dīcar | audiam | audiar |
| | 2 | amēs | amēris (-re) | habeās | habeāris (-re) | dīcās | dīcāris (-re) | audiās | audiāris (-re) |
| | 3 | amet | amētur | habeat | habeātur | dīcat | dīcātur | audiat | audiātur |
| Pl. | 1 | amēmus | amēmur | habeāmus | habeāmur | dīcāmus | dīcāmur | audiāmus | audiāmur |
| | 2 | amētis | amēminī | habeātis | habeāminī | dīcātis | dīcāminī | audiātis | audiāminī |
| | 3 | ament | amentur | habeant | habeantur | dīcant | dīcantur | audiant | audiantur |

### Imperfect Subjunctive

| | | 1 Act. | 1 Pass. | 2 Act. | 2 Pass. | 3 Act. | 3 Pass. | 4 Act. | 4 Pass. |
|---|---|---|---|---|---|---|---|---|---|
| Sing. | 1 | amārem | amārer | habērem | habērer | dīcerem | dīcerer | audīrem | audīrer |
| | 2 | amārēs | amārēris (-re) | habērēs | habērēris (-re) | dīcerēs | dīcerēris (-re) | audīrēs | audīrēris (-re) |
| | 3 | amāret | amārētur | habēret | habērētur | dīceret | dīcerētur | audīret | audīrētur |
| Pl. | 1 | amārēmus | amārēmur | habērēmus | habērēmur | dīcerēmus | dīcerēmur | audīrēmus | audīrēmur |
| | 2 | amārētis | amārēminī | habērētis | habērēminī | dīcerētis | dīcerēminī | audīrētis | audīrēminī |
| | 3 | amārent | amārentur | habērent | habērentur | dīcerent | dīcerentur | audīrent | audīrentur |

|  | 1 Act. | 1 Pass. | 2 Act. | 2 Pass. | 3 Act. | 3 Pass. | 4 Act. | 4 Pass. |
|---|---|---|---|---|---|---|---|---|
| **Present Imperative** | | | | | | | | |
| Sing. | amā | amāre | habē | habēre | dīc★ | dīcere | audī | audīre |
| Pl. | amāte | amāminī | habēte | habēminī | dīcite | dīciminī | audīte | audīminī |
| **Future Imperative** | | | | | | | | |
| Sing. | amātō | | habētō | | dīcitō | | audītō | |
| Pl. | amātōte | | habētōte | | dīcitōte | | audītōte | |
| **Present Infinitive** | | | | | | | | |
| | amāre | amāri | habēre | habēri | dicere | dīcī | audire | audīri |
| **Present Participle** | | | | | | | | |
| | amans –ntis | | habens –ntis | | dīcens –ntis | | audiens –ntis | |
| **Gerund** | | | | | | | | |
| | amandum | | habendum | | dīcendum | | audiendum | |
| **Gerundive** | | | | | | | | |
| | amandus –a –um | | habendus –a –um | | dīcendus –a –um | | audiendus –a –um | |

★ an irregular form: see chapter 16 Morphology

357

# VERBS: THE PERFECT SYSTEM

|  |  | 1 | 2 | | 3 | | 4 | |
|---|---|---|---|---|---|---|---|---|
|  |  | Act. | Pass. | Act. | Pass. | Act. | Pass. | Act. | Pass. |

## Perfect Indicative

|  |  | Act. (1) | Pass. (1) | Act. (2) | Pass. (2) | Act. (3) | Pass. (3) | Act. (4) | Pass. (4) |
|---|---|---|---|---|---|---|---|---|---|
| Sing. | 1 | amāvī | amātus sum | habuī | habitus sum | dīxī | dictus sum | audīvī | audītus sum |
|  | 2 | amāvistī | amātus es | habuistī | habitus es | dīxistī | dictus es | audīvistī | audītus es |
|  | 3 | amāvit | amātus est | habuit | habitus est | dīxit | dictus est | audīvit | audītus est |
| Pl. | 1 | amāvimus | amātī sumus | habuimus | habitī sumus | dīximus | dictī sumus | audīvimus | audītī sumus |
|  | 2 | amāvistis | amātī estis | habuistis | habitī estis | dīxistis | dictī estis | audīvistis | audītī estis |
|  | 3 | amāvērunt (–ēre) | amātī sunt | habuērunt (–ēre) | habitī sunt | dīxērunt (–ēre) | dictī sunt | audīvērunt (–ēre) | audītī sunt |

## Pluperfect Indicative

|  |  | Act. (1) | Pass. (1) | Act. (2) | Pass. (2) | Act. (3) | Pass. (3) | Act. (4) | Pass. (4) |
|---|---|---|---|---|---|---|---|---|---|
| Sing. | 1 | amāveram | amātus eram | habueram | habitus eram | dīxeram | dictus eram | audīveram | audītus eram |
|  | 2 | amāverās | amātus erās | habuerās | habitus erās | dīxerās | dictus erās | audīverās | audītus erās |
|  | 3 | amāverat | amātus erat | habuerat | habitus erat | dīxerat | dictus erat | audīverat | audītus erat |
| Pl. | 1 | amāverāmus | amātī erāmus | habuerāmus | habitī erāmus | dīxerāmus | dictī erāmus | audīverāmus | audītī erāmus |
|  | 2 | amāverātis | amātī erātis | habuerātis | habitī erātis | dīxerātis | dictī erātis | audīverātis | audītī erātis |
|  | 3 | amāverant | amātī erant | habuerant | habitī erant | dīxerant | dictī erant | audīverant | audītī erant |

## Future Perfect Indicative

|  |  | Act. (1) | Pass. (1) | Act. (2) | Pass. (2) | Act. (3) | Pass. (3) | Act. (4) | Pass. (4) |
|---|---|---|---|---|---|---|---|---|---|
| Sing. | 1 | amāverō | amātus erō | habuerō | habitus erō | dīxerō | dictus erō | audīverō | audītus erō |
|  | 2 | amāveris | amātus eris | habueris | habitus eris | dīxeris | dictus eris | audīveris | audītus eris |
|  | 3 | amāverit | amātus erit | habuerit | habitus erit | dīxerit | dictus erit | audīverit | audītus erit |
| Pl. | 1 | amāverimus | amātī erimus | habuerimus | habitī erimus | dīxerimus | dictī erimus | audīverimus | audītī erimus |
|  | 2 | amāveritis | amātī eritis | habueritis | habitī eritis | dīxeritis | dictī eritis | audīveritis | audītī eritis |
|  | 3 | amāverint | amātī erunt | habuerint | habitī erunt | dīxerint | dictī erunt | audīverint | audītī erunt |

## Perfect Subjunctive

| | | 1 | | 2 | | 3 | | 4 |
| | | Act. | Pass. | Act. | Pass. | Act. | Pass. | Act. | Pass. |
|---|---|---|---|---|---|---|---|---|---|
| Sing. | 1 | amāverim | amātus sim | habuerim | habitus sim | dīxerim | dictus sim | audīverim | audītus sim |
| | 2 | amāverīs | amātus sīs | habuerīs | habitus sīs | dīxerīs | dictus sīs | audīverīs | audītus sīs |
| | 3 | amāverit | amātus sit | habuerit | habitus sit | dīxerit | dictus sit | audīverit | audītus sit |
| Pl. | 1 | amāverīmus | amātī sīmus | habuerīmus | habitī sīmus | dīxerīmus | dictī sīmus | audīverīmus | audītī sīmus |
| | 2 | amāverītis | amātī sītis | habuerītis | habitī sītis | dīxerītis | dictī sītis | audīverītis | audītī sītis |
| | 3 | amāverint | amātī sint | habuerint | habitī sint | dīxerint | dictī sint | audīverint | audītī sint |

## Pluperfect Subjunctive

| | | 1 | | 2 | | 3 | | 4 |
| | | Act. | Pass. | Act. | Pass. | Act. | Pass. | Act. | Pass. |
|---|---|---|---|---|---|---|---|---|---|
| Sing. | 1 | amāvissem | amātus essem | habuissem | habitus essem | dīxissem | dictus essem | audīvissem | audītus essem |
| | 2 | amāvissēs | amātus essēs | habuissēs | habitus essēs | dīxissēs | dictus essēs | audīvissēs | audītus essēs |
| | 3 | amāvisset | amātus esset | habuisset | habitus esset | dīxisset | dictus esset | audīvisset | audītus esset |
| Pl. | 1 | amāvissēmus | amātī essemus | habuissēmus | habitī essēmus | dīxissēmus | dictī essēmus | audīvissēmus | audītī essēmus |
| | 2 | amāvissētis | amātī essētis | habuissētis | habitī essētis | dīxissētis | dictī essētis | audīvissētis | audītī essētis |
| | 3 | amāvissent | amātī essent | habuissent | habitī essent | dīxissent | dictī essent | audīvissent | audītī essent |

359

## VERBS: THE PERFECT SYSTEM (cont.)

| | 1 | | 2 | | 3 | | 4 | |
|---|---|---|---|---|---|---|---|---|
| | Act. | Pass. | Act. | Pass. | Act. | Pass. | Act. | Pass. |
| **Perfect Infinitive** | amāvisse | amātus esse | habuisse | habitus esse | dīxisse | dictus esse | audīvisse | audītus esse |
| **Future Infinitive** | amātūrus esse | amātum īrī | habitūrus esse | habitum īrī | dictūrus esse | dictum īrī | audītūrus esse | audītum īrī |
| **Past Participle** | | amātus –a –um | | habitus –a –um | | dictus –a –um | | audītus –a –um |
| **Future Participle** | amātūrus –a –um | | habitūrus –a –um | | dictūrus –a –um | | audītūrus –a –um | |
| **Supine** | amātum | | habitum | | dictum | | audītum | |
| | amatū | | habitū | | dictū | | audītū | |

## VERBS: IRREGULAR

The following verbs are irregular in the imperfect system; their perfect forms being regular are not given here:

(a) verbs in –iō with present infinitive in –ere;

(b) *ferō ferre tulī lātum* and its compounds.

## Present Indicative

| | capiō (Act.) | capior (Pass.) | ferō (Act.) | feror (Pass.) |
|---|---|---|---|---|
| Sing. 1 | capiō | capior | ferō | feror |
| 2 | capis | caperis (–re) | fers | ferris |
| 3 | capit | capitur | fert | fertur |
| Pl. 1 | capimus | capimur | ferimus | ferimur |
| 2 | capitis | capiminī | fertis | feriminī |
| 3 | capiunt | capiuntur | ferunt | feruntur |

## Imperfect Indicative

| | Act. | Pass. | Act. | Pass. |
|---|---|---|---|---|
| Sing. 1 | capiēbam | capiēbar | ferēbam | ferēbar |
| 2 | capiēbās | capiēbāris | ferēbās | ferēbāris (–re) |
| 3 | capiēbat | capiēbatur | ferēbat | ferēbatur |
| Pl. 1 | capiēbāmus | capiēbāmur | ferēbāmus | ferēbāmur |
| 2 | capiēbātis | capiēbāminī | ferēbātis | ferēbāminī |
| 3 | capiēbant | capiēbantur | ferēbant | ferēbantur |

## Future Indicative

| | Act. | Pass. | Act. | Pass. |
|---|---|---|---|---|
| Sing. 1 | capiam | capiar | feram | ferar |
| 2 | capiēs | capiēris (–re) | ferēs | ferēris (–re) |
| 3 | capiet | capiētur | feret | ferētur |
| Pl. 1 | capiēmus | capiēmur | ferēmus | ferēmur |
| 2 | capiētis | capiēminī | ferētis | ferēminī |
| 3 | capient | capientur | ferent | ferentur |

## Present Subjunctive

| | Act. | Pass. | Act. | Pass. |
|---|---|---|---|---|
| Sing. 1 | capiam | capiar | feram | ferar |
| 2 | capiās | capiāris (–re) | ferās | ferāris (–re) |
| 3 | capiat | capiātur | ferat | ferātur |
| Pl. 1 | capiāmus | capiāmur | ferāmus | ferāmur |
| 2 | capiātis | capiāminī | ferātis | ferāminī |
| 3 | capiant | capiantur | ferant | ferantur |

## Imperfect Subjunctive

| | Act. | Pass. | Act. | Pass. |
|---|---|---|---|---|
| Sing. 1 | caperem | caperer | ferrem | ferrer |
| 2 | caperēs | caperēris (–re) | ferrēs | ferrēris (–re) |
| 3 | caperet | caperētur | ferret | ferrētur |
| Pl. 1 | caperēmus | caperēmur | ferrēmus | ferrēmur |
| 2 | caperētis | caperēminī | ferrētis | ferrēminī |
| 3 | caperent | caperentur | ferrent | ferrentur |

## Present Imperative

| | Act. | Pass. | Act. | Pass. |
|---|---|---|---|---|
| Sing. | cape | capere | fer | ferre |
| Pl. | capite | capiminī | ferte | feriminī |

## Future Imperative

| | Act. | Act. |
|---|---|---|
| Sing. | capitō | fertō |
| Pl. | capitōte | fertōte |

## Present Infinitive

| Act. | Pass. | Act. | Pass. |
|---|---|---|---|
| capere | capī | ferre | ferrī |

## Present Participle

| | |
|---|---|
| capiēns –ntis | ferēns –ntis |

## Gerund

| | |
|---|---|
| capiendum | ferendum |

## Gerundive

| | |
|---|---|
| capiendus –a –um | ferendus –a –um |

361

# VERBS: IRREGULAR (cont.)

The following verbs have only active forms; they are irregular in the imperfect system; their perfect forms being regular are not given here:

## Present Indicative

| | | | | | | | |
|---|---|---|---|---|---|---|---|
| *Sing.* 1 | sum | possum | volō | nōlō | mālō | eō | fīō |
| 2 | es | potes | vīs | nōn vīs | māvīs | īs | fīs |
| 3 | est | potest | vult | nōn vult | māvult | it | fit |
| *Pl.* 1 | sumus | possumus | volumus | nōlumus | mālumus | īmus | — |
| 2 | estis | potestis | vultis | nōn vultis | māvultis | ītis | — |
| 3 | sunt | possunt | volunt | nōlunt | mālunt | eunt | fiunt |

## Imperfect Indicative

| | | | | | | | |
|---|---|---|---|---|---|---|---|
| *Sing.* 1 | eram | poteram | volēbam | nōlēbam | mālēbam | ībam | fīēbam |
| 2 | erās | poterās | volēbās | nōlēbās | mālēbās | ībās | fīēbās |
| 3 | erat | poterat | volēbat | nōlēbat | mālēbat | ībat | fīēbat |
| *Pl.* 1 | erāmus | poterāmus | volēbāmus | nōlēbāmus | mālēbāmus | ībāmus | fīēbāmus |
| 2 | erātis | poterātis | volēbātis | nōlēbātis | mālēbātis | ībātis | fīēbātis |
| 3 | erant | poterant | volēbant | nōlēbant | mālēbant | ībant | fīēbant |

## Future Indicative

| | | | | | | | |
|---|---|---|---|---|---|---|---|
| *Sing.* 1 | erō | poterō | volam | nōlam | mālam | ībō | fīam |
| 2 | eris | poteris | volēs | nōlēs | mālēs | ībis | fīēs |
| 3 | erit | poterit | volet | nōlet | mālet | ībit | fīet |
| *Pl.* 1 | erimus | poterimus | volēmus | nōlēmus | mālēmus | ībimus | fīēmus |
| 2 | eritis | poteritis | volētis | nōlētis | mālētis | ībitis | fīētis |
| 3 | erunt | poterunt | volent | nōlent | mālent | ībunt | fīent |

## Present Subjunctive

| | | | | | | | |
|---|---|---|---|---|---|---|---|
| Sing. 1 | sim | possim | velim | nōlim | mālim | eam | fīam |
| 2 | sīs | possīs | velīs | nōlīs | mālīs | eās | fīās |
| 3 | sit | possit | velit | nōlit | mālit | eat | fīat |
| Pl. 1 | sīmus | possīmus | velīmus | nōlīmus | mālīmus | eāmus | fīāmus |
| 2 | sītis | possītis | velītis | nōlītis | mālītis | eātis | fīātis |
| 3 | sint | possint | velint | nōlint | mālint | eant | fīant |

## Imperfect Subjunctive

| | | | | | | | |
|---|---|---|---|---|---|---|---|
| Sing. 1 | essem | possem | vellem | nōllem | māllem | īrem | fierem |
| 2 | essēs | possēs | vellēs | nōllēs | māllēs | īrēs | fierēs |
| 3 | esset | posset | vellet | nōllet | māllet | īret | fieret |
| Pl. 1 | essēmus | possēmus | vellēmus | nōllēmus | māllēmus | īrēmus | fierēmus |
| 2 | essētis | possētis | vellētis | nōllētis | māllētis | īrētis | fierētis |
| 3 | essent | possent | vellent | nōllent | māllent | īrent | fierent |

## Present Imperative

| | | | | | | | |
|---|---|---|---|---|---|---|---|
| Sing. | es | – | – | nōlī | – | ī | – |
| Pl. | este | – | – | nōlīte | – | īte | – |

## Future Imperative

| | | | | | | | |
|---|---|---|---|---|---|---|---|
| Sing. | estō | – | – | nōlitō | – | ītō | – |
| Pl. | estōte | – | – | nōlitōte | – | ītōte | – |

## Present Infinitive

| | | | | | | |
|---|---|---|---|---|---|---|
| esse | posse | velle | nōlle | mālle | īre | fierī |

## Present Participle

| | | | | | | |
|---|---|---|---|---|---|---|
| *sens –tis | *potens –tis | volens –ntis | nōlens –ntis | – | iens euntis | – |

## Gerund

| | | | | | | |
|---|---|---|---|---|---|---|
| – | – | – | – | – | eundum | – |

## Gerundive

| | | | | | | |
|---|---|---|---|---|---|---|
| – | – | – | – | – | – | – |

* *sens* is only used in compounds; *potens* is only used as an adjective.

363

# APPENDIX A

## Authors and Works

References to authors and works were given in abbreviated form throughout this course. Expansion of the abbreviations, and very brief details about each author, will be found in the following list.

Apul.　APULEIUS, rhetorical and narrative writer (b. AD 123)
　　　　*Apol.* = *Apologia*
August.　St AUGUSTINE, early Christian writer (AD 354-430)
　　　　*Conf.* = *Confessiones*
Caes.　CAESAR, historian (102-44 BC)
　　　　*B.G.* = *de Bello Gallico*
Cato　CATO, agricultural writer (234-149 BC)
　　　　*Agr.* = *de Agricultura*
Catul.　CATULLUS, love poet (c.85-c.54 BC)
　　　　(*Carmina* = 'Poems')
Cic.　CICERO, orator, writer on philosophy and rhetoric (106-43 BC)
　　　　*Amic.* = *de Amicitia*
　　　　*Arch.* = *pro Archia*
　　　　*Att.* = *Epistulae ad Atticum*
　　　　*Cael.* = *pro Caelio*
　　　　*Catil.* = *in Catilinam*
　　　　*de Orat.* = *de Oratore*
　　　　*Div.* = *de Divinatione*
　　　　*Div. Caec.* = *Divinatio in Q. Caecilium*
　　　　*Fam.* = *Epistulae ad Familiares*
　　　　*Fin.* = *de Finibus*
　　　　*Leg.* = *de Legibus*
　　　　*Mur.* = *pro Murena*
　　　　*N.D.* = *de Natura Deorum*
　　　　*Off.* = *de Officiis*
　　　　*Orat.* = *Orator*
　　　　*Parad.* = *Paradoxa Stoicorum*
　　　　*Phil.* = *Philippicae*
　　　　*S.Rosc.* = *pro S. Roscio Amerino*
　　　　*Sen.* = *de Senectute*
　　　　*Tusc.* = *Tusculanae Disputationes*
　　　　*Ver.* = *in Verrem* [(I) / (II)1-5]

Claud.   CLAUDIAN, epic poet (fl. AD 395)
         *Carm. Min. = Carmina Minora*
Col.     COLUMELLA, agricultural writer (fl. AD 60)
         (*de Re Rustica*)
Hor.     HORACE, lyric and satirical poet (65-8 BC)
         *Carm. = Carmina* ('Odes')
         *Ep. = Epistulae*
         *Epod. = Epodi*
         *Saec. = Carmen Saeculare*
         *Serm. = Sermones* ('Satires')
Juv.     JUVENAL, satirical poet (fl. AD 100)
         (*Satirae*)
Liv.     LIVY, historian (c.59 BC-c.AD 17)
         (*Ab Urbe Condita*)
Lucr.    LUCRETIUS, philosophical poet (c.94-55 BC)
         (*de Rerum Natura*)
Mart.    MARTIAL, epigrammatist (c.AD 40-101)
         (*Epigrammata*)
Nep.     NEPOS, biographer (c.99-24 BC)
         (*Vitae*)
         *Cha. = Chabrias*
         *Han. = Hannibal*
         *Them. = Themistocles*
Ov.      OVID, epic and amatory poet (43 BC- c.AD 17)
         *Am. = Amores*
         *Ars = Ars Amatoria*
         *Her. = Heroides*
         *Met. = Metamorphoses*
         *Pont. = Epistulae ex Ponto*
         *Rem. = Remedia Amoris*
         *Tr. = Tristia*
Pac.     PACUVIUS, tragic dramatist (220-c.130 BC)
         *incert.* = (uncertain)
Petr.    PETRONIUS, prose satirist (fl. c. AD 50)
         (*Satyricon*)
Pl.      PLAUTUS, comic dramatist (c.254-184 BC)
         *Am. = Amphitruo*
         *Aul. = Aulularia*
         *Capt. = Captivi*
         *Cist. = Cistellaria*
         *Cur. = Curculio*
         *Men. = Menaechmi*
         *Mer. = Mercator*
         *Mos. = Mostellaria*
         *Per. = Persa*
         *St. = Stichus*
         *Trin. = Trinummus*
         *Truc. = Truculentus*

Plin.   PLINY THE ELDER, encyclopaedic writer (AD 23-79)
        *Nat. = Naturalis Historia*
Plin.   PLINY THE YOUNGER, letter writer (c.AD 61-c.114)
        *Ep. = Epistulae*
Prop.   PROPERTIUS, love elegist (c.55-15 BC)
        (*Elegiae*)
Quint.  QUINTILIAN, educationalist (c.AD35-?)
        *Inst. = Institutiones Oratoriae*
Sall.   SALLUST, historian (86-c.34 BC)
        *Cat. = Catilina*
        *Jug. = Jugurtha*
Sen.    SENECA (THE YOUNGER), philosopher and tragic dramatist
        (c.5 BC - AD 65)
        *Ben. = de Beneficiis*
        *Dial. = Dialogi*
        *Ep. = Epistulae*
        *Oct. = Octavia* (spurious)
        *Q.N. = Naturales Questiones*
Tac.    TACITUS, historian (c.AD 55-?)
        *Ann. = Annales*
Ter.    TERENCE, comic dramatist (c.185-159 BC)
        *Eu. = Eunuchus*
Tib.    TIBULLUS, love elegist (c.48-19 BC)
        (*Elegiae*)
Val.Max. VALERIUS MAXIMUS, historian (fl.AD 27)
        (*Memorabilia*)
Var.    VARRO, scholar and antiquarian (116-27 BC)
        *R.R. = Res Rusticae*
Verg.   VIRGIL, epic, didactic and bucolic poet (70-19 BC)
        *Aen. = Aeneis*
        *Ecl. = Eclogae*
        *Georg. = Georgica*
        [V.] *Copa* (spurious)

# APPENDIX B

## Original Form of Adapted Latin Passages

This appendix lists in unaltered form all the Latin passages which were altered or abbreviated on their first appearance, and were therefore marked with a small asterisk. Omissions which do not affect the syntax and add only minimally to the context are indicated by "...". "E" and "R" refer respectively to the Examples and the Reading section of each chapter.

CHAPTER 2

E1    nam illic homo tuam hereditatem inhiat quasi esuriens lupus. (Pl. *St.* 605)

E3    pauper locupletem optare podagram
nec dubitet Ladas, si non eget Anticyra nec
Archigene. (Juv. 13.96)

E4    domum suam istum non fere quisquam vocabat. (Cic. *S.Rosc.* 52)

E5    tunc scito esse te omnibus cupiditatibus solutum, cum eo perveneris ut nihil deum roges nisi quod rogare possis palam. (Sen. *Ep.* 10.5)

R1    atqui, inquit, si Stoicis concedis, ut virtus sola, si sit, vitam efficiat beatam, concedis etiam Peripateticis. (Cic. *Fin.* 5.78)

R2    ... paupertatis, quam nemo gravem sentit nisi qui putat. (Sen. *Dial.* 12.12.1)

R3    animus hominis dives, non arca appellari solet. (Cic. *Parad.* 44)

R6    beata est ergo vita conveniens ad naturam suam, quae non aliter contingere potest quam si primum sana mens est et in perpetua possessione sanitatis suae, deinde fortis ac vehemens. (Sen. *Dial.* 7.3.3)

R10   quid enim prohibet nos beatam vitam dicere liberum animum et erectum et interritum ac stabilem, extra metum, extra cupiditatem positum? (Sen. *Dial.* 7.4.3)

## CHAPTER 3

E4  beatus autem esse sine virtute nemo potest. (Cic. *N.D.* 1.48)

R1  luce sacra requiescat humus, requiescat arator. (Tib. 2.1.5)

R6  velut haec meretrix meum erum miserum sua blanditia intulit in pauperiem. (Pl. *Truc.* 572)

R8  infelices quidam non sine voluptate, immo ob ipsam voluptatem sunt, quod non evenerit si virtuti se voluptas inmiscuisset, qua virtus saepe caret, numquam indiget. (Sen. *Dial.* 7.7.2)

## CHAPTER 4

R7  fuerit mihi eguisse aliquando pretium tuae amicitiae, qua apud meum animum nihil carius est. (Sall. *Jug.* 110.3)

R8  paucis carior fides quam pecunia fuit. (Sall. *Jug.* 16.4)

R9  nihil est enim, mihi crede, virtute formosius, nihil pulchrius, nihil amabilius. (Cic. *Fam.* 9.14.4)

## CHAPTER 5

E2  profecto non tam perspicue nos istorum maleficia videremus, nisi ipsos caecos redderet cupiditas et avaritia et audacia. (Cic. *S.Rosc.* 101)

E3  vitiorum ... quae eo magis latent, quo maiora sunt. (Sen. *Ep.* 53.5)

E5  luxuria victrix orbis immensas opes
iam pridem avaris manibus, ut perdat, rapit. (Sen. *Oct.* 434)

R3  quamquam sacrilegium, furtum, adulterium inter bona haberi prorsus persuasimus. quam multi furto non erubescunt, quam multi adulterio gloriantur! nam sacrilegia minuta puniuntur, magna in triumphis feruntur. (Sen. *Ep.* 87.23)

R5  contra evenit in his morbis quibus afficiuntur animi: quo quis peius se habet, minus sentit ... quare vitia sua nemo confitetur? (Sen. *Ep.* 53.7)

R9      nam si ratio et prudentia curas,
non locus effusi late maris arbiter aufert,
caelum non animum mutant, qui trans mare currunt.
(Hor. *Ep.* 1.11.25)

## CHAPTER 6

E3  in primis autem et illos numero qui nulli rei nisi vino ac libidini vacant. (Sen. *Dial.* 10.7.1)

E4      "artibus" inquit "honestis
nullus in urbe locus".          (Juv. 3.21)

R1  an ille mihi liber cui mulier imperat? (Cic. *Parad.* 36)

R3  videt igne micantis sideribus similis oculos. (Ov. *Met.* 1.498)

R5  "sed naturale est" inquis "ut desiderio amici torquear; da ius lacrimis tam iuste cadentibus. naturale est opinionibus hominum tangi et adversis contristari: quare mihi non permittas hunc tam honestum malae opinionis metum?" nullum est vitium sine patrocinio; nulli non initium verecundum est et exorabile, sed ab hoc latius funditur. (Sen. *Ep.* 116.2)

R7    numina sint precibus non inimica meis. (Ov. *Pont.* 2.8.38)

R8    nam cui aliquid accedere potest, id imperfectum est; cui aliquid abscedere potest, id imperpetuum est: cuius perpetua futura laetitia est, is suo gaudet. omnia autem quibus vulgus inhiat ultro citroque fluunt: nihil dat fortuna mancipio. (Sen. *Ep.* 72.7)

R9    non irascetur sapiens peccantibus. quare? quia scit neminem nasci sapientem sed fieri, scit paucissimos omni aevo sapientis evadere, quia condicionem humanae vitae perspectam habet; nemo autem naturae sanus irascitur. (Sen. *Dial.* 4.10.6)

R10   sed multi mortales, dediti ventri atque somno, indocti incultique vitam sicuti peregrinantes transigere: quibus profecto contra naturam corpus voluptati, anima oneri est. (Sall. *Cat.* 2.8)

## CHAPTER 7

E1    et quia pecori bonus alendo erat ... (Liv. 29.31.9)

R1    tres viros coloniae deducendae agroque dividendo creaverunt. (Liv. 8.16.14)

R3    nunc quod satis est ad omnis miserias leniendas, sapientibus me viris dedi. (Sen. *Dial.* 12.5.2)

R4    at in ea quidem spernenda et repudianda virtus vel maxime cernitur. (Cic. *Leg.* 1.52)

R10   quid ais Eruci? tot praedia, tam pulchra, tam fructuosa Sex. Roscius filio suo relegationis ac supplici gratia colenda ac tuenda tradiderat? (Cic. *S.Rosc.* 43)

## CHAPTER 8

E1    censores, vacui ab operum locandorum cura propter inopiam aerarii, ad mores hominum regendos animum advertunt. (Liv. 24.18.2)

E3    magis illa iuvant quae pluris ementur. (Juv. 11.16)

E4    nam quis est, pro deum fidem atque hominum, qui velit, ut neque diligat quemquam, nec ipse ab ullo diligatur, circumfluere omnibus copiis atque in omnium rerum abundantia vivere? (Cic. *Amic.* 52)

R1    est enim proprium stultitiae aliorum vitia cernere, oblivisci suorum. (Cic. *Tusc.* 3.73)

R2    si isti callidi rerum aestimatores prata et areas quasdam magno aestimant ... quanti est aestimanda virtus? (Cic. *Parad.* 51)

R2    nam amator meretricis mores sibi emit auro et purpura.
      ...
      pulchra mulier nuda erit quam purpurata pulchrior:
      poste nequiquam exornata est bene, si morata est male.
      pulchrum ornatum turpes mores peius caeno collinunt.
      (Pl. *Mos.* 286)

R3    at vero in M. Caelio ... nulla luxuries reperitur, nulli sumptus, nullum aes alienum, nulla conviviorum ac lustrorum libido. (Cic. *Cael.* 44)

R5    verum si quis est qui etiam meretriciis amoribus interdictum iuventuti putet, est ille quidem valde severus; abhorret non modo ab huius saeculi licentia verum etiam a maiorum consuetudine atque concessis. (Cic. *Cael.* 48)

R7     unum exemplum luxuriae aut avaritiae multum mali facit: convictor delicatus paulatim enervat et mollit, vicinus dives cupiditatem irritat, malignus comes quamvis candido et simplici rubiginem suam affricuit. (Sen. *Ep.* 7.7)

R10    quanto rerum minus, tanto minus cupiditatis erat: nuper divitiae avaritiam et abundantes voluptates desiderium per luxum atque libidinem pereundi perdendique omnia invexere. (Liv. *pr.* 12)

CHAPTER 9

E3     sed lacte fieri debet sincero et quam recentissimo. (Col. 7.8.1)

E4     si quid superfuerit post solstitium, acetum acerrimum et pulcherrimum erit. (Cato *Agr.* 104.2)

E5     scilicet in tantis opibus, quas, optima matrum,
terra parit. (Ov. *Met.* 15.91)

R1     et virum bonum cum laudabant, ita laudabant, bonum agricolam bonumque colonum. amplissime laudari existimabatur qui ita laudabatur. (Cato *Agr.* 1.2)

R2     quasi vero mihi difficile sit quamvis multos nominatim proferre, ne longius abeam, vel tribulis vel vicinos meos qui suos liberos, quos plurimi faciunt, agricolas assiduos esse cupiunt. (Cic. *S.Rosc.* 47)

R8     cum enim Gyges regno Lydiae, armis et divitiis abundantissimo, inflatus animo Apollinem Pythium sciscitatum venisset an aliquis mortalium se esset felicior, deus ex abdito sacrarii specu voce missa Aglaum Psophidium ei praetulit. is erat Arcadum pauperrimus, sed aetate iam senior terminos agelli sui numquam excesserat, parvuli ruris fructibus et voluptatibus contentus. (Val. Max. 7.1.2)

R9     nunc contra villam urbanam quam maximam ac politissimam habeant dant operam. (Var. *R.R.* 1.13.7)

R10    protrahatur etiam avaritia latentium indagatrix lucrorum, manifestae praedae avidissima vorago, neque habendi fructu felix et cupiditate quaerendi miserrima. (Val. Max. 9.4.intr)

CHAPTER 10

E1     divitias alii praeponunt, bonam alii valetudinem, alii potentiam, alii honores, multi etiam voluptates. (Cic. *Amic.* 20)

E3     patria, quae mihi vita mea multo est carior. (Cic. *Catil.* 1.27)

R6     potest enim non solum aliud mihi ac tibi, sed mihimet ipsi aliud alias videri. (Cic. *Orat.* 237)

R7     labor optimos citat; senatus per totum diem saepe consulitur, cum illo tempore vilissimus quisque aut in campo otium suum oblectet, aut in popina lateat, aut tempus in aliquo circulo terat. (Sen. *Dial.* 1.5.4)

R10    at populo Romano numquam ea copia fuit, quia prudentissimus quisque maxime negotiosus erat, ingenium nemo sine corpore exercebat, optimus quisque facere quam dicere, sua ab aliis benefacta laudari quam ipse aliorum narrare malebat. (Sall. *Cat.* 8.5)

## CHAPTER 11

E3    haud facul ... femina una invenietur bona. (Pac. *incert*. 35W)

E4    eheu quid faciant, dic, homines, cuive habeant fidem? (Catul. 30.6)

R9    pro qua quis bonus dubitet mortem oppetere? (Cic. *Off*. 1.57)

## CHAPTER 12

E2    id egit rerum natura ut ad bene vivendum non magno apparatu opus esset. (Sen. *Dial*. 12.5.1)

E4    sunt homines quos libidinis infamiaeque suae neque pudeat neque taedeat. (Cic. *Ver*. 35)

R1    quem enim Romanorum pudet uxorem ducere in convivium? (Nep. *pr*. 6)

R5    quid tum? omniane bonis viris quae facere possunt facienda sunt, etiamne si turpia, si perniciosa erunt, si facere omnino non licebit? ... licet autem quod legibus, quod more maiorum institutisque conceditur. neque enim quod quisque potest id ei licet, nec si non obstatur propterea etiam permittitur. (Cic. *Phil*. 13.14)

R6    sileatur de nocturnis eius bacchationibus ac vigiliis; lenonum, aleatorum, perductorum nulla mentio fiat; damna, dedecora, quae res patris eius, aetas ipsius pertulit, praetereantur. (Cic. *Ver*. 1.33)

R8    cuius consuetudinis atque instituti patres maioresque nostros non paenitebat. (Cic. *Div. Caec*. 69)

## CHAPTER 13

E3    decrevit quondam senatus uti L.Opimius consul videret ne quid res publica detrimenti caperet. (Cic. *Cat*. 1.4)

E4    non ita civitatem aegram esse ut consuetis remediis sisti possit. (Liv. 3.20.8)

R2    non enim libenter erat ante oculos suorum civium, quod et vivebat laute et indulgebat sibi liberalius quam ut invidiam vulgi posset effugere. (Nep.*Cha*.3.2)

R5    ac philosophia quidem tantum abest ut laudetur ut ... a plerisque neglecta, a multis etiam vituperetur. (Cic. *Tusc*. 5.6)

R6    ne nimis laetae res essent, pestilentia civitatem adorta coegit senatum imperare decemviris ut libros Sibyllinos inspicerent; eorumque monitu lectisternium fuit. (Liv. 7.27.1)

R8    hae ingenti summa ab ignotis etiam ad commercium gentibus accersuntur, ut matronae nostrae ne adulteris quidem plus sui in cubiculo quam in publico ostendant. (Sen. *Ben*. 7.9.5)

R10   pestilentia in agris forisque et conciliabulis et in urbe tanta erat ut Libitina funeribus vix sufficeret. his prodigiis cladibusque anxii patres decreverunt ut et consules, quibus diis videretur, hostiis maioribus sacrificarent et decemviri libros adirent. eorum decreto supplicatio circa omnia pulvinaria Romae in diem unum indicta est. (Liv. 40.19.3)

CHAPTER 14

E1    lucra petens habili tauros adiungit aratro
et durum terrae rusticus urget opus. (Tib. 1.9.7)

E2    invenietis omnia prospera evenisse sequentibus deos, adversa spernentibus. (Liv. 5.51.5)

E3    impiger extremos curris mercator ad Indos,
per mare pauperiem fugiens. (Hor. *Ep.* 1.1.45)

R4    vitis ... quam serpentem multiplici lapsu et erratico, ferro amputans coercet ars agricolarum, ne silvescat sarmentis et in omnis partis nimia fundatur. (Cic. *Sen.* 52)

CHAPTER 15

E2    quam si sequemur ducem, numquam aberrabimus. (Cic. *Off.* 1.100)

E4    at mihi felicem vitam, si salva fuisses,
fingebam demens. (Tib. 1.5.19)

R7    non igitur potestis voluptate omnia derigentes aut tueri aut retinere virtutem. (Cic. *Fin.* 2.71)

CHAPTER 16

R6    colligere incertos et in ordine ponere crines
docta neque ancillas inter habenda Nape,
...
accipe et ad dominam peraratas mane tabellas
perfer et obstantes sedula pelle moras. (Ov. *Am.* 1.11.1)

CHAPTER 17

R5    L.Sulla exercitum, quem in Asia ductaverat, quo sibi fidum faceret, contra morem maiorum luxuriose nimisque liberaliter habuerat. loca amoena, voluptaria facile in otio ferocis militum animos molliverant: ibi primum insuevit exercitus populi Romani amare, potare, signa, tabulas pictas, vasa caelata mirari. (Sall. *Cat.* 11.5)

R7    voluptatibus itaque se mergunt quibus in consuetudinem adductis carere non possunt, et ob hoc miserrimi sunt, quod eo pervenerunt ut illis quae supervacua fuerant facta sint necessaria. (Sen. *Ep.* 39.6)

R10    si quae non nupta mulier domum suam patefecerit omnium cupiditati palamque sese in meretricia vita collocarit, virorum alienissimorum conviviis uti instituerit ...: cum hac si qui adulescens forte fuerit, utrum hic tibi, L.Herenni, adulter an amator, expugnare pudicitiam an explere libidinem voluisse videatur? (Cic. *Cael.* 49)

CHAPTER 18

E4    et cum rogationem promulgassent ut ager ex hostibus captus viritim divideretur ... (Liv. 4.48.2)

R1    quid fles, Asterie, quem tibi candidi
primo restituent vere Favonii
    Thyna merce beatum
      constantis iuvenem fide
Gygen?   (Hor. *Carm.* 3.7.1)

R6 veteres illic Sueborum praedae et nostris e provinciis lixae ac negoti-
atores reperti, quos ius commercii, dein cupido augendi pecuniam,
postremo oblivio patriae suis quemque ab sedibus hostilem in agrum
transtulerat. (Tac. *Ann.* 2.62)

## CHAPTER 19

R4 mandemusque memoriae quod vir mitissimus et ob hoc quoque
maximus Thrasea crebro dicere solebat: qui vitia odit, homines odit.
(Plin. *Ep.* 8.22.3)

R5 invictus patriam defensum revocatus bellum gessit adversus P.Sci-
pionem. (Nep. *Han.* 6.1)

R7 sed ubi labore atque iustitia res publica crevit, reges magni bello domiti,
nationes ferae et populi ingentes vi subacti, Carthago, aemula imperi
Romani, ab stirpe interiit, cuncta maria terraeque patebant, saevire
fortuna ac miscere omnia coepit. (Sall. *Cat.* 10.1)

R9 omnia praeteribo quae mihi turpia dictu videbuntur, neque solum quid
istum audire, verum etiam quid me deceat dicere considerabo. vos,
quaeso, date hoc et concedite pudori meo ut aliquam partem de istius
impudentia reticere possim. (Cic. *Ver.* 1.32)

## CHAPTER 20

E2 Rhodum venimus ubi, quas mercis vexeram,
omnis ut volui vendidi ex sententia. (Pl. *Mer.* 93)

R4 omnes nationes servitutem ferre possunt: nostra civitas non potest, nec
ullam aliam ob causam, nisi quod illae laborem doloremque fugiunt,
quibus ut careant omnia perpeti possunt, nos ita a maioribus instituti
atque imbuti sumus, ut omnia consilia atque facta ad dignitatem et ad
virtutem referremus. (Cic. *Phil.* 10.20)

R10 "nihil ignoveris!" immo aliquid, non omnia. "nihil gratiae causa
feceris!" immo resistito gratiae, cum officium et fides postulabit.
"misericordia commotus ne sis!" etiam, in dissolvenda severitate; sed
tamen est laus aliqua humanitatis. "in sententia permaneto!" vero, nisi
sententiam sententia alia vicerit melior. (Cic. *Mur.* 65)

## CHAPTER 21

E3 si acum, credo, quaereres,
acum invenisses, si appareret, iam diu. (Pl. *Men.* 238)

R2 quod si quis deus mihi largiatur ut ex hac aetate repuerascam et in cunis
vagiam, valde recusem. nec vero velim, quasi decurso spatio, ad
carceres a calce revocari. quid habet enim vita commodi? quid non
potius laboris? (Cic. *Sen.* 83)

## CHAPTER 22

E3 promitto tibi te ex eius amicitia magnam voluptatem esse capturum.
(Cic. *Fam.* 13.77.2)

E4 memento promisisse te, si quisquam hanc liberali
causa manu adsereret, mihi omne argentum redditum iri! (Pl. *Cur.* 490)

## CHAPTER 23

E1    gubernatores, cum exsultantes lolligines viderint, aut delphinos se in portum coniicientes, tempestatem significari putant. (Cic. *Div.* 2.145)

## CHAPTER 24

E1    videamus ea quae sequuntur primum deorumne providentia mundus regatur, deinde consulantne di rebus humanis. (Cic. *N.D.* 3.65)

E2    quid paulo ante, inquit, dixerim nonne meministi? (Cic. *Fin.* 2.10)

E3    cuius de adventu cum fama in Graeciam esset perlata et maxime Athenienses peti dicerentur propter pugnam Marathoniam, miserunt Delphos consultum quidnam facerent de rebus suis. (Nep. *Them.* 2.6)

E5    dici non potest quam sim hesterna disputatione tua delectatus vel potius adiutus. (Cic. *Tusc.* 2.10)

R6    isne tibi melius suadet qui, rem facias, rem,
si possis recte, si non, quocumque modo rem,
ut propius spectes lacrimosa poemata Pupi,
an qui Fortunae te responsare superbae
liberum et erectum praesens hortatur et aptat?
(Hor. *Ep.* 1.1.65)

R7    duplex est enim vis animorum atque natura; una pars in appetitu posita est, quae est ὁρμή Graece, quae hominem huc et illuc rapit, altera in ratione, quae docet et explanat, quid faciendum fugiendumve sit. ita fit ut ratio praesit, appetitus obtemperet. (Cic. *Off.* 1.101)

## CHAPTER 25

E2    nego in Sicilia tota, tam locupleti, tam vetere provincia, tot oppidis, tot familiis tam copiosis, ullum argenteum vas, ullum Corinthium aut Deliacum fuisse, ullam gemmam aut margaritam, quicquam ex auro aut ebore factum, signum ullum aeneum, marmoreum, eburneum, nego ullam picturam neque in tabula neque in textili quin conquisierit, inspexerit, quod placitum sit abstulerit. (Cic. *Ver.* 4.1)

E4    hoc homini amplius, quod addidit rationem, qua regerentur animi appetitus, qui tum remitterentur, tum continerentur. (Cic. *N.D.* 2.34)

E5    itaque non deterret sapientem mors, quae propter incertos casus quotidie imminet, propter brevitatem vitae numquam longe potest abesse, quominus in omne tempus rei publicae suisque consulat. (Cic. *Tusc.* 1.91)

R1    post autem apparatu regio accepti sermonem in multam noctem produximus, cum senex nihil nisi de Africano loqueretur omniaque eius non facta solum, sed dicta meminisset. deinde ut cubitum discessimus, me et de via fessum et qui ad multam noctem vigilassem artior quam solebat somnus complexus est. (Cic. *Rep.* 6.10)

R4    qui ... cum domus patris a foro longe abesset, quo facilius et nostras domus obire et ipse a suis coli posset, conduxit in Palatio non magno domum. (Cic. *Cael.* 18)

# APPENDIX C

## Vocabulary for Learning

The following vocabulary list assembles in alphabetical order the Vocabulary to Learn given at the end of each chapter.

ā/ab (prep w.abl) = from, by
ad (prep w.acc) = to
ager agrī (m) = land, a field
alius –a –ud = different, other
amō –āre –āvī –ātum = to love
amor –ōris (m) = love
animus –ī (m) = the mind, spirit
at (conj) = but
atque/ac (conj) = and
audiō –īre –īvī –ītum = to hear
aut (conj) = or
aut... aut (conjs) = either ... or
autem = however, but
beātus –a –um = happy
bonus –a –um = good (adv: bene)
capiō –ere cēpī captum = to take (hold of), seize, capture
cognoscō –ere cognōvī –itum = to get to know
cum (prep w.abl) = with, together with
dē (prep w.abl) = from, about
deus deī (m) = a god (nom.pl: dī)
dīcō –cere –xī –ctum = to say, speak of, call
diēs –ēī (m) = day
dīves –itis = rich, wealthy
dīvitiae –ārum (f.pl) = riches, wealth
dō dare dedī datum = to give, grant
domina –ae (f) = a mistress
domus –ī/-ūs (f) = a house, home
ē/ex (prep w.abl) = from, out of
ego = I
enim = for
eō īre iī itum (intr) = to go
erus –ī (m) = a master
et (conj) = and
et...et (conjs) = both ... and
etiam = also, even
faciō –ere fēcī factum = to make, do

fēlix –īcis = fruitful, fortunate, happy
ferō –rre tulī lātum = to carry, bear, bring
fore: see sum
fortis –is –e = strong, courageous
fugiō –ere fūgī = to run away from
fuī: see sum
futūrus: see sum
gaudeō –dēre gāvīsus (intr) = to rejoice
habeō –ēre –uī –itum = to have, possess, consider (to be)
hic haec hoc = this
homō –inis (m) = a human being, man
iam (adv) = now, already
ille –a –ud = that, this
imperō –āre –āvī –ātum (w.dat) = to order, command
in (prep w.acc/abl) = into / in, on
infēlix –īcis = unfruitful, unfortunate, unhappy
ipse –a –um = himself, herself, itself, etc.
is ea id = this, that
ita (adv) = so, in this way
itaque (adv) = and so
labor –ōris (m) = labour, toil
lātum: see ferō
magnus –a –um = great
māior –ior –ius = greater, older; (m.pl) ancestors
meus –a –um = my (own)
miser –era –erum = pitiable, wretched, unhappy
mittō –ere mīsī missum = to let go, send
mulier –eris (f) = a woman
multus –a –um = much, many
nam = for
nē = not; (conj) that ... not
negō –āre –āvī –ātum = to say no, refuse, deny
neque/nec (conj) = and ... not, nor
neque/nec ... neque/nec (conjs) = neither ... nor
nēmō –inis (m) = no-one
nihil/nīl (n.indecl) = nothing
nisi (conj) = if not
nōn = not
nōs = we
noster –tra –trum = our (own)
nox –ctis (f) = night
nullus –a –um = not any, no
numquam (adv) = never
nunc (adv) = now
omnis –is –e = every, all
pars –tis (f) = a part
pater –tris (m) = a father
paupertās –ātis (f) = poverty
petō –ere –īvī –ītum = to make for, seek

pōnō pōnere posuī positum = to place, put
possum posse potuī = to be able (to)
puella –ae (f) = a girl
puer –erī (m) = a boy
pulcher –chra –chrum = beautiful
quaerō –rere –sīvī –sītum = to look for, ask
quam (w.compar) = than
–que (conj) = and
quī quae quod = who(ever), which, what
quis? quid? = who? what?
quis qua quid = anyone, anything
quisque quaeque quidque = each person or thing
ratiō –ōnis (f) = reason
rēs reī (f) = a thing, matter
saepe (adv) = often
sapiens –ntis = wise
sē / sēsē = himself, herself, itself, etc.
sed (conj) = but
semper (adv) = always
sequor –quī –cūtus = to follow
sī (conj) = if
sum esse fuī = to be (fut.infin: fore; fut.part.: futūrus)
suus –a –um = his, her, its (own), etc.
tamen (adv) = nevertheless, yet
tempus –oris (n) = time
tū = you
tulī: see ferō
tuus –a –um = your (own)
umquam (adv) = ever
ūnus –a –um = one, a single
urbs –bis (f) = a city, the city of Rome
ut (conj) = that
veniō venīre vēnī ventum (intr) = to come
vērus –a –um = real, true; (adv: vero) in truth, in fact; (adv: vērum) but
    in truth
vester –tra –trum = your (own)
video vidēre vīdī vīsum = to see
videor vidērī vīsus (intr) = to appear, seem (to)
vincō –ere vīcī victum = to conquer, defeat
vir virī (m) = a man
virtūs –ūtis (f) = virtue
vīta –ae (f) = life
vitium –[i]ī (n) = a fault, vice
vīvō –vere –xī –ctum (intr) = to live
vocō –āre –āvī –ātum = to call, invite
volō velle voluī = to want, wish (to)
voluptās –ātis (f) = pleasure
vōs = you

# APPENDIX D

## A Note on Pronunciation

A full account of how Latin was pronounced in classical antiquity can be found in W.S. Allen *Vox Latina* (2nd ed. Cambridge 1978). For practical purposes Latin can be pronounced more or less as it is written. It should be noted however that *c* and *g* are **always** hard consonants (i.e. as in English "cat" and "god").

Latin vowels can be long or short. In this course long vowels are printed with a "long" mark, e.g. *beātus*; vowels before *-nf* and *-ns* are lengthened in pronunciation but are not printed with a long mark, e.g. *mons* (pronounced *mōns*); all other vowels printed without a long mark are short, e.g. *dominus*. Vowels of doubtful length, which are found in some common Latin words, are left unmarked.

Similarly Latin syllables can be long or short. A syllable is long if it contains a long vowel or a diphthong or a short vowel followed by two or more consonants; otherwise it is short.

In Latin words of two or more syllables, one syllable carries an "accent". It is now believed that in antiquity this was a stress accent rather than a tonal accent. In words of two syllables the first syllable is stressed, e.g. *puer*, *māter*. In words of three or more syllables the last but one syllable is stressed if it is long, e.g *imperātor*, *voluptās*; otherwise the preceding syllable is stressed, e.g. *animus*, *videor*.